Innovative communities

Innovative communities: People-centred approaches to environmental management in the Asia-Pacific region

Edited by Jerry Velasquez, Makiko Yashiro, Susan Yoshimura and Izumi Ono

United Nations University Press

TOKYO · NEW YORK · PARIS

© United Nations University, 2005

The views expressed in this publication are those of the authors and do not necessarily reflect the views of the United Nations University.

United Nations University Press
United Nations University, 53–70, Jingumae 5-chome,
Shibuya-ku, Tokyo, 150-8925, Japan
Tel: +81-3-3499-2811   Fax: +81-3-3406-7345
E-mail: sales@hq.unu.edu   general enquiries: press@hq.unu.edu
http://www.unu.edu

United Nations University Office at the United Nations, New York
2 United Nations Plaza, Room DC2-2062, New York, NY 10017, USA
Tel: +1-212-963-6387   Fax: +1-212-371-9454
E-mail: unuona@ony.unu.edu

United Nations University Press is the publishing division of the United Nations University.

Cover design by Rebecca S. Neimark, Twenty-Six Letters

Printed in Hong Kong

ISBN 92-808-1116-9

Library of Congress Cataloging-in-Publication Data

People-centred approaches to environmental management in the Asia-Pacific region / edited by Jerry Velasquez ... [et al.].
    p. cm.
  Includes bibliographical references and index.
  ISBN 9280811169 (pbk.)
  1. Sustainable development—Asia. 2. Sustainable development—Pacific Area.
3. Environmental management—Asia. 4. Environmental management—Pacific Area. I. Velasquez, Jerry.
  HC415.E5P44   2005
  338.95′07—dc22   2005025242

Contents

v

Water management

List of tables

List of figures

Preface

This book was motivated by the realization that change and innovation at the community level are critical to the creation of a sustainable society. The first step was the launching of a joint research project by the United Nations University (UNU) and the United Nations Environment Programme (UNEP) focusing on "Innovative Communities: Community Centered Approaches to Sustainable Environmental Management". This joint initiative looks at the concept of innovativeness as applied to the community level and explores its implications for local environment management. In highlighting successful examples of community innovation, and exploring the reasons behind their success, this research initiative aims to add to our understanding of the key factors that provide an enabling environment for community innovation. A more thorough understanding of these factors will be of great assistance to local communities (internally) in their efforts to promote innovation and change for sustainable environmental management and also to the local, national and international stakeholders (externally) working with them.

The focus of both the research project and this book is the Asia-Pacific region, which is characterized by its diversity in ecological and cultural situations, political systems and economies. Although the region has achieved rapid economic growth, which has contributed to a reduction in poverty and improvements in welfare and well-being, it has faced difficulties in ensuring an equitable distribution of improvements. At the same time, it has struggled to protect the environment from air and water pollution, water scarcity, solid and hazardous waste, deforestation, land degradation and biodiversity loss. Nonetheless, the Asia-Pacific region is characterized by rapid change and dynamism, as well as a willingness to try new approaches and bring about seemingly impossible societal changes. A careful examination of the initiatives carried out in the region provides a number of useful lessons about what communities and key stakeholders can do to ensure the successful implementation of their innovative processes.

Within the book, the concept of community innovation is developed through a detailed analysis of cases and the identification of key "innovative elements" that contribute to successful community-centred local environmental management. The aim is to highlight the successful tools, methodologies and processes used by innovative communities that might be of use to other communities and stakeholders, particularly in developing countries, that face the challenge of effecting change at the community level in the hope of a more sustainable future.

Acknowledgements

This book would not have been possible without a great deal of hard work and the dedication of many people. They have helped at various stages and we would like to express our appreciation for all of their helpful suggestions and insights. First and foremost we would like to acknowledge Hari Srinivas for initiating the idea for developing the book. We would like to extend our thanks to Shona E. H. Dodds and Randal Helten for their commitment in assisting us in editing the chapters during the preliminary stages and to Selena Malhan for her editorial assistance during the final stages of publication. We would also like to thank Naoko Ikeda for her contribution and valuable comments on the chapters. Last, but by no means least, we are sincerely grateful to the authors who made this book possible and to the communities that made it a reality by sharing their experiences and providing a true insight into their lives.

About the editors

Jerry Velasquez is a Programme Specialist at the United Nations Environment Programme in Nairobi, Kenya. He was previously an Academic Programme Officer at the United Nations University (UNU) and Coordinator of the UNU Global Environment Information Centre, Tokyo, Japan.

Makiko Yashiro is a Research Associate at the UNU Global Environment Information Centre, Tokyo, Japan.

Susan Yoshimura is a researcher in leadership and environmental governance and a former campaigner at Greenpeace Japan.

Izumi Ono is a Programme Associate at the UNU Global Environment Information Centre, Tokyo, Japan.

Contributors

Evan Anthony Arias is a Planning Officer and Head of the Provincial Planning and Development Office, Guimaras, the Philippines.

Victor B. Asio is a Professor of Soil Science and Geo-ecology, and Head of the Terrestrial Ecosystem Division, Institute of Tropical Ecology, Leyte State University, the Philippines.

Marlito Jose M. Bande is a Community Organizer at Cienda-San Vicente Farmers Association, and a forest management specialist at the Terrestrial Ecosystem Division, Institute of Tropical Ecology, Leyte State University, the Philippines.

Luc Bellon is a researcher in anthropology at EHESS, Centre of Anthropology for Contemporary Worlds, Paris, France, and at the Epistemology and Hermeneutic Department of the University of Milan, Italy.

Amit Chanan is Strategy and Policy Officer at Sydney Catchment Authority, Australia.

Darryl Romesh D'Monte is chairperson of the Forum of Environmental Journalists of India and President of the International Federation of Environmental Journalists.

Nathaniel von Einsiedel is a former Regional Coordinator for Asia and the Pacific, UNDP/UNCHS (Habitat)/World Bank Urban Management Programme.

J. Marc Foggin is executive director of Plateau Perspectives, Quebec, Canada, and a chief adviser to the Upper Yangtze Organization.

Andrew C. Farncombe is Director of Programming, International Programs Office, Canadian Urban Institute, Toronto, Canada.

Francis E. Gentoral is Southeast Asia Regional Manager of the Canadian Urban Institute, the Philippines.

Walter Jamieson is Dean at the School of Travel Industry Management, University of Hawaii at Manoa, and Managing Director of Integration Planning & Management Co., Ltd., Thonburi, Thailand.

Rika Kato is a Chief Officer at Icograda 2003 NAGOYA Secretariat, Japan.

Charles Landry is the author of *The creative city: A toolkit for urban innovators* and director of Comedia, a leading UK think tank and consultancy on the future of cities.

Pawinee Sunalai is a Project Coordinator at the Canadian Universities Consortium, Urban Environmental Management Project, Asian Institute of Technology, Pathumthani, Thailand.

Sundjaya is a Programme Manager in Conservation International Indonesia, and is involved in community-based nature resources management programmes in the Togean Islands, Central Sulawesi, Indonesia.

Diane Warburton is a writer and researcher specializing in community participation and sustainable development working with community organizations and national bodies including WWF-UK and the Countryside Commission.

Teruhiko Yoshimura is a researcher at the United Nations Centre for Regional Development, Nagoya, Japan.

1

Introduction and overview

Jerry Velasquez, Makiko Yashiro, Susan Yoshimura and Izumi Ono

Since the United Nations Conference on Environment and Development (UNCED) in 1992 (also known as the Rio Earth Summit), the critical importance of innovation and change has been repeatedly highlighted within efforts to create a more sustainable society. These efforts have enjoyed a certain amount of success in that they have increased awareness of the principles of sustainability and helped to change the way that governments think and act. Many of the principles enshrined in the introduction to *Agenda 21*,[1] for example, are now reflected in government policy-making and in the actions of local authorities. Yet, despite all the efforts that have been made, environmental conditions across the globe are still deteriorating; prevailing consumption patterns are still unsustainable; and there are still no proper regulatory frameworks in place to prevent the free market's negative impact on the environment. Many more steps need to be taken if we are successfully to transform the sustainability principles and slogans that arose from the 1992 Rio Earth Summit into actual practice.

The need for innovation and change

The environmental problems faced by the world are characterized by their complexity and uncertainty and the fact that they require dynamic approaches by society if they are to be successfully addressed. The issue of climate change, for example, needs to be understood from many

1

Sustainable development is ...

... a process of change in which the exploitation of resources, the direction of investments, the orientation of technological development, and institutional change are made consistent with future as well as present needs.
(World Commission on Environment and Development 1987: 9)

---

angles because it impacts on biodiversity, land degradation, natural disaster rates, agricultural production, and more. Understanding climate change requires the utilization of a wide range of knowledge and skills from different fields such as science, economics and politics.

The solution to most environmental problems must also reflect this complexity and must be implemented through the close coordination of the efforts of different stakeholders with a diversity of knowledge and skill sets. Such coordination often requires drastic changes to existing environmental management structures. Add to this a high level of scientific uncertainty and the constantly changing nature of global environmental problems and it becomes clear that society must be responsive, dynamic and willing to experiment with new and innovative approaches if sustainable development is to be achieved.

The importance of the community level

It was already clear in 1992 that innovation and change for the creation of a sustainable society cannot be achieved without active involvement at the local community level. There is widespread acceptance that sustainable development requires community participation in practice as well as in principle. This is reflected in the text of *Agenda 21*, where the importance of local community action is mentioned in almost all of its 40 chapters.

Now there is even more evidence to suggest that the causes and pressures of any of today's environmental problems can be traced back, directly or indirectly, to the local level – and to the lifestyles, choices, values and behaviours of local communities. Adding to the evidence is the failure of conventional approaches to sustainability, such as top–down authoritarian approaches, and the clear necessity for a change in attitudes and behaviour right down at the individual and everyday level. As a result, the Plan of Implementation adopted at the 10-year follow-up to UNCED, the World Summit for Sustainable Development in Johannesburg in 2002, reaffirmed the crucial need to enhance and support actions at the local level in order to accelerate sustainable development.

This strengthened recognition of the necessity for innovation and change and the important role played by local communities has generated a number of innovative experiments at the local level. Communities have been implementing a wide range of innovative initiatives that can be characterized by certain key factors such as public participation, stakeholder partnerships and the utilization of local knowledge and resources. Yet, whereas some communities have been successful in implementing these innovations, others have faced great difficulties. Challenges have included problems in generating the political momentum necessary to experiment with, and eventually accept, new ideas. Strong political resistance is linked to the fact that innovation and change are often associated with the need for fundamental changes to political and governance structures. It is critically important, therefore, that we develop a better understanding of how communities can successfully bring about innovation and change to establish a sustainable society by identifying and examining the key elements that help foster community innovation at the local level.

What is a community?

There are several ways of defining the term "community", including "a group of people living in the same locality and under the same government" or "a group of people having common interests".[2] The first definition brings thoughts of a place of belonging, the other definition brings thoughts of common understanding. In this book we define a "community" as a combination of the above: a group of people who are involved in collective action in a specific geographical location. The main distinction is that our definition of communities does not always include all residents or only residents of a particular area. What links them together is their sharing of common local environmental issues and collective action towards solving these issues.

Although not all of the residents are covered in our description of a community, this definition allows all the local residents to participate if and when they become aware of these issues. In this regard, a "community" is something that can be scaled-up in its coverage of participants, depending on each local situation.

What is community innovation?

Innovation, which is generally discussed in relation to the introduction of new technologies and approaches in the business sector, can be defined in numerous different ways. It is not easy to develop a single definition and a detailed examination of the definition of the term itself is outside the scope of the discussion here. It is commonly agreed, however, that innovation as a concept implies something new and unconventional. When it is applied to communities, it implies the development of new cultures, a new ethos, changed behaviours and roles, as well as institutions.

Community innovation can be characterized as a collective human activity that often involves a change in the processes through which things are carried out, and requires a fundamental change in political and governance structures. An innovative community is therefore able to bring in new methods and ideas that can improve its environment and initiate changes through the imaginative ideas or artistic ability of its people.

What does it take for a community to be innovative? Why are some communities innovative and others not? Much has been discussed on the broader relevance and transferability of best practice approaches to community innovation. One of the key questions addressed in this study is whether the strategies and actions that work in one community will necessarily be equally successful in another. In this respect, it has been widely recognized that the effectiveness of tools and methodologies is influenced largely by local circumstances and is not, therefore, easily replicated or directly transferable. Furthermore, as Charles Landry notes in Chapter 3, community innovation is usually influenced by conditions such as time, location and culture. This means that approaches that might seem to be innovative for a certain community may not be innovative for other communities.

What is critical for all communities, however, is that they possess or develop certain preconditions, including a general atmosphere that enables people or organizations to plan and act innovatively with both creativity and imagination. A preliminary analysis of the case studies prepared for this book highlights a number of essential features that characterize the innovative potential of communities:

- a shared community recognition of a relatively urgent sustainable development need or challenge;
- established, flexible local governance structures that can be adapted to accommodate and sustain multi-stakeholder mechanisms;
- the availability of relevant local culture, knowledge and indigenous practices that can combine with new and introduced ideas and technologies to generate innovation;
- strong local community leadership and a pioneering spirit.

The multi-stakeholder partnership and participatory processes described in this book are vehicles for developing stakeholder coherence. In Chapter 4, for example, Nathaniel von Einsiedel mentions that, for innovation to take place, different roles and perspectives of multiple stakeholders are essential but, at the same time, diversity of opinions and interests could be a barrier to innovation. Similarly, Luc Bellon says in Chapter 5 that diversified and conflicting interests are, "simultaneously, the trigger of innovation and the biggest threat to innovative mechanisms". It is therefore important to have an effective system in place in the community to ensure an active dialogue among stakeholders and to promote coherence, while maintaining the diversity of roles, interests and opinions of stakeholders.

It is also worth noting that this book does not specifically identify full ownership as a key component of community innovation. Although this is an important aspect of the effective implementation of solutions, the cases explored in this book show that ownership of issues and solutions affects only the pace at which innovation takes place. For example, in Chapter 5, which describes a case of sustainable hunting in Pakistan, Luc Bellon describes incremental innovation in the use of game guards, their allocation and roles. Most of the other cases, however, describe situations in which external facilitators created the initial input of ideas, funding and initiative, which were then taken on board by the host communities. In these cases, at the beginning, a certain amount of innovation is injected into the community, which then adopts the new ideas and makes them its own.

These features are the key ingredients that need to be considered in defining what drives a community to become innovative. Yet, it is still important to recognize that innovation is unique to each community and its particular circumstances. Even though there are a number of features that can help to establish, or signify, an enabling innovative environment, it is still up to each community to convert these features into locale-specific procedures and working methodologies that will achieve a specific result. The precursors might exist in many communities, but to be innovative a community still has to work out the best way to take advantage of them and put them into practice.

What is an innovative community?

In this book we use the term "innovative community" to refer to a group of people who are able to bring about change and innovation in order to establish a sustainable society. They are willing to take unconventional approaches, often by making dramatic changes in people's attitudes, perceptions, mindsets, roles and behaviours, as well as developing new ethoses, cultures, institutions and governance structures.

About the book

Innovative Communities is designed to provide readers with a better understanding of how selected communities in the Asia-Pacific region fostered their creativeness and adopted innovative methodologies to address pressing environmental issues and promote sustainability. In addition to the careful examination of the systems, processes and methodologies applied by the communities, an effort is also made to analyse the factors and conditions that nurtured their innovative capacities.

The primary purpose of the book is to build upon our preliminary understanding of the concept of innovative communities by providing a comprehensive analysis of a series of case studies collected from the Asia-Pacific region. The objective underpinning the book, and also the collaborative research project upon which it is based, is the identification of critical elements that facilitate sustainable community innovation. Through an analysis of each case study, the book intends to clarify the crucial importance of local community-level innovation.

Through analysis and discussion from many different angles, the book also provides readers with tips on how communities can foster innovation and make changes that lead to a sustainable society. In doing so, the book intends to assist communities, community-based organizations, decision makers who are involved in community-based environmental initiatives and also those who provide support to communities at various levels of governance from the local to the global.

The book is divided into two parts. The first part is made up of three conceptual chapters written by experts in the field of community development, urban planning and local environmental management. These chapters are aimed at providing an introduction to the conceptual and theoretical background of sustainable community development and innovation. Chapters 2 and 3 give an overview of societal trends and recent discussions regarding communities and sustainable development. They explore the implications of innovativeness in creating a sustainable society as well as some of the critical issues to be considered in discussing community innovation. Although Chapter 4 focuses exclusively on Asia from a local government policy perspective, it draws out a number of lessons about how to overcome key barriers and to scale up or mainstream community innovation.

The second part of the book comprises nine case-study chapters written by community leaders, local government officials, journalists, representatives of non-governmental organizations (NGOs) and academics. These chapters highlight a number of innovative community-based environmental initiatives in the Asia-Pacific region and cover a wide range of issues, including natural resource management, ecotourism, forest management, solid waste management and water management. The communities targeted in the case studies vary significantly in their size, economy, politics, culture, environment and many other respects. What they have in common, however, is that they have applied innovative methodologies and made changes to their communities that resulted in an improvement both in their environmental conditions and in the extent of local empowerment.

The insights gained through the theoretical and conceptual chapters, along with the lessons learned from the case studies, will be used to identify the key elements that help communities to develop an enabling environment in which innovation can flourish and take hold. The aim is to demonstrate how the initiatives undertaken at the community level succeeded not only in addressing environmental problems but also in strengthening and empowering the communities. At a broader level, the intention is to explain the ways in which the concept of innovativeness fits into the overall processes of societal development at the community level. This is achieved by highlighting the ways in which the innovativeness of the communities themselves can assist these processes.

The conceptual chapters

In Chapter 2, Diane Warburton and Susan Yoshimura provide a conceptual background for our understanding of the terms "community" and "sustainable development", both of which are critical when considering community innovation. They highlight some of the key challenges of bringing together the social, economic and environmental aspects of sustainable development and emphasize the need for innovative approaches to the translation of the principle of sustainable development into action.

According to Warburton and Yoshimura, citizen involvement in decision-making and action is a crucial factor in promoting innovation and change. In addition, they argue that it is important to promote community involvement as both an end and a means. What is needed is an open community where people can participate in decision-making processes, experiment with new approaches, and own the process of change and innovation. It is also important to conduct an assessment of the nature of community involvement in order to better understand the effectiveness of community involvement mechanisms and achieve continuous improvement. In this regard, Warburton and Yoshimura introduce the frameworks for analysing community involvement that have been developed by Arnstein, Oakley and Warburton and examine their effectiveness. According to the authors, because communities are unique culturally, politically and in many other ways, it is important to adapt non-hierarchical participatory approaches and focus on examining the suitability of different styles of participation for different communities. The process of community involvement should be designed in such a way that it fits well with the unique conditions of each community.

Warburton and Yoshimura also discuss the barriers to promoting community participation, such as the lack of interest and willingness to change in governmental institutions, the lack of awareness of the benefits of community involvement among officials and politicians, as well as the lack of strategic planning by public authorities. Finally, the authors touch upon the vital role of learning and capacity-building in enhancing the level of skills that institutions, groups and individuals are able to apply to achieving sustainable development.

In Chapter 3, Charles Landry suggests that the world is experiencing a drastic transformation in its economic, political, societal and environmental conditions. This makes it essential for communities to respond to their environmental problems in "unconventional" ways, in many cases by adopting new and innovative approaches with imagination and creativity.

Landry argues that, although a large number of innovative initiatives are implemented at the individual and project levels, it is difficult to find truly creative and innovative communities. This is partly owing to the complexity of interests, cultures, insights, perspectives and power configurations that make up communities. In order for communities to become innovative, therefore, there needs to be a system of forums in place where such diverse factors can be coordinated through open-minded discussion and communication, allowing people to think and act in innovative ways. Unsupportive governments and an unwillingness by private sector actors to incorporate sustainability principles into their policies and practices also make it difficult for innovation to be mainstreamed. This is compounded by the limited capabilities of existing measurement scales of economic growth, progress and well-being.

Landry emphasizes that community innovation is a cultural process and that the development of innovative capacity requires communities to utilize their intangible assets, such as cultural knowledge. In order to achieve innovation, communities need to produce, recognize and codify cultural knowledge by understanding and describing possibilities for innovation better. They need to generate a local ethos that directs innovative thinking and the initiatives of communities, developing innovative projects based on the ethical framework and providing opportunities for continuous learning. In order to develop the momentum for innovation and to mainstream it within the community, it is important to have embedding strategies, which foster a sense of ownership among community stakeholders.

Different types of creativity and innovativeness are necessary to deal with the complexity and diversity of communities. Creative solutions and innovation can be generated by any stakeholders, including public, private or voluntary sectors, as well as individuals. The key challenge·at the community level is to develop an innovative milieu based on preconditions that are culturally determined and should be unique to each community. It is critical that communities identify and understand their distinctive features and utilize them in achieving innovation to promote sustainability.

In Chapter 4, Nathaniel von Einsiedel provides an overview of the environmental challenges encountered by selected cities in Asia and illustrates how these cities used innovative approaches in an effort to overcome them. He also reviews the obstacles cities confronted when implementing innovative policies and, based on their experiences, suggests ways in which these can be overcome.

Many cities in Asia face a series of environmental problems, including land encroachment, water supply and sanitation, solid waste disposal, traffic congestion and air pollution. All these problems have had negative effects on human health, social structure and economic activities in urban areas. In order to improve the situation, many urban communities in Asia have tried to carry out innovative environmental initiatives that have required local governments to adopt new policies and processes. These cities are now experiencing difficulties in adopting, replicating and scaling up innovative approaches for environmental management owing to tension among stakeholders, a resistance to change and social complexity.

Von Einsiedel notes that the key to the successful implementation of innovative environmental policies is the promotion of coherence among stakeholders. In this respect, he highlights the effectiveness of promoting multi-stakeholder participation and partnership in local government decision-making and implementation processes. He presents a number of practical tools and mechanisms that can facilitate effective participatory environmental planning. He also emphasizes the importance of local "champions" who play key roles in planning processes. In addition, von Einsiedel highlights the need to understand the factors that affect decisions at the policy level, including possible negative reactions to change, and the need to secure support not only in the decision-making process but also in the implementation process.

Case-study chapters

The nine case studies, from eight countries in the Asia-Pacific region, deal with a variety of environmental issues, ranging from natural resource management and ecotourism to solid waste management. The case studies were selected on the basis of two criteria: they involve a strong combination of environmental management and community building; and they involve communities that have succeeded in adopting innovative methodologies in addressing their environmental problems.

Within each case, the authors were asked to: examine how the community operates; describe the innovative features of the case; explore in detail the processes and methodologies used that led to the success of the solution; outline the actors who played the key roles in implementing the initiative; and describe any internal and external support provided. They were also asked to highlight any factors that acted as a barrier to communities in their efforts to adopt innovative approaches, along with any other critical elements that helped to create an enabling environment for community innovation.

In Chapter 5, Luc Bellon reviews the innovative wildlife conservation initiatives conducted by the Pashtun community in Torghar, in the northern Balochistan Province of Pakistan. According to Bellon, the notion of innovation consists of two distinct features. One is radical and revolutionary and involves making drastic changes to the existing system. The other is incremental and involves constant minor improvement and adaptation. It is the combination of the two features that ensures effective change.

Bellon argues that, despite prevailing perceptions to the contrary, change and innovation are often integrated into existing social dynamics within traditional rural communities such as Torghar. He describes how the community in Torghar planned and implemented a number of wildlife conservation activities that required drastic changes in and by the community, including the prohibition of hunting, and how these affected the community's social, economic and cultural systems.

Bellon also reviews some of the challenges faced by the community within the processes of innovation, such as the conflicting interests of different social groups. He uses his case study to illustrate how a sense of collective responsibility for the holistic management of mountain biodiversity was generated. Based on a careful examination of the initiatives in Torghar, Bellon argues that innovation emerges through "a complex social process" in which the different interests of social groups conflict and negotiate with each other. In this sense, innovation is seen as an unstable process that requires constant adaptation and occurs when there are needs and appropriate conditions in place in the community.

In Chapter 6, J. Marc Foggin reviews the conservation initiatives implemented by the Suojia community on the Tibetan plateau. He introduces the complexities of the decisions and policies that affect the environmental conditions of the Suojia community and discusses some of the government policies, such as the sedentarization of pastoralists, that have had a negative impact on the local environment.

Foggin focuses primarily on the conservation work conducted by the

Upper Yangtze Organization (UYO), one of the first civil society organizations established in the region. Being founded and led by local community leaders, UYO has successfully implemented a number of sustainable land management and nature conservation initiatives. These were achieved by involving local people and through networking actively with a range of external actors such as the local government and domestic and international NGOs.

Foggin analyses several community features, such as strong leadership, the pioneering spirit of community leaders, active internal and external communication and networking, effective consensus-building mechanisms and local ownership, that have enabled the community to adopt innovative approaches. He also demonstrates the vulnerability of community-based initiatives to sudden policy changes and undemocratic decision-making at the higher levels. This reinforces the importance of democratic community empowerment and the need for greater community input into decisions that affect their lives.

In Chapter 7, Walter Jamieson and Pawinee Sunalai review a sustainable tourism initiative implemented in the community of Klong Khwang in Thailand. With growing recognition of the importance of public involvement in local planning processes in Thailand, the community-driven tourism development has been attracting increasing attention. There is also a growing awareness within the tourism sector of the need to incorporate the principles of sustainable development into tourism activities.

Jamieson and Sunalai show how the community in Klong Khwang has successfully incorporated the principles of sustainable development into its tourism initiatives, with substantial technical support provided by the Canadian Universities Consortium Urban Environmental Management Project (CUC UEM). Based on their experience of working with the Klong Khwang community as CUC UEM members, Jamieson and Sunalai review and describe in detail the approaches and activities that the community adopted to implement sustainable tourism. They analyse the factors that enabled the community to adopt an innovative approach to sustainable tourism. They conclude that the combination of external forces, such as technical assistance from academic institutions, local governments and NGOs, with internal forces such as community leadership and the active participation of locals is critical for the community to be innovative.

In Chapter 8, Sundjaya introduces the ecotourism initiatives undertaken by the community of Lembanato on the Togean Islands of eastern Indonesia. Surrounded by a beautiful environment with rich biodiversity, the community has developed a unique tradition and culture that is based on a close relationship between people and nature. The rich traditional culture and knowledge of Lembanato have been deteriorating, mainly because of the intrusion of external culture. Sundjaya describes the community's ecotourism initiatives, illustrating the efforts that have been made by a variety of stakeholders to use local traditional knowledge and culture to integrate the tourism business and the conservation of mangrove forests.

This case study shows how even the most successful innovative ecotourism initiatives can be vulnerable to external factors such as political, economic and social instabilities at the national, regional and international levels. Sundjaya stresses the need for the community to conduct comprehensive assessments and become aware of external factors and threats. He also highlights the importance of the continued financial and technical assistance provided by external organizations, the establishment of transparent systems in the community to ensure the equal distribution of income, and the involvement of customary institution or community leaders in the planning process.

In Chapter 9, Victor Asio and Marlito Jose Bande highlight the innovative rural communities of Cienda and San Vicente in Baybay on Leyte Island in the Philippines. In order to control illegal logging and promote sustainable forest management, these communities have successfully implemented various forest management initiatives. With external assistance, the communities have successfully adopted a "rainforestation" approach that has enabled them to protect their forests and generate an income for local people. Asio and Bande illustrate some of the key factors that helped the community adopt an innovative approach, including environmental awareness, strong local commitment and a sense of volunteerism, the utilization of local knowledge, and the strong leadership of some community members. In particular, they highlight the criticality of financial and technical support from NGOs, academic institutions and international organizations. Such support is crucial for communities that are initiating and implementing innovative activities, although too much dependence on financial assistance from external organizations can harm the sustainability of initiatives.

In Chapter 10, Teruhiko Yoshimura and Rika Kato review the citywide solid waste management initiative implemented in Nagoya City, Japan. This initiative is characterized by the strong leadership shown by the local government, as well as the active participation of community-based organizations throughout the implementation process. Owing to a sudden shortage of waste disposal sites, Nagoya faced an urgent need to reduce the amount of solid waste generated in the city. As a result, in February 1999, the city launched a new policy that required citizens to make efforts to reduce waste by radically changing their waste management practices. Yoshimura and Kato closely examine the approaches taken by the local government as well as the structure of the different community-based groups, such as the neighbourhood association, municipal health commissioners, ward administration commissioners and NGOs, and the distinctive roles played by them.

Yoshimura and Kato also introduce the concept of *Machi-zukuri*, an urban planning approach adopted in Japan, which focuses on promoting the role of communities as key players in community development processes, and apply the concept to examine to what extent the Nagoya City's initiatives were "community-centred". Analysing the innovative features of approaches taken by the local government and citizens, the authors conclude that it was the combination of top–down management by the local government in providing an effective system for recycling and bottom–up incremental efforts by citizens that enabled Nagoya City to achieve remarkable results.

In Chapter 11, Andrew Farncombe, Francis Gentoral and Evan Anthony Arias review a solid waste management initiative implemented in the province of Guimaras in the Philippines. This initiative was established and implemented under the strong leadership of the provincial government of Guimaras as part of a trend toward decentralization of responsibility for the delivery of basic services, including waste management. A key feature of this initiative, which receives external technical assistance, is the multi-stakeholder mechanism that enabled NGOs, civil society groups and the private sector to participate in the planning and implementation of waste management activities. Farncombe et al. describe the initiative in detail and explain how the mechanism has effectively harmonized the views and activities of different actors. They also highlight the role of external institutions and the infusion of external knowledge in the formulation and implementation of innovative initiatives.

In Chapter 12, Amit Chanan illustrates the integrative catchment management system introduced in the Hawkesbury-Nepean basin near Sydney, Australia. Nearly 200 years of uncontrolled development, in conjunction with intensive dam construction on the upper reaches, have severely damaged the environment of the Hawkesbury-Nepean catchment. In response to increasing awareness of the need to manage the river and its catchment properly, the Hawkesbury-Nepean Catchment Management Trust was established by the New South Wales state government. This unique organizational structure succeeded in promoting partnerships among different stakeholders and ensured the active participation of local communities and other interest groups in the management of the catchment area.

Chanan examines the innovative organizational features of the Trust and illustrates how these contributed to the improvement of the environment and led to the empowerment of the community as an advocate, watchdog and educator. The state government's closure of the Trust, despite its obvious successes, reaffirms the difficulties that communities experience in achieving a balance between the need for independence and the need for government support and cooperation to achieve common goals. More importantly, this case study demonstrates the need for a democratization of governance structures. This is critically important if communities are to be fully involved in the decision-making that directly affects them and gain control over the sustainability of their innovative initiatives.

In Chapter 13, Darryl Romesh D'Monte reviews the community-based water management initiatives implemented in the Alwar district of Rajasthan, India. Facing serious deforestation and droughts, the communities in Alwar, with the facilitation of a local NGO, implemented an innovative initiative by using the traditional water-harvesting structure called *johad*. According to D'Monte, the full utilization of traditional knowledge and local labour forces within the initiative resulted not only in the improvement of environmental conditions and local financial well-being, but also in the enhanced self-confidence of the local community.

The success of these initiatives can also be attributed to the catalytic role played by the local NGO, which focused on promoting self-help attitudes among the local people. Also key was the active involvement of traditional village self-governing bodies, such as village assemblies, through which people in the communities participated in the planning and implementation processes. By analytically reviewing the barriers they faced, and the steps taken by the communities in an effort to overcome them, D'Monte highlights the critical role of external organizations in conjunction with the utilization of indigenous self-governing mechanisms and local traditional knowledge and technologies.

Conclusion

The intention of this book is not to suggest a package of best-practice approaches that can be replicated under certain conditions but, rather, to draw out the key lessons from each case study in order to identify the main elements that constitute an enabling environment for community innovation. The existence, or deliberate creation, of such an environment fosters creativity at the community level and enables the adoption of innovative approaches to environmental and sustainable development challenges. Following the conceptual and case-study chapters, a final concluding chapter will combine the theoretical insights provided in the earlier chapters with the lessons drawn from the case studies to highlight what appear to be the critical preconditions for community innovation.

Notes

1. *Agenda 21* is a comprehensive plan of action for a sustainable future that was developed at the 1992 Rio Earth Summit.
2. *The American Heritage® Dictionary of the English Language*, 4th edn, copyright © 2004, 2000 by Houghton Mifflin Company.

BIBLIOGRAPHY

Asian Development Bank (2001) *Asian environment outlook 2001*. Manila: ADB.
Carley, M. and C. Ian (2000) *Managing sustainable development*. London and Stering, VA: Earthscan.
Hemmati, M. (2002) *Multi-stakeholder process for governance and sustainability*. London and Stering, VA: Earthscan.
Henderson, H. (1997) "Development beyond economism: Local paths to sustainable development", in Hildegarde Hannum (ed.), *People, Land, and Community*, pp. 89–104. New Haven, CT: Yale University Press.
Smith, D. and K. Jalal (2000) *Sustainable development in Asia*. Manila: Asian Development Bank.
United Nations Department of Economic and Social Affairs, Division for Sustainable Development (1992) *Agenda 21*; available at: 〈http://www.un.org/esa/sustdev/documents/agenda21/index.htm〉.
Warburton, D. (1998) "A passionate dialogue: Community and sustainable development", in D. Warburton (ed.), *Community and sustainable development: Participation in the future*. London and Stering, VA: Earthscan.
World Commission on Environment and Development (1987) *Our common future*. Oxford: Oxford University Press.

Part I

Community innovation for sustainable development: Concepts and approaches

2

Local to global connections: Community involvement and sustainability

Diane Warburton and Susan Yoshimura

Introduction

A growing body of knowledge demonstrates that sustainable development requires community participation, both in principle and in practice.
Local communities have a central place in *Agenda 21* – the agenda for
sustainable development in the twenty-first century that was produced at
the United Nations Conference on Environment and Development
(UNCED) in Rio de Janeiro in 1992; almost every chapter emphasizes
the need for community involvement in managing and solving the problems covered in the document. Along with this recognition at the international level, it has become increasingly common for community involvement to be given a central role in public policy, programmes and
projects on sustainable development at the national and local levels.

Despite growing acceptance of community approaches in principle,
however, the engagement of communities in practice still remains the exception rather than the norm. This chapter addresses the theory behind
community-level programmes and policy aimed at sustainability, in order
to provide an analysis of where we currently stand and to offer ideas on
where to go from here. We analyse the nature of the concepts of community and sustainable development, and also aim to provide some insight
into the importance of community involvement in sustainability schemes.
As well as addressing issues faced when assessing community involvement, we consider issues that are central to discussions about community involvement, such as good governance and the links between local

19

initiatives and global-level repercussions. Finally, we offer some ideas on how to foster learning to achieve better community involvement.

The nature of community

The concept of community is often taken to be unproblematic, but there remain many different understandings and definitions. Some common understanding of the term is required in order to establish how it may link to sustainable development, although it is recognized that a range of different meanings is likely to exist at any one time.

Community is usually understood as being to do with "locality", with "actual social groups", with "a particular quality of relationship" that is "felt to be more immediate than society". When used in conjunction with other activities, such as "community politics", it is "distinct not only from national politics but also from formal local politics, and normally involves various kinds of direct action and direct local organizations 'working directly with people'" (Williams 1988). Community thus often links people (individually and collectively) to a "sense of place" in a particular relationship.

The attachment to place – not just natural places, but urban places too – is one of the most fundamental of human needs ... The important thing about places, of course, is that they are shared. Each person's home area is also other people's. The sense of place is therefore tied to the idea of "community". (Jacobs 1995: 20)

"Community" is that web of personal relationships, group networks, traditions and patterns of behaviour that develops against the backdrop of the physical neighbourhood and its socio-economic situation. (Flecknoe and McLellan 1994: 8)

"Community" exists somewhere between individualism and traditional collectivism, between family and the more distant "society", with a predominantly local and geographical focus, although not necessarily one that equates with any formal geographical boundaries (including nation-states).

There are, however, almost always different sorts of communities within geographical areas: communities may define themselves by religion, history, ethnic origin or sexuality. Indeed, communities are rarely homogeneous; they are more often diverse, may be fragmented and conflicted, and are constantly changing. Influences for change in communities may come from many directions, because communities are rarely completely isolated and may be linked vertically to all other levels of governance (regional to global) and horizontally (to other communities with common concerns), especially as new communication technologies become more widely available.

In spite of the complexities, "community" provides a useful focus for government policies, and modern politics often now invokes it in a number of ways:

- as an **aim** – community is used to explain *why* we are doing various programmes, what we want to achieve, and how we want to live (e.g. to "build" or "rebuild" community or communities); here, community becomes the ideal society made up of people who know and care about each other;
- as **participants** – community is used to describe *who* is involved in policy (e.g. the "local communities" involved in developing and implementing plans, policies and programmes);
- to describe the **process** – community action is used to mean *how* things should happen (e.g. through participation and involvement, the grass roots, local action, self-help);
- as the **location** for policy – community is used to describe *where* policy is enacted (e.g. the local neighbourhood, small town or village, places where we can know and be known).

Many policies and programmes targeting the community have been welcomed by those working in the field of community development and by local communities themselves. The idea that communities themselves contain great resources and have the power to take responsibility to make things better themselves has been recognized as being particularly effective in long-term programmes (e.g. Taylor 1995). It is important, however, to avoid the dangers of failing to examine any underlying assumptions about what we mean by community. These assumptions include the following:

- Everyone shares a view about what "community" means, and that it relates in some way to idealized communities (often rural) of the past. In practice, there is no shared view of what an ideal community is or would be, and few specific examples of previous communities (other than in fiction) exist that epitomize those ideal communities.
- Poverty and social exclusion are essentially "community issues" for poor people themselves to solve by gaining skills (through capacity-building and training) and access to new opportunities. This assumption avoids any suggestion that poverty and social exclusion may be structural problems created by the nature of current economic and political systems.
- Community is a solution for poor people and not for everybody. The focus in community development, community regeneration, etc., tends to be on the poorest and most disadvantaged neighbourhoods and not

(until recently) on wider neighbourhoods, towns or whole parts of major cities, irrespective of the varieties of wealth they contain.

- Disadvantaged people need to have their "capacity" built before they can participate in community action or in decisions that affect their lives and those of their neighbours. No one would suggest that stockbrokers or journalists need to have their capacity built before they can engage in political/democratic activity or community action, although they are no more likely to be able to create responsible, caring, supportive, inclusive community relationships than are those living in poorer neighbourhoods.
- The social exclusion of disadvantaged communities is about economic status and skills, and not about politics or power. Generally, much less attention has been paid to political exclusion than to social, economic and environmental exclusion.
- Communities are always good and positive. In practice, judgements have to be made about the nature of the community being sought. Historically, communities have not always been ideal; they have often been oppressive, divisive, hierarchical, rigid, sexist and racist. Contemporary communities have some additional negative images – as ghettos or as exclusive, gated communities.

Visions of a "good" community are now beginning to be developed. One of them describes a community that is diverse (with mixed ages, skills and professions, ethnic backgrounds, religions, wealth, and so on), welcomes difference, is active, has many opportunities for involvement, and is based on extensive social relationships and strong formal and informal networks. However, such a community is not something that can be "rebuilt" or "returned to" as if there were a golden age of community from some past era. In practice, "community" may best be seen as an aspiration rather than a return to something, and as a choice rather than an inheritance.

Sustainable development background

The concept of sustainable development is as poorly understood and as contested as the concept of community, but for different reasons. Whereas most people may assume they understand what is meant by "community", "sustainable development" is more often simply a new idea. It is useful, therefore, to trace the historical background of sustainable development before further examining the relationship with community.

The generally accepted starting point for the concept of sustainable development was the report *Limits to Growth*, first published in 1972.

The analysis was undertaken by an international group of scientists, researchers and industrialists (the Club of Rome), which met to discuss the future of the planet and its inhabitants. The resulting report provided a powerful critique of the problems (and ultimate impossibility) of pursuing conventional approaches to economic growth in a finite global system, but they also proposed the following:

It is possible ... to establish a condition of ecological and economic stability that is sustainable far into the future. The state of global equilibrium could be designed so that the basic material needs of each person on earth are satisfied and each person has an equal opportunity to realize his individual human potential. (Meadows et al. 1983)

Limits to Growth provided a critique of conventional growth and development and an outline of the environmental problems facing the world (especially the use of finite natural resources and increases in pollution), alongside the concept of meeting basic human needs now and into the future. These factors reappear in all subsequent discourses on sustainable development to varying degrees.

The Club of Rome report was followed by a whole series of initiatives under the auspices of the United Nations and other bodies, including the Brandt Commission on international development and North/South inequalities and the World Conservation Strategy (both published in 1980). Both these initiatives explored similar ideas of how to solve problems of poverty and inequality while tackling environmental problems and limits.

The World Commission on Environment and Development (WCED) was established in 1983, led by Gro Harlem Brundtland, the former Norwegian prime minister and former director-general of the World Health Organization. The Brundtland Report created the following definition of sustainable development, which has been used as the basis for almost all subsequent national and international work in the field:

Humanity has the ability to make development sustainable – to ensure that it meets the needs of the present without compromising the ability of future generations to meet their own needs. (WCED 1987: 8)

The next major turning point was the UN Conference on Environment and Development (UNCED) in Rio de Janeiro in 1992 – known as the Earth Summit – at which *Agenda 21* was signed. After Rio, there were initiatives in many individual countries and across global regions to develop more specific strategies for sustainable development, and the ideas of sustainability also increasingly came to underpin wider approaches to development and environmental protection. The UN World Summit on Sustainable Development in Johannesburg in 2002 marked 10 years since the Earth Summit, reviewed progress and established new priorities.

It is worth recalling exactly what was important in *Agenda 21*. The first paragraph reads:

Humanity stands at a defining moment in history. We are confronted with a perpetuation of disparities between and within nations, a worsening of poverty, hunger, ill health and illiteracy, and the continuing deterioration of the ecosystems on which we depend for our well-being. However, integration of environment and development concerns and greater attention to them will lead to the fulfilment of basic needs, improved living standards for all, better protected and managed ecosystems and a safer more prosperous future. No one nation can achieve this on its own; but together we can – in a global partnership for sustainable development. (*Agenda 21*, para. 1.1)

The environmental implications have always only been *part* of sustainable development, but it has been the environmental aspects that have received most attention. This priority has always been a matter for debate. Indeed, the Brundtland Commission's report specifically says that:

When the terms of reference of our Commission were originally being discussed in 1982, there were those who wanted its considerations to be limited to "environmental issues" only. This would have been a grave mistake ... the "environment" is where we all live; and "development" is what we all do in attempting to improve our lot within that abode. The two are inseparable. (WCED 1987: xi)

Although the environment is only one aspect of sustainable development (alongside social and economic development), it must be recognized that, without the involvement of environmentalists and the environmental movement in debating and promoting sustainable development, it is unlikely that the concept would have retained its centrality to policy. However, the focus on the environmental dimensions of sustainable development in policy-making has meant that the social and economic elements have received far less attention and remain contested.

The debates on the economic aspects of sustainable development have tended to polarize between the need for what Brundtland called a different "quality of growth" and the insistence of most Western governments on maintaining high levels of economic growth and employment as key economic aims, assessed through conventional economic indicators such as gross domestic product (GDP) and the proportion of people in full-time employment. Various types of indicator for Brundtland's "different quality of growth" have been proposed (e.g. MacGillivray and Zadek 1996), but these have yet to be widely accepted.

The social aspects of sustainable development tend to be less fundamentally contentious, perhaps because they are even less well developed. The following social issues tend to arise most often in relation to sustainable development:

- health and safety
- well-being and quality of life
- poverty and disadvantage (including social exclusion and environmental equality)
- fairness and equity (within and between countries, and within and between human generations)
- governance issues (including accountability, legitimacy, openness)
- democracy and participation (including political inclusion and social capital)
- human rights and responsibilities (including cultural diversity, citizens' and/or consumers' rights)
- values, ethics and morality (including ethical trade, business and industry)

In recent years there have been new debates around concepts such as resource productivity (which includes making better use of finite natural resources and re-using waste) and on sustainable production and consumption. These new ideas are bringing together the social, economic and environmental aspects of sustainable development more effectively, but they may still fall short of the radical action required. There remain considerable differences in views, some detailed below, not only about how best to work for sustainable development but even about the inherent priorities.

- Many environmentalists have accepted the imperative of development – in order to tackle poverty, deprivation and inequality – but some continue to argue that no further development is possible if the Earth is to survive. They argue that priority should be given to the search for the scientific evidence that will win the technical argument for environmental protection or for the professional solution that will solve the problem. For them, sustainable development is just the next stage in the battle for environmental issues to be taken seriously in public policy and commercial strategies.
- Many in the development movement internationally have accepted that development proposals need to take all the social, economic, environmental and political impacts of development into account. Here too, however, there are different viewpoints, and some in the development movement have not accepted the analysis that led to the concept of sustainable development, and continue to argue for conventional

economic growth, wealth accumulation and trickle-down approaches to development.

It is clear that some of the more fundamentally challenging implications of "sustainable" development are far from universally accepted. But, for those who do support the wider principles, sustainable development offers a new way of thinking about development and a new model of progress – one that requires new analyses of the ways in which development needs to be done, and of what the negative impacts may be and how they can be reduced, and new methods of measuring success, progress and "growth".

As the concept of sustainable development becomes more widely articulated internationally, the struggles to understand the real practical implications continue. The importance of the new *processes* required for sustainable development was recognized from the start. The Brundtland Report states quite clearly that it is not just the old methods of economic development that need to change: "The time has come to break out of past patterns. Attempts to maintain social and ecological stability through old approaches to development and environmental protection will increase instability. Security must be sought through change" (WCED 1987: 309). The Brundtland Report recognized that innovation – in environmental protection as much as in social and economic development – is key to achieving sustainability. A crucial part of this innovation is a political system that ensures citizen involvement in decision-making and community action for change.

Community involvement in sustainable development

Sustainable development requires innovation – major changes in the way institutions, organizations and individuals operate. It cannot be "business as usual" alongside some minor environmental concessions. Some of the necessary innovations are about reforming internal management approaches to achieve change; some are about new technologies; some relate to the nature of monitoring, regulation and enforcement through globally agreed standards and reporting mechanisms. Central to all these necessary changes is the participation of stakeholders, especially local communities.

The importance of the community's role in achieving sustainable development has been widely acknowledged. The Brundtland Commission argued that the very first requirement in the pursuit of sustainable development should be "a political system that secures effective citizen participation in decision making" (WCED 1987: 65). It recognized the following:

The law alone cannot enforce the common interest. It principally needs community knowledge and support, which entails greater public participation in the decisions which affect the environment. This is best secured by decentralizing the
management of resources upon which local communities depend, and giving these
communities an effective say over the use of the resources. It will also require
promoting citizens' initiatives, empowering people's organizations, and strengthening local democracy. (WCED 1987: 63)

Agenda 21 contains extensive references to community involvement
and empowerment, including much emphasis on capacity-building (Warburton 1998), within the wider principle that sustainable development requires engagement from all sectors of society. For example:

Sustainable development must be achieved at every level of society. People's organizations, women's groups and non-governmental organizations are important
sources of innovation and action at the local level and have a strong interest and
proven ability to promote sustainable livelihoods. Governments, in co-operation
with appropriate international and non-governmental organizations, should support a community-driven approach to sustainability. (*Agenda 21*, para. 3.7)

Commitment to working towards sustainable development at the community level is required from more than just the international community. Many local governments have also recognized the importance of
community-level work. A major example of this is Local Agenda 21
(LA21), which has produced some impressive innovation in community
participation, including bottom–up, neighbourhood-based LA21s (Warburton 2002), working groups, forums, visioning and "future search" exercises, community audits and other mapping exercises, work with
schools and young people, state of the environment reports, environmental networks, and round tables (Church 1995). These and many other initiatives continue to build on the experience of innovators who have
worked to make links between environmental issues and community
action over past decades.

The increasing importance of community participation can be seen
as resulting from three main areas of pressure, which have influenced
the following wide range of policy areas including sustainable development:

• **Effectiveness**. Conventional, externally driven and expert-led projects
  and programmes (e.g. to tackle urban regeneration, poverty and inequality, agricultural productivity, wildlife conservation, countryside
  management) have failed to achieve the significant long-term effects
  sought (WCED 1987; Oakley 1991; Hastings et al. 1996; Rahman
  1993); immediate improvements were not valued or maintained locally,
  and the necessary long-term changes in individual people and social

structures did not materialize. Innovative approaches that involve citizens in the development and long-term sustainability of their own communities are therefore being tried. Participatory approaches that bring otherwise marginal groups into development processes and wider decision-making are seen to contribute further to greater effectiveness by reducing the social divisions that can lead to conflict.

- **Ethics**. The ethical arguments for community participation have shifted over recent years, with a growing focus on the "right" to participate: "Forgotten somehow is the fact that participation in the institutions that shape one's life is not a gratuitous privilege, but a basic right" (Kasparson, quoted in Hallett 1987: 5). The rights-based discourse has a long tradition in United Nations institutions and beyond, with rights to development, to environmental health and safety, and to overarching human rights being agreed in the past 50 years. The United Nations Development Programme's *Human Development Report 2000* argues that "the fulfilment of human rights requires democracy that is inclusive", and it has been suggested, therefore, that "elections are not enough" (Gaventa 2002). The focus on rights has moved the debate on participation beyond mechanistic approaches providing for minimal community consultation, which depends on the responsiveness of institutions for efficacy, and taken it into the more powerful political arena in which communities and individual citizens are rightful and legitimate participants in the processes that affect them (Gaventa 2002).

- **Demand**. There is a growing split, particularly in certain Western countries, between declining participation in the formal processes of democracy (especially voting and membership in political parties) and growing interest in other forms of political participation, including protest movements and direct action. A growth of these new forms of political action is now apparent in many parts of the world. Governments are perceived to have lost power in a globalized economy (although this is possibly no more than a self-fulfilling prophecy by those who are happy to see such a loss of power). There is no doubt, however, that people have less trust in the ability and willingness of governments to act on their behalf (see, for example, Beck 1992; Fukuyama 1995), and alternative and more direct participatory processes – locally, nationally and globally – have grown in importance. In addition, direct authority of all kinds is increasingly challenged, and "experts" (including scientists) are less trusted. Non-governmental organizations (NGOs) are more trusted than governments or official bodies by the public, as well as having considerable political clout as a result of their large memberships. Public demand for involvement in the decisions that affect individuals is growing through all these mechanisms, leading to the growing confidence and expertise of all these bodies.

There is a key distinction between community involvement, or participation, that uses the resources of local people as a method for improving the efficiency and effectiveness of projects and community involvement as a part of the *purpose* of the project (Oakley 1991). This has been described as a distinction between *instrumental* and *transformative* (or developmental) participation (Nelson and Wright 1995). The literature suggests that unless community involvement is explicitly part of the overall purpose of the project – an end as well as a means – then the initiative in question is unlikely to be sustainable.

There are actually both instrumental and transformative reasons for ensuring that community involvement is an end as well as a means in projects, programmes and policy-making. Treating community involvement simply as an instrumental means of getting a better project or programme can result in disjointed approaches to gaining involvement (project by project) and thus to participation overload. When particular groups are constantly bombarded with requests for their involvement this leads to growing cynicism about the value of these exercises and eventual withdrawal. Planning for community involvement as an end in itself (transformative), and seeing civil renewal as an ultimate goal that depends on active citizens, can provide the rationale for developing coherent strategies for community involvement, for investment in the capacity-building that is needed (for public, private and voluntary organizations as well as for communities), and for changes in institutional structures that ease citizen access to decision-making processes and wider active engagement. Participation can then become a virtuous circle of involvement and positive action.

Clearly, local action alone will not transform the global political arena. But the community level can have a key role in contributing to wider innovation and change – by raising awareness of the global implications of local decisions and by creating new social norms that can influence individual values, activities and behaviours. Sustainable development will never be achieved without major changes to the priorities and choices of individuals. As long as personal (and national) success is judged in terms of financial wealth and material consumption, the pressure on finite natural resources is increased and the potential for reducing inequality is reduced. Legislation and regulation will play a part in shaping individual priorities and choices, but it also requires changes to the hearts and minds of individuals, communities and society as a whole, which can be developed through new participatory processes. The United Kingdom's Royal Commission on Environmental Pollution put it this way:

Achievement of sustainable development may well depend on the extent to which the principle of reconciling environmental protection, material well-being and equity becomes an internalized value. There is some evidence that this is already happening to a significant extent ... Values are an essential element in decisions about environmental policies and standards. People's environmental and social values are the outcome of informed reflection and debate. To ensure such values are articulated and taken into account, less familiar approaches need to be used to extend and complement present procedures for consultation and participation. (RCEP 1998)

Recent work on environmental citizenship has begun to focus more on this development of a shared sense of the common good and the rights and responsibilities of citizens within the common good. Individual values, attitudes and behaviours are thus connected with the social pressures that enable people to find the "right" thing to do through interaction with others in new and conventional participatory processes that connect individual and collective virtue and justice. The role of the community in exerting moral coercion (informed social pressure) is central to the achievement of environmental citizenship through creating a critical mass of citizens who "practise what they preach" in terms of environmental responsibilities and promoting and enforcing principles of environmental justice (Bell 2003). Stated another way, "[l]ocal community remains essential as a site for the realisation of common values in support of social goods" (Robert Sampson, quoted in Blunkett 2003).

Community-level action for sustainable development thus helps create the new social norms and moral values that underpin global sustainable development, and without which other actions will fail. It becomes possible, then, to see the following three clear roles for communities in sustainable development:

- as **consumers/customers** of services and products, particularly public goods and services – "The quality of public goods and services is highly dependent on the trust between the provider and user of that service" (Skidmore et al. 2003);
- as **co-producers** of public goods and services, sharing responsibility as well as rights – citizens are not simply the passive recipients of services delivered by the state on their behalf, "in fact their consent and active participation is [sic] crucial to the quality of goods and services they receive ... they are best understood as being 'co-producers', citizens and the state working together" (Skidmore et al. 2003);
- as **citizens** operating in the political sphere where decisions are made about public priorities and resources, taking into account the needs of others – people "think and act differently as citizens than we do as consumers" (Skidmore et al. 2003) and decisions about public goods and public value are inherently political contests that require the public to engage as citizens not consumers.

Appropriate participatory processes can enable communities to become a force for the innovation that is essential to sustainable development, through the development of new roles for individuals and groups in the provision of goods and services by public and private sectors, through the development of personal values and social norms, and through new forms of political action.

Sustainable development provides the framework for the processes through which appropriate behaviours, policies and priorities are debated and determined: "sustainability is concerned as much with process as with product ... the journey is as important as the destination" (Selman 1995). The quality of the process will determine the legitimacy, effectiveness and acceptability of its policy outputs, and thus the extent to which the public (and other stakeholders) will value, accept and "own" the changes that will be required in lifestyles and aspirations.

Such an open system in communities, in which people can participate in decision-making processes using their knowledge and creativity, is the opposite of a top–down authoritarian system. It allows people to communicate with each other, try new approaches and make changes to the existing system. It is therefore vital to examine the participatory sustainable development processes being applied to achieve innovation at the community level, and to determine if they are indeed "open" to the community. By assessing the nature of the community involvement that exists, lessons can be learned and progress made in improving both those processes and their outputs and outcomes. If no one knows what success looks like, it cannot be repeated or improved upon.

Assessing community involvement in practice

The benefits of community involvement

Much of what is written about community involvement relies on qualitative assessments of the benefits, based on experience rather than detailed quantitative and statistical evidence (for example, Hallett 1987; Oakley 1991; Wilcox 1994), and tends to focus on the following benefits:

- Better and more locally appropriate projects can be developed to tackle specific locally understood problems and opportunities by bringing together expert advice and local knowledge in project design, development and management.
- Local people are more likely to look after something if they have been involved in deciding what is needed and creating it, thus reducing repair and maintenance costs on the public purse and prolonging the relationship of care and concern.

- The potential for conflict can be limited if all the likely stakeholders are involved at an early stage of project development, reducing major problems and costly delays at later stages.
- Communities and individuals can be strengthened by community involvement. Community organizations can become more secure, and individuals can become more confident, more aware and better able to do more.

There are significant debates about who the "beneficiaries" of community activity actually are, and the extent to which they gain qualitatively from the experience. The beneficiaries may include those running the community project, the users of the facilities or services developed, as well as those who live locally and benefit from wider, less tangible improvements in community safety, pride and spirit. For those most directly involved, there can be a range of quite tangible benefits, especially in developing personal skills and confidence and in dealing with public institutions in ways that lessen damaging feelings of powerlessness and alienation. New social relationships can also lead to benefits such as improved social status and an increase in hopes and aspirations (perhaps to learn in more formal settings), as well as more immediate practical benefits such as improved access to local services and involvement in wider networks that may allow access to further training and employment opportunities. All these benefits depend on a satisfactory experience of involvement, which essentially requires giving participants some evidence that they have made some difference.

There is some quantitative evidence of the benefits of community involvement, although these tend to be from the perspective of public agencies rather than local communities. For example, an early study by the World Bank (1994) examined the costs and benefits of participatory and non-participatory programmes funded by the Bank. The findings showed that, overall, participation by beneficiaries was "the single most important factor in determining the overall quality of implementation" and made a significant contribution to project effectiveness, including lower operational costs (e.g. maintenance). A separate study by the UK Department of Health (HEMS 1998) found that those who felt empowered to make their own decisions, who were engaged in community activities and who lived in places with strong neighbourhood social capital were less likely to report poor health and less likely to have unhealthy lifestyles.

Approaches to community involvement

Work is continuing to develop broad indicators of community involvement so that more effective evaluations of the immediate and long-term costs and benefits can be made. Many studies draw on the idea of social capital, developed by Robert Putnam, as a key indicator of a strong civic community. Such a community is "marked by an active, public-spirited citizenry, by egalitarian political relations, by a social fabric of trust and co-operation" (Putnam 1993: 15), expressed in strong social institutions and networks, from labour unions to choral societies. Putnam argues that social capital is a moral resource and public good that activates the latent human capital of individuals and populations.

Although social capital can be seen as the product of, and essential lubricant for, strong and involved communities, other analyses focus on levels of power and control. The classic version is Arnstein's ladder of participation (Arnstein 1971), which was devised in 1969 and has been used to analyse levels of community and public participation ever since. Arnstein's ladder has eight levels: the first three rungs (manipulation, education and information) are generally regarded as non-participative approaches; participation starts at level four (consultation, although this can include passive, perhaps tokenistic, involvement), rising to full control at level eight by those participating (see Table 2.1).

Peter Oakley's analysis suggests three different broad levels of power related to participation (Oakley 1991):

- **Participation as contribution:** control and direction are not passed to local people, who are just asked to contribute resources.

Table 2.1 Arnstein's ladder of participation

Level	Approach	Participation
Level 1	Manipulation	These two levels assume a passive audience,
Level 2	Education	who are given information that may be partial or constructed
Level 3	Information	People are told what is going to happen, is happening, or has happened
Level 4	Consultation	People are given a voice but not the power to ensure their views are heeded
Level 5	Involvement	People's views have some influence, but traditional power holders still make the decisions
Level 6	Partnership	People can begin to negotiate with traditional power holders, including agreeing on roles, responsibilities and levels of control
Level 7	Delegated power	Some power is delegated
Level 8	Citizen control	Decision-making and action are fully delegated

Source: Arnstein (1971).

- **Participation as organization:** organizations and institutions are created and/or developed as an important element in participation. A participatory process may result in formal organizations (such as local trusts), as well as in informal groupings in which the development of a new (or changed) organization involves some delegation of power and control.
- **Participation as empowerment:** the relationship between power and participation is made explicit – participation is developmental, and power and control are devolved.

Oakley stresses that the first of these types of participation (contribution) is fundamentally different from the other two – both organization and empowerment involve a transfer of control. The importance of Oakley's analysis is not just in his analysis of shifts of power but also in his recognition of the structural as well as the personal and practical changes that result from participatory action; it is about people as individuals and what they achieve, but also about the new structures (groups, associations, trusts) they establish that continue to provide mechanisms for participation in the long term.

One of the great strengths of these analyses is the recognition that power and resources are central to community involvement. However, the use of levels encourages the notion that some levels are *inherently better* than others, whereas in practice different levels of involvement are appropriate in different circumstances. Arnstein's ladder, in particular, also has some important omissions – for example, activities that contribute to democratic activity but are not commissioned, led or controlled by government or other institutions, including those that are essentially about protest. It also focuses only on community participation in decision-making, rather than including participatory (including community) *action*. This raises the important issue of what exactly is being participated *in*. In most cases, community participation is analysed in terms of participation in public policy programmes led by government, NGOs or other institutions, but this remains only part of the picture.

An alternative framework (developed by Warburton to evaluate community involvement in community energy projects) may be used to understand the following five different types of practical community involvement at the project level:

- **Involvement:** community involvement in schemes run for community benefit by public, private, voluntary or community organizations. This would exclude schemes established for private profit (because of the community benefit element). In this instance, community involvement could range from participation in the design and establishment of the project to community organizations providing services or goods.
- **Initiation:** schemes *initiated by* voluntary or community organizations,

with additional community involvement processes to ensure wider support and knowledge (beyond the group promoting the scheme).

- **Partnership:** schemes in which voluntary or community organizations are *partners* in a meaningful way; that is, not just token names on the project proposal but having, say, 50 per cent representation in the governing group.
- **Management:** schemes *managed by* voluntary or community organizations, through agreement with the developers or owners (for example, a management group or board made up of representatives of the local community).
- **Ownership:** schemes *owned by* the local community. Ownership could be through a community company, development trust or other community enterprise model, or through election of the governing group (that is, ownership through political control).

In this model, some projects may use several of these types of community involvement over time, such as a scheme initiated by a community group, but with wider community involvement, and then run in the long term by a partnership including that group but also others. To "count" as a community scheme, at least one of these types of involvement would need to be present.

The types of community involvement in this model cover many of Arnstein's levels of control and include involvement in both decision-making and action, but they are presented in a non-hierarchical framework, so none is presented as "better" than the others in all circumstances. They cover the full range of approaches, taking into account factors of control, involvement, leadership and input (see Figure 2.1).

It is important to consider all these various factors in analysing approaches to community involvement, particularly because communities are unique in their culture, resources and socio-political situation, and in many other ways. Although a sharing of power is important, there is no one method or approach – no magic technique – that will work universally. Processes for community involvement need to be designed so that

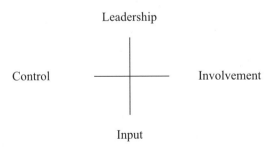

Figure 2.1 Factors in community involvement.

they are appropriate to the needs of the particular community and to the particular circumstances. By examining the balance between leadership, input, involvement and control, many different and equally appropriate patterns of community involvement can be identified and better evaluated.

Such an analysis can be undertaken only once an understanding has been reached of the types of activity in which voluntary and community organizations are involved at the local level. These activities can be categorized as follows (Home Office 2004):

* **Action to build social capital.** People take part in community initiatives that build relationships, trust, shared norms and networks through which a community's resource and opportunity bases are enriched for all its members, and that are essential for active citizenship.
* **Delivering services.** This covers: *autonomous services* provided by community organizations through mutual aid, etc., and supported by funds raised by members; *specialist services* supported by service agreements, contracts or grants by the public sector; and *statutory public services*, where some of these services have been devolved to more formalized community organizations and voluntary bodies through contracts and service agreements.
* **Involvement in governance.** People represent the interests of all local people or of particular groups in influencing decisions that affect their quality of life or in advocating community interests in public decision-making arenas or as users of public services.

Academic analysis of community involvement can provide only a partial picture. Any form of participation is a human experience, and the quality of that experience may best be captured by individual story-telling and participatory evaluations of experience, in which indicators and evaluation processes are developed, findings and essential lessons are shared and decisions about required action are made with participants. There are difficulties associated with this approach, including the need to balance the benefits of preserving the authenticity of the participants' own words against creating outputs that can be digested by institutions in the form of reports and recommendations, which may require "translation" by evaluators (Hunt and Szerszynski 1999). However, the potential for creating a more richly textured picture of the positive aspects and difficulties of any specific participatory project will help ensure that lessons can be identified for future work.

Stakeholders

Part of assessing the quality of community involvement will always be a review of the stakeholders involved. Clearly, the determination of which stakeholders are appropriate will depend on the context, but the basic definition of a stakeholder covers anyone who will be affected by, or may affect, the issues under consideration.

In practice, participatory projects are often directed at local groups and organizations such as community associations, village hall committees, volunteer groups, women's or youth organizations, tenants' organizations, conservation groups, and all the other interest groups that can be found in any community. Community involvement must also include those local people who may often be excluded from a lot of community activities: older people, people with physical disabilities, people from ethnic minority communities, young people, people struggling with poverty.

The nature of potential local beneficiaries has already been outlined. Going beyond the people who live locally, other stakeholders may also have an interest: visitors, including people involved in leisure pursuits; professionals with an interest in the particular project (foresters or conservationists, researchers, architects or engineers); developers; and others with a financial or commercial interest. Beyond these are stakeholders concerned simply with ensuring the continued "existence" of public and social goods they may never use or even see – for example, environmentalists concerned about rainforests on the other side of the world (Jacobs 1995). Such interests may be represented through formal NGOs or through far less formal networks and social movements.

Any discussion of stakeholders has to touch on issues of representation and accountability, especially as public institutions are often concerned that those they are working with are not representative of wider interests. In many cases locally, such a lack of representativeness is highly likely – many community groups are established to tackle a particular local problem and consist simply of those local people concerned enough to get involved. Local groups often make considerable efforts to encourage the widest possible involvement in their activity (not least because a large number of supporters encourages the authorities to take demands seriously), but these groups are not usually elected by all those in their apparent constituency, and generally they do not claim to represent anyone but themselves and their members.

Many local voluntary and community organizations do take accountability seriously, developing a range of formal and informal structures to ensure that their activities are open and transparent to anyone with an interest (Craig et al. 2001). However, such undertakings can use up significant resources, and thus tend to be more limited in poorly resourced small organizations than in public and private organizations with substantially greater resources. For many voluntary and community organizations, their legitimacy comes from their activities to give voice to citizens who would not otherwise be heard, and their commitment to participatory forms of organization is designed to support that activity by extending their accountability and representativeness to enhance their effectiveness (Craig et al. 2002). As always, organizations need to balance these activities with continuing to provide effective action and leadership.

The representativeness of certain groups may become an issue for government and public institutions if the group is delivering messages that challenge the current orthodoxy. In many cases, however, government and public bodies value the quality of the evidence that such groups can offer – in terms of new ideas and projects and closeness to the grassroots – more highly than formal representativeness (Craig et al. 2002).

Barriers to community participation

Community involvement remains a marginal activity, although its nature and benefits are now better understood by society than in the past. Most development (and conservation) is still undertaken conventionally, in an expert-dominated, externally driven and exclusive manner. Even when community involvement does happen, participatory action on the ground can be undermined or even neutralized by the governing institution's lack of willingness to change. Institutions often fail to recognize that a participatory approach is not just another step in the project process, but a fundamental change in philosophy. This can be difficult for agencies that are used to developing their own solutions away from the public gaze.

There are other barriers to effective and appropriate community involvement. Centralized decision-making can exclude those not within inner circles, and many powerful officials and elected politicians remain unconvinced of the merits of (or demand for) greater community involvement. Even when stakeholders are involved in early stages, they are rarely included in the actual decision-making, and they may be excluded from detailed planning and implementation, and almost certainly from any monitoring and evaluation. The implementation of decisions relating to sustainable development would be helped by a strengthened sense of ownership among participating stakeholders of the decisions and actions to be taken, but this rarely happens in practice.

At the other end of the scale, a lack of strategic planning by public authorities can create too much demand for involvement from certain key community groups, often within deadlines that are too short for them to consult their own members, as well as creating resource pressures that many groups cannot deal with. In addition, relationships between public institutions, communities and citizens have deteriorated over recent years in many parts of the world. As a result, the public may not trust that institutions will be willing, or able, to make any changes. Moreover, people often doubt their own ability to make any difference (Macnaghten et al. 1995).

To develop the appropriate governance systems for sustainable development, with the essential community involvement at their core, requires innovation and change in project and programme management systems and in the political policy and decision-making processes behind the practical work. This will necessitate considerable changes in the organizational cultures of public and voluntary bodies. For example, their procedures and decision-making must be more open and accountable, and their staff more familiar with and responsive to community-level processes.

Governance

The wider link between community involvement and sustainable development can be found by examining the importance of the new governance structures required for both. This chapter has already described the value of community involvement as a learning experience for both individual citizens and communities, and how it helps people to see more clearly the consequences of individual and local choices for society and the planet, and to discourage unsustainable attitudes and behaviours. Community-led projects and programmes can create more sustainable local solutions. But community involvement cannot flourish, or make lasting improvements, unless it is set within wider changes to governance structures.

Essentially, governance is about the *processes* and the political, legal and administrative *institutions* through which decisions are made, and about how these processes and institutions are managed and are accountable. Governance processes include, but go beyond, governments. The complexity of the decision-making needed for global sustainable development – and the web of impacts, rights and responsibilities across sectors, countries and continents – means that systems of governance are required that combine state governments, global governance structures, local governance, civil society and corporate activities.

> The greatest challenge posed by globalization is that of good governance in the broadest sense. (Annan 1998a: 3)

> Good governance is perhaps the single most important factor in eradicating poverty and promoting development. By good governance is meant creating well-functioning and accountable institutions – political, judicial and administrative – that citizens regard as legitimate, through which they participate in decisions that affect their lives, and by which they are empowered. (Annan 1998b)

In these statements, the Secretary-General of the United Nations high-lights the role of good governance, which involves the creation of institutions through which citizen involvement is achieved. Citizen involvement and good governance are not separate goals, but should be aimed for together and with good balance. Some in government fear a negative impact from community involvement, but it can and should inform and strengthen existing democratic forms.

There is, in short, no magic about community. The age-old tasks of government still have to be performed – creating legitimate authority and transferring it to new leaders when necessary, accounting for public money ... Every profession and public official should respect those who depend on their services and find ways of giving them a voice which cannot be disregarded. That calls for *more* sensitive and effective civic leadership, not less of it, from democratically accountable public authorities. (Donnison 1993; emphasis added)

Community involvement, however, does require traditional democratic institutions to change, so that the gap can be closed between community-based activities (and community involvement in policy-making) and mainstream projects, programmes and political decision-making, bringing together the systems of representative and participatory democracy. Innovation will be required to ensure better integration and joined up working between these currently separate strands of democratic activity. In this context, recent and future experiences should be rigorously monitored and evaluated to assess the most effective systems for different cultural contexts.

Learning and capacity-building – the way forward

The innovation needed to create the new systems and practices required to achieve effective community involvement, stronger democratic structures and sustainable development is fundamental and deeply challenging. Sustainable development is not a policy that can simply be agreed upon and enforced. Legislation and regulation are needed, but so too are learning and capacity-building in order to ensure that regulation is known about, understood and adhered to, and as a way of minimizing the need for enforcement by reducing undesirable activities before they happen.

Different sorts of learning methods are needed to develop the new values, attitudes and behaviours compatible with sustainable development. People do learn through the experience of community involvement, but this needs to be explicitly supported to enable people to turn experience into expertise and wider knowledge and wisdom. It is well understood that "sustainable development ultimately rests on national and local capacity for policy-making and implementation" (CSD 2002), and that capacity-building is needed to improve the ability of institutions, groups and individuals to work on these issues more effectively. The new knowledge and skills required for sustainable development can best be developed through new learning mechanisms. Such "capacity building requires a flexible process-driven approach that encourages learning, adaptive management, experimentation, a long-term commitment, the building of human skills and competencies, and a sensitivity to local culture, politics and context. It cannot be programmed in detail from the outset, but must involve government, civil society and private actors with social and environmental responsibilities" (CSD 2002).

Learning at the community level can be developed in a number of ways, from relatively formal learning experiences that focus on the benefits of participatory action (e.g., Scott et al. 1989), through to the learning that results from active participation and careful reflection on that experience. Values and social norms are developed through social interaction, and learning through involvement in debates, decision-making and practical action, which are key elements in the learning needed for sustainable development. Involvement techniques such as citizens' juries allow time for participants to learn about the issues they are dealing with, to take evidence and to question technical experts, and it is likely that other involvement mechanisms will need to build a learning element into plans more explicitly in future if the required capacity-building is to be achieved.

Professionals too must question and change their roles and activities. Robert Chambers (1997) has shown how conventional professional attitudes ("we know best") have led to errors, omissions and delusions, with spectacularly damaging results. New responsibilities are now placed on professionals to promote participatory approaches, requiring a new humility, sensitivity, nimbleness and willingness to change; the changes needed are personal as well as institutional (Chambers 1997). Education and learning in these terms go beyond any idea that professionals or experts (or educators) have all the answers.

Paulo Freire's concept of "conscientisation" proposes a mutual learning process through which people "learn to perceive the social, political and economic contradictions, and to take action" (Freire 1996). The mutuality of the learning process is crucial – it is not learning at the feet of a master, but joint learning based on the principles of dialogue between teachers and lay people in which the knowledge of all parties is respected, recognizing that "the educator himself needs educating".

As well as personal and professional learning and change, institutional learning will be required to support the transition to a sustainable society. It has been argued that hierarchical agency structures present particular barriers to participatory action because the tiers reduce communication and understanding as issues progress (Baxter 1996). Institutions therefore need to become "learning organizations" to deal with the dynamics of change over time (Bryden et al. 1995).

In short, the education and learning processes for innovative community action on sustainable development can cover a wide spectrum, from simple information provision to materials and activities that stimulate thought and discussion and enable people to develop their own views, values and beliefs. Techniques can range from basic materials that provide authoritative facts and figures, to interactive learning based on real engagement in policy development and/or practical projects. As learning takes place, it is important to include sufficient mechanisms to capture and evaluate the experience, draw out lessons, articulate those lessons more widely, and then change practices as a result, so that experience is not lost beyond the few individuals intimately involved.

Conclusion

"Community" is now deeply entrenched as a guiding principle in current political debate and public policy. Although it is a contested concept and there is certainly no shared idea of what "community" actually looks like, there are attempts to understand the potential characteristics of a sustainable community that is diverse, open and welcoming of difference.

It is clear that the *process* of community involvement is as important as the *product* of community-level action for sustainability; it is a learning experience and a voyage of discovery for all involved. That means it can be messy and difficult. It is equally clear that there is a need to assess whether the process has been a success. Only then will community involvement be done better in the future.

The subject is difficult to pin down because it works in the context of the ever-changing values of society against a background of the ever-greater complexities of the modern world. In such a state of flux, there can be no underlying consensus that can be reached if only we can find the right technique. Rather, the challenge is to find processes that allow society to struggle with the conflicts and uncertainties and to establish areas of agreement that will serve for the time being. Community involvement is one of those processes, and its appeal is likely to grow as people find satisfaction in being part of deciding their own futures. It is a profound challenge to policy makers – but it is a positive challenge that should enable future policy decisions to be more legitimate, accountable and appropriate, and implementation to be more successful in contributing to the innovations necessary to achieve sustainable development. Sustainable development does not offer a blueprint or model for community involvement, but it does offer a framework of principles and a growing understanding of those principles in global institutions, as well as in local governments, communities and other organizations. Some governments may find these principles difficult to accept, but numerous organizations and networks are working on these issues, from developing analyses to conducting direct action. It is likely that the debates will continue for many years to come as we try to find out more about the sorts of communities we want to create in a sustainable future.

REFERENCES

Annan, Kofi A. (1998a) "Report of the Secretary-General on the work of the Organization", General Assembly 53rd session, 7th plenary meeting, 21 September; available at: ⟨http://www.un.org/documents/a53pv7.pdf⟩.
——— (1998b) "Partnerships for global community", *Report of the Secretary-General on the work of the organization.* A/53/1, 27 August. New York: United Nations Department of Public Information.
Arnstein, Shelly (1971) "A ladder of citizen participation in the USA", *Journal of the Royal Town Planning Institute* 57: 176–182; first published in 1969 in *Journal of American Institute of Planners* 35: 216–224.
Baxter, S. H. (1996) *Experiences in participation: A review of current practice in rural development programmes.* Edinburgh: Scottish National Heritage.
Beck, U. (1992) *Risk society: Towards a new modernity.* London: Sage Publications.
Bell, D. R. (2003) "Environmental citizenship and the political", paper presented at the ESRC seminar on Citizenship and the Environment, Bath, UK, 10–15 October.
Blunkett, D. (2003) *Civil renewal: A new agenda.* London: Home Office, June.
Bryden, J., D. Watson, C. Storey and J. van Alphen (1995) *Community involvement and rural policy.* Arkleton Trust, Arkleton Centre, University of Aberdeen.
Chambers, R. (1997) *Whose reality counts? Putting the first last.* London: Intermediate Technology Publications.
Church, C. (1995) *Towards local sustainability: A review of current activity on Local Agenda 21 in the UK.* London: UNA Sustainable Communities Unit/ Community Development Foundation.
Craig, G., S. Monro, T. Parkes, M. Taylor, D. Warburton and D. Wilkinson (2001) "Willing partners? Voluntary and community organisations in the democratic process, Interim research findings", University of Essex, UK.
——— (2002) "Willing partners? Voluntary and community organisations in the democratic process, Final research findings", University of Essex, UK.

CSD [Commission on Sustainable Development] (2002) "Implementing Agenda 21", Report of the Secretary-General. Commission on Sustainable Development (United Nations Economic and Social Council) acting as the preparatory committee for WSSD. Advance unedited text.

Donnison, D. (1993) "Listen to the voice of the community", *The Guardian*, 10 September.

Flecknoe, C. and N. McLellan (1994) *The what, how and why of neighbourhood community development.* London: Community Matters.

Freire, P. (1996) *Pedagogy of the oppressed.* London: Penguin; first published 1970.

Fukuyama, F. (1995) *Trust: The social virtues and the creation of prosperity.* London: Hamish Hamilton.

Gaventa, J. (2002) "Exploring citizenship, participation and accountability", *IDS Bulletin* 33(2).

Hallett, C. (1987) *Critical issues in participation.* Sheffield: Association of Community Workers.

Hastings, A., A. McArthur and A. McGregor (1996) *Less than equal? Community organisations and estate regeneration.* York: Policy Press and Joseph Rowntree Foundation.

HEMS [Health Education Monitoring Survey] (1998) "Health in England (1998). Investigating the links between social inequalities and health", in *Health Education Monitoring Survey 1998.* London: The Stationery Office.

Home Office (2004) *Building civil renewal. A review of government support for community capacity building and proposals for change.* UK Home Office, Civil Renewal Unit, January.

Hunt, J. and B. Szerszynski (1999) "How was it for you? Issues and dilemmas in the evaluation of deliberative processes", in Tim O'Riordan, Jacqueline Burgess and Bron Szerszynski, *Deliberative and inclusionary processes. A report from two seminars.* CSERGE Working Paper PA99–06, Centre for Social and Economic Research on the Global Environment, University of East Anglia.

Jacobs, M. (1995) *Sustainability and socialism.* London: SERA (Socialist Environmental Resource Association).

MacGillivray, A. and S. Zadek (1996) *Accounting for change: Indicators for sustainable development.* London: New Economics Foundation.

Macnaghten, P., R. Grove-White, M. Jacobs and B. Wynne (1995) *Public perceptions and sustainability in Lancashire: Indicators, institutions and participation.* Lancaster University for Lancashire County Council.

Meadows, D., et al. (1983) *Limits to growth.* London: Pan Books; first published 1972.

Nelson, N. and S. Wright (1995) *Power and participatory development.* London: Intermediate Technology Publications.

Oakley, P. (1991) *Projects with people. The practice of participation in rural development.* London: International Labour Organization, through IT Publications.

Putnam, R. D. (1993) *Making democracy work: Civic traditions in modern Italy.* Princeton, NJ: Princeton University Press.

Rahman, M. D. A. (1993) *People's self-development: Perspectives on participatory action research.* London: Zed Books.

RCEP [Royal Commission on Environmental Pollution] (1998) *Setting environmental standards. Royal Commission on Environmental Pollution 21st report.* London: HMSO.

Scott, I., J. Denman and B. Lane (1989) *Doing by learning: A handbook for organizers and tutors of village-based community development courses.* Cirencester: ACRE.

Selman, P. (1995) "Local sustainability", *Town Planning Review* 66(3).

Skidmore, P., P. Miller and J. Chapman (2003) *The long game: How regulators and companies can both win.* London: Demo.

Taylor, M. (1995) *Unleashing the potential: Bringing residents to the centre of regeneration.* York: Joseph Rowntree Foundation.

United Nations Department of Economic and Social Affairs, Division for Sustainable Development (1992) *Agenda 21*; available at: ⟨http://www.un.org/esa/sustdev/documents/agenda21/index.htm⟩.

Warburton, D. (1998) "A passionate dialogue. Community and sustainable development", in D. Warburton (ed.), *Community and sustainable development. Participation in the future.* London: Earthscan.

——— (2002) "Evaluating participation in sustainable development", paper presented at EASY-ECO Conference, Vienna, 23–25 May.

WCED [World Commission on Environment and Development] (1987) *Our common future.* Oxford: Oxford University Press.

Wilcox, D. (1994) *Guide to effective participation.* Brighton: Partnership Books.

Williams, R. (1988) *Keywords.* London: Fontana; first published in 1976.

World Bank (1994) *The World Bank and participation.* World Bank Learning Group on Participatory Development, Operations Department, September.

3

Being innovative, against the odds

Charles Landry

Introduction

This chapter provides an overview of innovativeness and how it can be applied to the agenda of creating sustainable communities. Along the way, it draws on examples highlighting different aspects of innovative action. It stresses how it is easier to be innovative as an individual than as an organization, community or city, and spells out the obstacles that block imaginative action at nearly every turn. Most of these barriers are to do with entrenched economic and political interests; technology-related issues are far less of a problem. Promoting sustainability ultimately involves behavioural change and transformation. Because transformation often hurts, it frightens those who have something to lose. As a result, humanity has made far less progress than it should have on the agenda of sustainability.

This chapter also proposes a way of looking at innovative processes and how they can be encouraged. It suggests that, by creating innovative momentum in a community, a virtuous cycle of creativity can be generated. To drive momentum, the notion of trading power for creative influence is key – those with power need to understand that releasing their tight hold on power in fact unleashes great potential in communities by empowering them. In so doing, imaginative community leaders create the conditions within which it is possible for citizens to think, plan and act creatively. Successes build ambition and excitement, with the result that more obstacles are overcome, in the process changing the mindset of key individuals in a community and helping to create an innovative milieu. This process of change is essentially cultural, since agreeing to change involves a shift in values. Further, because values are about choices and choices are about politics, fostering sustainability is also a political issue.

I draw on my own direct experiences, mostly in more economically developed countries. Nevertheless, the attributes that make communities innovative can apply equally to developed and less-developed countries. The qualities of an innovative environment ultimately come down to a few features: taking measured risks, widespread leadership, a sense of going somewhere, having the strength to go beyond the political cycle, and, crucially, being strategically principled and tactically flexible, as well as recognizing the resources that come from a community's history and talents. To foster this situation, changes in mindset, perception, ambition and will are required. Each country, whatever its state of development, has projects that in their own way are inspiring. There are many examples of a community or city, whatever its problems at first sight, finding unusual ways of generating projects that are models of sustainability. They do this by assessing their local cultural circumstances and assets and by responding imaginatively to what is possible (and often seemingly impossible) in their context. What this requires is insight, courage, tenacity and determination, as well as a willingness to go against conventional thinking.

Setting the scene

People and organizations are often innovative

If one were to take a helicopter view of communities around the world, it would immediately become clear how many imaginative, innovative and courageous people have tried to change their communities for the better – and the same is true for organizations. One only needs to look at the databases of best practice from the United Nations Human Settlements Programme (UN-HABITAT), the Together Foundation[1] or the International Council for Local Environmental Initiatives (ICLEI)[2] or to scan the list of winners of the Right Livelihood Award (RLA)[3] to feel a sense of awe at what can be achieved. Many examples come to mind – people such as Wes Jackson, who developed a system of perennial farming for the American prairies, or Birsel Lemke, who campaigned to stop mining companies destroying the Turkish landscape; groups such as the Peoples Science Movement of Kerala in India, which played a crucial role in building Kerala's unique model of people-centred development, or the

Finnish Village Action Group, Kylätoiminta, which found dynamically innovative ways for rural regeneration and popular participation. The list is endless.

Communities have greater difficulty in being innovative

When comparing the efforts around the world of innovative *communities* toward sustainability, as distinct from *individual projects*, the results are disappointing. This is not for want of trying, however. An alarmingly small number of large-scale projects have been completed, which is a sad reflection of the current situation. A survey by Barton and Kleiner (2000), for example, revealed hundreds of eco-village or neighbourhood projects worldwide, but most were purely at the conceptual stage – often with impressive websites and high reputations in their networks. The new town of Bamberton in British Columbia, Canada, on the drawing board for a number of years, is representative of many such communities:

A steep site overlooking the Saanich Inlet on Vancouver Island is the proposed location for the new town of Bamberton. Thirty kilometres north of Victoria this 12,000 person community awaits approval from the government before it can go ahead. Until that time, it remains a city in the imagination of its designers. The planning of this town is visionary in many respects. Attempting to break from the uninspired model of suburban housing that characterizes many of our cities, the designers have studied a combination of historical models and new technologies. The hope is that this will make a progressive and workable community for the next millennium. Bamberton has been planned as a series of environmentally sensitive neighbourhoods. An emphasis on pedestrians over automobiles has changed the pattern of the street layout. Other issues such as building materials, waste management, and sewage treatment have been scrutinized and designed to create an ecologically sustainable town. The town will be wired with fibre optic trunks because it is intended that the majority of the residents will work at home. Telecommuting will reduce dependence on cars and public transportation. (Barton and Kleiner 2000: 80)

Barton and Kleiner's survey analysed 55 projects and revealed a rich variety of innovative communities that bill themselves as eco-neighbourhoods. They have great diversity in scale, location, focus and means of implementation, and include many different types – for example, rural eco-villages such as Crystal Waters in Queensland, Australia; tele-villages such as Little River near Christchurch in New Zealand; urban demonstration projects such as a high-density block of 150 dwellings with courtyards in Kolding, Denmark; urban eco-communities such as Ithaca Eco-Village in New York State in the United States; new urbanism developments such as Poundbury in the United Kingdom, initiated by the Prince of Wales, or Waitakere in Auckland, New Zealand; and ecological townships such as Auroville in South India, or Davis in California, United States.

The key impression of the survey is that there is only a tiny proportion of comprehensively innovative projects at the neighbourhood level. Many had a number of impressive buildings and high environmental standards, but very few combined these features with new sustainable economic activities or new political or social arrangements. As exemplary projects, all are praiseworthy. But their wider success is questionable. They are too small to be self-sustaining in any real sense and transport issues remain a problem, because many people work outside their community.

The obstacles to innovation

Lack of courage and blocked thinking

The main problem is that governments at the local, regional and national levels often "speak with a forked tongue" in spite of their public pro-sustainability stance. There are policy and practical obstacles over which a local community has little power. In many cases, "sustainable development" is a phrase more talked about than practised: "It is often used with casual abandon as if mere repetition delivers green probity" (Barton and Kleiner 2000: 6). This is a common problem. A recent survey conducted by Culture Intelligence in England looked particularly at the cultural uses of technology in cities.[4] Interestingly, it found that cities with a track record of innovation rarely used the term "sustainable development", although the concept of sustainability was embedded in many activities and policies. Striving or lagging cities, in contrast, continually advertised what they were going to do but often did not deliver results.

According to Barton and Kleiner's survey, well over 50 per cent of the projects reviewed involved fewer than 300 people, and, of the 14 projects (23 per cent) that aimed to involve at least 1,000 people, which is the size where economies of scale can begin to operate, only 4 had reached that scale or were complete. These are Lykovryssi in Greece, which focuses on solar energy; Puchenan in Linz, Austria, whose special feature is its district heating system; Auroville in India, which is acclaimed for its wasteland reclamation, but also focuses on spiritual and psychological growth; and Davis in California, whose 1974 general plan gave it a national reputation for energy conservation.

Of the smaller projects, most were rural and initiated by residents themselves. The analysis showed that the voluntary/community sector dominated as project initiators (69 per cent), followed by the public sector (22 per cent) and the private sector (9 per cent). The reasons for the dominance of the voluntary/community sector vary, but include being more in touch with local needs, being able to respond more rapidly, and being less constrained by commercial or regional and national agendas.

There is a gulf between projects emerging out of idealistic commitment and those that are delivered by the market system or the public domain. Some successes have been achieved by the private sector, particularly at the technical level, where problems have been solved using methods ranging from energy-saving techniques to more efficient methods of recycling waste or growing food. Also, as the book *Natural Capitalism* outlines (Hawken et al. 1999), there are many prototype products that could deliver greater sustainability. However, to put it bluntly, the inner logic of capitalism works against the principles of sustainability. Capitalism is not as risk taking as many think, so it avoids daring to be environmental. Moreover, having conquered the world, capitalism now steals our time by speeding up processes from building techniques to demands for commercial payback, and has reached the final frontier by scouring resources from a supposedly infinite future.

Meanwhile, the public sector often lacks the courage to develop the incentives and regulatory regimes that foster sustainability. Notable exceptions include Zurich's scheme to charge heavy users of energy more per unit than careful users. Clearly, there are admirable local projects driven by initiatives such as the iconic Local Agenda 21 programme (a programme described in Chapter 28 of Agenda 21 calling upon local authorities to consult with communities and develop and implement a local plan for sustainability through existing government strategies). However, neither governments (particularly at the national level) nor corporations have the determination to apply the principles that could change the landscape of our thinking and consequent actions. These principles are well summarized by Carew-Reid et al. (1994) as follows:

- the public trust doctrine, which places a duty on the state to hold environmental resources in trust for the benefit of the public;
- the precautionary principle, which both highlights caution and argues that lack of full scientific certainty should not be used as a reason for postponing cost-effective measures to prevent environmental degradation;
- the principle of intergenerational equity, which requires that the needs of the present are met without compromising the ability of future generations to meet their own needs;
- the principle of intragenerational equity, which requires that all people currently alive have an equal right to benefit from the use of resources, both within and between countries;

- the subsidiarity principle, which deems that decisions should be made at the lowest appropriate level; and, finally,
- the polluter pays principle, which requires that all costs of environmental damage should be borne by those who cause them.

These can be seen as normative requirements that must be debated primarily in the political domain.

An alternative template exists. Consider the paradigm-shifting conceptual breakthroughs that, if applied, would change our products, services and communities dramatically. They include the notion of *carrying capacity*, the concept of *ecological footprint*, and the focus on *resource productivity* as distinct from *resource exploitation*. These are explanatory and interpretative devices as well as methodologies for assessing effectiveness, but they are stated in new terms that foster environmental caring. They have immense potential for changing how we live.

The dominant market paradigm, by contrast, has at its core the notions of growth and money. Although these notions are extremely powerful, they are also simplistic. They do not capture the complexity of how social systems operate, measuring only a small part of community dynamics. For example, they do not accommodate good ways to measure work undertaken, effects on the environment, or the losses created by the growth paradigm. The reality is that our regulatory and incentive structures reinforce the dynamics of growth and money, yet they could just as easily be structured to create completely different outcomes. Applying the concept of resource productivity would be one such measure. Most importantly, the environment must be recognized as being not a minor factor of production but rather "an envelope containing, provisioning and sustaining the entire economy" (Daly 1997).

A question arises: When we know what should be done why are we not doing it? Nigel Taylor answers that there are "comfortable myths that we can tacitly ignore the central role of national governments and international capitalism which leads us to overplay the role of localities and design solutions" (Taylor 2000: 19). The unacknowledged obstacles are power, entrenched interests and lack of responsibility. When put kindly the obstacle is called inertia; those seeking to avoid the issue say environmentalism will not work in the real market. But the market is a flexible mechanism whose power lies in its adaptive qualities. It can adapt to the environmental agenda, just as it has adapted to the public goods agenda by providing public transport, health services or cultural facilities. An example suffices to make the point. Emscher Park, in the Ruhr industrial area of Germany, had been severely degraded by its past steel production and coal-mining activities. The regional government set high environmental (and aesthetic) standards in its 10-year renewal programme, encouraging public support for its overarching goals. In response, private and public operators (often leading the initiative) adapted, and in so doing generated new technologies for healing the environment, using the local area as the experimentation zone. Over time, a raft of companies were generated that now employ 50,000 people, and export markets opened up as other regions and countries strove to catch up.[5]

New boundaries of measurement

A further obstacle to innovation lies in the way we measure success and failure. Accounting systems are, of course, geared to an unsustainable paradigm and thus are narrowly based, focusing on benchmarks such as growth in gross national product or gross domestic product. Wealth is equated only with money, and by that measure growth in many countries has been huge, technological innovations have been astonishing, and living standards have shot up. But many people know intuitively that all this "growth" is not always making lives better. Real life for many has become less healthy, more stressful and more polluted. The risks involved in selecting what to measure were stated articulately by Daniel Yankelovich, the renowned American pollster:

> The first step is to measure whatever can be easily measured. This is okay as far as it goes. The second step is to disregard that which can't be measured or give it an arbitrary value. This is artificial and misleading. The third step is to presume what can't be measured isn't really important. This is blindness. The fourth step is to say that what can't be easily measured really doesn't exist. This is suicide! (Yankelovich, 1971)

Three examples serve to reinforce the point. In *If Women Counted*, Marilyn Waring explains the irony that a tree has a measurable economic value when it is chopped down and sold as wood, but not while it is alive and creating the oxygen we need (Waring and Steinam 1990). The second example is housework, whose monetary value remains unmeasured in national economies. Third, people in Los Angeles use petrol worth over US$800 million while sitting in traffic jams, which contributes to the growth of GNP (Boyle 2000). One must question these methods of measuring "progress".

Alternative measurement scales do exist, one of the best of which is the Index of Sustainable Economic Welfare (ISEW). The ISEW measures money but also subtracts the externalities that are often invisible within the formal economy, such as pollution, disease and depletion of natural resources (Mizrach n.d.). According to this index, many countries in the industrialized world reached their highest standard of living in 1974 and have been going downhill since, if we calculate the effects and associated costs of pollution, for example.

Technology is no longer the barrier

Innovative communities need to assess their ambit for being imaginative and where obstacles exist. We can classify the spheres of possible intervention according to end product, technology, technique and procedure, process, implementation mechanism, problem redefinition, target audience, behavioural impact, and professional context. In terms of problem definition, there is a wealth of experience and clarity, as there is in the development of technologies. Few real obstacles prevent the development of products and processes that are more sustainable than current ones, whether it be new housing and building techniques or the hydrogen-fuelled car. Similarly, many tried and tested participatory techniques already exist to involve communities in creating more environmentally friendly neighbourhoods. The key difficulty lies in shedding accepted ideas of "progress" in regulatory regimes.

By assessing the logic of the "factor four" concept (the doubling of wealth while halving resource use) described in *Natural Capitalism*, the nature of the required paradigm shift becomes clear (Hawken et al. 1999). The central argument, based on 50 real-life examples, is simple. Since the industrial revolution, "progress" has been defined by an increase in *labour productivity* aided by technology, even if that productivity required greater use of natural resources. Thus, the regulatory and incentive structures of markets do not currently reward resource efficiency. The "factor four" concept relates to a new measure of progress called *resource productivity*, and Hawken et al. give examples showing how at least four times as much wealth can be extracted from the same resources by employing the principle of "doing more with less". They argue that the benefits of new paradigms that integrate the "factor four" concept will be widespread, especially as profits for companies can increase when they readjust their thinking and corporate efforts are underpinned by the right regime of incentives. As the authors note, "businesses should sack their unproductive kilowatt hours, tonnes and litres rather than their workforce" (Hawken et al. 1999: 56). This will happen if labour is taxed less and resource use is taxed more. Crucially, the authors assert that the technologies are now in place to reduce resource use dramatically:

> there are not only new technologies, but new ways of linking them … When a series of linked efficiency technologies are implemented in concert with each other, in the right sequence and manner and proportion, there is a new economic benefit to be reaped from the whole that did not exist with separate technologies. (Hawken et al. 1999: 66)

Existing ways of doing things can hold professionals in a vice-like grip. Architects or engineers, for example, often argue that they are paid according to what they spend, not what they save, so efficiency can directly reduce their profits by making them work harder for a smaller fee, because the fee is usually based on a fixed percentage of costs. Another example is the almost universal practice of regulating electric, gas, water and other utilities in such a way that the utilities are rewarded for increasing the use of their services (the example of Zurich, cited earlier, is the exception). Transport planners often think in terms of *vehicle mobility* rather than *accessibility* for the whole population, thus undervaluing the needs or even rights of cyclists or pedestrians.

The examples in *Natural Capitalism* can all be applied to community or urban environments. Essentially they represent the best practices of business that are currently missing from the databases of innovations and best practices of governments and public bodies such as UN-HABITAT, Together Foundation and ICLEI. Examples include a product called "Superwindows", which integrate building design, natural lighting and energy systems, as in the Passivhaus building in Darmstadt and the ING building in Amsterdam (incidentally, "Superwindows" also had social effects – reducing absenteeism); technologies to reduce the energy use of appliances (including fans, pumps, motors and air-conditioning) by over 75 per cent; getting organizations, especially municipalities, to specify energy efficiency as a criterion in equipment procurement; and retrofitting energy and power management functions into existing equipment. Other examples are of mechanisms that often simply require a slight mind-shift, such as calculating governmental payments to public transport providers on the basis not of passenger numbers but of miles driven, which encourages public transport in less dense areas; offering incentives to share savings between providers and users; providing "density bonuses" to reward the co-location of houses and work-places or to reward proximity to public transport; and giving rebates for the efficient use of energy.

What is particularly innovative about the "factor four" concept is that it can create a form of profitable "eco-capitalism"; all the actors in a community – including, for example, businesses, local authorities and consumers – become involved in making their community more sustainable. A shift from using labour productivity to energy productivity as a measure would be revolutionary, because its implications cascade down into the whole of our economic and lifestyle structure. In particular, it should appeal to businesses' own self-interest, because it makes becoming more sustainable potentially profitable.

In summary, the key is to create regulatory frameworks that calculate the true ecological costs, which would reduce the competitive advantages of firms that currently damage the environment without paying the costs of restoration. Moving towards "factor four" will require all kinds of innovations in other parts of economic activity, of which changes in the regulatory regime remain key.

Enriching the idea of capital

Capital is in effect the "stock" of assets that a community considers to be valuable, which can be drawn upon in the form of "revenue" to sustain and enhance life. Although there are many forms of capital, shallow thinkers assume the trick is simply to amass one form alone – finance. Successful communities, in contrast, go out of their way to accumulate all types of capital. They understand capital in complex ways – how to amass it and how to use it. They nurture *human capital* – whose currency is talent, imagination, intelligence and the skills and special knowledge of their people; *social capital* – the complex web of relationships between the organizations, communities and interest groups that make up civil society and whose currency is trust, reciprocity, connectedness and networks; *cultural capital* – the heritage, memories, creative activities, dreams and aspirations of a place; *intellectual capital* – the ideas and innovative potential of a community; *creative capital* – the capacity to identify, nurture, attract, mobilize and sustain talent, ideas and potential; and *environmental or natural capital* – the built and natural landscape and the ecological diversity of an area.[6] Today the limiting factor to future economic development is the availability and functionality of natural capital, in particular life-supporting services that have no substitutes and currently have no market "value".

The market paradigm confuses terminology by appropriating key words such as *value* and *worth* that anchor a culture's view of the world. It is difficult to use a word such as "value" because there is uncertainty about whether one means "value" in the sense of monetary exchange or as some higher non-monetary measure. Related to this is the fact that most cities have a narrow view of capital as financial capital and often in the process deplete other forms of capital. However, an appreciation that renewal and sustainable growth can be achieved only through a more harmonious balance is on the rise. The day a city starts to see that every action or decision it takes can have a positive or negative impact on its stock of capital, and that a squandering of one form of capital will affect its stock of financial capital, is the day it takes control of its own destiny. Whereas central banks, financial markets and companies create financial capital, other actors play a more central role in generating the human or social capital of a community, including the formal and informal learning sectors, community-based organizations and public interest organizations.

An approach based on preferred futures asks: "Where do we as a community want to be and how do we get there?" One answer might be: "We want to be a culturally rich, self-sustaining community." This approach harnesses a community's capital by thinking forwards and planning backwards, by asking how the market can help to achieve those objectives rather than leaving it to the market to predetermine the scope within which it is possible to assess opportunities. In one instance, the market dominates; in the other, it is a servant.

In conclusion, what we see is a series of barriers to innovative community action at the macro level in terms of mindsets, conceptual frameworks, measurement systems, overarching entrenched interests and consequent policy instruments, and, finally, will and motivation. But let us not be disheartened. Although the small number of successful examples paints a dismal picture of where we currently are, momentum is growing and in many parts of the world it is approaching the point of critical mass. Many technologies already exist that can move us along the road to sustainability, and in some spheres positive signs are emerging, such as the increasing popularity of a new breed of energy-efficient cars. The behavioural patterns of large populations are changing, not through social engineering but through individual will, as seen in the rising recycling rates in Germany and the Netherlands for example. These may be isolated examples, but they are a signal that the market, even without the full range of incentives that we need to move it towards sustainability, is very slowly beginning to adapt.

Developing civic creativity

There is thus no shortage of innovative people, organizations and projects, or of technologies; the crucial issue is to determine whether there are truly creative and innovative communities. The difficulty is that, although we know enough about the qualities and mindsets of innovative individuals or organizations to assess their effectiveness, talking about innovative communities adds a layer of complexity. This is because, for a community to be creative, an amalgam of interests, cultures, insights, perspectives and, crucially, power configurations need to be aligned in such a way that innovative, open-minded processes of listening, talking and discussing can be embedded. These are preconditions for people to think, plan and act with imagination. After searching for communities that are innovative in every aspect of what they do, it is my conclusion that the communities more likely to be innovative were those that had key people who shared a certain culture and mindset and were able to withstand some of the pressures of simplistic market thinking. These communities seemed to have developed "civic creativity", which is imaginative problem-solving in the public interest – public actors become more risk-taking and entrepreneurial within a framework of accountability and private actors recognize that working for the public benefit is in their own longer-term interest. Examples elaborated later, such as the Huddersfield Creative Town Initiative in the United Kingdom, the Slow Cities movement in Italy, and Rotterdam's City Safari and Erasmus projects in the Netherlands, display these qualities.

The widening scope of innovation

Innovations invariably imply some process of creative or imaginative thinking; for example, the capacity to see a problem in a new way, perhaps even reformulating it as quite a different problem or issue with a different range of possible solutions. For Dalian in China, the simple notion of defining its strategic objective as to "strive for the best, but not the largest" in the Chinese context was an innovation with a raft of downstream effects.[7] This is because it focuses the city on assessing the world's best practices and getting away from the idea that bigger is better. Sometimes this creative leap can be quite fundamental, as, for instance, when it was suggested that resource productivity would be a better conceptual tool for assessing economic activity than labour productivity or resource exploitation, as seen in the ethos of Ithaca Eco-Village or the Crystal Waters settlement (Barton and Kleiner 2000: 273, 269). Another creative leap is thinking that traffic planning consists not in changing the city to accommodate the car, but in restraining the car in order to maintain the environment of the city; Groningen in the Netherlands is a celebrated example of this. Sometimes the leap is of a second order, not involving a fundamental paradigm shift but nevertheless redefining the problem and thus opening up different possibilities. One example can be found in Lowell, Massachusetts, where the town decided in 1997 to restore its old mill buildings rather than tear them down.[8]

The chain of innovation

There is an entire spectrum or chain of approaches to sustainability. Here I distinguish seven, of which the first five can be regarded as innovative, and the last two as negative responses to a community problem:[9]

- A **meta-paradigm shift** is a paradigm shift in the most basic sense, as originally suggested by Thomas Kuhn (1962) – a completely new way of ordering reality and conceptualizing the world. By definition, such a shift straddles and informs different policy areas in an overarching way. Shifts of this order of impact happen rarely. The notion of sustainability – which reorients the way we think about the principles of economics, the environment, and social and cultural life – is perhaps the most obvious example in recent years. At its heart is the idea of holistic, integrated thinking and acting and an attempt to understand impacts of every kind at every level. The notion of cultural diversity, which reorients our thinking away from seeing cultures as homogeneous, static things to dynamic, heterogeneous processes, might become a similar meta-paradigm shift. Unfortunately, the power of the concept of cultural diversity remains insufficiently appreciated.

- A **paradigm shift** is a basic redefinition of a problem, or perhaps the discovery of a new problem, such that the very objective of policy is changed. Examples from the past 20 years include the polluter pays principle; universal electronic communications systems; participative community planning; self-reliance projects for homeless people; traffic planning to restrain rather than facilitate vehicular traffic; and the shift in urban economies from declining sectors, such as manufacturing, into expanding ones, such as services.
- **Basic innovation** involves new ways of achieving objectives, almost invariably including an element of "fine-tuning" the definition of the problem. Examples include the pedestrianization of city centres (a very early example was Essen in Germany in 1904); zero-tolerance policing programmes; solar-powered villages; regeneration through the development of culture; public–private partnerships; and citizen budgeting (citizen involvement in the local government budgetary process).
- **Best practice** encompasses outstanding examples of practices that are generally regarded as unique. Examples include the pedestrianization of Copenhagen and Munich in the 1970s (in both cases inspired by the example of Essen); traffic calming; environmental auditing; the "Environment City" concept;[10] district heating systems; using children or women as planners; benchmarking; and the "new indicators" movement (promoting social or sustainability indicators).
- **Good practice** includes achievements that reach a standard benchmark, replicated in a number of other cases, that may be easily described in codes of practice or good practice guides. Examples include park and ride schemes; the refurbishment of industrial buildings for reuse; separate bins for recycling waste; conservation codes; and procedures for consulting communities.
- **Bad practice** involves continuing with a practice that has recognized weaknesses. Such practices invariably deny the possibility of sustainability, and they often arise from ignorance and/or inertia. Examples include building urban motorways that slice through established residential areas or central shopping areas; the creation of public housing ghettos; allowing the discharge of untreated sewage into rivers; building deck access high-rise housing developments; and ignoring community input into decision-making.

- **Appalling practice** includes activities that knowingly work against the principles of sustainability, such as deforestation or the use of gas-guzzling motor cars.

Best practice as the baseline

Any community that claims to be innovative needs to operate at a minimum level of good practice across the spectrum of sustainability. Yet the importance of good practice will be fully recognized only if a community has made the "mind-shift" involved in understanding sustainability principles at a visceral level, in every fibre of its being. Only then will the desire, motivation and will be generated to act sustainably. In order to generate this dynamic for innovation, it is crucial to see best practice as being the baseline, because then the chances for creating innovations are more frequent. Too often there is the danger of the word "sustainability" being used as a mantra to disguise inaction. If best practice is used as the baseline, communities are more likely to move away from the tendency to do one-off "sustainability" initiatives or pilot projects and instead make them a part of their mainstream activities.

Freiburg in Germany has generated such an innovative dynamic and can be described as an innovative community.[11] It is a small town of 220,000 inhabitants, where over the past 30 years transportation policy has increasingly been informed by an environmental perspective. Freiburg's public transport policy is an outstanding example of best practice, involving a reduction in individual car use; the continuous upgrading of the public transport network; improvements in public transport services; an emphasis on the social as well as the environmental dimensions of public transport; and the integration of public transport planning into other policy plans.[12] Between 1976 and 2000, car use declined from 60 per cent to around 40 per cent. In addition, despite population increase, the number of cars entering the city centre each day declined by 4,000 (from 236,000 to 232,000) – the only city in Germany where this occurred. Freiburg now has a worldwide reputation for ecologically focused urban development. The Fraunhofer Institute for Solar Energy Systems, an internationally oriented renewable energy institute, provides input to municipal environmental policies on energy saving through public transport, cycling and selection of building materials.[13] The Institute's reputation has attracted other innovative bodies to Freiburg, such as the Institute for Applied Ecology (Öko-Institute)[14] and the International Council for Local Environmental Initiatives (ICLEI).[15] A virtuous cycle was set up involving technical demonstration, awareness raising and public participation in eco-living, which was paralleled by a commitment from the municipality. Freiburg projects itself to the outside world as an innovator in the field, attracting yet more talent, ideas and resources.

"Innovation" is relative

The definition of something as a community innovation is both time and space dependent. What is innovative in one place or period may be common knowledge somewhere else. Some communities tend to develop innovations earlier than others and experience widespread diffusion of those innovations, whereas other areas may have barely begun to adopt them. Germany, for instance, pioneered the concept of pedestrianization of city centres, and it became standard in German cities in the mid-1960s, quite a long time before most other European cities. This difference in timing is partly related to factors such as levels of car ownership, which may mean that traffic restraint is not yet an issue in some places. More broadly speaking, the entire local resource base will determine the limits of the possible. The Finns developed the brilliantly innovative idea of rebuilding Kemi's economy on snow and ice to attract tourists, in effect creating an ice town. This would have been impossible in Andalusia in southern Spain, but equally the Finns could not have invented a solar village.

Intangible factors are also relevant: for example, cultural factors may mean that the implementation of a best practice in one case would be bad practice in another. Thus liberal democratic attitudes are seen as an a priori good in the West, but less so in Singapore. So the conceptual framework itself is value laden, with a series of assumptions that need to be made explicit. A single benchmark may be useful and possible for assessing innovations generally within "Western" society, but not on a global basis. This raises a fundamental question: Are there principles of sustainable development that hold true whatever the local circumstances and longer-term developments? Clearly there are, but how they are implemented is another matter and is culturally determined.

Innovation clusters

A related but different issue is that innovations do not necessarily come singly; rather, they seem to cluster in certain places at certain times, sometimes almost accidentally, sometimes as a matter of deliberate policy. Germany's Emscher Park project, mentioned above and elaborated below, was a deliberately planned cluster of projects that simultaneously pursued goals of economic restructuring, physical rehabilitation and environmental improvement – the whole complex of projects is much greater than the sum of the parts.

Importantly, in assessing the best practices listed in various databases, I discovered important clusters either in geographical areas or within countries. This is a result of the "inspiration effect", competitive pressure and learning capacity. In Brazil, for example, Curitiba (public transport), Porto Alegre (citizen budgeting) and Belo Horizonte (waste disposal) all provide different instances of innovative practice within a single country. There are also important environmentally sustainable clusters around northern Switzerland, southern Germany and Alsace-Lorraine in France, as well as in Italy's Emilia Romagna and in Vienna, Austria. They all focus strongly on generating a high quality of life. They seek to connect issues of economic inventiveness with sustainability and community empowerment, combined with rigorous benchmarking programmes to drive their development. High quality of life is used as a competitive tool, which reinforces their economic and social dynamic. It is noticeable that these groupings are all economically strong, highlighting that sustainable development is not necessarily a drag on the economy.

Trading power for creative influence: The innovative milieu

The concept of the "innovative milieu", helping the chain of innovation to spread and gain acceptance, is very relevant here. Chains of innovation today seem to emanate from highly networked places. These crucial networking capacities and mutual aid structures are rooted deeply in the social system and are very difficult to replicate in the short term, yet are vital for innovation to spread. This point is especially important for innovations related to sustainable development, which require behavioural change. Although this change in innovative capacity and culture has been achieved in some successful commercial organizations, especially in high-tech and cultural industries companies, it is infinitely more difficult to achieve in the community context as a whole, because communities are composed of a mix of actors – public, private, voluntary – each with their own organizational culture and agenda. Individual organizations within each sector might be creative and have the potential to be innovative, but the key issue is how they can network to be creative *together*, by establishing an enabling environment in which both innovative thinking and project implementation from whatever source, whether public, private or voluntary, can flourish.

For a community to keep ahead of the game, it is essential for it to see itself as a dynamic, innovative organism. It needs to have the necessary preconditions in terms of "hard" and "soft" infrastructure to generate a flow of ideas, inventions, knowledge of best practices and the capacity to reflect. This in turn can develop into a local ethos that through its vision and sense of itself generates the pressure to perform in ways we can describe as creative.

In our context, "hard" infrastructure is the nexus of buildings and institutions, such as research institutes or educational establishments, with deep knowledge of the broader sustainability agenda. In order to shift entrenched attitudes, these entities require credibility and local power. They achieve this in a plethora of ways, most commonly by solving an acknowledged problem. An example is the Kurokabe Corporation, a cooperative in Nagahama City, Japan, which revitalized the dying town centre (threatened by large superstores) through an innovative project to make it a centre of glass expertise for the country.[16] Its subsequent success in developing the cooperative into over 30 glass-related enterprises (which now attract a large tourist trade) has made Nagahama bolder. Clearly other aspects of "hard" infrastructure are cultural venues and other meeting places as well as support services such as transport. These need to be easily accessible physically and emotionally.

"Soft" infrastructure is the system of social networks and human interactions that underpins the flow of ideas between individuals and institutions. Whether through face-to-face contact in a variety of contexts or through information technology, wider networks of communication are able to develop, thereby helping generate the confidence, motivation and will to get projects implemented and communicated.

With this infrastructure in place, the innovative milieu then becomes an environment in which a critical mass of entrepreneurs, community activists, intellectuals, administrators, ordinary citizens and power brokers can operate in an open and tolerant environment, and where face-to-face interaction is encouraged, thereby facilitating the inventions that lead to greater sustainability. In most instances, however, competition between various layers of government or entrenched interests is so strong that communities constantly miss opportunities and fail to fulfil their potential. The key challenge in this situation is to remake institutions using the concept of the innovative milieu, in order to ensure that the open interaction between various stakeholders to enhance innovative ideas leading to greater sustainability is replicated. This implies changing the processes by which institutions are run, for example changing an operating culture from being hierarchical towards one of openness and responsiveness.

Cultural change as the source of innovation

Thinking culturally

At its core, the development of innovative capacity is a cultural process. Here, I use the concept of "culture" to mean "the webs of significance people have spun" (Weber, quoted in Geertz 1993: 5), or "piled up structures of inference and implication" (Geertz 1993: 7). This concept is linked to the concept of culture as the negotiation of values (Matarasso 1997: 8) and "judgement about significance and therefore what is kept as memory" (Pachter and Landry 2001: 16), as well as what is selected to become part of the officially accepted canon (Williams 1998: 87). Communities are seeking to reconnect to their pasts and what is important to them, and in this endeavour cultural resources, particularly those seen as virtues of a forgotten past, are key. Tapping these deeper resources can trigger the imagination, because people must find a way of re-empowering assets that may be intangible. Community self-renewal is a much more subtle and overarching process than previously appreciated. It involves more than simply technological innovations and more than just physical improvements. It involves innovation at every level of decision-making, including the social and political, affecting incentives and regulatory regimes, and how governance is adapted to new circumstances. Thus, organizational capacity and structure have been acknowledged to be tools for community development.

The ways in which innovators in communities see, perceive and think about themselves, their operating environment and their aspirations is embedded in their consciousness. This consciousness is cultural because it shapes their values and ideas and the plans they create, and the degree to which they allow information to affect them and subsequently their actions. Some communities – and one thinks here of communities of first peoples – seem to have a world view that is more connected to their natural environment than that in other communities. Thus, their "instinctive" response is to think in terms of ecological and holistic balances and not to let market thinking or apparently "rational" thought processes that break "wholes" into component parts get in the way. By perceiving things differently, such communities are led to do things differently – and, more importantly, to do different things. They do not suffer from premature interpretation, which occurs when communities find themselves funnelled down a pre-existing interpretative track of possibilities and cannot think their way out of a box. These communities see a problem, say the polluting effects of intensive car use, and their minds are flooded with pre-defined solutions that rarely challenge the underlying causes because broader power interests are not addressed.

Cultural knowledge

Thinking culturally about community or about urban possibilities and innovation assumes that all knowledge is cultural, including scientific or economic knowledge, whose process of production and trajectory is influenced by the value systems and ethics of the society within which it takes place. To highlight cultural knowledge is to assert the importance of subjective and experiential views as well as verifiable and objective knowledge. As a consequence, what are seen as the resources of a given place and their potential are equally culturally determined. Once these resources are utilized, they in turn shape the future progression of a particular culture. In the context of the environmental crisis, the need for cultural change is part of becoming innovative.

The challenge for communities that wish to be innovative by instinct, rather than by top–down decree, is to foster the "stickiness" of the cultural change so that it becomes deeply embedded into consciousness. Innovation needs to become "memetic". Memetics is a term coined by Richard Dawkins in his book *The Selfish Gene* (Dawkins 1989) and describes the process by which certain ideas flow, transfer and spread, replicating themselves like a virus and becoming dominant by hijacking pre-existing ideas. Those that are able to spread like an epidemic are then the most successful in evolutionary terms.

The connection between cultural diversity and innovative capacity

Respect for diversity requires communities to see their rich mix of history and diversity in local culture as an opportunity, not a threat, and as an anchor of the distinctiveness of a place. Mass mobility and global migratory patterns, however, have increased the layers of culture. New cultural influences need to be absorbed, and this is a process that often generates conflict. The traditional approach is to foster multiculturalism, which acknowledges and celebrates differences. From this approach, innovations can emerge in communities, enriching local food culture or introducing new stimuli for the local economy, for example. This approach is fine – as far as it goes.

The next step in enhancing local innovative capacity is to see how an exchange of ideas at a deeper level can create fusions and crossovers between different cultural perspectives. This is the intercultural agenda, and it is useful to consider principles of bio-diversity here. A rich culture is marked by a diversity of ever-proliferating forms, where the endogenous culture absorbs and adapts to external influences, whether they be ideas, products and services, new people or global trends. A vibrant community is one that creates mixes and hybrids in a constant interplay between the old and new, yet is anchored with a confident sense of self.

However, the dynamics of our emerging world foster the opposite of diversity. Options, choices and opportunity are often narrowed down. Consider these for a moment:

- the reduced range of shops in town centres the world over,
- the narrowing range of cultural products we consume (variety may be increasing but diversity is not),

- the "international style" of architecture that shapes our communities and cities, affecting the look and feel of places,
- less real choice of foods,
- the branding of our disparate experiences into a simple set of global core themes.

Underlying these tendencies is homogenization and a drift towards monoculture. At times this may be comforting; for example, as English becomes a global language, those for whom English is not their mother tongue are enabled to communicate with each other. Put another way, however, the effects can be seen as stark. There are currently 5,000 living languages worldwide, but this figure is predicted to dwindle to 2,500 by the end of the twenty-first century, when a majority of the world's populations will speak 12 languages (Dalby 2002: 24). This reduction in cultural diversity parallels the trends seen in the world's loss of bio-diversity. This process leads to losses in world views, in types of understanding and in the resources to create solutions to problems.

Four processes of cultural change

A cultural (i.e. values-based) perspective needs to move to the centre of thinking about communities and their possibilities of being innovative; it should not be seen as a marginal, add-on concept. Related to culture, the capacity to interpret local meaning and importance allows for a richer, more multi-layered description of what is happening, why it is happening and what could happen in a given place. This allows causalities, connections, relationships and dynamics to be understood. Community development processes need to function at a subtle and sophisticated level and they cannot do this without this depth of knowledge. In order to achieve its full potential for innovation, a community needs to initiate four distinct processes through which that cultural knowledge – the soil from which innovations emerge – is produced, legitimized and codified. The first is to describe possibilities better, the second is to develop a guiding ethos, the third is to develop innovative projects, and the fourth is to enable communities to become learning organizations to sustain the innovative momentum.

Richer descriptions of possibilities

The first step in cultural change is for a community to develop a vision that includes a multi-layered ethnographic description of its existing everyday life – not in the sense of the banal and relatively insignificant, but including the important deeper drivers of human existence such as power, relationships, happiness or aspiration. Look at any community plan and these are mostly missing. Descriptions are usually limited, and the tendency is to focus on social problems and pathologies, such as drunkenness, drugs, teenage pregnancy, hooliganism, housing needs, economic development initiatives, and so on. Important as these are, they leave out the potential for innovation. The focus needs to be on, for example, giving breathing space to assess what might be innovative, or providing the raw materials for future innovation, such as trends in new social uses of technologies, alternative lifestyle innovations for sustainable living, or working with people's hidden emotions, desires, dreams and aspirations.

A prime example is the "transformation plan" for South Tyneside in northern England, called "From Ordinary to Extra-ordinary: Transforming South Tyneside's Futures",[17] through which one of the United Kingdom's most deprived areas sought to shift the nature of local debate dramatically. It did this by trying to move the community of 150,000 inhabitants away from the victim mindset that had etched itself into the town's way of thinking. Prior to the project, issues were described only in negative terms, such as "the young are a problem", "industry and especially ship-building has died", "the population is ageing" or "drug use is rising". The new plan challenged the community to look at itself and its prospects in different terms. On closer examination, innovative opportunities were everywhere. Although traditional manufacturing had declined year on year for 15 years, closer examination of the data through a different prism showed that "green" manufacturing (i.e. environmental industries) had been rising annually. Further, skills in ship-building were found to be very similar to those required in the green industries. By viewing the area as a "beacon for the actively retired", and as older people came to be seen as active agents of regeneration, the ageing population problem was turned into an opportunity. South Tyneside may not yet be an innovative community, but it has begun the process by allowing a transformation plan to be written, by accepting its conclusions and by launching some initiatives.

Generating an ethos to drive innovation

The second step is to develop an ethos that can guide communities' initiatives. Innovation for the sake of innovation is not a good in itself. For example, many technological innovations are potentially harmful, such as genetic modification of foods. Furthermore, most literature on innovation favours technologically driven inventions rather than focusing on social, political or cultural innovations that could encourage us to change our lifestyles for the better. Innovation needs to be shaped by an ethical framework or an ethos. This happens at three main levels: first, grand notions of how a community can be transformed; second, how this set of overarching ideas is etched and embedded into the plans, projects and initiatives of partners and collaborators; finally, and perhaps most importantly, how its structures deal with day-to-day routine.

The ethos of the innovative community, not just the local authority but other partners and citizens as well, should be firm and strategic in its principles, yet tactically flexible in implementation. These principles are in fact becoming increasingly obvious. A brief look at the values that shape the Healthy Cities[18] or the Environment Cities movements, the European Union's social cohesion initiatives,[19] and UN-HABITAT's Best Practices shows that they all boil down to some common themes. These include (1) involving those affected by decisions in both the creation and implementation of solutions; (2) generating projects that are self-sustaining; (3) respecting local cultural and historical contexts; and (4) working with strategic partners on the basis of equality and respect.

The Slow Cities movement is an example of ethos-driven development. The movement developed out of the Slow Food movement, which started in Italy in the 1980s,[20] and is expanding the concept to cover all aspects of life. It emphasizes the importance of local identity through the preservation and maintenance of the local natural and built environments; developing and using infrastructure in harmony with the natural landscape; using technology to improve the quality of life and the natural and urban environment; encouraging the production of local foodstuffs using eco-sensitive methods; supporting production based on cultural traditions in the local area; and promoting the quality of local hospitality. The aim of the Slow Cities movement is to implement a programme of civilized harmony and activity grounded in the serenity of everyday life, by bringing together communities that share this ideal. The movement has developed a manifesto (which sets out the underlying principles) and a charter of association (which cities wishing to become "slow" must sign). To be a member and to be able to display the movement's snail logo, a city must meet a range of requirements, including increasing pedestrian access, implementing recycling and reuse policies, and introducing an ecological transport system. Working with the Slow Food movement, the Slow Cities movement is spreading the word about its "slow" brand of community connectedness.

Developing innovative projects

The third step involves developing a concrete project to accompany the community's plan and chosen ethical framework. For communities to be open to innovation, flexibility in the selection of projects is required. Further, a constant review of the selection criteria helps avoid fossilization of thinking. Often a community's ability to be innovative lies in its cultural history. For example, in places such as Florence or Siena in Italy, the weight of memory of a once-creative place tends to foreclose opportunities for innovation: communities tend to believe that the best possible scenario has already been achieved. In contrast, Rotterdam in the Netherlands, which was largely destroyed in the Second World War, is undergoing an intense process of innovation in areas such as community relations, the intercultural agenda, leisure policy, design guidelines and master planning.

Rotterdam's Erasmus project,[21] which is concerned with intercultural understanding, is a good example of an innovative project encompassing a wide variety of relatively small projects, all branded under the banner of Erasmus.[22] The project includes making the central library accessible to a culturally diverse public; moving the Rotterdam Conservatory curriculum away from a Eurocentric to a world music perspective; adapting primary health care services to a multicultural clientele; mobilizing a neighbourhood to develop more vital economic structures through art productions;[23] and adjusting the approach of the Zuidplein Theatre to suit the demands of an ethnically diverse community.[24]

Rotterdam's City Safari is another imaginative project that has invented a sustainable approach to tourism development. It was started as an economic development project to bring more resources from tourism to local people rather than intermediaries. The project identifies local people and organizations that are willing to be visited by tourists. By 2003 there were around 600 on the list. A visitor chooses the types of site or people to visit and is provided with a list of addresses and vouchers to give as payments to hosts, who are the direct beneficiaries. For example, someone's interest may be in speciality shops such as tattoo parlours or delicatessens; in spiritualist or religious groups; in fishing enthusiasts; in planning; or in unusual hobbies. For the visitor there is also the challenge of finding the locations in the city, which takes them completely off the tourist trail.[25]

Learning to be innovative

The final key process in cultural change is the notion of cultivation, learning and striving for perfection in relation to certain standards of attainment. Innovation is clearly fostered in environments where a certain type of learning is put centre-stage. This learning is essential in periods of rapid social transformation. Learning and reflection must be placed at the centre of our daily experience so that

- individuals continue to develop their skills and capacities, and better understand, for example, why the sustainability agenda is not an optional choice but a necessity;
- organizations and institutions recognize how to harness the potential and often-suppressed motivation of their workforce, resulting in a new sense of social responsibility;
- organizations and institutions respond flexibly and imaginatively to the opportunities and difficulties of this period of paradigm change;
- communities act responsively and adapt flexibly to emerging necessities; and
- societies understand that diversity and differences between communities can become a source of enrichment, understanding and potential.

The challenge for policy makers, then, is to promote the conditions in which a "learning community" can unfold. A learning community is much more than a community whose members are simply well educated. It is a place or a society where the idea of learning infuses everything – where individuals and organizations are encouraged to learn about the dynamics of where they live, how that place or society is changing, and what its emerging needs are. It is also, perhaps most importantly, a place or society that can learn to change the way it learns, based on an understanding of these dynamics.

An interesting approach to learning and nurturing of citizens that is linked with community innovation is found in Birmingham in the United Kingdom. The "learning city" concept is used to engender, encourage and drive a reflexive attitude to the city's development. Projects include the University of the First Age for young people, the University of the Third Age for retired people, the Young People's Parliament (housed in the city's Millennium Point building – a new signature building), and the Learning Zone website for students, which expresses the overall idea.[26] These projects were conceived and launched by the charismatic Tim Brighouse, who was head of the city's education department from 1992 to 2002.

Initiating and sustaining momentum

Building momentum

The most difficult task is to build and sustain momentum, and how this occurs differs from place to place. A number of lessons can be learned by looking at communities that have put the sustainability agenda centre-stage. The most important of the preconditions is a group of activists, some of whom are likely to be mavericks, with in-depth knowledge of sustainability issues. Ideally these people are connected in some way to power structures or, if not, have a strategy of influence to reach and have an impact on them. This group needs both dynamic thinkers and doers: innovation is not just about having ideas, but also about how these are managed and implemented. It also needs strong communication linkages internally and externally, to keep up with current thinking and best practice. A strategy of influence would be alert to unexpected opportunities, such as an environmental grants programme that might allow a pilot programme to be set up (as was the case with many projects in the databases of ICLEI or UN-HABITAT and the Together Foundation). Projects that involve advocacy can attract support in a variety of ways, for instance by addressing necessity, scarcity issues or cost. A good example is the Lykovryssi suburban workers' settlement north of Athens, where solar power now provides 80 per cent of all energy requirements at a low cost to 435 apartments.[27] Emscher Park in Germany, using obsolescence as an opportunity, appealed to the need to replace techniques, equipment or buildings and thus created spaces whose use could be reconsidered (Landry 2000).

Once preconditions are met, the challenge then is to find ways of bringing innovation into the mainstream of a community. Any campaign will involve ambition and aspiration in order to appeal to people's deeper wish to live in harmony with nature. Giving citizens the opportunity to envision their future in an unfettered way usually results in the description of an ecotopia or eco-Arcadia. For example, in early 2003 the mayor of Paris undertook a major consultation exercise to find out how Parisians wanted their city to develop. The result was a detailed description of neighbourhoods where walking is easy, face-to-face contact is the norm, local shops sell local produce and, most importantly, the environment is cared for and pollution dealt with. An element of opportunism and entrepreneurialism is key when trying to bring innovation into the mainstream. An example is the idea of marketing animal manure from zoos (ZooDoo) as compost for gardens. Initiated 20 years ago by the Bronx Frontier, a non-profit community-based organization in New York,[28] this idea has been replicated in zoos throughout the world. Responding to competitive pressure is effective, as communities compete for resources and recognition, and environmentalism increasingly becomes an important factor in inward investment decisions. Allied to the strategizing process, a culture of active participation, ideas-gathering and debate is essential. This culture can engender more sophisticated urban visions, which usually lead to learning from others and inspiration from outsiders, which in turn can create unexpected connections. As the development of Freiburg shows, finding a way to locate a centre of excellence in a community can be a real catalyst.

When all else fails, a political crisis or a change in leadership can be useful triggers for innovations, provided the background research and lobbying has been undertaken. Indeed, the need for an urgent response to structural crisis or instability may help overcome obstacles to innovation. Crisis situations need immediate solutions, and it is impossible to insist on old approaches if they are not immediately effective. In Benxi, a city in China, the fact that its heavy pollution was visible from a satellite led to the creation of its Local Agenda 21 programme to move from pollution control to pollution prevention.[29] Nowadays it is possible to generate a new form of "structured instability" or "controlled disruption" and this is being self-consciously developed by "urban visioning" or "triggered goal-setting". Community leaders can mimic the conditions of crisis by creating the desire and aspiration for sustainable development, thereby highlighting the disparity between the current reality and what could be. This in part lies behind the momentum within the cluster of cities in the region around Zurich, Basel, Karlsruhe and Freiburg, which are competing on a new terrain – a quality-of-life agenda driven by sustainable development.

Symbolic triggers are important in this process of change-making and help galvanize action. Triggers might be a statement of intent, a charter, a declaration or a manifesto, or branded concepts and local landmark events that act as rallying points, campaigns or benchmarks to stimulate action and innovation. Creating a Local Agenda 21 is one of the most powerful triggers to emerge in recent years. The same thing can happen when a community is persuaded to brand itself as a "green city". Such marketing slogans raise expectations and can be mechanisms to focus strategy on reducing the gap between hype and reality. In the end, clearly the ideal is for there to be clarity amongst stakeholders about what they intend to do and how to get there – yet that is rare.

Moving in an innovative direction

As the well-known expert on sustainability Hugh de Varine notes, culture "is the sum total of original solutions that a group of human beings invent to adapt to their natural and social environment",[30] a definition that highlights that the creative process is embedded within a dynamic culture. Yet it is not inevitable that communities are creative – societies or cities have moments of both progress and regress. Which is in the forefront depends on how values or "the order of things" are negotiated and the level of public recognition accorded to the value of new knowledge in, for example, science, ecology, human behaviour or the arts. Whereas creation and innovation are legitimized in fields such as science or technology, few communities have a deliberate and self-conscious overarching strategy to promote innovation as part of an ethos that embeds innovative thinking.

The Huddersfield Creative Town Initiative (CTI)[31] in the United Kingdom is an exception to the rule. An industrial town of 130,000 inhabitants located close to Leeds and Manchester in northern England, Huddersfield grew rapidly in the nineteenth and early twentieth centuries on an industrial and manufacturing base of woollen textiles, engineering and chemicals. In the 1980s it suffered a severe recession, as did much of the British economy, leading to mass unemployment and industrial restructuring. Workers now commute to neighbouring cities, thus draining skills and talent, and there is a concentration of poverty amongst Huddersfield's mainly Asian ethnic minorities.

Yet in 1997, Huddersfield was one of the winners of a European Union competition to find Europe's most innovative urban initiatives. Huddersfield's CTI proposal argued that creativity, a latent form of intellectual capital, exists in all walks of life – in business, in education, in public administration, in social care services, and among environmental activists, for example. The aim of the CTI was to change the perception that Huddersfield had of itself. A creative town, it argued in its publicity, must vaunt its creativity every time it communicates – face-to-face, through its printed material and through other media. Through a series of pilot projects, it sought to establish an innovative area of the town as part of a process of extending creative thinking throughout the town – embracing ways in which the unemployed can regain the confidence to re-educate themselves, developing routes to entrepreneurship, and setting up a network of creative thinking across all disciplines and sectors.

These projects were devised to achieve the aims of the "cycle of urban creativity".[32] Some were aimed at enhancing the town's capacity for generating ideas, such as the Creativity Forum and the Millennium Challenge, which consisted of small innovative social, environmental and economic urban projects sponsored by a local businessman in the year 2000. Other projects, such as the Creative Business Development Training Company, were intended to aid business development in small and medium-sized enterprises. The "Create!" project was at the centre of the network designed to promote and bring together creative thinkers in the town. The Hothouse Units were set up to get innovative businesses to work together in a favourable environment, and various vehicles of dissemination were set in motion, including discussion forums, a website and a database of creative projects.

The scale of impact of the CTI was somewhat unexpected. It succeeded in achieving a thorough reappraisal of how the town thought of itself, and launched a strategy to re-brand the town under the banner "Huddersfield – Strong Heart, Creative Mind", with the full support of the formerly critical media. It set out to establish – at regional, national and international levels – more favourable perceptions of Huddersfield, by identifying it as a town with a creative and innovative culture, a reputation for quality output, progressive businesses and institutions, active individual citizens and corporate bodies, a richness of multicultural diversity and an enterprising community spirit. In 1997, at the start of the CTI, creativity was seen by the leadership in Huddersfield as something vague and of relevance only to the arts. Five years later, it was recognized that enabling people and organizations to be creative is a means of unleashing talent and harnessing intellectual capital, and the concept of being innovative everywhere had been internalized by the main policy makers. Creativity is increasingly seen as an attribute that needs to be embedded in every process or project, and not merely in the new and obviously creative media industries.

Huddersfield did not arrive at this situation out of the blue. It was the result of an internal political struggle, key changes in personnel, and deep reflection on the community's future. Huddersfield realized that medium and small towns like itself, whose original locational advantages and resource and skills base have long since disappeared, exist all over Europe and, indeed, the rest of the world. Many have gone into decline after failing to adjust to the demands of the new globalized economy. Often suffering deep-rooted deprivation, with all the social consequences that entails, they experience a spiral of worsening difficulties. Huddersfield saw that it had only one resource: its people – their intelligence, ingenuity, aspirations, motivation, imagination and creativity. If these could be tapped, renewal and regeneration would follow. To operate in this new landscape, the town council needed to build relationships with an ever-growing range of other agencies. It needed to influence, to collaborate, to orchestrate and to scrutinize – roles that are not easily balanced; it needed a public information service to show who did what, since the council was increasingly commissioning services from others rather than supplying them itself. The council's style of urban management had to change dramatically. This required tenacity and a certain ruthlessness.[33]

Sustaining momentum: The "embedding strategy"

A persistent problem remains even with the best innovators: how do you sustain momentum over time? In the period of Huddersfield's CTI, the confluence of talent and interests between the political leadership, local officials and broader partnership stakeholders drove the project forward from 1997 to 2000. Then the leadership changed and the dynamic reduced. The key ingredient needed to spread an innovative vision and create the ambition to follow through is an "embedding strategy". The objective of such a strategy is to create a sense of "ownership" of an innovative process and to ensure it is understood and acted upon at every level of a municipality and among all community stakeholders. Normally visions, even community-led ones, are "owned" by a limited circle of people, but, in order to implement a plan successfully, the cooperation of a mass of people and organizations at all levels is required.

The London borough of Lewisham, which sought to weave a new vision called "Creative Lewisham" into its internal fabric, provides such an example. Although the plan was not exclusively environmentally focused, environmental issues formed an integral part. This visioning project sought to establish a strategic synthesis of artistic imagination, sustainable urban design, the potential of its local economy, the social inclusion agenda, and cultural thinking. It highlighted the need to enhance people's creative capacity to solve their own problems (with help). It used a series of "levers" to catalyse momentum. These included the local authority selling key assets at below market value to foster the development of businesses for young people. This was achieved by the property valuation department broadening its assessment measures because it recognized that short-term losses would have long-term benefits if judged within a multidimensional context, such as calculating the effects of talented people staying in or coming to the borough. Another lever was its Art of Regeneration programme, which worked with schools to draw out latent talent as a means of inspiring local people to raise their aspirations. A third lever was the building of the Laban dance centre, the largest in the United Kingdom, which combined a focus on excellence with a strong programme of community involvement.

The project's embedding strategy, centred initially on the local government authority, was to involve all public servants, from the cleaner to the chief executive, and from the accounts or administration and personnel departments to all functional divisions, such as environmental services or social affairs and economic development. Importantly, attempts were made actively to bring on board elected members, as well as external trainers and consultants working for the authority. The message spread out to partners, such as other public service organizations within the borough and the diverse contractors that work with the borough, as well as a to wider range of stakeholders, such as the voluntary sector, property developers and those involved in construction projects and other businesses in Lewisham. The plan also focused on the borough's educational establishments, some of which, like Goldsmiths College, are world class. Importantly it included transport organizations, from rail to road, because these often hold back innovation in local authorities.

What did embedding the "Creative Lewisham" agenda mean? For a start it was essential to give the stakeholders who were involved in generating the vision in the first place far more detail about Lewisham's vision and the aims and objectives for Creative Lewisham. Second, it involved educating them about precisely what the plan could mean for them, and how they could contribute to making Creative Lewisham a reality. Finally, it encompassed the sharing and exchanging of skills, knowledge and experience to achieve this.

A multi-stranded approach was developed to deliver this outcome, led by a dedicated external entity called the Creative Lewisham Agency and by staff within the authority. Key players were the executive management team in the local authority, the people who provide the learning and development function, and the communications department. In sum, the objective was to produce a report that would be more than a document that lies collecting dust on a shelf – something that is, unfortunately, a common experience. The plan was to orchestrate pacing devices and staging posts. The range of proposed activities fell schematically into various categories: celebratory events that engender a "feel-good" factor and respond to real achievements – for example, using 70 street representatives to generate projects to increase recycling or to create "artistic" recycling units that make recycling a joy; debate-style events to generate a culture of discussion; industry-focused events that effectively sell Lewisham as an experimentation zone; "revealing" events that make invisible assets visible; and advocacy-based events that argue the case for creativity and innovation.

Has this embedding process been successful so far? Yes and no. Yes, in the sense that innovative empowered community action is seen as the driver for development. No, in that inertia or bureaucratic weight is still a powerful force. Insiders feel that major changes have been made; for example, the property valuation department now includes environmental and social criteria in assessments. Outsiders, by contrast, feel that Lewisham has only reached the starting gate.[34]

Final thoughts

Differing types of creativity are needed to develop and address the complexities of a community, which constantly has to deal with conflicting interests and objectives. This creativity might be the creativity of scientists in solving problems related to pollution; of planners in generating new urban policies; of engineers in solving technical problems concerned with transport or other issues; of artists in helping to reinforce the identity of a place; of business people in generating new products or services that enhance the opportunities for wealth creation; or of those working to develop social innovations that might help with issues such as social fragmentation or social exclusion. Thus, creative solutions and innovations can come from any source, whether it be the public, private or voluntary sectors, or individuals operating on their own behalf.

The qualities of an innovative environment ultimately come down to a few features: taking measured risks, widespread leadership, a sense of going somewhere, being determined but not deterministic, having the strength to go beyond the political cycle, and, crucially, being strategically principled and tactically flexible, as well as recognizing the resources that come from a community's history, talents and products and services. To make the most of this environment, changes in mindset, perception, ambition and will are required. An understanding of the new competitive tools for community development is also key – tools such as the community's networking capacity, its cultural depth and richness, the quality of its governance, design awareness and understanding how to use symbolic and perceptual understanding, and, last but not least, eco-awareness. Using such tools, a transformation will have a strong impact on organizational culture. This type of transformation will not be achieved simply by following a business-as-usual approach.

These attributes can apply equally to developed and less-developed countries. Each country, whatever its state of development, has projects that in their own way are inspiring. Readers will know of many examples of towns or cities, whatever their problems at first sight, finding unusual ways of fostering projects that are models of sustainability. They do this by assessing their local cultural circumstances and assets and by responding imaginatively to what is possible (and often seemingly impossible) in their context. What this requires is insight, courage, tenacity and determination, as well as a willingness to go against conventional thinking. Being unconventional is key, because if we always do what we have always done, with the same mindset, we will end up with the same result, which is often what created the problem in the first place.

The world is changing so dramatically that it feels as if a paradigm shift is under way. Responding in routine ways will not address current problems. The cultural attributes and attitudes that made many communities great and successful in the past are precisely those that are likely to constrain them in the future. Today, communities and companies all over the world are seeking to replace hierarchies with networks, authority with empowerment, order with flexibility and creativity, no-holds-barred growth with sustainability, and paternalism with self-responsibility. These are the new seeds of success and, if they are ignored, the most talented of the young, the ambitious and the gifted will continue to leave, and as they leave their communities will decline. Therefore it is a question of developing an atmosphere, milieu and preconditions within which it is possible to act with imagination. Creating this atmosphere requires developing a culture of sustainable entrepreneurship and ambition, focused on drawing on the distinctive cultural resources of a community. How the community is governed, managed and organized will be affected, which implies addressing many obstacles that lie deep in local and international power structures.

The challenge, therefore, is to develop a culture of creativity that will make it possible to identify, harness, attract, nurture and sustain the talents that will revitalize communities. This in turn will make it possible to develop imaginative solutions to seemingly intractable problems. Although there might be general lessons to be learned, the main challenge is to find unique responses to emerging problems and opportunities. The goal in adapting to a changing world is to identify what is special and distinctive about each place and to be true to that. In the future, those communities that manage this trick are more likely to be successful. Many projects all over the world are already showing the way.

Notes

1. UN-HABITAT and the Together Foundation, "Best Practices Database", ⟨www.bestpractices.org/⟩.
2. ICLEI is an international association of local governments focusing on campaigns and projects related to sustainable development issues. See case studies at ⟨www3.iclei.org/iclei/casestud.htm⟩.
3. RLA Foundation, "Right Livelihood Award", ⟨www.rightlivelihood.org⟩.
4. Survey by Culture Intelligence (2002), which interviewed 52 local authorities in eastern England in order to assess the contribution of local authorities to the development of cultural uses of new technology. See ⟨www.audience.co.uk⟩.
5. Further information on Emscher Park can be found at ⟨www.iba-emscher-park.de/7913.html⟩ and ⟨www.iba.nrw.de⟩.
6. A useful summary of the "capital" debate can be found in Department for International Development (1999).
7. See the database of the International Council for Local Environmental Initiatives ⟨www.iclei.org⟩.
8. See ⟨www.ci.lowell.ma.us⟩.
9. This matrix was first developed in Hall and Landry (1997).
10. The Environment City notion was invented by the European Union in 1992. See ⟨www.environ.org.uk/e-city/index.php⟩.
11. The official website of the city is ⟨www.freiburg.de⟩.
12. Freiburg owed a great deal to the example of Basel, Switzerland, a city that implemented a variety of environmentally friendly measures in different areas of transport in the 1980s and early 1990s. Its "environmental" travel card has been copied by many other Swiss and German cities.
13. This Institute has the oldest solar-powered demonstration house in Germany (dating from 1978). See ⟨www.ise.fhg.de⟩.
14. Founded in 1977 to analyse and evaluate future environmental problems, it seeks to develop and implement environmental problem-solving strategies. See ⟨www.oeko.de⟩.

15. See ⟨www.iclei.org⟩.
16. Personal visit, December 2002.
17. Drawn up in 2002 by Comedia for the South Tyneside Local Strategic Partnership. Available from South Tyneside MBC, Town Hall, Civic Offices, Westoe Road, South Shields, NE33 2RL, United Kingdom.
18. The Healthy Cities concept was invented in 1985 and then taken up by the World Heath Organization as a means of promoting greater attention to the integrated problems of heath, safety, homelessness and environmental concerns. Over 1,000 projects are now affiliated. For further information, see ⟨www.oneworld.org/cities/cities_healthy.html⟩.
19. The European Union's social cohesion work can be explored at ⟨europa.eu.int/comm/regional_policy/index_en.htm⟩.
20. The Slow Food movement promotes the protection of local cultural diversity and the right to taste through the preservation of local cooking and eating traditions, and rejects the folly of fast food and "fast life". Details on its charter of association and related matters can be found at ⟨www.slowfood.com⟩.
21. Details can be found at ⟨www.fhk.eur.nl/english/rotterdam.html⟩.
22. "Erasmus" refers to a Rotterdammer, and a person of tolerance and humanism operating in an age of religious strife. This name has power, local resonance and significance.
23. For example, the Freehouse Project uses artists and cooperates with shopkeepers, small businesses and craftspeople resident in the culturally diverse neighbourhood of Oude Westen.
24. This theatre is hidden under underground on the outskirts of Rotterdam. In an attempt to connect with its culturally diverse environment, Zuidplein has radically reviewed its approach and evolved from being a theatre led by theatrical supply to one led by the demands of residents.
25. Details on the City Safari project can be found at ⟨www.citysafari.nl⟩.
26. See the Learning Zone website at ⟨http://icbirmingham.icnetwork.co.uk/students/thelearningzone/⟩.
27. See ICLEI case studies at ⟨www3.iclei.org/iclei/casestud.htm⟩.
28. ⟨http://www.bizspirit.com/bsj/archive/articles/steckel1.html⟩.
29. See the Best Practice Database of UN-HABITAT and the Together Foundation, ⟨www.bestpractices.org⟩.
30. Personal conversation with the author.
31. See ⟨http://www.huddersfieldpride.com⟩.
32. For details of the concept of the "cycle of urban creativity" see Landry (2000).
33. For details on the history of the Huddersfield Creative Town Initiative, see Landry (2000).
34. For details on Creative Lewisham, see ⟨www.creativelewishamagency.org.uk⟩.

REFERENCES

Barton, Hugh and Deborah Kleiner (2000) "Innovative eco-neighborhood projects", in Hugh Barton (ed.), *Sustainable communities*. London: Earthscan.
Boyle, David (2000) *The tyranny of numbers*. London: HarperCollins.
Carew-Reid, J., R. Prescott-Allen, S. M. J. Bass and D. B. Dalal-Clayton (1994) *Strategies for national sustainable development: A handbook for their planning and implementation*. London: Earthscan Publications, in association with International Institute for Environment and Development (IIED), London, and World Conservation Union (IUCN), Gland, Switzerland.

Dalby, Andrew (2002) *Language in danger*. London: Penguin.

Daly, Hermann (1997) "Uneconomic growth: From empty world to full world economics", paper presented at the DeLange-Woodlands Conference "Sustainable Development: Managing the Transition", Rice University, Houston, Texas.

Dawkins, Richard (1989) *The selfish gene*. Oxford: Oxford University Press.

Department for International Development (1999) *Sustainable livelihoods guidance*. London.

Geertz, Clifford (1993) *The interpretations of culture*. London: Fontana.

Hall, P. and C. Landry (1997) *Innovative and sustainable cities*. Dublin: European Foundation for Living and Working Conditions.

Hawken, Paul, Amory Lovins and Hunter Lovins (1999) *Natural capitalism, The next industrial revolution*. London: Earthscan.

Kuhn, Thomas (1962) *The structure of scientific revolutions*. Chicago: University of Chicago Press.

Landry, Charles (2000) *The creative city: A toolkit for urban innovators*. London: Earthscan.

Matarasso, Francois (1997) *Use or ornament: The social impact of participation in the arts*. Stroud, UK: Comedia.

Mizrach, Steve (n.d.) *GNP vs. ISEW: Developing an Index of Sustainable Welfare (ISEW)*, available at ⟨http://www.fiu.edu/~mizrachs/gnp-n-isew.html⟩.

Pachter, Mark and Charles Landry (2001) *Culture at the crossroads*. Stroud, UK: Comedia.

Taylor, Nigel (2000) "Eco-villages: Dream or reality", in Hugh Barton (ed.), *Sustainable communities*. London: Earthscan.

Waring, Marilyn and Gloria Steinem (1990) *If women counted*. Auckland: HarperCollins.

Williams, Raymond (1988) *Keywords*. London: Fontana Books.

Yankelovich, Daniel (1971) "The new odds", speech given at the 11th Annual Marketing Strategy Conference of the Sales Executives Club, New York, 15 October.

4

Mainstreaming innovative approaches to sustainable urban environmental management in Asia

Nathaniel von Einsiedel

Introduction

This chapter provides an overview of the environmental challenges facing many cities in Asia and demonstrates how a number of cities are addressing these challenges by attempting to bring innovative approaches to urban environmental management into the mainstream.[1] I discuss both the obstacles that cities are trying to overcome and the means through which they introduce, replicate and scale up innovations in urban environmental management. In particular, I highlight the practices of local authorities and suggest a process that could increase the probability of successful mainstreaming of innovations in regular municipal operations. In this respect, I make a particular effort to emphasize the criticality of participatory decision-making processes (whereby various local stakeholders work in partnership) for achieving environmental sustainability in cities in the region.

The insights provided in the chapter are based on my experience in overseeing the implementation of UN-HABITAT's Urban Management Programme (UMP),[2] which provided technical support for a number of cities in the Asian region. The specific case studies highlighted represent only some of the cities supported by the UMP. The details of each of the five case studies discussed are provided in the appendix at the end of the chapter.

Environmental and related challenges in Asia and the Pacific

Urbanization was particularly pronounced in the Asian region in the second half of the twentieth century. In 1995, the urban population of Asia was 1,150 million, or about one-third of the total population of 3,515 million (UN-HABITAT 2001a: 14–15). By 2025 the Asian region will become predominantly urbanized, with an urban population of 2.5 billion, or 55 per cent of the total population (UN-HABITAT 2001b: 268–269). This anticipated increase represents a massive economic and demographic transformation from rural to urban societies. It is a transformation that is drastically changing the nature and scale of humanity's impact on the environment.

Today, 9 out of the world's 13 mega-cities are located in Asia (mega-cities have a population of over 10 million). By 2025, this number will rise to 20. By then, more than half of Asia's inhabitants will live in mega-cities and another 300 million will live in 45 large cities with populations in excess of 5 million each (Asian Development Bank 2001: 6–8). Environmental management in these cities represents a major challenge if we are to meet the goal of sustainable development.

Despite the importance of urban environmental issues, they have traditionally been assigned only a low priority by local authorities in Asia. The result has been irreversible damage to human health, reduced productivity, weakened social structures and the undermining of long-term development. The shifts that are needed to redirect urban policy toward more sustainable environmental practices are not always clear and are never easy. This is particularly the case, given that urban environmental issues cannot be viewed in isolation from aspects of urban poverty and governance. As urban areas expand, the poor and the disadvantaged become increasingly concentrated in them. The accumulated backlog in urban housing, combined with the rapidly increasing population of urban poor, results in the proliferation of slums and squatter settlements (see Figure 4.1), severe shortages of urban infrastructure, including inadequate and poor-quality shelter, pollution of air and water, and growing problems of solid waste collection and disposal. The costs of these critical environmental problems fall most heavily on the urban poor, in terms of poor health, lower productivity, reduced income and poor quality of life.

Many urban communities in Asia are experiencing a transition in which populations are exposed to serious traditional health risks and, at the same time, are being introduced to modern environmental risks.[3] As a city's population size and density grow, people increasingly are exposed to environmental risks related to pollution. Some of the major environmental issues faced by Asian cities include insufficient management of

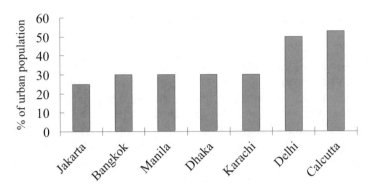

Figure 4.1 Urban slum populations in selected Asian cities, 1990.
Source: *State of the Environment in Asia and the Pacific*, UNESCAP, 1990.

air quality, waste water and solid wastes (see Table 4.1). This is partly owing to the low levels of investment for environmental management activities in Asian cities. The lack of capacity for wastewater treatment and for waste collection and disposal results in direct discharge of wastes to surface drains, which leads to increasing risks of health epidemics (see Table 4.2). In terms of air quality, the World Health Organization calculated that, in the 1990s, 12 of the 15 cities in the world with the highest levels of particulates, and 6 with the highest levels of sulphur dioxide in the atmosphere, were in Asia (Asian Development Bank 1999: 8–17).

In the late 1990s, the Asian Development Bank reported that the most serious environmental problems in Asia were associated with rapid and often uncontrolled population growth, industrialization and increasing vehicle densities (Asian Development Bank 1999: 8–17). Whereas the focus of environmental concerns has been on large cities with populations of 5 million and above, increasing attention is now being given to secondary cities.

The 1990s witnessed a number of efforts by government and industry to improve environmental conditions in urban areas, but the financial crisis that hit all of South-East Asia in 1997 brought these efforts to a complete stop. Worsening macroeconomic conditions in many Asian countries have led to a lowering in the priority of environmental concerns compared with job creation, especially for low-income countries grappling with the needs of public health rather than improvements to the environment. In fact, lack of political commitment and environmental awareness, and poor enforcement, are cited as major causes of low levels of investment in urban environmental management facilities, such as wastewater treatment facilities and sanitary landfills. The institutional framework for better environmental management is further complicated

Table 4.1 Solid waste generation in selected Asian cities

Solid waste	Calcutta (1994)	Dhaka (1994)	Jakarta (1993)	Karachi (1994)	Manila (1994)	Seoul (1994)	Shanghai (1993)
Generation (metric tons/day)	2,500	2,500	5,200	6,000	4,158	15,397	9,181
Collection efficiency (volume of waste collected as percentage of volume generated)	95	50	80	30	82	90	65

Source: Asian Development Bank (1996: 13).

Table 4.2 Urban water and sewerage coverage in selected Asian cities, 1997

Service	Bangkok	Calcutta	Dhaka	Jakarta	Karachi	Manila	Seoul	Shanghai
Water:								
Service coverage (%)	82.0	66.0	42.0	27.0	70.0	67.0	100.0	100.0
Availability (hours/day)	24	10	17	18	1–4	17	24	24
Production (million m^3/day)	3.85	1.20	0.78	0.97	1.64	2.80	4.95	4.70
Domestic use (litres/capita/day)	0.19	0.01	0.09	0.22	0.09	0.27	0.28	0.07
Sewerage:								
Service coverage (%)	10.0	3.2	28.0	–	83.0	16.0	90.0	–
Waste treated (%)	–	–	–	–	–	–	–	83.0

Source: Asian Development Bank (1996: 12).

where interventions must address multiple administrative boundaries, as in the case of a polluted river that flows though several municipalities in an urban metropolis such as Metro Manila.

The most critical issues currently faced by urban communities in Asia may be summarized as follows:

- **Land encroachment** – the spread of slums and marginal settlements of the urban poor often in ecologically sensitive and disaster-prone areas, including waterways and lowlands subject to annual flooding.
- **Water supply and sanitation** – chronic water shortages and lack of sanitation. Virtually all surface waters have become degraded, and excessive demand for groundwater in coastal cities has led to saline intrusion and lowered water table as well as ground subsidence in some cities. Water-related disease is the leading cause of death, and is found most commonly in low-income neighbourhoods.
- **Solid waste disposal** – characterized by inadequate management, with collection efficiency (ratio of volume of solid waste collected against total volume generated) averaging around 60 per cent, and related problems such as disposal in open water, leaching into groundwater, air pollution from open burning, and spreading insects and rodents as disease vectors. Most urban communities dispose of their solid waste in landfills and open dumps.
- **Traffic congestion** – very high levels, especially in mega-cities, where congestion has become endemic, resulting in lost income, urban sprawl, increased pollution and a progressively deteriorating quality of life.
- **Air pollution** – comes mainly from transportation, energy production and industrial fuel use. Growth in vehicle use has been exponential in Asia, more than doubling every seven years in some cities. Locally manufactured vehicles have poor emission characteristics; vehicle fleets are old and poorly maintained and turnovers are low; two-stroke motorcycle engines are common; diesel vehicles account for a greater portion of vehicle population and kilometres driven; fuels are among the dirtiest in the world. In terms of energy production and industrial fuel use, pollution comes from coal used for power, heating and industrial production (mainly in Chinese cities). The air quality of many urban communities in Asia poses a significant public health risk to their residents, which will become more severe in the near future if emission controls are not put in place.

Most of the recent improvements in the environmental conditions of urban communities in Asia carried out by local governments have not focused on traffic congestion and air pollution. This is not surprising, given that these two issues are beyond the capacity of local governments to address and require the intervention of higher levels of government. The following section describes the circumstances and challenges faced in implementing innovative urban environmental initiatives at the local government level.

The challenges for innovations at the local government level

In addressing many of the environmental problems mentioned above, urban communities in the Asian region have undertaken various innovative initiatives. Recent experiences in Asian cities demonstrate the critical importance of scaling up, replicating and mainstreaming successful initiatives at the community level to solve city-wide environmental problems. In searching for effective solutions to urban environmental problems, local governments are required to adapt or change policies as societal conditions change and to ensure the proper implementation of these policies. In addition to the traditional obstacles related to availability of resources, various other obstacles need to be faced during the planning and implementation of innovative policies, including the natural human tendency to resist change and the social complexity of the issues being addressed.

People's resistance when confronted by an innovative course of action derives partly from fear of the unknown and partly from not wanting to give up something that is familiar. Even when individuals understand that the innovation will be for the better, they are still likely resist because:

- embracing change takes time and effort, which the participants may not want to invest;
- taking on something new usually means giving up something else that is familiar, comfortable and predictable;
- annoyance or fear of disruption stops them from taking the first steps; and
- if change is imposed externally and not derived internally, resistance may be ego-related.

Another major obstacle in the planning and implementation of innovative urban environmental initiatives is the social complexity of the environmental issues faced in Asian cities. Social complexity refers to the already large and still rapidly growing number and diversity of stakeholders involved. These stakeholders are players in a social network around any specific urban environmental issue. On the one hand, their input and participation are important to crafting and implementing innovative solutions. On the other, some of these stakeholders have the power to stop, undermine or even sabotage the innovation if it threatens them or their mandated role.

Each of the stakeholders has his or her own individual experience, personality type, and style of thinking and learning, which make consensus difficult to achieve. Furthermore, each of these stakeholders comes from a different discipline, with its own specialized language and culture. Thus, achieving shared meaning and context with regard to the issue being addressed is especially difficult.

The social complexity of urban environmental issues goes beyond individual diversity and diversity among disciplines. A major issue when introducing innovative approaches is that the stakeholders represent different groups or organizations. Whether formal or informal, each organization has its own function and charter and its own goals, and is managed by its own chief executive officer. These organizations may even have divergent goals. When the stakeholders of an urban environmental management programme or issue come together to collaborate, they represent not only themselves but also their respective management chain in the hierarchy. Ideally, each one of them should be committed to the same goal, but operational objectives and agendas can be quite fragmented.

Although tension is inherent in urban environmental issues as well as in their solutions, this is especially severe in many Asian cities, especially those with large populations, high urban growth rates and great disparity between the rich and the poor. Directly related to these characteristics is the large number of groups with varying, even conflicting, interests, which tend to heighten tension. Despite the most carefully thought out plans, the dynamics of environmental issues tend to enhance chaos and fragmentation in an improvement programme. As these programmes grow in size, social complexity increases. Large programmes, such as city-wide waste reduction and recycling initiatives, typically have dozens of stakeholders representing the programme management team, residents, landowners, various government agencies, non-governmental organizations (NGOs), private businesses and civic organizations. As independent groups, they are likely to have different ideas about the real issues and what the criteria for success are.

A further major obstacle faced by innovative urban environmental management approaches is technical complexity. This refers to the more common issues of environmental management, such as the engineering considerations of a sanitary landfill or a wastewater treatment facility. However, technical complexity is not nearly so difficult to overcome as the human tendency to resist change and the phenomenon of social complexity.

Overcoming the obstacles

The most effective way for local authorities to overcome these obstacles and promote innovation – as demonstrated by several successful experiences – is to work closely with and ensure the strong commitment

of local communities, especially lower-income groups (including the inhabitants of illegal or informal settlements). Although the time and
energy invested initially may be high, the involvement of stakeholders in
planning and decision-making processes will result in their stronger commitment later. It is necessary to overcome the usual perceptions that
securing commitment is a huge task, that implementation can be exceed-
ingly slow, or that efforts are not getting anywhere.

Despite the effectiveness of involving local stakeholders in the initial
stages of the process of innovation, in many instances it is the way people
are approached – rather than the innovation itself – that causes resistance. Because of the relatively short term of office of Asian city mayors
and the need to pre-empt anticipated resistance, there is a tendency for
municipal governments to rush into a new programme, seeking to reach
full speed in a short time. However, this is very likely to backfire. There
is a better chance of developing synergistic working relationships, better
communication and greater involvement of municipal staff if the engagement of local stakeholders is pursued at a measured, deliberate pace. By
starting slowly, the change that accompanies innovation can ultimately be
incorporated at an accelerated pace.

A close investigation of recent experiences in a number of Asian cities
also shows how the issues of resistance to change and social complexity
have been addressed through the introduction of multi-stakeholder participation and partnership mechanisms in formal municipal decision-
making and implementation processes for environmental improvement
programmes. The lessons drawn from these experiences can be grouped
under three major headings: processes and tools for planning; partners
and stakeholders; and outputs and impacts.

Processes and tools for planning

The first step in an environmental improvement programme at the local
government level is the creation of a plan. Action plans come in various
formats, some of which are outlined below. Balancing short- and long-
term goals and focusing not only on process but also on institutional
changes are key. A participatory process at the planning stage is also
crucial to the success and sustainability of the programme.

In many Asian cities, the formal planning process typically begins with
the preparation by the local authority of Terms of Reference (TOR), laying down the objectives, activities, time frame and budget allocation for
the proposed activities. The TOR usually outlines a set of very specific
objectives requiring focused interventions. In Nonthaburi in Thailand,
for example, the single most important objective was the restoration and
preservation of the canal landscape (see Case Study 1). The TOR tends
to use the immediate concerns of the municipal authorities as "entry

points" based on the expectation among such authorities of immediate "visible" impact (Urban Management Programme 2002). The biggest drawback in this approach is that very often the decision-making process gets caught up in the specificities of the interventions without understanding or, consequently, influencing the bigger institutional picture. Environmental action plans inevitably require, or lead to, widespread cross-sectoral institutional changes.

Furthermore, in cities where the emphasis on process overshadows the specific "solutions" sought by stakeholders, the impact and sustainability of the exercise are also questionable. To address this issue successfully requires balancing the immediate requirements of the city with the demands of the process. This entails flexibility and customization on the part of the stakeholders. For example, in their efforts to address critical urban issues, Leshan in China (Case Study 2) and Phuket in Thailand (Case Study 4) defined their immediate objectives with respect to their longer-term vision, taking up the issue of environmental sustainability as a step towards increased tourism and economic productivity. In Mumbai (Bombay) in India, the prime issue of solid waste management expanded into a wider discussion about how to mobilize citizen participation in service delivery (see Case Study 5).

The preparation of a city profile, as well as other issue papers, is another critical component of a participatory environmental improvement process. Issue papers elaborate on the city's critical problems and serve as a reference in identifying and then engaging stakeholders. The city profile and issue papers provide the substantive framework for subsequent activities and deliberations. In a number of urban environmental improvement initiatives in Asian cities, the draft city profile was eventually transformed into an environmental status report. Stakeholders appear to hold the view that the purpose of the profile is not just to collect data and information about the city, but to identify key issues and priority areas for development of action plans. Thus, the city profiles and issue papers are often drafted initially by one of the participating stakeholder groups and subsequently finalized through inputs from other groups, often through focus group discussions and workshops. This step in the decision-making process is critical because this is when the real focus and direction of the process are established.

The action planning phase of the decision-making process is as crucial to the success of stakeholder participation as the action plans themselves. In cities where the municipal authority and the local community have identified common priorities and have accepted the need to work together, the likelihood of successful implementation is much greater. In Leshan, for example, restoration of some of the city's ancient gateways was completed even while stakeholder consultations were still in progress, based on a consensus between the municipal government, the businesses surrounding the gateways and the people who have inhabited the gateways for many years (see Case Study 2). By way of contrast, in Surat in India, the environmental management guidelines were prepared by an eminent academic institution without the participation of the city's key stakeholders and found no ownership in the municipal administration or even amongst other stakeholders. This was the case even though the guidelines were technically sound and made all the "right" recommendations for sustainable environmental management in the city (see Case Study 3).

Partners and stakeholders

Local "champions" are critical in promoting innovative solutions as well as participatory decision-making for urban environmental issues. To help facilitate the consensus-building process, these champions should ideally be based in the same city or in another city in the same country, especially if the municipal authorities and civil society organizations have a long history of conflict. Champions may be local community leaders or officials or research-oriented technical or academic institutions that are committed to the environment and to sustainable development issues. Whoever they may be, and whatever organization they may represent, they need to be experienced in community mobilization, on the one hand, and public policy implementation, on the other.

The role of the champion as consensus facilitator is likely to evolve a great deal in the course of the decision-making process. A wider variety of issues will almost certainly arise during the process, and champions can move on from simply facilitating workshops to become substantive advisers to the process. Some may even take on responsibility for consistent and continuous stakeholder engagement and conflict resolution. It is not always easy to find institutions with the range of capabilities to address a wide range of issues, especially if the issues are diverse and seemingly unrelated. In Dhaka, for instance, the city corporation highlighted revenue mobilization and financial management in addition to solid waste management as key areas of concern. To do justice to both issues, it was necessary for the city to mobilize two local institutions. Although both were technically competent, professional differences of opinion hampered their effectiveness, resulting in the initiative not fully achieving its objectives.

The identification of key stakeholders is an important step in participatory decision-making, being a precursor to the initiation of a dialogue on common concerns. In urban environmental management in Asian cities, the role of, and linkages between, government agencies at different levels are critical. Along with the local government, agencies such as water supply and sewerage boards, environmental protection agencies, pollution control boards and various line departments at the subnational and national levels all have a stake and a responsibility. In the experience of Nonthaburi in Thailand, the provincial government, 5 city governments and 11 *tambon* (village) administrations formed one important category of stakeholders, along with citizens. Industries, both manufacturing and service, form other important stakeholder groups. In Surat in India, the city's initiative to institutionalize its post-plague actions for improved public health services was co-sponsored by the South Gujarat Chamber of Commerce and Industry, the apex federation of manufacturing industries in the southern part of the state of Gurajat. This reflected their interest and commitment.

In cities where solid waste is the priority, community organizations – in particular, residents' welfare associations, neighbourhood societies and community-based organizations (CBOs) representing the slum dwellers – have an important stake and role to play. With such a broad range of stakeholder groups, identifying who they are, what interest they represent, what roles they play, and the linkages among them can make all the difference to the success of the city's urban environmental improvements.

For multiple stakeholder initiatives many, if not most, Asian cities have developed a wide variety of indigenous project management arrangements. The common practice in most of these is the multi-stakeholder "Steering Committee", which guides the process and oversees thematic working groups that develop action plans. In Phuket in Thailand, for example (Case Study 4), a Project Implementation Task Force (PITF), comprising 14 senior city officials and chaired by the director of the Environmental Health Division, was constituted. The PITF reports to the Urban Environmental Management Committee (UEMC), chaired by the mayor and with members drawn from various divisions of the city, the business sector, NGOs and community organizations, and relevant departments of the provincial and national governments. Five subcommittees, corresponding to the five priority areas of concern identified by the UEMC, were constituted and assigned responsibility for developing the action plans and monitoring environmental activities in the city. The entire structure, although originally established for drafting the city's urban environmental policy, has now been mainstreamed into the institutional framework of the city government.

The use of working groups proves to be effective in cities dealing with more than one major environmental issue or with distinct multiple outputs. The groups often lead to intensive and detailed discussions and the formulation of focused action plans. They also ensure that the various levels and sectors of the city administration and other stakeholders "buy in" to the process, thus facilitating implementation of the action plans.

Outputs and impacts

Various efforts to improve urban environmental conditions in many
Asian cities have led to many types of action, some extremely focused
and problem-specific, others broad and all-encompassing. In Dhaka, for
instance, clear recommendations were made for addressing two key
issues: solid waste management and revenue mobilization. In Surat, on
the other hand, an important output was a "Corporate Plan" for the city
with a five-year perspective. In Leshan, four specific activities were undertaken under the overall development framework provided by the
"Action Plan on Environmental Improvement and Tourism Development in Leshan", which set out a common vision for the city and identified a series of actions to achieve this vision.

A key accomplishment of recent efforts in many Asian cities since the
UN Conference on Environment and Development held in Rio de Janeiro in 1992 (the "Earth Summit") is a heightened awareness of urban
environmental issues and the responsibilities of different stakeholders. In
many cities, these efforts have led to the mainstreaming of innovative
"home-grown" initiatives, the convergence of existing policies and plans,
and the development of an integrated framework for implementation. In
Nonthaburi, for example, the development of horizontal linkages among
local administrations and civil society stakeholders and the initiation of
vertical coordination between provincial and local governments are key
achievements (see Case Study 1). As a result, the Canal Funding Initiative (Grum Rak Naam) has been successful in accessing substantial funding support from the national government as well as technical assistance
from donor agencies for promotional activities focusing on sustainable
canal environmental management. In Mumbai, several Advanced Locality Management committees worked to improve environmental conditions by scaling up "zero garbage" at the ward level (see Case Study 5).

The above discussion provides some examples of the tools and approaches used by Asian cities in implementing urban environmental
management initiatives, through the promotion of multi-stakeholder participation and partnership mechanisms. Innovative initiatives often require local governments not only to change policies but also to ensure
that these changes are properly implemented. Yet political risk still
arouses anxiety and conflict among stakeholders in relation to policy
change in many Asian cities. Individuals and groups that see themselves
as being helped or hurt by change react in ways that influence the situation. The more severe they perceive their potential loss to be, the more
vigorously they will oppose the change. No matter how difficult it may
be, however, innovative policy change is crucial if existing urban environ-

mental conditions in Asian cities are to be improved. Therefore, building the capacity for policy reform in government, especially local government, is essential because the capacity for policy change in managing the change process will ultimately determine whether the innovation succeeds or fails.

Based on the lessons from the examples discussed above, as well as other similar initiatives in the Asian region, the following section suggests a number of factors that need to be considered in order to mitigate opposition to policy changes and eventually to increase the probability of success.

Increasing the probability of success

An established environmental management policy or practice involves two sets of interests in a state of equilibrium. On the one hand are the interests of those who benefit from the established policy, and, on the other, those who are disadvantaged but have come to accept the policy for a variety of reasons. Obviously, those who benefit will not want the policy changed unless they are convinced that they will be better off or at least remain the same under a new policy. For example, in introducing user charges for solid waste collection and disposal, local authorities often encounter resistance from citizens who have traditionally received such services for free. Those who are disadvantaged come to accept a policy when they find that they cannot do anything about it or that attempts to change it are too costly. Thus a policy, once established, is balanced in an unchanging state.

Any initiative to alter that policy, whether it involves something innovative or not, will upset this equilibrium and trigger an attempt by each interest to influence the process of change in their favour. This reaction can take many different forms, from public protests against a proposal to passive resistance to its implementation, and can come at many points in the decision-making process as the nature of the change becomes visible to those affected. It is therefore crucial that the people involved in the policy-making processes understand the factors that affect policy decisions and possible reactions to policy changes, as well as the effective means to secure support in decision-making and implementation processes.

Identifying factors and conditions that affect policy decisions

In general, policy decisions are shaped both by the characteristics of individual policy makers and by the circumstances (or operating environment)

that bear on those individuals. The personal factors that influence an official's stance on a policy will include:
- ideological predispositions,
- professional expertise or training,
- memories of similar policy situations,
- position and power,
- political and institutional commitments and loyalties,
- personal attributes and goals.

These six factors may not each be relevant in every situation, and their relative importance may vary. Significant predictive knowledge can be gained by considering the stakeholders involved in a policy reform and thinking about the way each of the above factors might affect the individual's stance on a particular reform.

At the same time, policy makers operate in a social and political environment that has an influence on policy decisions. The factors include:
- societal pressure,
- historical context,
- economic conditions,
- administrative capacity,
- international context,
- other policies,
- other key institutions and stakeholders.

These seven factors represent conditions that exert a constant influence on the individual operating within a specific social and political system. The list does not include political and special interest pressures that vary by issue.

Knowing who the affected individuals or stakeholders are – their personal factors and the circumstances that influence their decisions – is an important first step in the change process.

Understanding possible reactions to policy changes

Reactions to innovative policy change are likely to occur primarily in either the public or the administrative arena. If the arena is public, opposition may be expressed in public protests, criticisms by the media, interest group pressure and loss of votes. If the arena is administrative, then opposition may manifest as non-allocation of the required funding or half-hearted efforts at implementation.

Whether public or administrative, the arenas of reaction are determined by two factors: impact and visibility. The key variable is the extent to which important stakeholders are affected or hurt, and how soon they know it. For example, the termination of street-cleaning jobs as a result of a new municipal waste reduction programme will hurt a lot of people and they will know it immediately; this is a high-impact, high-visibility policy. In contrast, a privatization programme for wastewater treatment may benefit many in terms of better public health but this will take longer to become known; it is a high-impact, low-visibility policy.

The characteristics of a proposed policy change in terms of its impact and visibility determine whether the arena for negotiation is public or administrative. It is useful for policy change proponents to determine the arena of reaction in order to predict where potential support and opposition may occur.

If some or all of the characteristics of the change are in the public arena, then proponents can predict and prepare for a public reaction. If this is likely to occur, the stakes are likely to be high for government, since its public political support is being questioned. Government's ability to deal with such a reaction will depend on its legitimacy and stability. It will need the support of the political coalition that is backing it and, if it has alienated an important faction, it could run into a lot of difficulty.

If some or all of the characteristics of the change are in the administrative arena, then proponents should focus on efforts in the administrative sector. What are the direct implications on the bureaucracy? Does it have, or can it quickly acquire, the capacity to implement the reform? In this case, what is at stake is the substance of the reform and the position of the individual who eventually decides whether to accept or reject it.

This knowledge helps policy change proponents to focus their efforts and to craft the appropriate strategies in mobilizing support and in countering opposition. Before taking the next step, however, it is important to re-emphasize the significant influence of the circumstances at the particular time that the reform is being proposed. If the circumstances are such that the political leadership perceives a crisis, experience shows that the stakes will be higher than under non-crisis conditions. Under crisis conditions, reform will be dealt with by officials at a more senior level, the process will occur rapidly and change is likely to be innovative or radical. Under non-crisis conditions, the opposite holds: the stakes are lower, there is less incentive to act, less senior officials are involved, and the reform is more likely to be incremental.

Mobilizing support for agenda-setting and policy formulation

The next step is to get the innovation proposal on the agenda. This may sound easy but, to get on the policy agenda, a proposal must be perceived to be of sufficient validity to be considered as an alternative or an addition to existing policies by those with the power to make policy decisions. Many brilliantly conceived proposals never reach the agenda. Influencing what gets on the agenda is a critical step in the change process because it is a time for gathering support by persuading important officials of the validity of the proposal, before they are confronted with the pressures of making a specific choice. In non-crisis circumstances, when there is no strong external pressure to act, this step is even more important because broad support is vital.

A range of people – so-called "gatekeepers" – are in a position to influence what gets on the agenda. Agenda-setting occurs at more levels of government than does actual decision-making. Frequently the agenda is composed by policy analysts or staff persons, who may bring up a proposal on their own initiative or at the request of a decision maker. These key people may be heads of planning units, critically placed staff in powerful ministries or technical assistants. The individuals will obviously vary from place to place, and from issue to issue, but it is essential for the proponent to know who they are and how to gain their support. A review of their personal factors and the circumstances influencing individual decisions is useful at this point.

Once the proposal is included on the agenda, fewer players and fewer proposals will be involved. As in the preceding step, the circumstances of crisis or non-crisis will provide significant information about what is likely to happen. In crisis circumstances, proposals already on the agenda that have been well developed and thought out and are bold enough to meet the requirements for decisive action will be favoured over those that are not.

When the agenda contains too many items, the transition from getting a proposal onto the policy agenda to securing its approval is an important filter. The person or group with the power to make policy decisions may or may not see the need for change. Their action is therefore crucial. Generally, at the local government level, three broad areas of concern will influence their judgement.

First, *political stability and support* are a consideration. Many local decision makers will ask how a change will affect first the political support and stability of their position, and secondly that of government. An ingredient of these considerations is the perception of important supporting and opposing stakeholder interests. Representatives of such groups may well have been consulted in earlier steps of the decision-making process and their views will probably be an important element in the ultimate decision. A proposal that is able to recognize these stakeholders and to predict their reactions stands a better chance of approval.

Second, *bureaucratic considerations* may exert a strong influence on the decision-making process, particularly in sectoral and non-crisis reforms. In policy change, high-level bureaucrats are often influenced by personal career objectives and considerations of power and organizational competition. These may take the form of access to financial resources, the potential for increases in staff benefits, responsibility for a greater range of activities, or just a desire to perform better. Bureaucratic considerations are especially important when decisions are made within specific agencies.

Third, *technical factors*, ranging from data suggesting a particular course of action to specific expertise on the part of the decision maker, may also exert an influence over the decision. More likely, some technocrats either within the bureaucracy or outside may have an important stake in an issue. For example, economists will have a strong influence on a decision to maintain a green belt around a city because they can calculate the economic cost, whereas doctors will have significant influence over issues of health policy.

There are obviously other considerations in particular situations, for example financial and economic factors, especially in countries experiencing economic difficulties. In many Asian countries, decision-making processes will already have some kind of criterion for evaluating policy or programme proposals. The relative weight given to each component of this criterion reflects the decision makers' perception of what considerations are important in the context of existing as well as likely future circumstances. In a crisis situation, political support and stability will likely be given the highest consideration, whereas, in a non-crisis situation, they may be considered on a par with financial implications. In any event, the particular circumstances remain the most powerful predictor of the decision-making process.

In situations where several policy proposals on the agenda are competing for limited resources, the decision-making process will involve bargaining between officials representing different interests. Understanding the power and influence of each of these officials is important in predicting the possible reactions. Personal factors and particular circumstances can again help provide this understanding.

Securing implementation capacity

Implementation is often a neglected part of proposals for innovative policy change. Once a decision has been made and a policy proposal has been accepted, there is frequently an assumption that it will be carried out as planned. Rarely does the decision-making process include an assessment of implementation capacity. Nor is much thought given to improving implementation capacity after the decision is made. Yet implementation is often more difficult than making the decision, especially when this involves innovations.

Getting approval for a policy proposal is different from securing a commitment to implement it. Ideally, these should go together but, more often than not, decisions to adopt innovative approaches do not produce the intended outcome because no commitment was given to implementation. Although there is a need for flexibility to adapt to changing circumstances or unanticipated events during implementation, evidence suggests that the capacity to implement a decision frequently does not exist at the time the decision is made.

Several actions are needed to improve this situation. First, as part of the decision-making process, decision makers need to assess whether the capacity exists to carry out the reform before they decide to approve it. Decision makers are usually senior officials who assume that their subordinates will carry out their decisions, but often their subordinates are not able to do this on their own. The senior officials' role, therefore, should be one of continued involvement, lending of authority, monitoring progress and supporting the implementation process. Another important action area is the development of the managerial capacity to carry out the tasks associated with the innovation, such as community mobilization, management of privatization programmes and revenue enhancement. Too often, the implementation of reform fails owing to the absence or weakness of managerial capacity, resulting in a widening of the rift between policy makers and implementers. Lastly, the above actions will happen only if the proposed innovation is accompanied by a specific implementation strategy. It is incumbent on the proponent of innovation to ensure that the proposal is well thought out from concept to implementation.

Conclusions

Given the scale, complexity and circumstances of the environmental problems in Asian cities, solving them requires nothing less than innovative approaches. The all too familiar scenes of uncollected garbage and open dumpsites, polluted rivers and canals, high levels of air pollution, and denuded forests are testimonies to the ineffectiveness of traditional approaches. Yet, despite the seeming intractability of these environmental problems, many communities throughout Asia have conceived and implemented innovative solutions, although often not at the scale of the entire city or town. What is further needed is for these approaches to be scaled up, replicated and brought into the mainstream of regular municipal operations.

The scaling up, replication and mainstreaming of innovative community-level approaches to solve city-wide environmental problems face several major obstacles. Apart from the inherent complexities of urban environmental issues, the two most formidable obstacles are resistance to change and social complexity. These phenomena are more often responsible for a lack of success than are difficulties of a technical nature. They are what Nonthaburi, Leshan, Surat, Phuket, Mumbai and many other cities in the Asian region are trying to overcome. The efforts of these cities, given their contexts, are innovations in themselves.

Resistance to change and social complexity are not necessarily always "bad" things, which need to be eliminated. They contribute to a condition that needs to be addressed. This condition is fragmentation – fragmentation of direction, of mission, of teamwork, even of how the issue or problem is understood. The antidote to fragmentation is coherence. This means the stakeholders must have shared meaning of key terms and concepts, they must be clear about their respective roles in the innovation, they must have a shared understanding of the background of the initiative and what the issues are, and they should have a shared commitment as to how the innovation will reach its objectives and achieve success.

Before coherence can be achieved, however, it is essential to determine who the stakeholders are and the circumstances in which they are operating; to predict the arenas for negotiation – whether public or administrative; and to devise strategies for mobilizing support and countering opposition. The role of innovation proponents, the "local champions", is crucial. Their ability to manage the change process will determine whether the proposed innovation succeeds or fails.

As demonstrated by the examples cited in this chapter, an effective way of building coherence is to adopt a participatory decision-making approach. This approach is particularly helpful in promoting urban environmental management innovations in Asian cities because of the need:

- to build consensus among many stakeholders on a number of controversial issues;
- to allow all stakeholders to influence decisions and build commitments to them;
- to balance vested interests in the face of the need for innovation to improve environmental conditions; and
- to allow wide-ranging and creative discussions and solutions.

Innovative approaches, by their very nature, take time to be internalized into the mindset, behaviour and action of the stakeholders concerned. Participatory processes can encourage continuous participation and speed up behavioural change by periodically creating conditions in which individual and group interests are heightened.

An analysis of recent initiatives in many Asian cities, including those mentioned in this chapter, reveals that participatory processes are both the means and the end. Most of the effort and energy of these initiatives is focused on making the process participatory. This is a major outcome and forms the core of what needs to be mainstreamed. Ensuring that the dialogue created during the process continues beyond one activity is a key challenge facing many Asian cities. The fact that participatory processes have an empowering effect makes these challenges somewhat easier to address. Communities indicate that the participatory process itself generates self-esteem. This empowering role is also expressed by municipal civil servants, and it appears to be a prerequisite for starting meaningful dialogue among the stakeholders if innovative approaches are to be considered, adopted and scaled up.

Formalization of what is in many cases a completely new way of working in a city understandably presents a serious challenge. Promoting the adoption of innovative approaches to urban environmental management issues requires the rigour of the scientific approach. However, the mainstreaming of innovation processes in urban environmental management, with its typically large number and diversity of stakeholders, is primarily social rather than individualistic. In the specific context of cities in the Asian region, the goal is not so much the "correct" answer but rather a solution that works and can be embraced by all stakeholders. In essence, the real challenge to innovation in urban environmental management is to look into the social domain to build effective collaboration.

Appendix: The case studies[4]

Case Study 1: Nonthaburi, Thailand

Nonthaburi is a province of 1 million people in the suburbs of Bangkok. In 1999, the municipality of Nonthaburi hosted an intergovernmental workshop to discuss the development of an action plan for the last remaining canal landscape of Greater Bangkok, located within Nonthaburi. The city canal landscape extends over approximately 40 km^2 and has an estimated population of 70,000, most of whom belong to low-income groups, living at high densities along the canal shores. A key lesson from the workshop was the apparent difficulties of intergovernmental cooperation and the diversity of interests.

Through a participatory decision-making process, Nonthaburi sought to develop a comprehensive action plan for the area, with a focus on environmental sustainability and cultural preservation. Increased intergovernmental networking and collaboration, coupled with enhanced public awareness and participation, was the overarching goal. Poverty alleviation was to be achieved through increasing land values and income opportunities.

The initiative formally started with the signing of a Memorandum of

Understanding between the province of Nonthaburi, 5 municipalities (Nonthaburi, Bang Muang, Bang Sri Mueng, Prai Bang and Bang Kruey) and 11 community governments (*tambon* administrations). The Canal Funding Initiative or Grum Rak Naam (GRN) was subsequently formed voluntarily to catalyse and synergize urban planning activities among these 17 governments and to facilitate consensus. The GRN is a consortium of representatives from all the local government entities involved in the initiative, whose main aim is to build close cooperation among these local governments in order to preserve the canal landscape. It also adopted the system of a rotating chairperson to ensure equal participation.

As might be expected, the implementation arrangement was complex and intricate because of the involvement of several local governments and the broad spectrum of issues being covered. To overcome this, the group agreed and developed a common vision for the Nonthaburi canal landscape, "Development without Destruction", which focused on enhancing the canal's economic growth without destroying its environmental and cultural assets. Based on this, a comprehensive action plan was prepared involving a range of interventions such as public investments in strategic environmental infrastructure, attracting private investments, especially in environmentally sound businesses, and image-building and marketing through cultural heritage preservation and eco-tourism development.

Case Study 2: Leshan, China

The city of Leshan, in the Sichuan province of the People's Republic of China, is known for its cultural heritage and unspoilt natural environment. The city has two World Heritage Sites identified by UNESCO – the Grand Buddha and Mount Emei – and it has become a prime tourist destination in recent years. Coping with increased tourism while maintaining environmental sustainability was the key challenge that the city sought to address through an initiative that began in 1999. Adopting a participatory approach, a series of multi-stakeholder workshops were organized by the Leshan municipal government (LMG). Key challenges were discussed and leading responsibility for different tasks was allocated as follows:

- ancient walls and gate protection and restoration: City Construction Committee and Cultural Department;
- primary planning and relief map of the green hub (an 18 km^2 environmental reserve in the heart of the city): Planning Department;
- planning and construction of model samples of farmers' houses: City Construction Committee;
- public awareness: City Environmental Department.

Following the first workshop, activities under the four identified areas proceeded apace. Under the ancient walls and gate renovation project, detailed site investigations were made and stakeholder workshops were held, which eventually led to action to preserve some key sites. Simultaneously, experts and professionals in the areas of hydrology, geology, tourism and horticulture came together to explore green-hub planning. In addition, an architectural design institution was entrusted with the task of developing a protection plan for the green hub. The LMG also initiated various innovative public awareness campaigns and other advocacy activities in the city, targeted at making citizens and stakeholders aware of key environmental and conservation issues.

Government departments, hotel associations, tourist agencies, schools and other educational institutions were all involved. On New Year's Day, 2001, 10,000 people ran a marathon to express their commitment to environmental sustainability. Between March and May 2001, the city witnessed a series of quiz competitions and drawing and photography exhibitions. On the occasion of World Environment Day (5 May 2001), citizens vowed to make Leshan a model city.

In October 2001, the LMG completed an action plan on Environmental Improvement and Tourism Development, which set out a common vision for the city and identified a series of actions to achieve this. The slogan "Love Our Leshan, Protect Its Environment" was widely publicized. The Leshan initiative demonstrates that it is crucial for decision-making processes to be flexible and contextually relevant, because situations vary from one city to another and, indeed, from one country to another.

Case Study 3: Surat, India

Surat, situated in the western state of Gujarat, is one of the fastest-growing cities in India. Rapid population growth owing to the in-migration of industrial workers has caused several environmental management problems for the city government. An outbreak of pneumonic plague in Surat during September 1994 was a manifestation of the incapacity of the civic authority to manage basic services. The plague created worldwide panic and severely affected the city as well as the entire nation's economy.

A remarkable turnaround in the solid waste management of Surat was observed by 1996 when it was declared the second-cleanest city in India. This transformation was attributed in large measure to a series of innovative initiatives by the elected council and the civic administration in partnership with local citizens and private businesses. Although civic participation had demonstrated its effectiveness in cleaning up the city after the plague, there was no "formal" mechanism to engage civil society, the chamber of commerce, industrial companies and other stakeholders in urban management. The city government therefore felt that it needed a mechanism that would institutionalize these efforts and provide for a participatory mode of urban management.

In 1997, the Surat Municipal Corporation (SMC) sought to undertake improvements in the city's environmental management within a participatory framework. The initiative particularly aimed to emphasize the development of institutional structures and administrative procedures to ensure that the efforts of the city government are sustained in the long term. The development of mechanisms to ensure the participation of key stakeholders in urban environmental improvement was also a major component of the Surat initiative. The officials of Surat city were conscious of the fact that their efforts to maintain a clean Surat are contingent upon a sound resource base and evolving public–private partnerships for service delivery.

Numerous meetings were organized with individual stakeholder groups to disseminate information and build participation in the programme in the city. These meetings reinforced environmental management and the development of public–private partnerships as particular thrust areas for the city. The main workshop, a City Visioning and Strategic Planning exercise, was organized in April 1998. It brought together all the stakeholders within the city – the city government and other public agencies, community organizations and the local business and industry sector – to prioritize the issues of concern within the thrust areas previously identified and to formulate feasible solutions. The day-long consultation session was jointly organized by the Southern Gujarat Chamber of Commerce and Industry and the Surat Municipal Corporation. Various experts, academics and donor agency representatives participated in the consultation.

Following several consultative workshops, various activities were undertaken. These focused on a variety of issues: the institutionalization of solid waste management, strengthening the zonal offices of the SMC, privatization of the bus transport system, a sewerage system for the city, etc.

Case Study 4: Phuket, Thailand

In early 1998, the municipality of Phuket in the southern part of Thailand felt it needed to improve its system of urban environmental planning and management. Phuket was no more than a sleepy cluster of fishing villages when it was upgraded from a sanitary district to a municipality nearly seven decades ago. It has come a long way since and, as Thailand's most popular tourist destination, now plays host to over 2.5 million tourists a year. Thus, the city initiated efforts to improve its environmental conditions and put in place institutional arrangements that would not only help in sustaining the tourism industry but also boost its contribution to Thailand's economic development. This was to be achieved mainly by strengthening the capacity of the municipal government in urban environmental planning and management, as well as its ability to bind together the various individual actions of the municipality's diverse stakeholders into a common vision of the future.

These efforts, which started in June 1998, involved two parallel tracks. One involved reviewing the plans and policies related to environmental management formulated by the national, provincial and local governments. The other involved initiating stakeholder consultations to prioritize the environmental challenges faced by the city and to engage various actors in a meaningful dialogue. In August 1998, the Project Implementation Task Force (PITF), comprising 14 members and chaired by the director of the Environmental Health Division, was constituted. Members were assigned the task of conducting community dialogues and a rapid training needs assessment for various stakeholder groups.

The PITF initiated human resource development activities by arranging regular bi-monthly sessions to provide training with a focus on urban environmental management/planning and sustainable development to key personnel from the municipality and other relevant agencies. The PITF also held meetings to build understanding of the principle of civil society participation in the urban development process. An informal public meeting was organized with the Ruam Nam Jai community in early October to introduce the city's objectives and activities. Representatives of 11 key community groups attended the meeting. In early 2000, the draft environmental policy was completed and consolidated. This was approved by the Urban Environmental Management Committee, chaired by the mayor of Phuket. Guidelines for Phuket's Urban Environmental Management were also submitted for approval.

The members of the Urban Environmental Management Committee were drawn from various divisions within the municipality, relevant departments of the provincial and national governments, the business sector, NGOs and community representatives. This committee is responsible for assisting municipal managers in formulating policies, guidelines and strategies in sustainable environmental management, prioritizing activities and projects, and effectively translating the draft environmental policy into action. To operationalize these policies, an Urban Environmental Management Subcommittee was also established in the municipality. Jointly chaired by Phuket's Deputy City Clerk and the director of the

Environmental Health Division, this subcommittee consists of 22 members representing various units within the municipality.

Case Study 5: Mumbai, India

Mumbai is India's industrial, financial and commercial capital. What was a cluster of seven small islets set in a coastal strip in the eighteenth century is now a mega-city, with a population of over 12 million and a sprawling area of nearly 450 km^2. The Municipal Corporation of Greater Mumbai (MCGM) administers the city, which is divided into 24 municipal administrative wards for civic administration. Each of these wards is practically a city in itself. Since 1997, Mumbai has witnessed increasing civil society participation in the management of basic urban services. Citizen groups were encouraged to form Advanced Locality Management (ALM) committees and to take on responsibility for the provision and/or maintenance of services and infrastructure. By 1998, there was a network of about 450 ALM committees in Mumbai. The key challenge lay in using them effectively, strengthening their capacity and facilitating the institutionalization of their interaction with the MCGM.

In November 1998, the MCGM initiated efforts focusing on solid waste management and decentralized governance. By early 1999, several consultation meetings had been organized to discuss the issues facing the residents of one ward in the western suburbs of Mumbai, which had a population of 500,000 at that time. These rounds of consultations involved residents' associations, ALM committees, prominent residents and various institutions.

Three major areas of interest emerged during the discussions: solid waste management; capacity-building for municipal personnel; and empowering ALM committees and institutionalizing citizen participation at ward level. In December 2000, the ward saw some significant improvements. The ALM committees and the ward office worked closely towards achieving the target of "zero garbage" in the ward. Vermi-composting was taken up in many localities. Rag-pickers were involved in waste segregation and door-to-door collection. The publication of a news bulletin was initiated for sharing information and experiences throughout the ward. The ward officials now meet citizen groups and ALM committees on a regular basis to discuss the most pressing development concerns facing the ward.

For some ALM committees, the process established by the MCGM was the first ever platform they had shared with other NGOs and CBOs, especially those representing the poor. The various groups learned to appreciate divergent points of view and the need for a dialogue to come to a common understanding and strategy. The citizens also learned to appreciate the constraints on municipal officials and were quite pleasantly surprised to see that the civic administration was open to criticism, introspection and innovative ideas.

Notes

1. The size of the cities discussed in this chapter ranges from small (Leshan, Nonthaburi, Phuket) to large (Mumbai). Although their contexts vary, I highlight them because of their experience in addressing urban environmental issues.
2. The UMP is a global technical cooperation facility of the United Nations aimed at strengthening the contribution that cities in developing countries make towards national socio-economic development. Launched in 1986, the UMP is the oldest and largest urban intervention of the United Nations, particularly in building the capacity of local authorities and stakeholders to address urban problems.
3. Traditional risks include a high incidence of poverty, malnutrition, dysentery, skin and eye infections, and other diseases related to water sanitation. Modern risks include exposure to hazardous and toxic waste, water pollution from industries, air pollution from industries and vehicles, noise pollution and urban stress owing to lack of space and lifestyle.
4. The source for these case studies is Urban Management Programme (2002).

REFERENCES

Asian Development Bank (1996) *Megacity management in the Asia Pacific region.* Manila: ADB.
——— (1999) *Sustainable cities: Environmental challenges in the 21st century.* Manila: ADB.
——— (2001) *Urban indicators for managing cities.* Manila: ADB.
UN-HABITAT (2001a) *The state of the world's cities.* Nairobi.
——— (2001b) *Cities in a globalizing world: Global report on human settlements.* London: Earthscan.
Urban Management Programme (2002) *UMP-Asia city consultations on urban environmental management.* Bangkok, pp. 9–15, 27–31, 37–39, 41–45, 47–51, 53–56.

Part II

Case studies from the Asia-Pacific region

5

From hunting to sustainable use: A Pashtun tribal group's innovations, northern Balochistan, Pakistan

Luc Bellon

Introduction

There are over 15 million Pashtuns around the world, with the majority distributed in Pakistan and Afghanistan (Jansson 1988).[1] This chapter focuses on an innovative initiative undertaken within a Pashtun population living in the north of Balochistan Province in Pakistan (see Figure 5.1). This initiative, known as the Torghar Conservation Project (TCP), is a sustainable use programme for the conservation of endangered wild animals. The main innovative aspects of the project relate to the direct involvement of local residents and include collective action for environmental management, the development of a conception of "community" goods and ownership of natural resources, and the promotion of equity and collective responsibility.

Remote rural communities, such as those in Torghar, are often mistakenly understood as being "traditional". That is, they are assumed to abide by a fixed set of social references that lead to the continual replication of an ancient way of life opposing the very idea of change. Examining the TCP initiative reveals, however, that change and innovation are not necessarily antithetic to the integrity of an established social set-up. The reality can be quite the opposite. Change and innovation can be, and often are, integrated into existing social dynamics. One of the difficulties in illustrating this lies with the fact that innovation itself is a complex process that does not obey simple mechanical laws. Innovations are often subdued by contradictory forces and are often unplanned rather

110

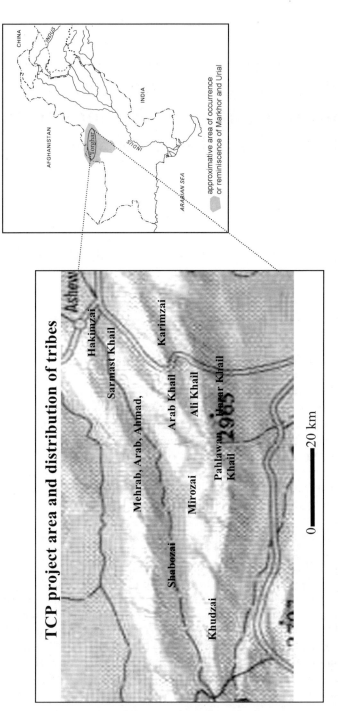

Figure 5.1 Map of the Torghar Conservation Project area.
Source: Nelles Maps, Munich, Germany; additions by the author.

than pre-planned. In this respect, innovative trends are sometimes not readily replicable.

The Torghar inhabitants as an "innovative community"

The TCP was initially designed to save two protected mammal species in the Torghar region by working with and involving the community of people living in the vicinity of their habitat. If the term "community" is understood as a social entity of which the concerned individuals recognize themselves to be a part, then the first question is whether the inhabitants in Torghar consider themselves to be members of a single community.

On the face of it, several criteria affirm the possibility of applying the notion of "community" to the inhabitants of Torghar. From a geographical perspective, all the inhabitants who live on the mountain are collective owners of the land. Economically, most of them have livestock and share the available pasture land. Environmentally, they all depend on the same natural resources. All the inhabitants are Jalalzai and subject to the authority of the Jogizai clan. From a socio-cultural perspective, the inhabitants are all Pashtuns who speak the same language, share customs, and intermarry.

Additional evidence suggesting that the people of Torghar are indeed a community relates to the way they reacted to the TCP. As the benefits of the project became increasingly clear to inhabitants, their willingness to work towards its sustainability increased. They very quickly appreciated the importance of conserving mountain biodiversity as a whole through concerted actions and via regulation. The people of Torghar can, therefore, be said to have reacted, and continue to react today, as a "community" with regard to the TCP initiative.

Outside the framework of the TCP, however, the social set-ups and identities of the Torghar people do not fit well into a defined group. Even though the community was unified in its general acceptance of the project, shifting power relations meant that this unity was regularly challenged. In fact, each group living on the mountain:

• strongly identifies itself as different from others and opposes others through territorial conflict;
• claims members outside the mountain who consider themselves to be co-owners of the land, thus benefiting from an extended social network;
• considers itself as belonging to an area far wider than the mountain range.

From this perspective, what initially appears to be the single "mountain community of Torghar" quickly becomes the "different Jalalzai groups of northern Balochistan and south-east Afghanistan". This is not simply a matter of academic definition, it is the daily reality on the ground.

The next question to be addressed is whether the Torghar community can be considered innovative. An innovative community can be defined as having "the proclivity to harness its people's innovativeness in such a way as to create sustainable lifestyles ... to bring in new methods, ideas, etc., to improve the environment and initiate changes" (UNU-UNEP 2002). But what does this really mean, and how can the concept of innovation itself be defined?

"The term 'innovation' is most often applied to the fields of science or economics and it encompasses two distinct features" (B. Bellon 2002). One type of innovation is "radical" or "revolutionary" and involves drastic changes at the expense of what currently exists. It is usually large scale and materializes as an irreversible breach in a process or structure. It can be characterized, therefore, as being singular, uncommon (if not rare), visible, and limited. The second type of innovation is "incremental" and involves minor improvements. Such innovations result from constant adaptations and responses to day-to-day situations. They are, therefore, permanent, unlimited, small scale and invisible at a given time.

These two types of innovation are interdependent and it is in combination that they ensure the effectiveness of change. It is within the context of these two features that the different innovative trends in the project area of Torghar are discussed.

The Torghar Conservation Project (TCP)

The Torghar Conservation Project was launched in 1985 in order to conserve two animal species, the Suleiman markhor (*Capra falconeri jerdoni*) – a wild goat – and the Afghan urial (*Ovis orientalis cycloceros*) – a wild sheep (see Figure 5.1). Both species are listed in the Third Schedule of the Balochistan Wildlife Protection Act 1974 as "protected animals", which means that they must not be hunted, killed or captured except in specific circumstances (Government of Balochistan, Agricultural Department 1977).

The markhor subspecies can be found only in a limited area that includes the mountains of western Pakistan (Takatu and Toba Kakar Ranges) and some of Afghanistan (Roberts 1997). It is listed as "endangered" under the US Endangered Species Act (ESA) (US Fish and Wildlife Services 1994; cited by Johnson 1997) and is included in Appendix I of the Convention on International Trade in Endangered Species of Wild Fauna and Flora (CITES 1973).[2] The Afghan urial is more widespread than the markhor, although not abundant (Roberts 1997). The urial is included in Appendix II of CITES.

One of the main outputs of the TCP has been that it has achieved a complete cessation of illegal hunting;[3] nearly 1,000 km^2 of conservation area is protected. The TCP, which was registered as a non-governmental organization (NGO) in 1994 under the name of the Society for Torghar Environmental Protection (STEP), is an entirely self-financing organization that obtains its income from trophy hunting.[4] STEP's management board includes tribal representatives of the people living in Torghar. The inhabitants themselves are not part of this board, but they have participated actively in the organization as game guards and they have successfully proposed, influenced and transformed its actions.[5] Their decision-making power has recently been enhanced through the creation of the Mountain Committee, which will be discussed in more detail below.

Collective action and the conception of common goods

Securing patronage

Upstream of the innovative trend, and the most radical change that has resulted from the project, is the prohibition on hunting. Hunting has played a significant role in patron–client relationships in Torghar (see the boxed text). The benefits of the hunting ban were not immediately apparent to the community, although it was still accepted by the mountain inhabitants. One of the main reasons for this was that the idea for the ban was actually launched by the area's leading figure, Nawab Temur Shah Jogizai, and was first implemented by his son Mahbub Jogizai. The involvement of the Nawab conferred legitimacy on the programme and also ensured the continuity of pre-existing power relations. Acceptance by the inhabitants was maintained over time through the ability of the chief and of his son to secure patronage and potential gains in terms of power that helped compensate for the losses incurred by the ban (see the boxed text).

Game guards and new roles

Another unprecedented result of the project was the creation of jobs for the game guards, whose purpose was to implement and control the hunting ban. At the start these jobs were primarily distributed among the inhabitants of Torghar by Mahbub Jogizai – representing his father, the Nawab. The first employees were selected on the basis of pragmatic criteria. They were recognized as being the best hunters on the mountain and as having enough authority or charisma to prevent other people from hunting. They also owed complete allegiance to the Nawab as well as to his clan. The position and role of the game guards were progressively enhanced because of the personal link to Mahbub Jogizai, their policing authority, and the monetary compensation they received. Although

Hunting in Torghar

Before the project started, hunting for food and pleasure was practised by the inhabitants of Torghar and individuals from off the mountain. Initially, primitive weaponry and the scarcity of ammunition
limited the number of animals that were killed. Although the most efficient hunters can claim to have killed more than 1,000 animals in a
life-long career (Samad Aka, in L. Bellon 2001–2002), the high level
of skill required limited the numbers of such hunters to just a few.
On the whole mountain – with a population of 200–300 households
(STEP 2000, 2001) – no more than 12 people out of the last generation
of hunters are said to have been outstanding hunters (Khoshalai, in
L. Bellon 2001–2002). Over-hunting became critical only with the outbreak of the Afghan war and the subsequent introduction of modern
automatic weapons in the late 1970s. By the early 1980s the markhor
and urial populations in Torghar were on the verge of extinction.

On the mountain, hunting involved well-recognized and admired
know-how. This knowledge partly concerned the behaviour of the animals and hunting ability, i.e. tracking and shooting. But it also implied
braving the supernatural creatures (called *perai*) that are believed to
own and guard the herds of wild sheep and goat. Some hunters are
said to have been killed as a result of the *perai*'s deadly wrath – the
last such reported case was 30 years ago (interview in Torghberg, Torghar, 9 May 2001). Admiration for the hunter's skills, bravery and
powers not only affected the status of the individual, but also benefited the group to which he belonged. It is not rare to hear a person
justifying the superiority of his own group by asserting that it contains
the most intelligent and most cunning people and has produced the
finest hunters.

More pragmatically, the skilled hunters were capable of hosting and
guiding influential game hunters from outside. Nawab Temur Shah Jogizai and his son Mahbub Jogizai, well-known hunting experts, regularly visited Torghar, as did other members of the Jogizai clan. Other
influential tribesmen as well as government officials would be invited
to do the same, either by a Jogizai or directly by residents of Torghar.
Obviously, this type of hunting was not linked to any subsistence
need. But it meant something beyond its practitioners' simple enjoy-
ment: allowing influential people to hunt played a dominant role in
the patron–client relationship prevailing in the region. Not only has
"hunting always been linked to politics" (Aurangzeb Jogizai, in L.
Bellon 2001–2002), but its importance increased as the animals progressively vanished.

Hence, much of social status and power relations was derived from
hunting. Abandoning such practices signifies loss on a much greater
scale than the meat that it used to provide.

they were integrated into the continuity of the prevailing power relations, the creation of the game guards generated a new status on the mountain.

The imposition of rules and restrictions

Over the years, implementation of the project has led to a series of incremental innovations. For example, once the idea of a hunting ban had been accepted by the mountain inhabitants, it had to be extended to all potential hunters. Amongst these were the nomadic tribes that passed through Torghar every year.[6] These tribes not only enjoyed free passage through these mountains, but they also benefited from a tacit right to make use of its resources. This included the hunting of wild animals for meat consumption. In an effort to extend the ban, tribesmen from Torghar undertook a campaign to meet and speak with the leaders of each nomadic group "at least ten times"[7] in order to convince them not to hunt.

· Hunting was not the only behaviour restricted under the project. Although paths for nomadic groups had been created by decades of passage through the mountain, some passing tribes would occasionally create new routes for grazing their herds, sometimes on the higher peaks, in order to take a short cut or to avoid the overpopulated regular trails. This presented a further threat to the mountain wildlife as their fodder was depleted. The people of Torghar forbade the nomadic groups from creating new paths.

As the Torghar tribesmen became increasingly aware of the importance of mountain biodiversity, they expanded a prohibition on cutting trees or green branches.[8]

Range management

Further incremental innovations include changes in attitude among the people in Torghar and also a set of necessary innovations concerning safeguarding the mountain's biodiversity. Agreements about change had to be made among the mountain people in relation to several issues. One of these agreements concerned a restriction on the local practice of cutting green trees to feed the leaves to livestock and to supply households with fuel wood. A special collective agreement (a *fatiha*, or oath)[9] on the matter was achieved in 1992. A similar oath was made about controlling grazing to prevent competition for grazing with the wild sheep and goats. This particular restriction was very sensitive because it concerns the main asset upon which the local economic system is built. It has, therefore, been hard to implement during recent years of severe drought, although the general principle behind the restriction has been largely accepted.

As climatic conditions have deteriorated and population pressures increased, additional innovations have been made in order to improve the environment and general living conditions. A major focus of these efforts has been water. Water spots have been created by the local inhabitants for the sole use of wild animals, others have been designated for human consumption, and others for herds and for agricultural purposes. These improvements were jointly conceived between the inhabitants and the TCP's board.

These recent innovations in range management show that the local people's understanding of the environment, in this case of animal behaviour, of the different types of grasses (for example, where and when they grow, their nutritive or other value, etc.), and of the ecological effects of their own behaviour, is acute.

Equity and ownership

The spread of the benefits

Although the funds from trophy hunting have made several other activities possible – such as medical support, the construction of water-related infrastructure, and the construction of roads – the game guard jobs have gradually come to be recognized as the main sustained benefit for the people. As a result, more inhabitants began to demand their "share" or "right" (*haq*) to be employed as game guards. This led to a dramatic increase in the number of game guards employed through the project. In the long run, the increase in jobs was based on tribal affiliations. This system was demanded by the groups themselves in response to both their own understanding of fairness (each tribal group should be given an equal share of jobs) and the project's guiding principle of equity (every individual on the mountain is entitled to a share of the benefits). The increase in game guard jobs, the gradual representation of tribal groups, and the time period over which this evolution took place, are depicted in Table 5.1.

Table 5.2 shows the distribution (as of 2001) of jobs in relation to tribal groups, their population, and the land they own. It is worth noting that the distribution of jobs is not always linked to tribal population or land ownership. This reveals the reactive rather than systematic approach of the project. Of all the groups, the Khudzai is the least favoured and it has also been the most reluctant to join the project.

The role of the game guard has evolved from the pragmatic duty of guarding the mountain to acquire an altogether new social status and an annuity derived from mountain ownership (rather than a salary paid for the performance of a duty). The selection criteria relating to ability to perform a specific duty have, in fact, become irrelevant to the status of the game guards. Most of the jobs are now considered to be for life and

Table 5.1 Evolution of game guard team, 1985–2001

Year	No. of groups	Group name	No. of game guards
1985–1986	Group 1	Single game guard group	12
1986–1995	Group 1	Shahizai	20
	Group 2	Others	22
1995–1997	Group 1	Shahizai (Kundar)	10
	Group 2	Shahizai (Khaisor and Tanishpa)	10
	Group 3	Others	11
1997–2001	Group 1	Shahizai (Kundar)	15
	Group 2	Shahizai (Khaisor and Tanishpa)	16
	Group 3	Shabozai	11
	Group 4	Others	16
2001+	Group 1	Shahizai (Kundar)	17
	Group 2	Hussaini (Tanishpa)	7
	Group 3	Pahlawan Khail	9
	Group 4	Shabozai	11
	Group 5	Mirozai	13
	Group 6	Khudzai	6

Source: STEP (2001); personal enquiries.

some game guards are employed even though they find it difficult to walk, hear or even see.

Wildlife ownership

Another fundamental step in the innovative process was the change in the conception of wildlife ownership. The project was based on the simple economic principle of distributing, among the people of Torghar, the benefits generated from scarce resources through trophy hunting. Thus, a direct link was made between the value of the wild animals and property rights. The benefits accrued to the "owners" of the wildlife and, therefore, of the mountain. This introduced a major change in the conception of ownership: from being considered the property of the *perai* (supernatural guardians – see the boxed text on page 114), the wild goats and sheep were now the property of human beings.

This change in the conception of wildlife ownership gave rise to much confusion. Some subgroups capitalized on their new capacity to claim ownership over the animals themselves. They claimed that animals belonged to specific parts of Torghar, which were the areas owned by them, regardless of the animals' capacity to migrate anywhere on the mountain (Frisina 2000). This claim enabled the subgroup to assert that "these animals are ours", thereby demanding entitlement to a larger share of the benefits. Others maintained that no one could claim property

Table 5.2 Distribution of people, land and game guard jobs across tribal subgroups in Torghar, 2001

Tribal group	Households in Torghar		People in Torghar		Land (%)[a]	Game guard jobs	
	No.	Per cent	No.	Per cent		No.	Per cent
Shahizai	123	52.2	1,013	53	47	32	53
Arab Khail	36	16.0	342	18	–	7	11
Ahmad Khail	22	9.0	169	9	–	3	5
Merhab Khail	12	5.0	105	5	–	4	7
Hazar Khail	25	11.0	165	9	–	4	7
Sarmast Khail	2	0.5	–	–	–	5	8
Pahlawan Khail	26	11.0	196	10	–	9	15
Ali Khail	2	0.5	36	2	–	0	0
Shabozai	35	14.8	291	15	16	11	18
Mirozai	34	14.0	269	14	14	13	21
Khudzai	43	18.0	356	18	23	6	8
Total	235	100.0	1,929	100	100	62	100

Note:
[a] Approximate figure.
Source: STEP (2001); personal enquiries.

rights over non-domestic animals and shifted the logic of distributing benefits from wildlife to land-based ownership. The confrontation between these two attitudes still continues today, although to a lesser degree.

This new way of conceptualizing possession dramatically transformed the relationship between the people and their environment. Hunters switched from trying to hunt as many animals as possible, to conservation and working towards a population increase. The competition with *perai* gave way to a new responsibility and, subsequently, a new power over the "natural resource". Consideration of the *perai* as the owner of the animals was incompatible with the way the project operated. It was therefore, if not forgotten, at least disregarded. The people's new sense of power over the mountain's resources helped to shape the concept of collective responsibility, which in turn opened the way to considering mountain biodiversity in a more holistic manner.

Collective responsibility

From the initial objective of safeguarding just two animal species on the mountain, it came to be recognized that it was necessary to pay attention to biodiversity as a whole. Sharing grazing, water preservation and saving trees all became relevant to the project and this made the need to act collectively obvious. Yet, uniform action around a common interest was in many ways an alien custom for the people of Torghar. The mountain is territorially divided amongst 12 groups, and ownership has always been based on these groups. Given this backdrop, achieving collective action to safeguard a separately owned good was a challenge.

The biggest hurdle was addressed by preventing existing conflicts from jeopardizing the project. Individuals had to iron out their differences in order to participate fully and some group representatives had to intervene in other groups' disputes in order to prevent negative repercussions. It was necessary, then, for some people (often game guards and/or their head) to acquire a new role as negotiators. This was accepted by the third parties despite the fact that these individuals would not normally have had such authority.

Introducing this new type of collective responsibility had an effect on all levels of social interaction and also included collective action with regard to outside forces.[10] Some groups were unhappy with the success of the project because it meant a loss of their own legitimacy, and so they attempted to discredit it. They engaged in such actions as encouraging people to poach and spreading negative rumours. These included the assertion that the programme was in fact a disguised attempt by the government to tighten its grip over this part of the province. It was also said to be un-Islamic and driven by alien non-Muslim forces that would eventually come to capture the mountain range.

This challenge was overcome when, through a concerted effort, a common acceptance was reached on the idea that the mountain was owned by different groups of people but was indivisible in terms of its management. This common acceptance was reached through an internal process of negotiations involving both debate and compromise. This can be described as a "soft" approach in that it did not involve the forcible imposition of decisions.[11] This approach was developed by the inhabitants themselves. It was not the result of one person's actions but involved several representatives. Nor was this innovative dynamic pre-designed; it emerged as a result of an organic process.

The innovations involved in the transition to collective action and responsibility induced a behavioural change among the mountain inhabitants without transforming the social structure. The project capitalized on the interdependence and pre-existing negotiating practices of nomadic groups. It utilized a widely practised and recognized custom by creating a new *fatiha*, and used the local governing institutions to obtain flexible political compromises. These innovations were a response both to the requirements of the project and to the generally declining environmental conditions of overgrazing, the depletion of water and grass, and the illness and death of livestock.

Features for sustainability

The above discussion has shown innovation to be far from alien to existing social practices. A "tribal community" does not abide by steadfast, unwavering or static "traditions" but is, on the contrary, driven by dynamics that comprise and provoke constant change. Innovation is not a limitless process – it does operate within constraints. To adopt a new approach to mountain biodiversity and act as a single "community" was undeniably innovative for the people of Torghar.

Yet, it is also in this domain that counter-innovative reactions find expression. For example, not all the changes to range management that were triggered during the implementation of the TCP were positive. Population growth, combined with the new and substantial income generated by the programme, actually led – until the recent six-year drought (1998–2004) – to a significant increase in the number of herds and their sizes, and this eventually caused the shepherds to abandon previous management practices.[12] This can be defined, in an indirect way at least, as a "perverse incentive" (McNeely 1988) of the project.

It is important when examining innovations within the Torghar community to address the issue of project sustainability in terms of the problems that may arise and any other developments that might affect the project. In particular it is important to look at the contradictions that have arisen from differing perceptions of community and conflicting interests. This issue of understanding and sustaining innovation can usefully be discussed in the context of recent efforts to reorganize the decision-making mechanisms of the Torghar Conservation Project.

Issues of community identity

Observing or working with a "community" assumes, by definition, that this community is bound by common interests. As discussed above, the "community" of Torghar came together in response to the TCP. Although common interests may exist, there are still conflicting interests that bring the nature of the community into question. If the cohesiveness of a community is even partially artificial, there will be repercussions for the innovation that is carried out by this community. It is crucial, therefore, to consider the roles of multiple social forces and conflicting interests when assessing the social structures of innovation. Concretely, this situation triggers contradictory reactions.

The idea of creating "Mountain Committees" for the grassroots management of the project was launched in 2001. Although everyone agreed that the committees were both necessary and beneficial to the project, the proposal faced resistance. Opposition arose from several directions: from influential people living outside the mountain area who were members of one of the Torghar sub-tribal groups; from groups laying claim to a portion of the mountain but not living there; from people living on the mountain who were scared of losing certain privileges; and from groups from the mountain that wanted to reverse inequalities.

The principles identifying the "Torghar community" were accepted by everyone. Yet, simultaneously, interactions that contradict the unity of such a community continued to prevail. This contradiction is not just between the conceivers of the project on the one hand (STEP's board of management) and the people of Torghar on the other; it is a contradiction within both groups as well.

Capturing innovation

As this case study shows, innovation is a complex process that is hard to measure or even observe (Henry 1991). Whether defined as a dual dynamic made up of both process and product innovation, each conducted through "invention", "innovation" and "diffusion" (Hall 1986), or as the sum of separate but intricate and interwoven mechanisms (Metcalfe

1986), innovation constantly challenges attempts to reduce analysis to mere mechanical cause-and-effect understanding. For example, as Metcalfe (1986) argues, a basically inefficient innovation can still lead to best-practice technology through the selection and diffusion mechanisms. The opposite is equally true.

The problem is all the more acute when focusing on the social organization of innovation or on innovations within a social context (Engel 1997). As in the case of Torghar, such innovations resist being clearly identified. In a social environment, innovation is better grasped by observing the processes underlying it, rather than its result (Lindblom 1990). One must also keep in mind that these processes are often diffuse, unintentional and epiphenomenal. Innovation should be understood as a complex social process rather than merely a matter of the transfer or dissemination of technologies or of knowledge and ideas. It is not a simple mechanical device.

To analyse such complex phenomena it is important to take into account the many conflicting forces within the particular social group. These include the way individuals or stakeholders can each have radically different perceptions of what their problems, goals and possible options are within the innovative frame. As Checkland and Scholes advocate (Checkland 1989; Checkland and Scholes 1990), "conflict" is inherent within any social group and any "cause-and-effect" phenomena can be jeopardized or annihilated by conflicting interests. From this, the question arises of whether or not it is possible, or even desirable, to have any kind of active or proactive influence over the innovation patterns of a given social group (Engel 1997).

Can innovation sustain itself?

Looking at innovative trends within a given social context, "'the best means to an end' does not exist. Numerous possible combinations of ends and means compete in the perception of those who will be involved in making a choice among possible actions" (Engel 1997: 22). What has been said of innovation processes in Torghar shows that the innovative trend was gradual. The "appropriate conditions" emerged as a result of conflicting interests, of different visions, of bargaining and of negotiations. Inflicting or forcing preconceived plans or actions upon inhabitants was never the norm within the TCP. In this respect the Torghar project in many ways exemplifies how innovation arises from the convergence of social forces – if, that is, this means accepting that "convergence" means nothing more than "a narrowed range of thoughts and attitudes" as opposed to a general agreement and perfect understanding which "never or rarely ... approaches a unanimity or consensus" (Lindblom 1990: 71).

The greatest strength of the project as a whole, and the key to its achievements, was its "let things happen" approach. Actors were left to act and, most importantly, no time limits for adaptations were imposed. But this had a cost. A failure to address conflicting forces puts the outcomes of an innovation at risk. Convergence derives not from mutually exclusive clusters of ideas, views or propositions, but from the issues that actors address when they outline the direction the innovation is to take (and with every experience, every new exposure, new discords creep in). Moreover, not only can each person's perception conflict with that of others; each person can also be confronted with his or her own conflicting interests and necessary choices. Respecting the plurality of social forces in the innovation process can lead one of these forces – group or individual – to act alternately in favour or against it.

A recent development in Torghar affairs provides a good example of this. Since its inception, the TCP has been confronted with demands by groups or by individuals regarding their rights (*haq*). The project had in fact become multifaceted, simultaneously serving different conflicting interests. The concept of *haq* precisely incarnates the array of interests that the TCP was unable to encompass within a single system, where it failed to generate unanimity or consensus. For a long time, decision-making for the TCP basically lay in the hands of a few people and this enabled others to argue that decisions were wrong because they were based on a lack of awareness of complex social realities. To rectify this situation, the organization's board attempted to delegate decision-making power directly to the "people who know", that is, the inhabitants themselves.

In 1998, independently from other members of STEP, two mountain groups decided to create another Council, which they chose to name "Committee". This Committee was to look after the specific interests of these two groups with regard to the project. Representation of each subgroup was based on population (an unusual criterion within the tribal setup) and the Committee was expected to meet three times a year. Yet again, internal disputes nullified the initiative and by 2002 the Committee had met only twice.

In view of the ineffectiveness of this attempt, between January and June 2002 STEP undertook a discussion exercise to reform its structure. Talks were carried out between members of the board and most of the mountain inhabitants. Three distinct entities were created as a result: (1) a Higher Council, representing all the programme's actors, (2) Committees of Elders, and (3) Mountain Committees – each committee representing a specific tribal group (this structure was inspired by the 1998 initiative). The objective was the devolution of decision-making power in order to achieve coherent initiatives. The proposed framework is illustrated in Figure 5.2.

124

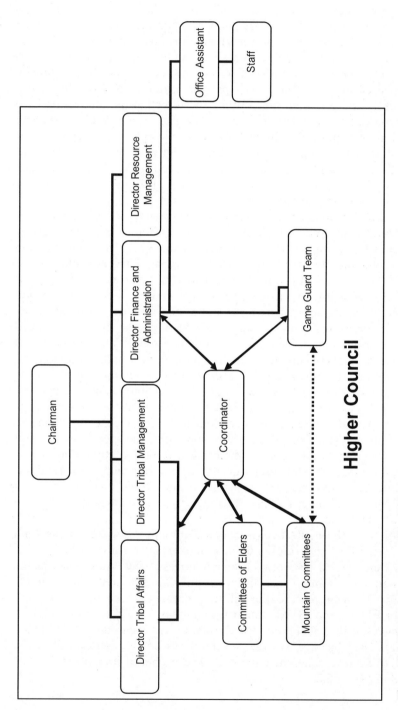

Figure 5.2 Proposed structure for STEP.
Source: Luc Bellon, 2002 field research.

The creation of a Higher Council gave each representative, except for the chairman, equal importance and authority in the decision-making process. This structure was the result of wide discussion and information exchange. Yet the end result still faced extraordinary opposition. Even though all the actors had agreed in principle, when the time came for implementation only one subgroup agreed to create the required Committee.

It is interesting to note that the proposed structure was designed to counter the flaws, constantly pointed out by Torghar inhabitants, of an overly flexible (non-directional) approach. The project's flexible structure had given enough latitude for existing power relations to operate, while at the same time becoming a tool for altering these relations. Some game guards, for example, used the programme to obtain authority over issues that had nothing to do with mountain conservation. Thus, inequalities were either enhanced or triggered by the project, which caused all its actors to protest. STEP's proposed reform meant rigidifying its structure and reducing the possibilities of using the project to favour conflicting interests.

The project in Torghar has managed to create conditions favourable to innovative processes, although these conditions are based on an unstable social equilibrium. The sustainability of these processes depends, therefore, on the possibility for the conflicting forces to be constantly in negotiation.

Conclusion

When the centipede was asked in which order he moved his hundred legs, he became paralysed and starved to death because he had never thought of it before and had left his legs to look after themselves. (Cited by Koestler 1968: 205)

This chapter has demonstrated that the "community" of Torghar, however pragmatic and relevant a grouping for a specific purpose, should not be seen and conceived as a holistic or autonomous social reality. The example of the TCP has also been used to show that "tribal" Pashtuns, despite often being described as "remote" or "traditional", welcome innovation. They do this not as an adaptation to recent changes, but as a customary trend in a constantly evolving environment. The tools for realizing this change are inscribed in their accepted social behaviours.

Finally, innovation has been shown to be a complex process that is non-mechanical and unpredictable. It has also been made clear that conflicting interests are, simultaneously, the trigger of innovation and the biggest threat to innovation mechanisms. If innovation is for the large part the result of social, creative, gradual and unplanned processes, the attempt to seize, control and direct it cannot be simple. Innovation can be understood as "emerging from the interplay in-and-between social practices" (Engel 1997: 125), and some networking between social actors can be seen as a particular social practice aimed at innovation. This leads to the conclusion that, as a result of active networking for innovation, forms of social organization emerge over time and have a momentum of their own. These networking practices leading to innovation concern a "met-practice" or "joint performance" (Gremmen 1993: 148) and they are best coordinated not necessarily by a centralizing force, but rather through mutual adjustment (Lindblom 1990).

There is a lot to learn from the centipede parable (cited above). One can suggest that the centipede has developed a system to make its legs work not because it designed the mechanisms of its own body, but both because it needed to walk and because the legs were available. In the same way, acting upon innovation processes has more to do with creating appropriate conditions than with suggesting specific actions. The innovation process may be constant, but it is also unstable. Sustainability is never secure, but is highly dependent on constant adaptation and reaction.

The arguments in this chapter have focused on the innovative processes resulting from essentially reactive behaviours. The question remains of whether or not proactive approaches are compatible with such reactivity. My contention is that the two are not dissociable, although the degree to which proactive reactions are understandable or welcomed varies according to the context. The consequences of premeditated actions are easier to manage if they are admitted to be subject to unpredictable reactions.

Glossary

fatiha: collective prayer, oath or commitment
haq: a "right" and/or entitlement collectively acknowledged by society
mullah: a man with religious authority and knowledge
perai: a supernatural creature, guardian of the mountain sheep and goats
pergor: indigenous fallow system applied to the management of the mountain grassland.

Acknowledgements

This chapter could not have been written without the valued support of Naseer A. Tareen, who guided and accompanied the research throughout; the very helpful knowledge and assistance extended by the STEP office (namely Paind Khan, Zahir Khan, Nawabzada Aurangzeb Jogizai, Jamshaid Ali Khan and Ubaidullah); the help, openness and warm welcome offered by the inhabitants of Torghar; and the indispensable backing of the International Foundation for the Conservation of Wildlife (IGF).

Notes

1. The region in which the Torghar Conservation Project was initiated is primarily inhabited by members of the Kakar tribe, with tribal authority lying in the hands of a subgroup called the Jogizai. Within the project area there are 2,000–3,000 inhabitants, each belonging to a different tribal subgroup.
2. For details, see ⟨http://www.fws.gov⟩.
3. Vis-à-vis the Pakistani state, the region falls into the "Provincially Administered Tribal Area" (PATA) category. This status was inherited from the colonial administrative system (Bruce 1900). In short, it implies marginality as regards the executive power (law and order are maintained by a local militia known as the "Levies Force") as well as legal power (specific laws and fiscal rights, etc.). Despite recent legal changes to this status, bringing these areas back into the mainstream (Ali and Rehman 2001), the region is still marginalized (L. Bellon 2002) and government institutions have little capacity to enforce some of the national laws, as is the case with hunting.
4. Hunting permits are granted by the Government of Pakistan and CITES. Prices of trophies have now mounted to US$25,000 for a markhor and US$15,000 for a urial. An average of two to three hunters comes each year to Torghar, although the mountain could sustain many more (Johnson 1997). During the period 1999–2002, STEP earned US$62,000 a year; its average yearly expenditure was US$90,000. The deficit – which was met by a bank overdraft – can mostly be explained by the war in Afghanistan and general political tensions in the region. The TCP has also benefited, although rarely, from occasional funding for specific projects.
5. STEP's board of management is composed of a chairman, a Director for Tribal Affairs, a Director for Tribal Management, a Director of Finance and Administration and a Director for Resource Management. Two of the directors have close tribal links with the Torghar inhabitants, but neither lives there. The other two directors each belong to an altogether different tribe. The responsibility of the board is to implement the decisions and policies of STEP, the latter being elaborated in close consultation with all people affected by the programme – meaning primarily the inhabitants of Torghar.
6. These tribes are numerous and belong to different groups. Some of the nomads belong to the same tribal group as those living in Torghar (Jalalzai, or Khulzai within the larger Kakar tribe – to which Jalalzai also belong), but others do not (Abdullahzai, Batzai, Merdanzai, Safi, Dotani, MariaNi, Shinwari, Mullah Khail, Aka Khail, Tor Naser, Hajigai, Nizam Khail, Niazai, Babozai, Suleiman Khail). For more details on the nomadic patterns of these tribes, see Mayne (1955), Robinson (1978) and Spain (1963).
7. Torghar tribesman, interviewed 10 July 2002 (in L. Bellon 2001–2002). The same person added: "We have informed all those tribes that when you [enter the mountain], even if it's a marriage party, you will not fire a shot. Even that is prohibited, so the rest you

can imagine. We have gone to every household that come this way and we go to their elders."

8. "And we have told them that on the way you will not touch the trees. Because these people had the habit of having an axe with them in order to chop branches to take the leaves to feed their animals. We told them not to do so" (Torghar tribesman, interviewed 3 September 2002; in L. Bellon 2001–2002).

9. Under a *fatiha*, representatives of households owning a resource get together and decide to limit the consumption of that resource – in this case, to use only dead wood for fuel, or ripe wild pistachio for feed – by swearing on the Koran that nobody will break the promise. The *fatiha* is supervised and ratified by a *mullah* (priest). According to this practice, those who do not act according to the collective decision will suffer God's damnation. Once the oath has been sworn, word is spread to all people potentially concerned. The number of people involved can vary from 2 individuals to 20 households, to the mountain as a whole or to a wider area.

10. "We have dealt with problems on household basis. From house to house we have involved people. Because in the beginning, when 7 or 8 people took their livestock to QS, there people tried to put some opposing ideas in their minds.... For example, if there are differences between [group A] and [group B] that we know will have negative effect on the program, then we voluntarily go and do the patch up. Usually we'll tell them that we have no interest. After all we are outsiders and we would like you to have no differences. Although the differences may be over something else, but we know that it can create problems for the program" (game guard, interviewed 15 April 2002; in L. Bellon 2001–2002).

11. "In the past, whenever we developed differences, we would beat up somebody here there, until one will give up. Ever since we started this program, we have not made anyone's nose bleed. The reason is that this program is tied to our conflicts" (interview with game guard, 7 September 2002; in L. Bellon 2001–2002).

12. Amongst these was *pergor*, under which specific grass areas were left fallow for several months. The areas, defined each year, were mostly on the mountain and were not allowed for grazing even to passing nomads. The herders would therefore move on to the plains, sometimes migrating all the way to Khorasan, and only those involved in agriculture would remain (collective discussion, Torghar, 11 September 2002; in L. Bellon 2001–2002).

REFERENCES

Ali, S. S. and J. Rehman (2001) "Indigenous peoples and ethnic minorities of Pakistan: Constitutional and legal perspectives", Nordic Institute of Asian Studies, Monograph Series No. 84, Curzon, Richmond.

Bellon, B. (2002) *L'Innovation créatrice*. Paris: Economica, Arte.

Bellon, L. (2001–2002) "Compiled interviews", Torghar, Qillah-Saifullah and Quetta, unpublished.

———— (2002) "Les zones tribales du Pakistan", *Alternatives Internationales* 5: 3–6.

Bruce, R. I. (1900) *The forward policy and its results*. London: Longman, Green and Co.

Checkland, P. B. (1989) "Soft system methodology", *Human Systems Management* 8: 273–289.

Checkland, P. B. and J. Scholes (1990) *Soft systems methodology in action*. Chichester: John Wiley.

CITES (1973) *Convention on International Trade in Endangered Species of Wild Fauna and Flora*, available at ⟨http://www.cites.org/eng/disc/text.shtml#II⟩; amended 1979.

Engel, G. H. (1997) *The social organization of innovation: A focus on stakeholder interaction*. Amsterdam: Royal Tropical Institute.

Frisina, M. (2000) "Suleiman Markhor (Capra falconeri jerdoni) and Afghan Urial (Ovis orientalis cycloceros) population status in the Torghar Hills, Balochistan Province, Pakistan", unpublished.

Government of Balochistan, Agricultural Department (1977) "Third Schedule of the Balochistan Wildlife Protection Act, 1974".

Gremmen, B. (1993) "The mystery of practical use of scientific knowledge", PhD dissertation, Twente University, Enschede, The Netherlands.

Hall, P. (1986) "The theory and practice of innovation policy: An overview", in P. Hall (ed.) *Technology, innovation and economic policy*, pp. 1–34. Oxford: Phillip Allan Publishers.

Henry, B. (1991) "The innovation process: Analysis, driving forces, obstacles, assessment", in B. Henry (ed.) *Forecasting technological innovation*, pp. 1–24. Dordrecht: Kluwer Academic Publishers.

Jansson, E. (1988) *India, Pakistan or Pakhtunistan*. Uppsala: Acta Universitatis Upsaliensis.

Johnson, K. (1997) "Status of urial and Afghan urial populations in the Torghar Hills, Balochistan Province Pakistan", in S. A. Mufti, C. Woods and S. A. Hasan, *Biodiversity of Pakistan*, pp. 469–483. Islamabad: Pakistan Museum of Natural History; Gainesville: Florida Museum of Natural History.

Koestler, A. (1968) "Beyond atomism and holism – the concept of the holon", in A. Koestler and J. R. Smythies (eds) *Beyond reductionism, new perspectives in the life sciences*, pp. 192–232. New York: Macmillan.

Lindblom, C. (1990) *Inquiry and change*. New Haven, CT: Yale University Press.

McNeely, J. A. (1988) *Economics and biological diversity: Developing and using economic incentives to conserve biological resources*. Gland, Switzerland: International Union for Conservation of Nature and Natural Resources (IUCN).

Mayne, P. (1955) *Journey of the Pathans*. Garden City, NY: Doubleday.

Metcalfe, J. S. (1986) "Technological innovation and the competitive process", in P. Hall (ed.) *Technology, innovation and economic policy*, pp. 35–64. Oxford: Phillip Allan Publishers.

Roberts, T. J. (1997) *The mammals of Pakistan*, revised edn. Karachi: Oxford University Press.

Robinson, J. A. (1978) *Notes on tribes of eastern Afghanistan*. Quetta, Pakistan: Nisa Traders; first published 1934.

Spain, J. W. (1963) *The Pathan borderland*. Karachi: Indus Publication.

STEP [Society for Torghar Environmental Protection] (1994) "Rules and by-laws of the Society for Torghar Environmental Protection", unpublished.

——— (2000) "Torghar census (population and livestock) May 2000", unpublished.

—— (2001) "Torghar census (population and livestock) June 2001", unpublished.

UNU–UNEP [United Nations University – United Nations Environment Programme] (2002) "Innovative communities: Community centered approaches to sustainable environmental management", Working Paper by the Innovative Communities Project, 1 April 2002; available at ⟨http://www.geic.or.jp/⟩.

6

Highland encounters: Building new partnerships for conservation and sustainable development in the Yangtze River headwaters, the heart of the Tibetan plateau, China

J. Marc Foggin

Introduction

Tibetan pastoralists have lived in the alpine grasslands of the Tibetan plateau for thousands of years. Living close to the land and dependent on the health of grassland ecosystems for their livelihood and well-being, these pastoralists have unique first-hand knowledge of the natural environment (Ekvall 1968; Foggin 2000; Goldstein and Beall 1990; Miller 1995; Wu 1997). Yet, as with many pastoralists worldwide, they have often been marginalized by government planners and development workers alike and their particular needs, concerns and aspirations, as well as their traditional land management practices and environmental knowledge, have been ignored (Bennett 1988; Blench 2001; Galaty and Johnson 1990; Humphrey and Sneath 1996; Loomis 1988; Miller 2000). In an attempt to help redress this situation, I have for many years now investigated how Tibetan herders value and use their natural resources, and how one community in particular, Suojia (pronounced *Swo-jya*), has worked to conserve grassland biodiversity for future generations.[1] Central to this complex endeavour are the multifaceted notions of community participation, local ownership of projects and activities, and the building of long-lasting partnerships for conservation (Berkes and Folke 1998; Bernard and Young 1997; Brown 2002; Ghai and Vivian 1992; Salafsky and Wollenberg 2000; Stevens 1997; Taylor-Ide and Taylor 2002).

This chapter focuses on the specific efforts in Suojia to protect the native biodiversity of the Tibetan plateau. Two main questions are asked:

- In what circumstances did the community initiate its forward-looking conservation work?
- What features of the community, or of its key individuals, have contributed most to their initial success?

In answering these questions, it is hoped that further insight will be provided into the nature of grassroots conservation in general and the character of innovative communities in particular.

I attempt to answer these questions by first reviewing the regional context and background of the environmental work undertaken by the people of Suojia and providing a description of the project area. This is followed by a brief history of the Upper Yangtze Organization (UYO) and a review of its relationships with several national and international partner institutions. This grassroots organization played the lead role in the nature conservation and sustainable development initiatives undertaken in the Suojia community. I then highlight some of the key innovative features of this community. Finally, a postscript will shed light on several important developments that are still unfolding in the project area.

Regional context and background

The Suojia community is composed almost exclusively of Tibetan pastoralists in the headwaters area of the Yangtze River, in south-west Qinghai Province, near the centre of the Tibetan plateau (see Figure 6.1). For residents of one of the harshest environments on Earth, who depend on grassland resources for their survival, the state of the environment is a matter of significant concern. At the same time, however, policy decisions made in distant Beijing, whether on grassland laws, market integration, infrastructure development or the establishment of national nature reserves, also have a significant impact on the community – sometimes with dire consequences. For this reason, it is important to consider a wide variety of perspectives in order properly to understand the circumstances and key elements of the conservation work carried out in Suojia. The rest of this section provides an overview of various environmental and developmental initiatives undertaken at national and provincial levels that have affected Suojia both directly and indirectly.

Although a large part of the population in Asia lives in urban settings, there are also vast regions of the continent that have relatively low population densities. This is most marked in China, where 95 per cent of the people live in only 45 per cent of the country's land area, and where over 50 per cent of the land is used primarily for extensive pastoralism (MOFA 2000; Xie 2000; Zhao 1994). Furthermore, many of the ecosystems in the sparsely inhabited regions of western China are threatened

Figure 6.1 The location of the Suojia community in the People's Republic of China.
Source: J. Marc Foggin.

with land degradation and loss of biodiversity (BWG/CCICED 2001: Edmonds 1994; He 1991; SEPA 2001; Smil 1993; Zhang 1998). This means that, although the human population is relatively small in such areas, the areas face serious environmental problems that affect not only the local people but also the millions more living downstream.

China is specifically composed of three major geographical regions: the Tibetan plateau, the Arid Northwest and Eastern Monsoon China (see Figure 6.1). The focus of this chapter is the Tibetan plateau, which accounts for roughly 25 per cent of the country's land area. Owing to its high altitude, which is on average over 4,000 metres above sea level, temperatures on the plateau are low. Permafrost is widespread, solar radiation is intense and high winds are frequent. Five of the world's largest rivers originate on the Tibetan plateau: the Brahmaputra, Salween, Mekong, Yangtze and Yellow rivers.

Although Suojia is located in the heart of the Tibetan plateau, its people are affected by many external factors. Because China is home to around one-quarter of the world's population, its primary concern is still to provide for the basic needs of the majority of its population. However, the uneven distribution of people and resources (for example, the Tibetan plateau has rich natural capital including oil, natural gas, precious minerals, hydropower and vast grasslands, but it comprises less than 1 per cent of the country's total population) means that these national priorities do not necessarily reflect the needs or particularities of remote mountain areas. Fortunately, however, many national leaders have come to recognize the importance of environmental protection, and the concepts of sustainable development and community participation have become fully ensconced in the country's development rhetoric. They are evident, for example, in the nation's current and most comprehensive drive toward modernization to date: the Western Development Strategy (WDS).

The WDS, which has been renamed by some scholars as China's "Go West" Campaign (e.g. Economy 2002), seeks, in particular, to address the needs of the ethnic minority people in China's vast hinterland, as well as the growing and evolving needs of the much larger population in the east. At the same time, the WDS has as its goal the protection of the environment for the benefit of future generations. In grand terms the WDS is very commendable. Yet its potential to benefit rural communities (what it means to the Tibetan herders of Suojia, for example) is questionable. Although most international agencies understand that the WDS is meant to include not only large-scale infrastructure development projects (or mega-projects) but also social development projects, actual funding almost exclusively targets the former. Some of the largest projects of the WDS include:

- construction of the Golmud–Lhasa railway;
- construction of a 3,000 km west-to-east gas pipeline;
- a colossal south-to-north water diversion project;
- the relocation/resettlement of millions of people in connection with these and other development projects.

These activities are likely to have several impacts on the community of Suojia; for example:

- the railway will bring new immigrants to the area and generally open the region to all sorts of new enterprises (but with the risk of excluding local communities);
- costly state projects will shift funds away from the provision of essential social services;
- serious disturbance to the natural flow of the Yangtze and Yellow rivers will disrupt their ecological balance; and
- relocation and sedentarization projects will bring about dramatic socioeconomic and demographic changes in the region, together with equally insidious ecological problems arising from the sedentarization of pastoral populations.

Although the WDS has also generated some environmental initiatives, these too appear to be mostly mega-projects that rarely engage with local people. These projects may not provide direct benefits to the communities and they may still prove to be associated with as yet unknown pitfalls. Almost all mega-projects carried out around the world have been ill fated and it remains to be seen if there will be a different outcome in China.

Provincial initiatives

Qinghai Province is the second administrative level at which major decisions affecting the people of Suojia are made. As part of its bid to participate in and access the national funding available for the development of China's western regions, the province has also proposed several large initiatives. Noting in particular its unique position as the source of three great rivers – the Yangtze, Yellow and Mekong rivers[2] (see Figure 6.1) – the province has concentrated primarily on projects framed as "ecological construction" work. So-called environmental projects include, among other things, the extraction of mineral resources; ecotourism development; the "modernization" of pastoral practices (i.e. the abandonment of traditional grazing methods); and the restoration of arid lands via the wide-scale introduction of a woody shrub, *Atriplex canescens*, and other species as part of a national programme to restore degraded land. The most prominent environmental initiative has been the establishment of China's newest protected area, the Sanjiangyuan Nature Reserve (SNR).

Qinghai Province also continues to forge ahead with its poverty alleviation programme, which aims to provide herders with permanent homes, livestock shelters, grassland fencing and winter forage for their domestic animals. Although such plans may give rise to some benefits (e.g. improved living conditions), the long-term benefits are not guaranteed. International development experience has in fact shown repeated failure in both human and environmental terms – from Morocco to Mongolia – in programmes that aim to promote sedentary lifestyles in pastoral or grassland systems (see, for example, Barfield 1993; Blench 2001; Ellis and Swift 1988; Galaty and Johnson 1990; Humphrey and Sneath 1996; Swift et al. 1990; Williams 1996).

Sanjiangyuan Nature Reserve

The Sanjiangyuan Nature Reserve (SNR), in which much of Suojia now unexpectedly finds itself, is one of the country's most publicized attempts to protect the fragile ecology of the upper reaches of the Yangtze River. The SNR aims specifically to conserve Tibetan biodiversity, especially

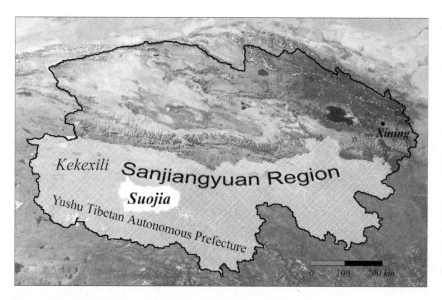

Figure 6.2 Qinghai Province and the Sanjiangyuan Region.
Source: J. Marc Foggin.

wetland habitat, and to enhance and sustain the livelihood and well-being of local people. With between 15 and 49 per cent of the water flow for the Yangtze, Yellow and Mekong rivers originating in the Sanjiangyuan region (see Figure 6.2), the SNR is extremely valuable not only for local communities but also for the entire nation. The SNR is divided into three main management zones: core zones for wildlife protection, buffer zones where limited animal husbandry can continue, and a large research area (*China Green Times* 2003). As a provincial project, the SNR initially included the entire Sanjiangyuan region, comprising 18 counties in southern Qinghai Province with a land area of 318,000 km^2, or 44 per cent of the provincial area. In January 2003, however, the SNR was upgraded to a national-level nature reserve and it now encompasses only 152,300 km^2 – with an estimated price tag of US$307 million (Xinhua News Agency 2003a). Although the delineation of management zones has yet to be finalized, it appears that Suojia is now included partly in the reserve's largest core zone and partly in an adjacent buffer zone. Only time will tell the ways in which local herders will benefit (or not) from the establishment of this reserve.

Each of the above frames of reference, whether it be the national or provincial perspectives on land management issues or the question of the newly established nature reserve, points to the complexity of decisions and their impacts on the Suojia community. How these initiatives will ultimately influence the future of conservation efforts by the Suojia people remains to be seen.

The environment and people of Suojia

The Yangtze River headwaters consist of several habitat types. Alpine and swamp meadows, which comprise mainly *Kobresia* sedges, provide the best forage for domestic animals. The arid steppe, covered with grasses and a variety of forbs, also provides some forage for livestock, especially horses. Among the wild ungulates, Tibetan gazelle, wild ass, blue sheep and, in lesser numbers, Tibetan antelope, wild yak, argali and white-lipped deer all make their home in Suojia's wide plains and gently rolling hills. Other mammals include large carnivores such as the wolf, Tibetan sand fox, snow leopard, Pallas' cat and brown bear, and a variety of smaller mammals such as Himalayan marmot, Tibetan hare, zokor and plateau pika (see Foggin 2000; Schaller 1998; Smith and Foggin 1999). Likewise, many birds are common even in the heart of the plateau, including many raptors (such as the Himalayan griffon, bearded vulture or lammergeyer, golden eagle, upland buzzard, saker falcon), game birds (e.g. Tibetan snowcock), passerines (e.g. snow finches, rose finches, accentors, larks) and others (see Foggin 2000; Lai and Smith 2003). The internationally endangered black-necked crane is particularly noteworthy, too, because it is found in relatively large numbers in Suojia's wetlands.

Environmental conditions on the Tibetan plateau are generally too severe for agriculture and are favourable only for pastoralism. It should be noted that the Tibetan rangelands developed over millennia under long-term grazing pressure by wild ungulates. Historically, until the early 1960s, several semi-nomadic hunting tribes lived in the region. Animal husbandry was introduced to the area as a new way of life with the establishment of the Suojia Commune in 1972. As one elderly woman in the Suojia community (interviewed in July 1998) recollects:

"I'm now 78 years old. When I was around 2 or 3 years old [c. 1920], my father came here with me to hunt wildlife because our family was poor. We weren't nomads but hunters. I don't remember exactly where we lived, but we joined a group of 20 people and we lived and hunted together ... Many years later I moved back to this same place, this time with my own family. That was when Suojia was established [around 1972]. We now live in the fourth brigade [village], Muqu, the last one to be established. Nobody wanted to move here because it's much too cold, but we didn't have any choice. So now this is my home again."[3]

A quarter of a century later, and three-quarters of a century after her first arrival as a child, this woman still lives close to the land. Every day she collects water from a spring and her daughter-in-law and grand-daughters milk the yak and undertake many other daily chores. Her grandsons herd the yak, and her son oversees heavier chores around the tent. Although wildlife is scarcer now than in the past, old wild yak horns are still used as milk pails, antelope horns are used to soften leather and gazelle horns are used to pull yak hair (instead of cutting it), in order to make better-quality rope. Despite the similarities of yesterday and today, many aspects of local livelihoods, and especially the local environment, are changing. For example, the stream that used to run next to the old woman's tent dried up around 1990, and the spring itself dried in 1995. Grassland vegetation composition is also changing, owing in part to regional climatic changes and in part to unsustainable grazing practices and severe soil erosion.

Today, unlike in the past when people hunted and migrated by following wildlife throughout the year, the people in Suojia now manage their own land and over 95 per cent of them herd livestock, mostly sheep and yak. In its basic form, pastoralism consists of several seasonal moves between summer and winter pastures within each family's parcel of land. Some of these herders seek to manage their rangeland in sustainable ways, moving livestock conscientiously from one pasture to another and culling animals in the autumn. Others, however, seek only to feed their livestock for the day and they give little forethought to the longer-term ecological consequences of their actions.

The government is currently introducing new policies that seek to sedentarize the people by providing them with winter homes, livestock shelters and grassland fencing (Richard 2000). Although these policies are aimed at protecting the grassland, it is likely that in many cases they may instead cause further harm to the environment. In fact, when mobility is removed from the grazing systems, as is now being encouraged in most pastoral areas in China, there is an increased risk of grassland degradation, which can result in large-scale environmental and human disasters. The concept of "ecological refugees" has already been used for herders in some parts of the Qinghai Province.

Another major environmental issue faced in Suojia is the decrease in numbers of wildlife as a result of illegal hunting. When gold was discovered in 1984 in the Kekexili desert (see Figure 6.2) – a large uninhabited area north-west of Suojia – nearly 30,000 prospectors made their way into a wilderness that had previously remained largely untouched by humans. Soon after, not only were thousands of people engaged in illegal mining, they also began to hunt Tibetan antelope, wild yak, snow leopard and many other endangered species. At first the poachers hunted only in winter when the ground was frozen and more suitable for vehicle transport.

Figure 6.3 Community-based protected areas in Suojia.
Note: Six community-initiated protected areas (PAs) have been established in total, five to protect key focal species (as indicated on the map) and one to protect an important wetland habitat (in Yaqu village, but not clearly delineated).
Source: J. Marc Foggin.

However, particularly as the trade in *shatoosh* (fine Tibetan antelope hair) grew, poachers began to hunt in the summer as well, when female antelope gather in large flocks en route to and from their remote birthing grounds. As a result, by the mid-1980s the decrease in wildlife was one of the major environmental problems facing the Suojia community.

Around 4,000 people currently live in Suojia, divided among four village-level administrative units: Muqu, Yaqu, Jiongqu and Dangqu villages (see Figure 6.3). Each village is further divided into subunits comprising 30–50 households. In terms of the socio-economic development of Suojia, few people have had even basic education and over 95 per cent of women are illiterate. The average household income is relatively low and the quality of people's health, especially that of women and children, is extremely poor.[4]

Development of the Upper Yangtze Organization

One of the main features contributing to the success of environmental management initiatives in the Suojia community is active community participation. This is augmented by enhanced communication among

the herders themselves, between herders and the government, and between herders (or community representatives) and international non-
governmental organizations (NGOs). Improved community participation
and communication, particularly in recent years, has been enabled by
progressive leadership in township, county and prefecture government[5]
and also in the Upper Yangtze Organization (UYO). The UYO is a
grassroots NGO that was established in Zhiduo County in 1998. The
UYO has played a critical role in the environmental work conducted in
Suojia, both as a designated community representative and as an advocate for culturally appropriate and sustainable change. In particular, the
UYO has proven itself to be uniquely able to listen to the people and to
mobilize them, and also to liaise effectively with regional planners and
government decision makers. In the rest of this section I describe the history and main initiatives undertaken by the UYO. The descriptions and
analysis will lend understanding of what has enabled the Suojia community to be successful in carrying out its environmental management work.

Creating the vision

The beginning of environmental protection work in Suojia can largely be
traced to the vision and initiative of Sonam Dorje, a local community
leader in the 1980s and early 1990s – officially as township leader and
later as county vice-governor. Sonam dreamed of protecting Suojia's
wildlife because he recognized an intrinsic aesthetic and cultural value in
biodiversity, in addition to its economic value. Although he was clearly
concerned for his people, what set him apart from his colleagues was his
appreciation of nature.

In the mid-1980s, Sonam Dorje first ventured into the Kekexili desert,
initially to protect the area's mineral resources from illegal gold miners
who had descended upon the area, but also to determine whether these
resources could be exploited to meet the financial needs of the county
government. As the level of illegal poaching increased, Sonam's understanding of the environment became much broader and more holistic.
To him, the wildlife gradually became a resource that was also worth protecting, and he came to consider the native biodiversity of the Tibetan
plateau to be a resource that was even more valuable than gold itself.

According to China's first NGO, Friends of Nature, Sonam had made a
dozen trips in the Kekexili with the Wild Yak Brigade, a semi-official
anti-poaching patrol, and they captured illegal hunters on eight occasions. In November 1994, when they came upon 18 poachers with around
2,000 Tibetan antelope skins in their possession, a gun battle ensued and
Sonam was killed. He was 40 years old.

The mission to protect wildlife was then taken up by his brother-in-law,

Zhaba Dorje. In Zhaba's four years with the Wild Yak Brigade, 250 sus-
pected poachers were arrested, and 60 guns, 10,000 rounds of ammunition, 57 vehicles and 3,717 skins and pelts of various endangered animals
were confiscated. To achieve this, the Wild Yak Brigade had only the
simplest equipment – fewer than 10 rifles, all borrowed, and 3 old jeeps.
The patrol ate and slept outdoors, climbed over glaciers and waited out
poachers on even the bitterest of days (Friends of Nature 1999; Xu 2001).
    After the unexpected death of Zhaba Dorje in November 1998, Sonam
Dorje's work was taken over and expanded by his former close friend
and colleague Drashi Dorje. Like his predecessors, Drashi Dorje had a
vision equally for the place, for a better future with abundant wildlife
and for improved living conditions for the people. To enact this vision,
Drashi Dorje brought together several friends, and they established a
new grassroots social organization, the Upper Yangtze Organization.[6]

Building civil society

Registered in May 1998, the UYO was declared "the first people's organization in the history of Zhiduo County" with a "complete working
structure, well-defined goals and objectives, and a representative membership" (Zhiduo County Civil Affairs Bureau 1998). The organization
aims to develop the area in environmentally friendly ways and to protect
the environment of the Yangtze River headwaters. The UYO was initially made up of six board members and around 100 regular members,
over 80 per cent of whom were local pastoralists. Five years later, the
composition was similar, with representatives of around 10–15 per cent
of Suojia families as well as a growing number of academics and journalists from the provincial capital and from throughout the nation. In 2003,
the number of active core members was eight people, although they all
also had other full-time salaried jobs and therefore had to carry out
UYO activities in their spare time.
    Early in its work, the UYO also sought external assistance.[7] Since
1998, many projects and activities have been planned and implemented,
with most funding and expertise coming from or introduced by the Canadian NGO Plateau Perspectives.[8]
    The work of the UYO has evolved into an innovative example of a lo-
cal conservation effort. Despite several requests that it expand its work to
neighbouring counties, it has restricted the geographical scope of its work
to Zhiduo County in order to focus on establishing a good, replicable
model for conservation and development in Tibetan plateau grasslands.
The organization has recently further refined its work by designating
three working groups for young people's education, culture and environment, and sustainable development.

Although formal establishment as an NGO was an obvious high point for Drashi Dorje and his team, some of the UYO's most significant challenges still lay ahead. An initial challenge was achieving legitimacy in the eyes of the government. Even today, few leaders in China truly understand the concept of "non-government" work and often assume it to be, at best, distinct from government work, or, at worst, in opposition to it. For decades, every development in China has been planned, organized and implemented by the government alone. In the UYO's early days, an unexpected roller-coaster ride ensued, with some people encouraging the fledgling grassroots organization, others watching attentively from the sidelines, and still others questioning its necessity, even its legitimacy. Since the national authorities recognized the country's first NGO, Friends of Nature, in 1994, civil society has come a long way. In less than a decade, over 200,000 organizations had sprouted in almost every corner of China, some working quasi-independently, others in close partnership with governmental agencies (Knup 1997; Viederman 1998). Equally as important, the UYO now also has a proven track record of good projects and thus is accepted as profitable to the area's development.

What makes the UYO particularly special is not only the fact that it is a non-governmental organization, which is a relatively new phenomenon in China, but also that it was founded by local Tibetan herders. Furthermore, one of the UYO's main strengths is that it capitalizes on maintaining and building relationships within the local community as well as with external agencies and advisers. The UYO thus bridges many divisions, enhancing the flow of ideas between a diverse array of people, organizations and bureaus, both national and international, who have a stake in the future of the Yangtze River headwaters. Five years after its inception, it was this exchange of ideas, translated into tangible action, that had enabled the people of Suojia to remain on the land, indeed even to be co-stewards of the land and its biodiversity.

Enhancing capacity for environmental management

The UYO has spearheaded several environmental activities. The first was the formulation of a multiple-use land management plan in collaboration with the Suojia government (i.e. the township, or sub-county, government). The plan was designed to allow for four different local protected areas. The "core zones" were determined on the basis of the abundance and distribution of four focal species: the snow leopard, the Tibetan antelope, the Tibetan wild ass and the black-necked crane. A protected area for wild yak and a large wetland were added at a later stage (see Figure 6.3), and the snow leopard core zone was extended to include its entire relatively contiguous rugged mountain habitat in Suojia. What is particularly unusual in this early work is that many herders were consulted in the process, and all agreed not to hunt – and agreed to discourage others from hunting – within the designated zones.

Although village-level governance in China already has democratic elements (for example, the election of village leaders), the new participatory approach introduced in the initial formulation of a regional land-use plan for Suojia is unique because it scales up the participation of local people to a regional level, across several villages, and engages with them to consider the actual content of projects and plans, not simply the selection of which person will implement policy designed from afar (Kelliher 1997). The UYO and its first international partner, Plateau Perspectives, jointly introduced the notion of public participation as an important ingredient in the process of community development, and the Suojia township government sanctioned the plan by adopting it as its own. Although no comprehensive map of the protected areas has been drawn, local people know the boundaries well and marker stones have been erected. According to local herders, snow leopard and wild ass populations are increasing as a result of this action (based on direct sightings and increased predation of livestock), and there is a sense of pride among local residents that their native wildlife and grassland habitat remain among the most pristine in the Tibetan plateau region.

A second strategic move of the UYO and the Suojia community was to organize, in concert with the township government, a group of local herders to serve as wildlife monitors. This group is now known as Suojia's Ecological Protection Committee (EPC). In practice, it was decided by the UYO and local government that village leaders would serve as the monitors since they generally have better education, they travel more than most people and, as democratically elected leaders, they generally are held in high esteem within the community. Through the establishment of the EPC, an informal environmental extension service has been put in place and valuable data are now being collected on the seasonal abundance and distribution of key wildlife species. This model has been replicated in the neighbouring Qumahe community, which is located north of the Yangtze River, because it resonates well with the government and the Tibetan herders themselves. This approach to conservation (i.e. involving herders in resource management, including the monitoring of wildlife populations) has also been introduced to government leaders as an effective way to carry out and even enhance regional conservation plans, as well as to reconcile, at least in part, local conservation and development objectives through community participation.[9]

A third main area of the UYO's work supported by the community has been the promotion of basic education, with a strong emphasis on environmental education. After long discussion about how best to serve the people of Suojia, the local government, the UYO and Plateau Perspectives agreed that education could play a central role in the community's future. Yet, when the issue was first raised with local herders, the idea of sending their children to school, even to local tent schools, received mixed reactions at best. For example, in Yaqu village of Suojia (see Figure 6.3), most household leaders initially showed little interest in sending their children to school. After the UYO's presentation of the importance of basic education, however, and with further discussions among the community in their own meetings over the next year, community members decided that formal education was critical for their children's future and they took the project forward. The project had become *their* project. Within a matter of months, the local people developed a management plan to start a new school, which was launched in September 1999 with 20 students studying Tibetan, Chinese and mathematics. Now the school has about 70 students, and children from about one-quarter of the community's households attend. Following two training workshops in 2001 and 2002, ecology classes were begun at the school. Similar tent schools have also begun to appear in other parts of Suojia and elsewhere in Zhiduo County. In Muqu village (see Figure 6.3), over 60 children, representing about 30 per cent of families in the community, now receive basic education. In addition to this, the school in Muqu has become a de facto "community centre", and ongoing vocational training in areas such as primary health care, veterinary care and rangeland management is being planned. In this way, a seed idea taken up by the community can bring about genuine hope and change.

Through the above and other activities, community and individual awareness about environmental issues has been raised, and the capacity for wildlife conservation in Suojia has been considerably enhanced. A sense of hope has emerged as people have seen that they are capable of affecting their own future.

The role of external influence

The Western Development Strategy and an uncertain future

As stated earlier, the most important development now affecting the area may be the onset of China's Western Development Strategy (WDS). In Qinghai Province, the WDS has led to several massive environmental projects, including the establishment of the Sanjiangyuan Nature Reserve (SNR) and projects to restore vast areas of degraded land. Although the WDS has attracted some favourable attention to the conservation work already begun in Suojia (BWG/CCICED 2001), it also has within it the potential to destroy much if not all of the community's work undertaken to date. In China as elsewhere in the world, analyses and planning activities conducted at higher levels will not always reflect the needs or plans of local communities.

In the present case, the main divergence of opinion has arisen in the form of suggestions that the people of Suojia should relocate (or be relocated) to other parts of the province, in the name of "environmental protection". This would not only undermine community structure and potentially lead to many significant social and cultural costs – as witnessed, for example, in past relocations of native groups to reservations in North America and Australia and in the sedentarization of pastoralists in North Africa and the former Central Asian republics. Such moves would also incur severe environmental costs. In Suojia, despite current hardships, almost everyone indicates that they would not wish to move, but want to remain on the grassland where they have lived their entire lives.

Ironically, the suggestion of relocation may have arisen in part because of the initial success of the conservation work in Suojia. Early plans for the SNR had in fact designated a neighbouring township to serve as one of the national reserve's main core zones. During a field investigation in 2001, however, it was discovered by national researchers that several community-based protected areas had already been established in Suojia, over three years previously, and that much more wildlife was present there than in the proposed area. According to local herders, wildlife populations were in fact increasing in Suojia as a result of the UYO's efforts to educate the people about biodiversity and of the community's self-imposed ban on hunting. Thus, because of the success of the wildlife conservation by the Suojia community, the draft plan for the national nature reserve was amended to designate Suojia as one of the largest potential core zones. The question then arose of whether the people of Suojia would be moved out of the core zone, since by definition core zones should have no human disturbance. Fortunately, after months of consultations and discussion within the community, it now seems unlikely that the people of Suojia will be asked to move because of the SNR, although no final decision has been officially made.

The relocation of people to other regions is not ideal for two main reasons. First, the simple presence of people in the area will continue to serve as the best deterrent to poachers, who until recently constituted the primary threat to wildlife in the nearby Kekexili desert and arid steppe. Secondly, the situation in Suojia remains unique, with the existence of a strong desire by local residents – and not just higher-level government plans – to develop the area in ways that maintain and protect the native biodiversity. Therefore, there are possibilities for the local community to develop plans that reflect their own needs and capacities and to collaborate with the higher government authorities in implementing their ideas, such as the training of local herders who will serve as wildlife monitors. Whether the local community will be able to build a genuine long-term partnership with the government and other stakeholders, as well as participate actively in decision-making processes for the management of the nature reserve, remains to be seen.

Partnerships with external agencies

The UYO has been able to access expert assistance and funds from a variety of foundations and NGOs in China and abroad (including financial assistance from the Global Greengrants Fund, Children in Crisis and NORAD, and technical expertise from the Biodiversity Working Group, Lähetyksen Kehitysapu and Fauna and Flora International) as well as from Chinese media and various levels of government. In addition, awards and acknowledgements by external institutions recognizing the initiatives in Suojia were instrumental in building people's confidence in the community. For instance, the government of Yushu Tibetan Autonomous Prefecture (see Figure 6.2) recognized and approved the UYO in August 2001 as a good "home-grown model" of civil society, an example of how local people should promote conservation and development in line with policies outlined by the national government. In addition, at the national level, Drashi Dorje, founder and director of the UYO, received an Earth Award in May 2002, presented by the State Forest Bureau and by Friends of the Earth (Hong Kong) for his outstanding conservation work.

However, there are also problems associated with partnerships with external organizations, whether government agencies or the international conservation community. These problems partly result from varied interpretations of the concept of "participation" (see Cooke and Kothari 2001; Ghai and Vivian 1992; Pretty 1995). In some cases, it is used to involve people in all stages of project planning, implementation and evaluation, and at other times it is used only for utilitarian purposes (i.e. to mobilize the masses for pre-set purposes). At worst, participation can be used to manipulate people and communities to endorse externally devised plans. Likewise, the concepts of sustainability, local ownership and partnership are interpreted and applied in many different ways (Westing 1996). Consequently, one danger for external organizations is that (knowingly or unknowingly) they appropriate for themselves ownership of work that in fact is the intellectual property of other people, often the local or indigenous people. In Suojia, this problem has already occurred on at least two occasions when external agencies acted as though the community had undertaken no previous work of its own and all the efforts made by the community were futile without the external assistance. There also have been problems with a lack of respect given to UYO members by external partners because of their lack of formal education. Although partnerships have continued for pragmatic reasons, lack of genuine participation and mutual respect has led on some occasions to a loss of confidence among the local people, resulting in a loss in project sustainability.

Innovative features of Suojia community

Several important features of the Suojia community, or of key individuals, played critical roles in the success of environmental initiatives undertaken in Suojia, such as the establishment of the community-based protected areas, wildlife monitoring and the establishment of tent schools (see Table 6.1).

The establishment of the UYO has been instrumental in much of the conservation work described in this chapter. Within the context of China, this in itself was extremely innovative because civil society has played little if any role in decision-making processes for several decades. Only in the early 1990s did work by the non-governmental sector finally gain recognition as a legitimate pursuit, and it has taken even longer for the notion to be fully adopted in China's remote inland regions. To undertake such a venture, strong **leadership** skills and a **pioneering spirit** were necessary, as found in the UYO director, Drashi Dorje. Because there are no quick fixes to the environmental problems addressed, a **long-term vision** was also required and, perhaps most importantly, an **ability to mobilize people**, first for the establishment of the organization itself, and secondly to carry out the UYO's plans. It is also noteworthy that Drashi Dorje set early goals for the organization to nurture new leaders, which was done through members' attendance at formal workshops (e.g. computer training, environmental education, policy meetings) as well as through personal mentoring relationships.

Similarly, a **pioneering spirit** and the ability to build a sense of **local ownership** in the work were necessary for regional land-use planning and the establishment of local protected areas in Suojia. Whereas most significant decisions in China are made at the provincial and national levels, in Suojia it was the local community who decided that protection of native wildlife was important and that local protected areas should be established. Given that most of the actual burden of this plan was to be incurred by the herders themselves (e.g. loss of grazing land), their support was essential for success. This was gained by opening **lines of**

Table 6.1 Innovative features of environmental initiatives undertaken in Suojia township

Main environmental initiatives in Suojia township	Main international partners				Innovative features
	PP[a]	BWG[b]	UM[c]	FFI[d]	
Establishment of the Upper Yangtze Organization (UYO)[e]	From 1998				Leadership, pioneering spirit, ownership, long-range vision, ability to network broadly
Regional land-use planning, including the establishment of community-based protected areas	From 1998	1999–2001			Pioneering spirit, ownership, communication
Biodiversity conservation research (including biological and socio-economic surveys)	From 1998		2001–2004	2001–2003	Strategic planning, desire to learn, communication
Capacity-building (gathering information and other resources, attending environmental conferences, etc.)	From 1998	1999–2001		2001–2003	Strategic planning, desire to learn, communication
Establishment of the Ecological Protection Committee (EPC); i.e. Suojia's wildlife monitors	From 1999	1999–2001			Encouragement, hope for future
Establishment of village-level schools, with an emphasis on environmental education	From 1999	1999–2001			Consensus-building, ownership, encouragement, hope for future
Regional survey of environment and health needs in pastoral areas of Yushu Tibetan Autonomous Prefecture	From 2000		2001–2004		Strategic planning, ownership

Notes:

[a] Plateau Perspectives (PP) has worked with the UYO since its inception in May 1998 (expertise and funding).

[b] The Biodiversity Working Group (BWG) of the China Council for International Cooperation on Environment and Development (CCICED) has partnered PP and UYO since 1998, bringing both funding and national-level patronage to the work.

[c] The University of Montreal (UM), sponsored by the Social Sciences and Humanities Research Council of Canada, has partnered PP, UYO and the Yushu Health Bureau to undertake a regional health needs assessment in Suojia and five other townships.

[d] Fauna and Flora International (FFI) has partnered the provincial Environmental Protection Bureau (EPB) and UYO, as well as PP in 2001, to help further develop a regional co-management plan for Suojia.

[e] A brief description of the UYO's work to date is also summarized in a special report by China Development Brief (Young 2001).

communication among herders, and between herders and government, so that the value of biodiversity protection was properly discussed and all opinions expressed and heard. As a result, a consensus was reached that key wildlife areas in Suojia should be set aside for the protection of special or endangered wildlife species. This has visibly led to improved protection for many native species of the Tibetan plateau. Unfortunately, although these community-based protected areas were subsequently incorporated into larger plans (by their inclusion in, or proximity to, the SNR's largest core zone), the unique work undertaken by the people of Suojia has not always been explicitly recognized.

Another innovative feature of Suojia and the UYO is a **desire to learn** from international experience in conservation and sustainable development, and through this process to equip themselves to make appropriate **strategic plans** for the future. This outward-looking attitude has been cultivated and encouraged largely by Drashi Dorje, himself mentored earlier by the visionary Sonam Dorje. Several other leaders have also worked to enhance the community's vision, for example by organizing a trip for 16 Tibetan herders to Beijing in 1996. Two of them later became founding members of the UYO. An environmental and health needs assessment now nearing completion is also proving valuable for making long-term development plans in Suojia, particularly by differentiating between opinion and fact through standard survey methodologies (see Foggin et al. 1997; Oths 1998), leading to scientifically informed decisions and focused interventions.

According to local participants, the establishment of Suojia's Ecological Protection Committee (EPC) has succeeded largely because of the early **encouragement** given by Plateau Perspectives, expressed in various forms of support including training and donations of equipment necessary for wildlife monitoring activities. The seed of hope that this has engendered for the EPC – in particular, through a realization that it was not alone in feeling its work was important – led the 16 wildlife monitors to persevere in their endeavour despite extremely difficult working conditions. These monitors have since received further training in wildlife survey techniques on several occasions, and they may yet become full and active participants in the management of the SNR. Thus, **hope** can also be a potent driving force for change, directly and indirectly, especially where local people have previously felt helpless, unheard or otherwise unable to help guide their own future (Bernard and Young 1997).

A final area of work that deserves mention again is the establishment of local village tent schools. The most important factor leading to the success or failure of such projects was the time invested in **consensus-building** within the community prior to the official start of the project. In this case, the process was facilitated primarily by the UYO. Without such consensus-building and a sense of **local ownership**, the projects would quickly dissolve, just as many externally devised plans in fact do. For each school project, as well as for other community development projects in Suojia, over a year was spent discussing and exchanging ideas with the community. As a result of this participatory approach, the people of Suojia now consider that the tent schools and the environmental education taking place in the schools belong to the community.

In summary, most environmental work undertaken in Suojia has been dependent on effective communication, on a free flow of information between parties and on a sense that all partner agencies are working toward the same goal, that is, biodiversity conservation and sustainable management of grassland resources. The UYO has played a particularly important role in this endeavour, serving both as community representative and as an agent of change. As previously stated, the organization is uniquely positioned to listen to and mobilize the local people, and to liaise with national decision makers and the international community. By seeking to establish genuine partnerships based on mutual respect and learning, the UYO has helped local communities to gain a greater sense of ownership of projects, which is a precursor of sustainability.

Conclusion

In what circumstances has Suojia initiated its work? What features of the community have contributed most to the initial successes observed? The short answer is that, even though civil society is still young in China, the establishment of a grassroots organization, the UYO, has been the primary enabling factor for successful conservation in Suojia. Furthermore, the capacity of the UYO to plan and implement appropriate projects has rested largely on the ability of several key individuals in the organization[10] to draw together disparate stakeholders – including Tibetan herders, government bureaus, national and international organizations, and expert advisers – into working partnerships. Although not all of the resulting partnerships are perfect, they are important steps in the right direction. The main challenge now is to ensure that external agents seeking to join such community-based conservation work, first, do not undermine the local initiatives by usurping the community's rightful ownership of the work, and, second, support the organization and community as equal partners instead of taking the role of leaders. In this way, the people of Suojia stand a fair chance of developing their own culturally and ecologically appropriate conservation strategies, for their own direct benefit as well as that of the nation, now and in the future.

Lessons to be learned for other communities and organizations are simply to continue learning, to encourage pioneering spirits, and to focus on opening lines of communication, consensus-building and other participatory approaches. In these ways it is possible to maintain and promote local ownership of every initiative, which, together with genuine partnerships among stakeholders, will go a long way to creating the right conditions for successful, innovative, community-based environmental management and conservation efforts.

Postscript, May 2003

Since the first draft of this chapter was written in December 2002, several important changes have taken place that affect the people of Suojia. It seems that they will no longer be relocated in connection with the establishment of the SNR per se, although other large environmental and poverty alleviation schemes of the WDS may affect the herders in similar ways. According to several recent press releases, large areas of grassland in Qinghai Province have been closed for the indefinite future and grazing restrictions placed on even larger areas to allow the renewal of degraded land. In a parallel plan, nearly 28,000 local residents in the province will also be relocated over the next few years (Xinhua News Agency 2003b). The latter scheme has been called "ecological emigration" by some authorities and aims "to shake off poverty" at the same time as it "restores ecological balance" in the "Go West" campaign (*China Daily* 2003). Permanent residential areas for former herdsmen are also planned, with the explicit aim "to encourage them [local herders] to abandon grazing" (Xinhua News Agency 2003c).

If the Suojia community is asked to move off the land, much of its environmental work to date may become irrelevant (apart from the experience gained and lessons learned). Many local herders have already heard rumours of relocation plans, and they have started to ask their cultural and religious leaders if and when they should begin to sell their livestock. Perhaps the above grassland restoration projects will not come to fruition in Suojia itself but, should they do so, local Tibetan herders may once again, most dishearteningly, become but recipients of life-changing decisions made far away. It is still unclear what final decisions will be made for Suojia, but it is sincerely to be hoped that even now the local community will yet be brought back into the decision-making process, for indeed it is the herders who remain the primary stakeholders, the first people to gain or lose from the changing environmental conditions in Tibetan plateau grasslands.

These factors obviously constrain to some degree the community's ability to be innovative, particularly in managing its grassland resources.

However, as before, the community continues to move forward with a variety of responses. On the one hand, discouraged by increased uncertainty in their lives, some people have retreated into more traditional, passive, even fatalistic attitudes. Other people, though, including the majority of UYO members, are still making plans for the future and even enlisting the support of external agencies for new projects in health, education and environmental protection. And herein lies the greatest innovation for the community and the UYO: by building partnerships that enhance their legitimacy and strengthen their capacity to meet their own long-term goals, and by focusing on the more positive elements of current government plans, each has learnt to move with the ebb and flow of government policies. In this way, within their own unique socio-political context, the people of Suojia have come a long way over the past few years, and they indeed comprise a truly innovative community.

Acknowledgements

I wish to thank the UNU–UNEP Innovative Communities project team as well as Dr Marion Torrance-Foggin and Dr Andrew Smith for their helpful comments on earlier drafts of the manuscript. I would also like to thank the Centre for Research into Environmental and Ecological Modelling (CREEM) at the University of St Andrews for office space and especially for being inspiring colleagues during my sabbatical leave in Scotland in 2002–2003.

Except when noted otherwise, information in this chapter is based on my interviews and informal discussions with Drashi Dorje since 1997, and with other UYO members.

Notes

1. Begun as part of my doctoral research, this work is now an integral part of the community-based, integrated conservation and development work undertaken by Plateau Perspectives, a Canadian NGO focused on social and environmental issues in the Tibetan plateau region of China (see ⟨http://www.plateauperspectives.org⟩). A more detailed description of this case study is also available in Chapter 8 of my doctoral dissertation (Foggin 2000).
2. Known in Chinese as the Sanjiangyuan (Three River Sources) region.
3. An interview conducted during a field trip in July 1998 (Foggin 1998).
4. Based on my interviews with local leaders (since 1998) and on preliminary findings of the project "Health Status & Risk Factors among Tibetan Pastoralists of Southwest Qinghai Province" undertaken cooperatively by Plateau Perspectives, the Yushu Tibetan Autonomous Prefecture Health Bureau, the Upper Yangtze Organization and the

Department of Geography at the University of Montreal. The data are from 50 house-hold interviews conducted in Suojia in February 2002 (Foggin et al. 2003).

5. In administrative terms, Suojia is the western township (*xiang*) of Zhiduo County, itself the western county (*xian*) of Yushu Tibetan Autonomous Prefecture (*zangzu zizhi zhou*). Qinghai Province is composed of seven prefectures. The "villages" and "sub-villages" of Suojia are the former brigades (*dadui*) and work units (*xiaodui*) of the commune era.

6. In Chinese, its name is *Qingzang Gaoyuan Huan Changjiangyuan Shengtai Jingji Cujin-hui* (literally, the Tibetan Plateau Yangtze River Headwaters Ecology Economy Promotion Committee).

7. Drashi Dorje first contacted me in December 1997, since when several years of research and reciprocal learning have ensued, as well as much of the environmental work described in this chapter. Initial contact was made fortuitously after a Chinese environmentalist suggested that Drashi Dorje meet "the Canadian biologist" (i.e. me) who was then conducting graduate research in the province.

8. I am also founder and director of Plateau Perspectives. Some of the UYO's projects and activities have been undertaken without direct financial cost, whereas others have required US\$100–5,000. Most funding needs from 1998 to 2002 were met from international sources, but in-country assistance is now increasing. More important than funds, though, have been the various forms of expertise and capacity-building and the encouragement given to the UYO at this critical stage in its development.

9. Several key recommendations for biodiversity conservation, based on initial field experiences in Suojia, were recommended to provincial and national government leaders at the Workshop on Biodiversity Conservation in Qinghai Province organized by the Biodiversity Working Group (BWG) of the China Council for International Cooperation on Environment and Development (CCICED) in Xining in June 2001. Further details are available at ⟨http://www.chinabiodiversity.com⟩.

10. Although the UYO's work was initially promoted largely by one person, since then the overall vision has become shared by a larger group of about seven or eight key people and is supported by many families in Suojia. This "decentralization" in UYO leadership was further enhanced in 2002 when Drashi Dorje reduced his direct involvement (as executive director) in the UYO's work in order to support the development of another prefecture-wide NGO, the Snowland Great Rivers Environmental Protection Organization (⟨http://www.snowland-great-rivers.org⟩). This move has led several UYO members greatly to increase their involvement and leadership in their organization, thus further strengthening its foundation.

REFERENCES

Barfield, T. (1993) *The nomadic alternative.* Englewood Cliffs, NJ: Prentice Hall.

Bennett, J. (1988) "The political ecology and economic development of migratory pastoralist societies in Eastern Africa", in D. Attwood, T. Bruneau and J. Galaty (eds), *Power and poverty: Development projects in the third world*, pp. 31–60. Westview Special Studies in Social, Political and Economic Development, Boulder, CO: Westview Press.

Berkes, F. and C. Folke, eds (1998) *Linking social and ecological systems: Management practices and social mechanisms for building resilience.* Cambridge: Cambridge University Press.

Bernard, T. and J. Young (1997) *The ecology of hope: Communities collaborate for sustainability*. Gabriola Island, B.C.: New Society.

Blench, R. (2001) *Pastoralism in the new millennium*. London: Overseas Development Institute.

Brown, K. (2002) "Innovations for conservation and development", *Geographical Journal* 168(1): 6–17.

BWG/CCICED [Biodiversity Working Group/China Council for International Cooperation on Environment and Development] (2001) *Conserving China's biodiversity (II)*. Beijing: China Environmental Science Press.

China Daily (2003) " 'Go West' concerns: Poverty, ecology", 10 March.

China Green Times (2003) 20 February; translated and reported in US Embassy, *Beijing Environment Science and Technology Update*, 7 March 2003, "New Nature Reserve in Key River Source Area".

Cooke, B. and U. Kothari, eds (2001) *Participation, the new tyranny?* London: Zed Books.

Economy, E. (2002) "China's Go West campaign: Ecological construction or ecological exploitation?", *China Environment Series* 5: 1–11.

Edmonds, R. (1994) *Patterns of China's lost harmony: A survey of the country's environmental degradation and protection*. New York: Routledge.

Ekvall, R. (1968) *Fields on the hoof: Nexus of Tibetan nomadic pastoralism*. New York: Holt, Rinehart & Winston.

Ellis, J. and D. Swift (1988) "Stability of African pastoral ecosystems: Alternate paradigms and implications for development", *Journal of Rangeland Management* 41: 450–459.

Foggin, J. M. (1998) *Recent accounts from the source area of the Yangtze River*. Xining, China: Plateau Perspectives.

——— (2000) "Biodiversity protection and the search for sustainability in Tibetan plateau grasslands (Qinghai, China)", PhD dissertation, Arizona State University, Tempe, USA.

Foggin, P., O. Farkas, S. Shiirev-Adiya and B. Chinbat (1997) "Health status and risk factors of seminomadic pastoralists in Mongolia", *Social Science and Medicine* 44: 1623–1647.

Foggin, P. M., M. E. Torrance-Foggin, J. Torrance and J. M. Foggin (2003) *Community health report: Zhiduo County 2002*. Xining, China: Plateau Perspectives, April.

Friends of Nature (1999) "On the frontlines of the battle to save the Tibetan antelope", *Friends of Nature Newsletter* 2: 3–4.

Galaty, J. and D. Johnson, eds (1990) *The world of pastoralism: Herding systems in comparative perspective*. New York: Guilford Press.

Ghai, D. and J. Vivian, eds (1992) *Grassroots environmental action: People's participation in sustainable development*. London: Routledge.

Goldstein, M. and C. Beall (1990) *Nomads of western Tibet: The survival of a way of life*. Hong Kong: Odyssey.

He, B. (1991) "China on the edge: The crisis of ecology and development", San Francisco: China Books and Periodicals.

Humphrey, C. and D. Sneath, eds (1996) *Culture and environment in inner Asia*.

Volume 1: The pastoral economy and the environment. Cambridge: White Horse Press.

Kelliher, D. (1997) "The Chinese debate over village self-government", *The China Journal* 37: 63–86.

Knup, E. (1997) "Environmental NGOs in China: An overview", Woodrow Wilson International Center for Scholars, Environmental Change and Security Project, *China Environment Series*, Issue 1, pp. 9–15.

Lai, C. and A. Smith (2003) "Keystone status of plateau pikas (*Ochotona curzoniae*): Effect of control on biodiversity of native birds", *Biodiversity and Conservation* 12: 1901–1912.

Loomis, D. (1988) "Desert rangeland livestock management in Soviet Central Asia", *Journal of Arid Environments* 17: 1–12.

Miller, D. (1995) *Herds on the move: Winds of change among pastoralists in the Himalayas and on the Tibetan plateau.* ICIMOD Series No. MNR 95/2, Kathmandu: International Centre for Integrated Mountain Development.

―――― (2000) "Tough times for Tibetan nomads in Western China: Snowstorms, settling down, fences, and the demise of traditional nomadic pastoralism", *Nomadic Peoples* 4(1): 83–109.

MOFA [Ministry of Foreign Affairs] (2000) *China's population and development in the 21st century.* Beijing: MOFA.

Oths, K. (1998) "Assessing variation in health status in the Andes: A biocultural model", *Social Science and Medicine* 47: 1017–1030.

Pretty, J. (1995) "The many interpretations of participation", *In Focus* 16: 4–5.

Richard, C. (2000) "Rangeland policies in the eastern Tibetan plateau", *Issues in Mountain Development* 4: 1–4.

Salafsky, N. and E. Wollenberg (2000) "Linking livelihoods and conservation: A conceptual framework and scale for assessing the integration of human needs and biodiversity", *World Development* 28: 1421–1438.

Schaller, G. (1998) *Wildlife of the Tibetan steppe.* Chicago: University of Chicago Press.

SEPA [State Environment Protection Agency] (2001) *China's second national report on implementation of the Convention on Biological Diversity.* Beijing: SEPA.

Smil, V. (1993) *China's environmental crisis: An inquiry into the limits of national development.* Armonk, NY: M. E. Sharpe.

Smith, A. and M. Foggin (1999) "The plateau pika (*Ochotona curzoniae*) is a keystone species for biodiversity on the Tibetan plateau", *Animal Conservation* 2: 235–240.

Stevens, S. (1997) "New alliances for conservation", in S. Stevens (ed.), *Conservation through cultural survival: Indigenous peoples and protected areas*, pp. 33–62. Washington, DC: Island Press.

Swift, J., C. Toulmin and S. Chatting (1990) "Providing services for nomadic people: A review of the literature and annotated bibliography". Staff Working Papers No. 8, New York: UNICEF.

Taylor-Ide, D. and C. Taylor (2002) *Just and lasting change: When communities own their futures.* Baltimore, MD: Johns Hopkins University Press, in association with Future Generations.

Viederman, D. (1998) "Save the planet, build civil society: Democracy gains from Chinese environmental effort", *Global Beat Issue Brief*, No. 37, 22 June.

Westing, A. (1996) "Core values for sustainable development", *Environmental Conservation* 23: 218–225.

Williams, D. (1996) "Grassland enclosures: Catalyst of land degradation in Inner Mongolia", *Human Organization* 55: 307–313.

Wu, N. (1997) "Indigenous knowledge and sustainable approaches for the maintenance of biodiversity in nomadic society: Experiences from the eastern Tibetan plateau", *Die Erde* 128: 67–80.

Xie, Z. (2000) *The atlas of population, environment and sustainable development of China*. Beijing: Science Press.

Xinhua News Agency (2003a) "China plans big nature reserve at sources of three major rivers", 19 February.

——— (2003b) "Degenerate grassland in west China to enjoy recess from grazing", 16 April.

——— (2003c) "Saving the Yellow River", 22 April.

Xu, Z. (2001) "Chiru's guardian angels shedding blood, tears", *China Internet Information Centre*, 18 January.

Young, N., ed. (2001) *250 Chinese NGOs: Civil society in the making*. Beijing: China Development Brief.

Zhang, W., ed. (1998) *China's biodiversity: A country study*. Beijing: China Environmental Science Press.

Zhao, S. (1994) *Geography of China: Environment, resources, population and development*. Wiley Series in Advanced Regional Geography, New York: John Wiley.

Zhiduo County Civil Affairs Bureau (1998) *Document of the Zhiduo County Civil Affairs Bureau (1998: 05)*. Zhiduo County Government, 26 May.

7

Sustainable tourism planning and management in Klong Khwang, Thailand

Walter Jamieson and Pawinee Sunalai

Introduction

A significant interest in local-level planning initiatives in Thailand has been created by the emphasis on public participation brought about by changes to the 1997 Constitution. Moving from a top–down model of planning and decision-making has required officials, and the communities themselves, to develop capacities that enable local communities to become an effective part of the planning and development process.

One sector in which the importance of public involvement has been increasingly recognized in Thailand is tourism. With the potential for quick economic gain, it is possible that ecological, social and cultural goals may be sacrificed by short-sighted and damaging tourism development schemes that ultimately harm both communities and tourists alike. Public involvement is essential to preventing these types of projects and ensuring sustainable tourism development. How this should occur is not yet clear, however, and the search for practical approaches that allow for community-driven tourism development continues.

As part of this process of testing new approaches to sustainable tourism, a range of community-based tourism planning and management methods has been established in the community of Klong Khwang in Thailand. This community serves as the focus of this chapter, in which we aim to describe and analyse how the principles of local determination and participation were positively introduced and implemented within the community's sustainable tourism project.

The nature of tourism

Although tourism is most often perceived as being economic in nature, it also has a number of non-economic objectives and benefits. These range from social (e.g. educational and recreational activities) to environmental (e.g. conservation of natural resources) and cultural (e.g. sharing of cultural traditions and events). Tourism is a socio-economic phenomenon made up of the activities and experiences of tourists and visitors who are away from their home environment and being serviced by the travel and tourism industry in host destinations. The sum total of this activity – experience plus services – is the tourism product.

Understanding the interrelationships among the different parts of the tourism system enables tourism stakeholders to improve the effectiveness of planning and management, thus assuring the likelihood of success that benefits the poor. Essentially, this system can be described in terms of supply and demand. Tourism planning should strive for a balance between demand (market) and supply (development). This requires an understanding, not only of market characteristics and trends, but also of the planning processes that aim to meet market needs. In addition, it is crucial that all the different aspects of demand and supply are carefully monitored and managed. That is, ecological, political, social, cultural and other factors in the external and internal environments of the visitor must be carefully observed and considered.

The dynamic nature of the tourism system makes it vital regularly to scan the external and internal environments of the destination and to be prepared to make any necessary changes to ensure a healthy and viable tourism industry. The tourism system is not only dynamic but also complex because of the many factors and sectors that are linked to the provision of the tourist experience and the generation of tourism revenues and markets.

Sustainable tourism and community planning

Since the 1987 release of the Brundtland Commission Report, *Our common future* (WCED 1987), more and more communities and planners have started to consider the principles of sustainable development as they prepare plans and policies for future development. Although there is still a great deal of rhetoric associated with sustainable development, some of the principles are now having an impact on how communities approach their planning and development processes.

The tourism community over the past decade has also adopted sustainable tourism practices. Sustainable tourism and sustainable community planning share the same objectives and principles. These include:

- **Participation**. Residents of a community must maintain control of tourism development by being involved in setting a community tourism vision, identifying the resources to be maintained and enhanced, and developing goals and strategies for tourism development and management. Residents must participate in the implementation of strategies as well as the operation of the tourism infrastructure, services and facilities.
- **Stakeholder involvement**. Tourism initiatives should be developed with the help of broad-based community input.
- **Local ownership**. Tourism development must provide quality employment for community residents. The provision of fulfilling jobs must be seen as an integral part of any tourism development at the local level.
- **Sustainability of the resource base**. Sustainable tourism development has to provide for intergenerational equity, with equitable distribution of the costs and benefits of tourism development occurring among both present and future generations.
- **Community goals**. Harmony is required between the needs of the visitor, the place and the community. This is facilitated by broad community support and a proper balance between economic, social, cultural and human objectives.
- **Cooperation**. Cooperation between local attractions, businesses and tourism operators is essential given that one business or operation can be directly affected by the performance or quality of another.
- **Carrying capacity**. There is a definite need for impact assessment of tourism development proposals in order to distinguish between plans that encourage mass tourism and those that encourage quality tourism. The capacity of sites must be considered, including physical, natural, social and cultural limits.
- **Monitoring and evaluating**. Guidelines have to be established for tourism operations, including requirements for impact assessment. Codes of practice should be established for tourism at all levels – national, regional and local.
- **Accountability**. Tourism planning must move away from a traditional growth-oriented model to one that focuses on opportunities for employment, income and improved local well-being while ensuring that development decisions reflect the full value of the natural and cultural environments.
- **Training**. Sustainable tourism development requires the establishment of education and training programmes to improve public understanding and enhance business, vocational and professional skills, especially for the poor and for women.
- **Promotion**. Sustainable tourism development involves promoting appropriate uses and activities that reduce poverty and draw from and re-

inforce landscape character, sense of place, community identity and site opportunities.

We are now at a stage in community planning and tourism development where the key challenge is to ensure that the above principles are actually implemented. The case study we discuss in this chapter has attempted to incorporate as many sustainable development principles as possible, which is why it was selected as a good example of sustainable development. The strong merits of this case were also recognized by the Asia-Pacific Economic Cooperation (APEC) Tourism Working Group when it examined various community planning initiatives in Asia (Hatton 1999).

Study background

In 1998, we became involved with the Klong Khwang community as members of the Canadian Universities Consortium Urban Environmental Management (CUC UEM) Project, based at the Asian Institute of Technology (AIT) in Bangkok and funded by the Canadian International Development Agency (CIDA). Prior to choosing this project in cooperation with the Tourism Authority of Thailand, the project team assessed a number of communities where sustainable tourism planning and participation processes could be implemented. The criteria for selecting a community included:

• tourism potential,
• community receptivity to tourism development,
• political support,
• accessibility.

Klong Khwang was chosen because it had the potential, motivation and capacity to be part of a demonstration project that would experiment with a variety of community development approaches within a tourism development setting.

At the beginning, the project team's role was to provide technical advice and support, whereas the community would be responsible for actually managing the process and eventually developing the tourism plan. Unlike other aid initiatives, the project provided little financial support to the community, which raised its own funds to implement plans. This was a unique situation for government officials, because foreign governments typically provide capital and operating financial resources.

The project team included Thai professionals and expatriates with backgrounds in tourism planning and management, architecture and urban environmental management. Day-to-day discussions were the responsibility of members of the Thai team and the community. The expatriates provided technical advice and direction and developed a strong relationship with the village headman and other community members. A capacity-building exercise was also part of the project. This was designed to ensure that tourism and other local officials were updated regularly on the project's approaches and lessons learned through publications, briefing notes, manuals and videos (Jamieson 2001a, 2001b).

Tourism in Klong Khwang

Klong Khwang is in the Province of Nakhon Ratchasima (Korat) in the north-east region of Thailand. It is 30 minutes, by automobile, west of the provincial capital city of Korat. The village belongs to the Sema Tambon (sub-district), which comprises 13 villages and the Amphoe District of Sung Noen with a population of 75,000. The village has about 100 households and is led by a headman who is elected by the community.

Klong Khwang's economy is based on agriculture, and rice is its main crop. In order to generate additional income, it was the community itself that identified tourism as a potential source of economic development. Before the project first began in 1999, tourism activities in the community were very limited. The village normally hosted small groups of local tourists who came to pay their respects to the Reclining Buddha and the Stone Wheel of Thamma, and also to visit an archaeological site near the community (see Figure 7.1). Visitors typically spent only an hour visiting Klong Khwang. They contributed about 10,000 baht (US$250) to the temple each month, which was used primarily to help maintain the community's temple (*wat*).[1]

The Klong Khwang community, led by an enthusiastic and capable headman, was convinced that tourism in the area had the potential to increase income and job opportunities and generally to improve the villagers' quality of life. At this early stage, community members did not have a defined concept of tourism development. What they wanted to do was put together a plan that would increase visitors' experiences and generate extra income, while not damaging the environment or the community's social and cultural characteristics.

Approaches and activities for community participation

When the project began, the community knew little about tourism. As a result, a number of awareness and involvement techniques were used to ensure that the community played an integral role in the ongoing development process and that future actions met residents' expectations. The approaches that were employed ranged from public consultation tech-

Figure 7.1 Tourism attractions in Klong Khwang.
Source: Walter Jamieson and Pawinee Sunalai.

163

niques and focus groups to an integrated simulated tourism experience. The techniques were adapted to the community's particular characteristics and capacity levels.

Public consultation

Throughout the planning process, CUC UEM held regular tourism planning meetings with the village headman and the community committee, which helps the headman with a variety of village activities (see boxed text). The intent initially was to determine why the community wanted to develop tourism, the type of tourism products that could be offered to visitors, the expected benefits of tourism, and the level of tourism the community could absorb. At first villagers thought that a tourism plan would be developed for them (a common practice), but over time this

---

The key actors in community-based tourism development of Klong Khwang

Support for the planning process came from a number of key actors, including the village headman, the community committee, the Sub-district Administration Organization, the community cooperative, provincial government offices and the Tourism Authority of Thailand. Not all of these stakeholders worked together at the same time.

Village headman and community committee

The headman, responsible for villagers' quality of life, is elected every four years. His main role in relation to the community-based initiative was to provide tourism information to villagers, solicit their views and encourage them to participate in the planning process. The community committee helps the headman with a variety of village activities.

Sub-district Administration Organization

This local government body was responsible for providing basic facilities and infrastructure in the area, including local roads, electricity, telephones, water supply and solid waste management.

Community cooperative

The cooperative was locally formed to work on the development of local products, e.g. agricultural products and souvenirs. Most of the members are women and elderly people.

Figure 7.2 Public consultations.
Source: Walter Jamieson and Pawinee Sunalai.

perception changed and the villagers realized the importance of their involvement in the overall decision-making process.

The community was encouraged to define its own tourism vision. As part of that process, a map of local resources and infrastructure facilities was produced that identified tourism resources and involved the community in the planning process. Visualization techniques were used to provide residents with a look at how proposed changes would affect their village. This also helped the community "see" the future through a user-friendly medium. This open visual process proved to be the most effective communication method and it has been used in a number of community planning exercises in North America (Jamieson et al. 1997).

A series of focus group discussions and interviews were conducted to give the community an opportunity to have an input into tourism development guidelines for decision-making. This process was facilitated by the village headman, who had a clear vision for the community and was able to provide direction and support for other members. The community had strong views about the areas and kinds of activities they wanted to open up to visitors. In some cases, suggestions came directly from the community. At other times, with the community's acceptance, the project team discussed, modified and adapted ideas in the process of developing the community's overall tourism vision. The community was guided by principles put forward by the King's Project (Royal Development Projects Board 1997).[2]

The headman assumed leadership of the process and was involved in describing the advantages/disadvantages of tourism and the proposed activities for the community. There was general agreement that tourism represented a desirable path for development. Yet, at the beginning of the development process, some villagers were concerned that it was not appropriate to profit financially from the Buddha and the temple. The

Figure 7.3 Mock tourism day.
Source: Walter Jamieson and Pawinee Sunalai.

headman explained to the villagers that this money would be used to protect and enhance the community's cultural and religious resources as well
as contribute to increasing the income of the local people.

The community was introduced to a number of potential tourism and
community development initiatives, such as creating an information
centre, providing parking, developing agricultural products and souvenirs, and establishing a savings group.

Simulated tourism day

Although effective community participation is an essential principle of
sustainable development in theory, it is often one of the most difficult
tasks to carry out in practice. To build community readiness and capacity
to embrace tourism, Klong Khwang villagers conducted a full-scale simulated "mock tourism day" with assistance from the project team.

This event had several objectives. It was designed primarily to provide
villagers with an opportunity to experience a large volume of visitors and
learn to deal with a variety of tourism and resident issues. It also tested,
first-hand, the community's infrastructure from a visitor's perspective and
evaluated the attractiveness of the site as a tourism destination. Finally, it
allowed residents to decide whether they really wanted to accept and develop tourism as a village activity over a longer period of time.

In the mock tourism exercise, a multinational group of 40 volunteers
assumed various tourist roles. It was the village headman and community
members who in effect developed the day's programme and activities.
These included the provision of English-speaking tour guides, planning a
sightseeing itinerary, and serving a buffet lunch prepared by the women's
group.

An evaluation confirmed that the "tourists" had an enjoyable and educational day; more importantly, the community had experienced the demands and opportunities associated with hosting a group of tourists. The tourism day provided opportunities for determining the feasibility of large tour groups, the timing of visits, the adequacy of existing facilities and infrastructure including waste management, the location of toilet facilities, the distribution of economic benefits, and the influence on daily community life.

One major finding was that a restaurant for tourists, run by local people, might not be feasible if it depended on volunteer labour. The women realized that, given their agricultural activities in the community and taking care of family needs, they had little time to take on new responsibilities. If a restaurant were to be developed, it would have to be staffed by paid employees and could not be seen as an additional responsibility for women in the community.

Developing the tourism plan

Experience has shown that tourism destinations must develop appropriate organizational structures, carry out a range of planning and design activities, be deeply and directly involved in marketing the destination, and view product development as an essential element in the overall tourism development process (Jamieson and Noble 2000). It is also crucial that economic and environmental goals be met (Jamieson 2001a).

With assistance from the CUC UEM Project, Klong Khwang developed a community tourism plan that proposed tourism development scenarios involving different levels of activity, from minimal intervention to large-scale tourism initiatives. The community proceeded with a moderate-scale model for tourism development that would produce modest numbers of visitors. It was felt that this moderate level of development would position tourism as a seasonal activity separate from, and for the most part not disruptive to, the community's existing agricultural base. Villagers believed that this would be the least intrusive option for the community and provide much-needed income at certain times of the year.

It was recognized that this modest approach required a much lower level of resident involvement and a smaller financial investment. This kind of tourism development also took into consideration the limited carrying capacity of the community, budget realities, the committee's modest economic goals, and the need to protect Klong Khwang's agricultural base. Tourism was seen not as lacking in value or importance, but simply as one component of the community's overall development objectives.

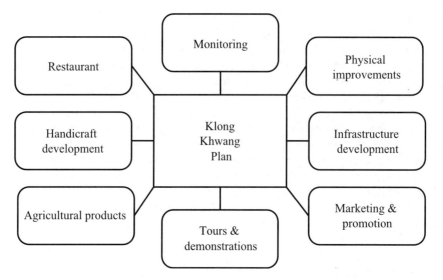

Figure 7.4 The components of the Klong Khwang tourism plan.
Source: Jamieson and Sunalai (1999).

The tourism plan

Following the preparatory stage, the community developed a detailed
tourism plan with the assistance of CUC UEM.[3] A number of plan components are briefly covered here to provide a sense of the overall direction adopted by the committee to use tourism as a cultural and economic
development tool. The plan's various components are shown in Figure
7.4.

- Women and older people in the village were interested in making
  handicrafts (e.g. mat weaving) as a source of extra income. There will
  be a need, however, for assistance in developing products that meet
  market standards and demands.
- The community was convinced that an opportunity existed to develop
  additional income by producing new agricultural products (e.g. banana
  chips and banana candy) and adding value to those currently grown in
  the community.
- The community saw the possibility of raising money through tours and
  exhibitions. Demonstrating traditional lifestyles, e.g. weaving, could be
  incorporated into an overall visitor experience to provide tourists with
  a glimpse of traditional ways of life in this part of Thailand. Tour
  guides would have to be trained, some would have to learn English,
  and there was a need to develop guiding skills. This was seen as a way

Figure 7.5 Local handicrafts.
Source: Walter Jamieson and Pawinee Sunalai.

for younger people in the community to earn extra income and develop new skills and knowledge. A small charge would be levied for these walking tours and demonstrations.

- The community felt that objectives in terms of visitor numbers would not require a significant marketing initiative or ambitious promotional efforts. The Tourism Authority of Thailand (TAT) could work with the community to identify specific target groups and initially raise the community's profile in Korat. This would ensure that, at various times of the year, there would be sufficient tourists to justify community investment and provide reasonable financial returns.
- The project team helped Klong Khwang develop marketing and promotional materials, e.g. brochures and postcards. Local officials were responsible for supplying information, e.g. key points of interest in Klong Khwang and text for print materials. The plan recognized the need for a kiosk located in a prominent position to provide visitors with information, such as the history of the reclining Buddha, the Wheel and the village itself.
- The community acknowledged that it would have to provide sufficient toilets, drinking water for visitors and effective directional signage. Security and medical services would also be required for larger events.
- To make the community more attractive to tourists and facilitate visitor activities, a number of physical changes were proposed to the plan,

Figure 7.6 Improvements to the village entrance.
Source: Walter Jamieson and Pawinee Sunalai.

including improving the entrance to the community (see Figure 7.6). It was also proposed that the area near the *wat* be improved to provide a resting and meeting place for tourists and community residents (see Figure 7.7).

• Part of Klong Khwang's tourism product is its traditional village character. As incomes rise and tastes change, the physical form of the community might also change if new housing and building materials were introduced. If these changes were to alter the character of the community, a large part of the tourism appeal of Klong Khwang would be lost. This produced a great deal of discussion. To maintain the existing character – an important community objective – some form of development controls would have to be put in place. Figure 7.8 demonstrates how original materials could be reintroduced to maintain the traditional community fabric.

• With the help of TAT and local district officials, it will be necessary for Klong Khwang to monitor the impact of economic, physical, environmental, social and cultural issues every year. With the support of the project team, the community has developed a series of simple indicators that can be easily monitored. These are described in further detail later in the chapter.

Figure 7.7 Improvements to the *wat* plaza area.
Source: Walter Jamieson and Pawinee Sunalai.

Figure 7.8 The use of traditional materials and form.
Source: Walter Jamieson and Pawinee Sunalai.

Implementing the tourism plan

After the tourism plan was developed at the end of 1999, Klong Khwang began its implementation on a gradual, measured basis. Independently, the community has sought assistance and support from various organizations such as the provincial government offices. The community also enjoyed several other major achievements, some of which will be discussed below.

Organizational structure

When the tourism plan was first being implemented, the village headman pointed out that "a plan is a bridge for the future". He and the community recognized that, to implement the plan and strengthen local people's involvement in managing tourism activities, an appropriate organizational structure was required. From the beginning of the planning process the community set up a tourism committee to serve as an advisory board for tourism-related development activities. This committee included a monk, a teacher, volunteers and an appointee who would look after the interests of the monastery. The committee, functioning in a businesslike manner, helped to guide tourism development and the community.

Establishment of community cooperative

In accord with the moderate tourism development model adopted by the community, a cooperative was established with a small investment of 9,400 baht (US$240). It consists of five working groups: production, marketing, finance, auditing and sales. Each group has a selected head and the village headman acts as chairperson of the cooperative as a whole. The objectives of the cooperative are to:
• generate additional income for villagers from tourism,
• reduce the number of unemployed people,
• promote Klong Khwang village and local goods made from agricultural products.
In 2000, the headman reported that the cooperative had 60 members, of whom 25 per cent participated in group activities. To encourage members to get involved in the working groups, there is an agreement that anyone who regularly participates receives a monthly dividend of 75 per cent of the profits generated from tourism activities and local goods made from agricultural products; 15 per cent of the profits go to the cooperative fund, which provides loans to cooperative members and assistance for medical expenses or funeral ceremonies; those who do not work get 10 per cent annually.

Figure 7.9 Community cooperative.
Source: Walter Jamieson and Pawinee Sunalai.

Product development

Training in agricultural product development has been provided by provincial government agencies. Profits from the sale of these local products are around 12,000 baht (US$300) per month. To maximize profits, every effort is made to purchase raw materials locally from Klong Khwang villagers.[4]

A small amount of souvenir production generates about 10,000 baht (US$250) a month.[5] Because of a lack of human resources, villagers who do not make souvenirs themselves hire others to do the work. The headman encourages and trains unemployed villagers to do this job. Although the income generated from the sale of local products appears to be small, it is an important source of extra income for the residents.

Figure 7.10 Local products.
Source: Walter Jamieson and Pawinee Sunalai.

Facilities, services and infrastructure

Road connections to Klong Khwang have been improved, providing good access to the community. A new parking area has been identified to avoid any damage to the Reclining Buddha caused by vibration from visiting vehicles. Public telephones and washrooms have also been provided. With support from TAT, there is now signage in Thai and English from the main road right into the village. The community did not want to provide home stays or build guesthouses because of the potential social and cultural impact.

Environmental protection

The tourism development approach adopted by Klong Khwang was designed to have minimal environmental impacts on the community. Increases in solid waste or waste water are minimal given that Klong Khwang does not provide accommodation or restaurants for the visitors. There is very little noise pollution because tourists spend only short periods of time in the community.

Income distribution

One key concern in relation to tourism development is that the economic benefits are often not distributed in an equitable manner. In Klong Khwang, donations are directed primarily to improvements and the maintenance of the temple and its facilities. Profits from agricultural products are equally distributed through the cooperative to members. Net profits from the sale of souvenirs are given to villagers and the cooperative. This example of managing profits is an excellent model for income distribution. From the beginning, the community was less concerned with individuals benefiting from the development process and more interested in ensuring that the entire community would profit once tourism activities were under way.

Monitoring tourism impacts

One problem associated with tourism development is that resources are often not devoted to monitoring activities (Jamieson et al. 2000). It is important that Klong Khwang monitor the success or failure of its management strategies. Without this activity it will be very difficult for Klong Khwang to determine its ability to meet future challenges. Simple monitoring indicators developed by the project team were presented in the Klong Khwang tourism development plan (see Table 7.1).

Table 7.1 Monitoring indicators

Issues	Monitoring indicators
Economic	The money the community obtains from tourism is categorized as follows: • donations • food and drink • souvenir sales • sale of agricultural products • walking and demonstration tours • jobs created by tourism activity
Physical	Damage to the reclining Buddha Whether grass and foliage are getting trampled or destroyed Damage to the roads/parking lot caused by buses and other vehicles
Environmental	Problems with solid waste Problems with waste water Noise pollution from tourists and buses Air pollution from buses/vehicles
Socio-cultural	Changes to the behaviour of the community Changes in housing styles Changes to the dress of the local people

Source: Jamieson and Sunalai (1999).

At the end of 2001, a year after the tourism plan was implemented, the project team returned to the Klong Khwang community and discussed the monitoring of tourism impacts with the headman. Simple methodologies to collect information involved observation, discussion with the headman and interviewing the community members. Based on the monitoring indicators presented in Table 7.1, the following are the results of tourism impacts on the Klong Khwang community.

• **Economic impacts**. Data collected by local people show that the number of tourists increased from 1,100 in 1999 to 3,000 per month in 2000, with associated increases in the income of local people.
• **Physical impacts**. As yet there have been no negative physical impacts from tourism development because of the gradual and careful process adopted by villagers.
• **Environmental impacts**. There have not yet been any environmental impacts from the disposal of solid waste or dealing with waste water, but, if tourism levels increase, formal infrastructure initiatives will have to be undertaken. The headman has been active in encouraging villagers to reuse and recycle materials to reduce the amount of waste being generated within the community and to earn extra income from selling recycled products.

- **Socio-cultural impacts**. From the village headman's point of view, the community is now more positive toward tourism. The community is friendlier and provides information to tourists. Modes of dress have changed and residents wear Thai clothes more often than before. Given the type of tourism planning process that is in place in the community, there are also indications that the villagers are working together more cooperatively.

Management issues/barriers

Although the experience has been positive overall, there are still several unresolved issues. It is too early to determine the willingness and ability of the villagers to continue sustainable control and management of the tourism process. At this stage, ongoing community guidance and support are still required.

Initially it was thought that very little marketing would be required. It is now clear that the community needs to develop a set of marketing and promotional tools to position its products in a more effective way. This raises the question of how a community such as Klong Khwang can best be positioned and promoted. Currently promotion is mainly by word of mouth. Responsible government agencies, such as the regional TAT office or the provincial government, must support Klong Khwang as one of the destinations on the Korat tourism circuit. The community cannot function alone or in isolation as a destination but must be seen as part of a larger series of activities. This was stressed in the recommendations of the CUC team to the community.

Given the community-driven nature of the process, the community is learning to determine its own activities as it gains experience. Yet there are other competitive destinations in the region and a need exists for Klong Khwang to develop its tourism product professionally in order to continue to attract sufficient income. There is also a need for professional advice on how to develop new markets for both agricultural and handicraft products.

Lessons learned

Klong Khwang has been recognized by the Nakhon Ratchasima provincial government as an excellent community-based initiative and is becoming well known to other communities in the province. The headman has been invited to talk to other communities about how to get villagers involved in community activities and how to strengthen their unity in working together to improve their quality of life through tourism development. Klong Khwang also accommodates a number of study tours from within Thailand and internationally.

It was acknowledged by all major stakeholders that the technical assistance provided by national and local governments and the project team was instrumental in ensuring important issues were identified, technical advice and direction were available to committee members, and an overall understanding of community-based tourism was established. The community was receptive to accepting technical advice and, most importantly, was committed to a planning process. In addition to the assistance provided by outsiders, the success of the community-based tourism development in Klong Khwang is the result of committed, high-quality leadership. The process would not have worked without the headman's ability. His personal vision and commitment to making the community a better place are clearly important ingredients in the success of this innovative initiative. This type of leadership may not always exist, so it is essential to develop such capacities and commitment. It takes time and effort but undoubtedly pays off in the long term.

Another lesson learned is that, if communities are to assume responsibility for their future, they need time to develop the necessary skills and knowledge and to recognize the importance of sustainable approaches to community development. Traditional classrooms for education and training may not be required; it is more effective to have informal discussions and meetings with focus groups, to walk around the village to identify issues and tourism products, and to use maps and other visual illustrations as guides for physical development.

The approach adopted within the process allowed all community members to think independently about issues as opposed to being driven by political processes. This resulted in a constructive process of information and skills development. It may not always be possible to replicate this situation, but independent teams, unconstrained by governmental structures and policies, are best suited to work with communities and help them achieve their objectives.

Another major reason for the success of the planning initiative was that the community realized the importance of a sustainable planning process. It is interesting to note that the community is following through on the plan very closely. Community members feel a strong sense of "ownership" of the plan. This has led to a high level of commitment to tourism activities and to ensuring success. A plan that was developed "outside" would probably not have achieved the same level of success.

Capacity-building also played a key role in the initiative's success. This occurred at a number of levels and included an effort to improve the ability of project team members to increase the community's capacity to manage its own affairs. One interesting result of the process is that the village headman has now become increasingly recognized by various governments and organizations as someone who can articulate a sustainable process of community-based tourism planning and development. He is a living example of the ability of communities to manage their own affairs if they have access to technical advice and support. For example, the headman was a guest speaker, along with academics and professionals, at a major international conference on community destination management.

If the planning process is to succeed, the major actors must be able to think "outside the box". For example, the notion of a cooperative was not originally viewed as part of the overall implementation process, but the community was adamant about the need for such an approach. It has turned out to be one of the most important tools for ensuring the equitable distribution of tourism resources.

The use of simulation and visualization techniques also proved to be successful. Technical assistance projects would do well to adopt similar approaches, especially if they are dealing with communities that are visually oriented.

The final lesson is that the nature of the community's values and spiritual way of life was essential in producing a plan with an equitable distribution of resources. The project team initially approached the community planning situation as one in which individual efforts would be encouraged and recognized. It soon became clear that the community, based on a Buddhist and rural way of life, saw things quite differently. The notion of sharing and commitment to the community's spiritual and cultural resources was seen as a priority.

Applicability to other communities in Asia and the Pacific

Given the multiplicity of different factors and forces at work in any community tourism development process, it is clear that the Klong Khwang process described here cannot be reproduced in its entirety in another situation. This said, our work in similar situations in several other countries has demonstrated the importance of incorporating sustainable tourism principles as guiding elements in any planning process. Without a careful implementation of these principles, it is not likely that a community will be able to achieve a sustainable tourism plan and development process.

The overall process employed within this case study provides an excellent framework for the structuring of a tourism planning and development process. It is nonetheless critical that each community develop its own set of organizational and management strategies that take into account the full range of stakeholders who have an influence on the eventual tourism product. The tourism planning process should adopt a comprehensive approach involving a detailed inventory and assessment process, the incorporation of pro-poor tourism concerns, and the development of destination plans that include visitor management strategies. It is clear that marketing information and promotional capacities are also essential and that any tourism development process must ensure that there is coordination between the various tourism initiatives taking place within the community and its original context.

One of the deciding factors when determining how successful a community might be in its tourism planning and development is the level of support it might receive from various governmental and nongovernmental organizations and technical assistance agencies. Without this type of support, it is almost impossible to believe that a community without the necessary resources could achieve a sustainable tourism product.

Finally, it is absolutely essential that communities do not adopt tourism as a major engine of economic growth at the expense of their traditional means of income generation. Tourism by its very nature is cyclical and is very vulnerable to events outside the control of the community. The impacts of the tragedy of 11 September 2001 in the United States, the Bali bombings in 2002, the SARS epidemic of 2003 and downturns in the world economy are all warning signs that communities should adopt tourism as only one of their sources of economic development. The case study developed within this chapter clearly demonstrates how a community chose to add to its economic activity and build on its traditional activities while still achieving the benefits of tourism development.

Conclusion

In assessing the success of the community-based tourism initiative in Klong Khwang, it is useful to identify the internal and external forces that were essential to the development process. A number of external forces helped support the process of community involvement and plan development, including the interest and support of the Tourism Authority of Thailand, the support of the district government and the work of the project team. Without them it would not have been possible for the community to succeed.

Although these forces were influential, it was the internal workings of the community that were the "key to success". The headman's leadership and the willingness of the community to participate in the process and support the development of a sustainable tourism development plan are seen as significant dimensions within the larger development process. The combination of internal and external forces has been essential to the overall effort.

Whether the Klong Khwang experience can be replicated as a "package" in other situations is uncertain at best. However, there is no doubt that many of the elements described in this chapter are relevant to other community tourism planning situations. It is hoped that funds will be made available for similar types of initiative to allow officials and community members to develop their knowledge of community development and planning. Only then will it be possible fully to understand the role of technical advice and innovative techniques in helping to support community-based tourism plans.

Notes

1. These statistics were provided by the village headman.
2. His Majesty's principles for community development include: (i) "no order", which means that people are not ordered to follow his initiatives, which should be done on a voluntary basis, (ii) "self-reliance", (iii) "people participation", (iv) "democracy", (v) "consistency", which means that local conditions and characteristics including topography, environment, culture and tradition should be taken into consideration when implementing His Majesty's development work, (vi) "community strengthening", which builds the foundation for living that will lead to the state of self-reliance in a sustainable fashion, and (vii) "education", which means encouraging people to obtain knowledge about making a living and practising agriculture using proper technology.
3. The full plan document can be found at ⟨http://www.integrationmgt.com/publications1. htm⟩.
4. These statistics were provided by the village headman.
5. These statistics were provided by the village headman.

BIBLIOGRAPHY

Getz, D. and W. Jamieson (1997) "Issues, opportunities and entrepreneurship in native tourism: A case study in Alberta, Canada", in D. Getz and S. Page (eds), *The business of rural tourism*. London: Routledge.
Hatton, M. J., ed. (1999) "Community-based tourism in the Asia-Pacific: Klong Khwang village: Planning for tourism development", Asia-Pacific Economic Cooperation (APEC). The School of Media Studies at Humber College, Canada.
Jamieson, W. (1999) *Guidelines on integrated planning for sustainable tourism development*. New York: United Nations Economic and Social Commission for Asia and the Pacific.
———, ed. (2001a) *Community tourism destination management: Principles and practices*. Canadian Universities Consortium Urban Environmental Management Project.

————, ed. (2001b) *Recommendations for sustainable village tourism development for the Greater Mekong Subregion*. Training and Technology Transfer Program, Canadian Universities Consortium Urban Environmental Management Project at AIT.

———— (2001c) "Interpretation and tourism", in W. Jamieson (ed.), *Community tourism destination management: Principles and practices*. Canadian Universities Consortium Urban Environmental Management Project.

———— (2001d) "Defining urban tourism destination management", in W. Jamieson (ed.), *Community tourism destination management: Principles and practices*. Canadian Universities Consortium Urban Environmental Management Project.

———— (2001e) "Managing urban heritage resources within a cultural tourism context", in W. Jamieson (ed.), *Community tourism destination management: Principles and practices*. Canadian Universities Consortium Urban Environmental Management Project.

Jamieson, W. and T. Jamal (1997a) "Contributions of tourism to economic development", in C. Gee and E. Fayos-Sola (eds), *International tourism: A global perspective*. Madrid: World Tourism Organization.

———— (1997b) "Tourism planning and destination management", in C. Gee and E. Fayos-Sola (eds), *International tourism: A global perspective*. Madrid: World Tourism Organization.

Jamieson, W. and P. Mandke (2002) "An exploration of the national policy issues related to the use of tourism development in poverty reduction in Southeast Asia", *Proceedings of the Fifth Biennial Conference: Tourism in Asia: Development, marketing and sustainability*.

Jamieson, W. and A. Noble (2000) *A manual for sustainable tourism destination management*. Training and Technology Transfer Program, Canadian Universities Consortium Urban Environmental Management Project at AIT.

Jamieson, W. and P. Sunalai (1999) *Klong Khwang plan*. Training and Technology Transfer Program, Canadian Universities Consortium Urban Environmental Management Project at AIT.

Jamieson, W., D. Getz and T. Jamal (1997) *Planning for sustainable tourism development at the local level*. Calgary: Centre for Environmental Design and Research.

Jamieson, W., D. Getz, T. Jamal and A. Noble (2000) *Local level planning for sustainable tourism development*. Canadian Universities Consortium Urban Environmental Management Project at AIT.

Noble, Alix and Walter Jamieson (2000) *A manual for interpreting community heritage for tourism*. Training and Technology Transfer Program, Canadian Universities Consortium Urban Environmental Management Project at AIT.

Royal Development Projects Board, Department of Technical and Economic Cooperation and United Nations Development Programme (1997) *Concepts and theories of His Majesty the King on development*. Bangkok: 21 Century Co.

Sustainable Community Tourism Destination Management (2000) 15-minute video for Canadian Universities Consortium Urban Environmental Management Project at AIT.

WCED [World Commission on Environment and Development] (1987) *Our common future*. Oxford: Oxford University Press.

8

Mangrove conservation through ecotourism development by the Bobongko people in the Togean Islands, Indonesia

Sundjaya

Introduction

Since the 1980s, ecotourism in Indonesia has been underlain by the search for a suitable biodiversity conservation strategy that can be complemented by a profit-generating scheme for local communities. This has been coupled with an increased awareness of the importance of a sustainable approach to ecotourism in areas such as national parks or nature reserves. In general, ecotourism is perceived as providing two basic benefits. One benefit is the conservation of nature, and the other is welfare improvement for local communities in conjunction with the maintenance of their culture (Lindberg and Hawkins 1995: 8).

Ecotourism is a business that requires adequate capacity within local communities and institutions, in order to prevent them from being marginalized in a development process that is often introduced by global industry.[1] When global industry does endeavour to involve local communities in an ecotourism business, there are several key issues that need to be addressed. For example, there is the question of how the local people should respond and exactly what type of practices should be carried out at the community level.

This chapter describes the process of ecotourism development undertaken by the Bobongko people of Lembanato village, on the Togean Islands of eastern Indonesia. Discussion focuses on how the people in this indigenous ethnic group have applied their local knowledge systems and responded to ecotourism from within their own particular social and cul-

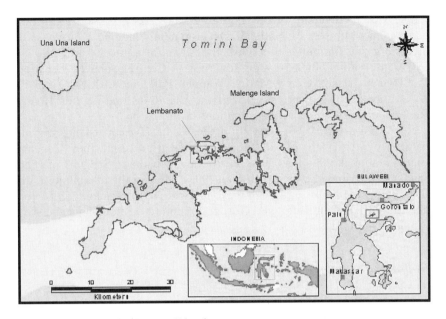

Figure 8.1 Map of the Togean Islands.
Source: Conservation International, Palu Office, 2003.

tural setting. I attempt to identify the various factors that have influenced the ecotourism development process and to draw out lessons that might assist other communities trying to develop similar initiatives.

Togean Islands at a glance

The Togean Islands are located in Tomini Bay, Central Sulawesi Province, Indonesia. They cover a land area of around 700 km^2 and a sea area of approximately 1,300 km^2 (see Figure 8.1). Biological surveys have revealed that the islands are home to 400 coral species, 26 of which are new to science (Allen and McKenna 2001). The diversity of this coral creates rich and colourful reefs that attract many visitors. The islands are also home to the hawksbill turtle (*Eretmochelys imbricata*) and the green turtle (*Chelonia mydas*). Some of the islands are also known to be a habitat for the endangered and protected giant coconut crabs (*Birgus latro*). Roughly 60 per cent of the islands are covered by lowland forests that are rich in various endemic protected animal species, including the Togean macaques (*Macaca togeanus*), Togean lizards (*Varanus togeanus*), babirusa (*Babyrousa babyrussa*), Sulawesi cuscus-bear (*Phalanger ursinus*), and tarsiers (*Tarsius togeanensis*) (Supriyadi et al. 1996).

The rich biodiversity of the Togean Islands has been well acknowledged. The Ministry of National Development Planning's *Biodiversity action plan for Indonesia* (1993) lists the islands as a priority area for marine conservation. In 1990, the Governor of Central Sulawesi declared the Togean Islands area a Marine Tourism Park. In 2002, the Ministry of Culture and Tourism categorized the islands as one of four Highly Recommended Ecotourism Destinations in Indonesia.

According to the 1997 population census, the Togean Islands are inhabited by approximately 30,000 people of various ethnicities: Togean, Bajau, Bobongko, Saluan, Bugis, Gorontalo, Minahasa, Sangir, Cina and Javanese (National Statistical Bureau 1998). Most of the inhabitants earn their living as farmers, although the Bajau people work mainly in fishing and the settlers from Bugis and Gorontalo tend to be merchants and government employees.

Bobongko people of Lembanato

Life and culture

Local mythology suggests that the ancestors of the Bobongko people came from mainland Sulawesi, south of the Togean Islands, although there is no concrete evidence of this. The Bobongko people are spread all over settlements on the Togean Islands, including the villages of Tumbulawa, Baulu and Lembanato. Some have them have married into other ethnic groups and live outside their ethnic community.

Most of the inhabitants of the village of Lembanato are Bobongko. The village is sheltered by a fairly dense mangrove forest on the Kilat Bay in the centre part of the islands (see Figure 8.1). In 2000, the village was home to 243 households and 1,143 people who mostly made their living by working in the *ladang* (dry-land agriculture) growing coconut, cocoa, clove, paddy, cassava, corn, fruits and vegetables. Although some people make their living from sea fishing, they will still own some *ladang*. The most reliable economic commodity for the locals is coconut, which is sold in the form of copra.

Key elements of Bogongko tradition and culture form the foundation of daily life in Lembanato. These include language, traditional medicine and spiritual beliefs regarding magic as well as traditional paddy-planting ceremonies or rituals held when opening up a forest area for *ladang* or starting the planting season. Events that mark the human life cycle – celebrating the birth of a baby, wedding ceremonies and death rituals – have also been carried out in the traditional ways of the Bobongko although they have also been influenced by other cultures, particularly Islam.

Local knowledge about mangrove ecosystems

Traditional ecological knowledge represents a collective understanding of the relationship between a community and the earth that is derived from particular places over long periods of time (Doubleday 1993).[2] To describe how the biodiversity of the mangrove forest has influenced the development of the cultural systems and livelihood patterns of the Bobongko people, and how traditional ecological knowledge has been formed, it is vital briefly to explain the relationship between the mangrove forest and the people's livelihoods.

Some of the unique traits of the Bobongko ethnic group, compared with other ethnicities in the Togean Islands, lie in their utilization of the mangrove forest (*wakatan*). According to Bobongko mythology, their ancestors planted and grew a particular type of mangrove tree that was used as the price paid to a Bobongko woman who was about to become a bride. For their ancestors, the marriage present, or price paid, was sacred and highly valued. As a result, they conscientiously grew the mangrove plants and handed them down to their children and grandchildren. This mangrove species is still called *wakatan sompaknyo*, which means "bride price" in the Bobongko language. The fruit of the *wakatan sompaknyo* is used by Bobongko women for making a traditional powder that has a cooling effect and is used as a cosmetic to nourish and protect skin from the sun.

The extent of Bobongko traditional ecological knowledge about mangroves is evident in the local taxonomy system, in which certain mangrove tree species are classified according to their physical characteristics.[3] Although the classification of mangrove species can also be found in other Togean communities, the Bobongko system is more complex and reflects the many uses the people have for mangrove resources. Utilization of the mangroves is also linked very closely to their cultural practices. The Bobongko have, for example, made cooking salt from the root of the *bambar* species of mangrove. This practice of root-salt production is not found in other ethnic groups, even though the *bambar* is available in almost all parts of the Togean Islands. In the production of mangrove root-salt the Bobongko people are bound by rules of custom that guide them on how to cut the root of the *bambar* properly so that the tree will still grow. Rules also forbid the Bobongko people from making mangrove root-salt during the paddy-planting season.

The Bobongko people utilize almost every part of the mangrove tree for various purposes. The trunk of the tree is used as firewood, for example, and for making boats, buildings and piers. The leaves and fruit are sometimes used in traditional medicines and cosmetics. The root is processed as salt and as an organic pesticide, which is effective enough to control paddy pests, and the bark is often used as the basic material for colouring fishing nets. It is not only the mangrove plant itself that is utilized in the daily lives of the Bobongko people, but also the many fauna that live in the mangrove forest ecosystem. These include the mangrove clam (*Geloina ceyloinica*), which is of economic value to Bobongko families and is also used for consumption.

As is the case with many other ethnic groups around the world, the traditional ecological knowledge of the Bobongko people is slowly eroding. A 2001 study, conducted by Conservation International (CI) Indonesia and the Pijak Foundation,[4] showed a significant gap in traditional mangrove knowledge between the older and younger generations of the Bobongko community (Conservation International Indonesia and Pijak Foundation 2001). Many young people no longer recognize the local names of certain species of mangrove tree, including the tree that is used for making root-salt.

This fading of traditional culture and knowledge can be attributed to many factors, but it is mainly the result of the intrusion of external culture. This culture has been regarded as suitable for the needs of the Bobongko people at this stage in their local development, but it has been adopted without careful attention to its impacts on local culture and knowledge. Another factor is the absence of mechanisms to transfer local knowledge to the younger generations. The two are strongly interconnected. The traditional knowledge possessed by the older generations is generally practical and is utilized in their daily lives. This means that, as the Bobongko people begin to prefer manufactured salt over traditional salt, the practice of making mangrove root-salt will slowly fade. The knowledge and techniques required for salt-making will become irrelevant and unused in everyday life.

Ecotourism development by the Bobongko people

The beauty of nature and the biological diversity in the Togean Islands, both marine and forest, have attracted many overseas tourists, mainly backpackers from European countries. In 1989, the authority of Central Sulawesi Province recognized the large potential for tourism in the Togean Islands and recommended designation as a Marine Tourism Park. A year later, 1,000 km² of sea around the islands was provisionally designated a Marine Tourism Park by Governor's Decree.

Introducing ecotourism to the Togean Islands

The idea for an ecotourism initiative in the Togean Islands was first introduced by the Togean Consortium, an organization that was established in Palu, the capital of Central Sulawesi Province, in 1995 to promote sustainable tourism in the Togean Islands. The Consortium was founded jointly by Conservation International (CI) and the Indonesian Foundation for the Advancement of Biological Sciences (IFABS), which worked on biodiversity conservation programmes in the Togean Islands.[5]

Although the Consortium did not officially begin its work until 1996, it conducted a survey in 1995 showing that the number of tourists visiting the Togean Islands during 1994–1995 was between 1,500 and 1,800. Most of these visitors were from Europe and their average length of stay was 7–10 days. During 1996–1997, records show that the number of visitors dramatically escalated to between 3,000 and 4,500 (Suhandi 1998). Along with the growing number of tourists, there was also an increase in accommodation provided by cottages and home stays, operated either by locals or by investors from outside the Togean Islands or from overseas. Between 2000 and 2002, Indonesian entrepreneurs and foreign investors collaboratively established three tourism, dive and accommodation facilities. There is also another dive operation in the east of the Togean Islands that is fully owned by an Italian.[6] Only three of the islands' sets of accommodation are fully owned by local people.

The Togean Consortium examined tourism development in the Poso district of Central Sulawesi and noted that only 1 per cent of the revenue was going to the local community. The majority was going to external investors who managed accommodation and transportation, and also to the local government in the form of taxes (Languha 1998). To ensure that this situation was not repeated on the Togean Islands, the Consortium developed a community-based multi-stakeholder concept of ecotourism and introduced it to the local community.

In 1997, training began for local guides. An ecotourism seminar, held in April that year, produced a community agreement to form the Togean Ecotourism Network (TEN). This network was to be facilitated by the Togean Consortium as part of an effort to increase local people's access to tourism activities. The Consortium invited local people from several different villages to be members of the network. Membership included fishermen, farmers, accommodation owners, local guides, tour operators and handicraft makers. The main aim of TEN was to derive an economic benefit from tourism in the Togean Islands and at the same time to preserve the rich biodiversity that was tourism's main commodity. Thus the network's two main objectives were to boost local people's earnings through tourism activities and to reduce the negative environmental impacts of tourism activities.

The next step in introducing ecotourism was the Consortium's programme, conducted through TEN, to assist members to develop tourism products while at the same time building skills in biodiversity conservation. The Consortium aimed to enhance the role of local people in community-based conservation in the Togean Islands through TEN. To further this goal, the Consortium provided the network with training, funding and technical assistance in product development. The Consortium also helped TEN members to manage biodiversity in certain areas of the Togean Islands by assisting in the development of nature tourism attractions and other supporting activities.

Other examples of support provided by the Consortium include creating trails for trekking in the primary forest of Malenge Island, making bookmarks out of recycled wood on Papan Island, and developing a mangrove forest boardwalk attraction managed by the Bobongko people in Lembanato village. TEN manages these attractions and serves as a network for any local people involved in tourism. TEN's biggest success came in 1999, when it received a "Tourism for Tomorrow" award from British Airways in the category of "Highly Recommended Project for Pacific Region". British Airways recognized TEN as a local institution that had succeeded both in providing the local community with access to the benefits of tourism and also in conserving the islands' biodiversity.[7]

Initiating the tourism project in Lembanato

Innovation in a community often does not emerge collectively. It often emerges through the efforts of one person who is eager to develop something different for his or her community. The idea of developing an ecotourism product by constructing a mangrove forest boardwalk in Lembanato can be credited to a Bobongko man called Ghalib Labatjo. This man is an official of the village government of Lembanato and a board member of TEN. He is also the key person in TEN who played a major part in transferring the idea of ecotourism, as it was originally promoted by the Togean Consortium, to other villagers. It was Labatjo, with help from the Consortium, who hit the "start button" launching the innovation within his community.

Labatjo was well aware of the potential of the Togean Islands, with their rich biodiversity, to be an attractive ecotourism destination. This was particularly the case with regard to Luok Tingki, a mangrove forest habitat in Kilat Bay. Luok Tingki was the natural habitat for many unique species of birds, deer (*Carvus timorensis*), various species of fauna endemic to Sulawesi, and also babirusa (*Babyrousa babyrussa*). Compared with other mangrove forests in the surrounding area that were being cut by local people, mostly for firewood, Luok Tingki was still in pristine condition. Labatjo saw that the forest's rich biodiversity could be shown to tourists to generate income while at the same time preserving the ecosystem and protecting it from over-harvesting by locals.[8]

After intensive consultation with the Togean Consortium, a plan was eventually produced by Labatjo and the Consortium to construct a mangrove boardwalk attraction. Labatjo held a series of meetings with key members of the Bobongko community to share ideas and review the technical process involved in constructing the boardwalk. These key community members were invited to participate by Labatjo on the basis of friendship relationships, level of interest and support for the plan, and age. Because older people have more traditional knowledge about the mangrove forests, it was thought that they would gain more respect and have more success in protecting the mangrove forest. At these meetings, local people involved in the initiative agreed on role and task distributions among themselves and agreed on the name – the Wakatan group.

Construction of the boardwalk was conducted by the Wakatan group with funding from TEN and the Consortium. The Togean Consortium also acted as a facilitator for the group by offering valuable input and ideas, providing a package of activities for tourists, and assisting in the group management of the attraction. In particular, the Consortium sent an expert to do a biodiversity survey on the attraction location, identify tourist sites, produce a guidebook and provide training for Wakatan group members in tour guiding. An officer from the Consortium lived with the community for several months to provide intensive assistance so that any problems faced during the project implementation stage could be addressed quickly. Further advocacy on the part of the Consortium led to the Wakatan group's receiving additional funding from the Tourism Office of Central Sulawesi Province.

In June 1998, the mangrove boardwalk was officially opened (see Figure 8.2). Because the Wakatan group members agreed not to disturb the mangrove trees during construction, the boardwalk has many curves as it turns to avoid trees. It is made of wood, and is 400 metres in length and 1 metre wide. It has one shelter, a wooden house where briefings are provided for visitors before they start sightseeing. The boardwalk also has a pier for a motorboat and a signboard providing information, in English, for tourists on mangroves and on the regulations. There is also a charity box at the entry gate so that tourists who sympathize with the Wakatan group's efforts can donate money.

Enhancement of management skills

Once the boardwalk infrastructure was constructed, the social infrastructure for managing the attraction had to be put in place. Business management of this sort was new to the Bobongko people and their knowledge system and culture did not have the resources to aid in this activity. Because of the economic value of the boardwalk, it was obvious that some

Figure 8.2 Mangrove boardwalk tourist attraction in Luok Tingki.
Source: Togean Consortium.

form of business management system would need to be adapted to the social life and knowledge system of the community. The chart in Figure 8.3 depicts how the input of local knowledge from Wakatan group members and the introduction of new business management knowledge from outside came together within the broader process of innovation development. It also shows the activities and the management structure that resulted from the merging of internal and external knowledge and values.

The most crucial element of external assistance to the Wakatan group within the process of developing the management system was the Togean Consortium's capacity-building assistance. The Consortium provided training and held periodic meetings and discussions to introduce commercial business principles to the community and to address problems as they arose. The aim was to reach agreement among members on how the boardwalk mangrove should be managed in order to maximize the number of tourists attracted.

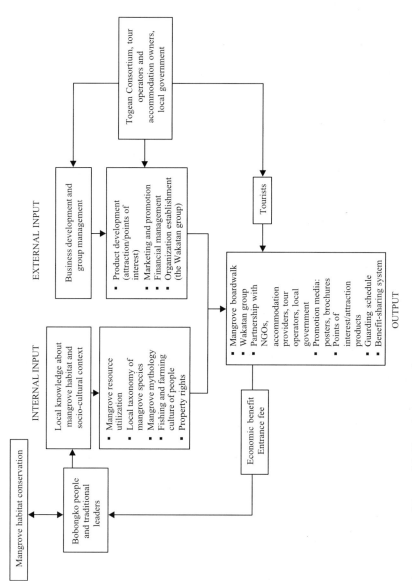

EXTERNAL INPUT

Togean Consortium, tour operators and accommodation owners, local government

Business development and group management

- Product development (attraction/points of interest)
- Marketing and promotion
- Financial management
- Organization establishment (the Wakatan group)

Tourists

INTERNAL INPUT

Local knowledge about mangrove habitat and socio-cultural context

- Mangrove resource utilization
- Local taxonomy of mangrove species
- Mangrove mythology
- Fishing and farming culture of people
- Property rights

Mangrove habitat conservation

Bobongko people and traditional leaders

OUTPUT

- Mangrove boardwalk
- Wakatan group
- Partnership with NGOs, accommodation providers, tour operators, local government
- Promotion media: posters, brochures
- Points of interest/attraction products
- Guarding schedule
- Benefit-sharing system

Economic benefit Entrance fee

Figure 8.3 Development of a management system for the mangrove boardwalk.

The areas that have been strengthened by the development of the mangrove boardwalk management structure can be clustered under three main categories: management of the working schedule, product development and marketing, and benefit-sharing through financial management.

Management of the working schedule

A schedule was developed among 15 members of the Wakatan group for the guards who would be stationed on the boardwalk and who would double as guides. The schedule involved two guards being stationed each day, with working days chosen according to members' preferences. This approach proved to be effective because the system enabled the members of the Wakatan group to strictly monitor the tourists who visited the area and to collect entrance fees. Because the mangrove forest of Luok Tingki is located about an hour by rowing boat from the village, without an appropriate guarding system it would be difficult to monitor the visitors. Quite often, tour guides brought tourists into Luok Tingki without informing the group in advance, causing a loss of earnings from uncollected entrance fees.

Improved management of the working schedule also brought about another benefit to the community. Because all group members were primarily engaged in some other work such as farming in *ladang* and fishing, it was impossible for them to guard the boardwalk all the time. With a guarding schedule of two people per day, each person had to sacrifice only one day off from *ladang* or fishing each week.

Product development

A crucial aspect of management was product packaging and marketing of the mangrove boardwalk attraction. The Wakatan group members felt that they needed to strengthen their abilities in tour guiding, marketing and promoting their product. The Consortium and the group therefore agreed to organize meetings aimed at improving the group's tour guiding techniques. They also agreed to develop networks with local guides and accommodation operators to promote the boardwalk attraction to tourists.

In the process of developing their marketing skills, the Wakatan group members made an interesting discovery. They soon realized that it was the uniqueness of Bobongko culture with regard to the management and utilization of mangrove forests that had the real value to be promoted as a commodity for tourists, rather than the boardwalk itself. In addition to the natural biodiversity of Luok Tingki, the group started to package information about traditional ecological knowledge relating to the management of mangroves, including root-salt production techniques.[9] As a part of these activities, the Togean Consortium and the Wakatan group collaborated to document other elements of traditional knowledge in a guide-book to be used by group members while guiding visitors. This included information on the indigenous taxonomical system, patterns of mangrove forest utilization, and the mythology of the mangrove forest.

Product marketing and promotion

A key aspect of the promotion and marketing scheme for the board-walk was network-building with tourism operators outside the commu-nity. Brochures, posters and press releases were designed and distributed by the Togean Consortium. The Consortium also developed a marketing network with local accommodation providers, who were asked to pro-mote the mangrove boardwalk to visiting tourists. The Consortium was able to promote the area to tour operators throughout Indonesia, even at the international level, through the distribution of posters and bro-chures at various seminars and symposiums.

Transparency and benefit-sharing

The introduction of a financial management system has brought two benefits to the community: enhanced transparency and an equal sharing of benefits. In this regard, several actions were undertaken by members of the Wakatan group:

- A treasurer was chosen from among the group members to be re-sponsible for financial management, which included bookkeeping of the group's cash flow.
- 30 per cent of the collected entrance fees was designated as group funds, and the rest was to be given to the member who was on duty.
- Tips given by tourists were the property of the member who was on duty.
- Money deposited in the locked charity box at the entrance gate of the boardwalk was collected by the member on duty and given to the trea-surer. Part of the funds collected was to be equally divided amongst members every three months; the remainder was to be kept by the or-ganization as reserve funds to maintain the boardwalk and other urgent needs.
- In order to maintain transparency, members took a guest book on duty. Based on the visitor record in the guest book, all members of the group could calculate the amount of money made.

Positive outcomes

Efforts by the Bobongko people in the Togean Islands to integrate tour-ism business and mangrove conservation through the strengthening of lo-cal ecological knowledge were highly innovative. This type of initiative, and the related management system developed by the Wakatan group, were completely new not just to the Togean Islands but to the Sulawesi region in general. The initiative introduced the idea that the mangrove forest, which was once commonly considered simply a wet and muddy place useful only for extraction purposes, could attract tourists who would enjoy its rich biodiversity and learn about local ecological knowledge. The mangrove forest could provide many benefits for the people, not the least of which was that it could serve as a source of income for local people. These benefits are explored in more detail below.

Income generation

Between 1998 and 1999 the Wakatan group reported that more than 100 tourists visited the mangrove boardwalk. During that period, the group's earnings reached more than 2 million rupiah (US$200–250).[10]

Strengthening of ethnic identity

In 1999, the Governor of Sulawesi and some officials from the Central Sulawesi provincial government and the Poso district government visited the mangrove boardwalk and met with the Wakatan group members. During the visit the head of the district and some officials donated money to the group, and this was reported by local newspapers in Central Sulawesi.[11] For the Bobongko people, who traditionally respect their leaders, this act symbolized respect for their people and it strengthened the self-confidence of the Bobongko ethnic group. The fact that outsiders, especially tourists, came and spent a lot of money in order to see and understand the Bobongko culture also encouraged the Bobongko people to implement ecotourism in the area.[12]

Mangrove habitat protection

Labatjo reported that, since the mangrove boardwalk had been built in Luok Tingki, no trees had been cut down because the Bobongko people know that the Wakatan group guards the location. Because Wakatan group members are the elderly of the Bobongko, the group's existence has been fairly well respected by others in the Lembanato community. Another factor in the protection of Luok Tingki was a regulation initiated by the Wakatan group and the villagers. This regulation, which was supported by the head of the village, forbade the cutting of mangrove trees in Luok Tingki while still allowing the Bobongko people to utilize mangrove resources at other locations in Kilat Bay.

A survey conducted by Conservation International and the Pijak Foundation confirms the positive effects that the initiative has had on biodiversity conditions (CI Indonesia and Pijak Foundation 2001).[13]

Problems faced in the process of innovation

The Wakatan group has faced many problems in its effort to implement ecotourism through the development of the mangrove boardwalk.

Unexpected challenges for tourism in the Togean Islands

Although the initiative has been successful in many respects, it has suffered from several setbacks that have affected its future. In 1998, for example, only a few months after the official opening of the boardwalk, its wooden shelter was destroyed by fire. The cause of the fire is unknown. The burgeoning numbers of tourists in Togean that year suggested that the boardwalk had a reasonably promising chance of providing an alternative income. As a result, the Wakatan group members rebuilt the shelter on their own without outside funds.

The biggest challenge, which turned out to be the turning point for the initiative, came in 2000 when social unrest and turmoil erupted in the capital city of Poso, which lies approximately 250 km from the Togean Islands. The poor security situation and political instability damaged Indonesia's image as a tourist location and the number of tourists visiting the country fell dramatically. The Ministry of Culture and Tourism reported that, during the period from 1998 to 1999, more than 4.4 million tourists visited Indonesia. This number fell to 3.1 million during the period from January to October 2000, the period of economic crisis and instability in several parts of Indonesia (Ministry of Culture and Tourism 2002). This also had an impact in the Togean Islands, where the number of tourist visits declined over a short period of time. Some lodgings reported that they received no tourists for several months.[14]

This disaster for tourism in the Togean Islands had significant effects on the number of tourists who visited the mangrove boardwalk in Luok Tingki. It became harder for the Wakatan group to obtain income from the initiative when poor security conditions continued into 2001. During this period, the motivation of group members slowly diminished because they no longer believed that the initiative had the potential to improve their economic welfare. As an alternative, they chose to focus their energy, time and attention on farming and fishing. As a consequence, some parts of the wooden mangrove boardwalk slowly began to decay because of a lack of maintenance owing to limited funds. At one point, the group had to close the boardwalk temporarily because it was too dangerous to be used.

During 2001–2002, there were intermittent visits by tourists, but the frequency and number were far less than the boom experienced between 1998 and 1999. On occasion, no Bobongko people were available in Luok

Tingki to serve as guides even when tourists visited the boardwalk. Although some tour guides visited Lembanato village to ask the members of the Wakatan group to act as guides, other tour guides often took tourists onto the unguarded boardwalk without acquiring permission from the group.

Since mid-2002, along with the gradual improvement in the security situation in Indonesia, the number of tourists visiting the Togean Islands has started to increase. These figures are, however, still far below the 1996 figures.[15] The Wakatan group members have made some effort to repair the boardwalk. This has included fund-raising activities aimed at NGOs and local government, which have unfortunately been unsuccessful. At the time of writing, group members were still making efforts to repair the boardwalk and to recapture the tourism market that had recently started to recover in the Togean Islands.

Internal problems

Language barriers

The effectiveness of the tour guides in Luok Tingki was handicapped significantly by their lack of English language ability. The Wakatan group members were completely dependent on the guides to interpret their stories about mangroves and their local knowledge when they accompanied tourists. Because these guides did not have an adequate understanding of the traditional knowledge and culture of the Bobongko community, stories could be misinterpreted. Although some efforts have been made to address this problem, including the provision of English language lessons for group members, the language barrier continues to be a serious challenge.

Benefit-sharing

Efforts were made to ensure the equal sharing of benefits among Wakatan group members through the introduction of the management system discussed above. In some cases, however, conflicts still arose within the group because of unequal profit-sharing. Each member's earnings were largely determined by the number of tourists who visited the boardwalk during his or her day on duty. For instance, one member of the Wakatan group might have guided 10 tourists in a week because tourists coincidentally visited the boardwalk when that member was on duty. Another member might not have earned any money for an entire month because there were no visitors while he or she was on duty. This problem was partly addressed by the group through the equal sharing of the group's savings every three months. Despite this effort, unequal earnings have continued to be a problem and this has led to a decline in motivation among group members to undertake guard duties. In response to this problem, the Wakatan group let its members choose freely whether or not to carry out their tasks. Most members remained active and stayed motivated to operate and maintain the boardwalk, even when there were no tourists. Others, though, chose to work in the *ladang* instead.

Support for innovation

The innovation developed by the Wakatan group was supported by various institutions and individuals both internally and externally. The flowchart in Figure 8.4 depicts the influences that some parties had on the Wakatan ecotourism development. The contributions of key actors are outlined below.

Togean Consortium

The Togean Consortium's main interventions were to introduce the ecotourism concept and provide capacity-building in business management to the Wakatan group members, both directly and in cooperation with the Togean Ecotourism Network. Ecotourism was complementary to the Consortium's own mission, which was to promote community-based biodiversity conservation in the Togean Islands.

Labatjo and the Togean Ecotourism Network (TEN)

As a member of TEN, Labatjo played the key role in developing the idea of how the Bobongko people could engage in an ecotourism business in the Togean Islands. TEN contributed funds during the early phase of boardwalk construction and also included the Wakatan group as one of its members. In addition, TEN assisted in promoting the mangrove boardwalk attraction through its promotional media such as brochures.

Local government

When local government officials visited the mangrove boardwalk and offered donations this convinced Wakatan group members that their work was appreciated. The Central Sulawesi Provincial Tourism Office and Poso District Tourism Office also donated funds to the development and maintenance of the boardwalk attraction. Unfortunately, the relevant local government institutions have not demonstrated any further support of significance to the local community. Such support could include a budget allocation for training local people in product development and tour guiding, or the development of regulations that require external tourism investors in the Togean Islands to build partnerships with local people.

198

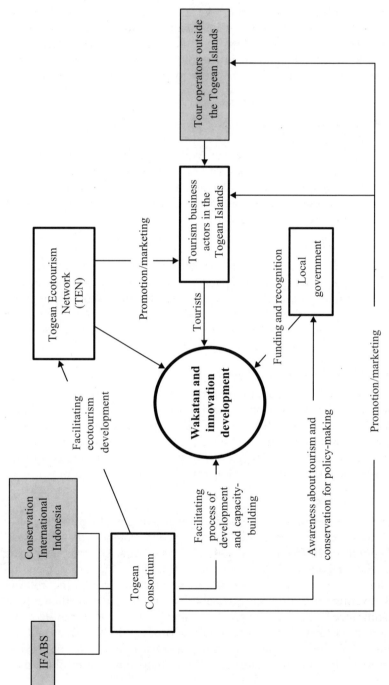

Figure 8.4 Influences on and support for the development of the Wakatan group's ecotourism initiative.

Tourism-related businesses

Some accommodation owners have supported the Wakatan group by rec-
ommending the mangrove boardwalk attraction to their guests. Accommodation owners also assisted the Wakatan group and TEN by allowing
them to display posters and distribute brochures for tourists.

Traditional leaders

There are two main traditional leaders in Lembanato. One is the village
head, whose role is regulated under National Law No. 22/1998. The other
is the leader of the *adat*, an indigenous institution that governs various
social and cultural aspects of the community such as traditional rituals
or conflict resolution. These two traditional leaders of the Bobongko
people assisted in identifying and presenting the indigenous knowledge
and culture of the Bobongko to tourists at the boardwalk attraction. Furthermore, the leaders gave the Wakatan group the authority to utilize the
mangrove forest in Luok Tingki, which according to traditional values
was common property to which all the Bobongko people had equal rights.
To avoid conflicts, a review of property rights over Luok Tingki was conducted by the Wakatan group, the village head and traditional leaders
before the initiative was started.

The village head and the Bobongko people

The village head played an important role in pushing forward the initiative in Luok Tingki, which was under the administrative authority of
Lembanato village. The village head participated in group discussions
and problem-solving sessions. The head also played a key role in mobilizing moral support for the initiative among the Bobongko people.

Lessons learned from the Bobongko

Tourism in the Togean Islands has been taking place since the mid-1990s.
Ecotourism, which focuses both on the preservation of natural resources
and on income generation for the local community, is a new approach in
Togean. This has meant that, when the concept of ecotourism was introduced and applied in the Bobongko community, various changes were required. These included the acquisition of the skills required to manage an
ecotourism attraction, such as product marketing and promotion, financial management, tour guiding and an ability to speak English. The management system that was formulated within the community was adapted
to fit in with the social and cultural norms of the community.

The Wakatan group, which consists of Bobongko people, is the only
community in the Togean Islands ever to implement an ecotourism

initiative. The combination of mangrove habitat conservation and the provision of income-generating opportunities for the local community is evident within the management of the mangrove boardwalk project. This has resulted in the achievement of habitat conservation objectives in Luok Tingki. At the same time, the potential for economic benefits has been an important driving force motivating the Wakatan group members to work on the initiative.

Tourism is a global issue with complex characteristics that cross national borders. When a local community becomes involved in this sector, it becomes part of a very extensive business network. The Togean Islands experience indicates the fragile nature of the tourism industry with regard to national and international political and security factors. For example, the extreme political and security instability that severely affected the Wakatan group's ecotourism initiative was completely unexpected. This proves that, even when tourism initiatives are developed at the community level, it is crucial to take into consideration a number of aspects on a larger scale. It is important, for example, to consider political, social and economic stability at the regional, national and global levels, as well as the potential effects on the tourism market. The local community therefore needs to be made aware that ecotourism, although economically beneficial in many cases, is also vital for the sustainable management of the community's natural resources. When the economic benefits from tourists decrease, for whatever reason, it is important that the local people are still motivated to conserve biodiversity.

Some of the major lessons that can be extracted from the Wakatan experience and may represent a good resource for other communities planning to initiate similar programmes include:

• There should be a comprehensive assessment of external factors and threats that could have a negative impact on the initiative. For each identified threat, the communities should prepare responses in advance, with assistance from external groups if necessary.
• The most effective way to solve problems that need immediate solutions in the early stages of development – for example, product management, tour guiding, biodiversity monitoring – is continual assistance by external facilitators or groups, who work closely and live together with the local people.
• Local communities often lack the ability to undertake financial management of the initiative. Open management systems that value transparency and equal profit-sharing should be introduced to avoid internal conflict among community members.
• Ecotourism attractions depend greatly on natural resources and these are considered to be common property in indigenous communities.

When an initiative does not involve all the members of the community, but obtains benefit from a common property area, the involvement of a customary institution or village chief during the planning process is crucial so as to avoid conflict within the community regarding rights to use natural resources.

Tourist visits to the boardwalk are increasing slowly now that the security situation in Indonesia is improving and Wakatan group members are trying to repair the boardwalk to recapture an income from tourists. It is notable that, without any assistance from outside institutions, Wakatan group members still have the motivation to continue. Labatjo reports that the mangrove boardwalk has made the Bobongko more widely recognized by other people, even from abroad, and this has greatly strengthened the consciousness of this ethnic community.

Labatjo and other Wakatan group members recognize, however, that contributions from other parties such as the Togean Consortium are still needed to reactivate the boardwalk project. This is particularly the case with regard to funding and technical assistance.

Glossary (Bobongko language)

adat: indigenous institution that governs the social and cultural aspects of the community
bambar: mangrove species used to make root-salt
ladang: dry-land agriculture
wakatan: mangrove forest
wakatan sompaknyo: mangrove tree species (*Kandelia kandel*), means bride-price mangrove

Acknowledgements

I wish to thank Ghalib Labatjo, all members of the Wakatan group and the Bobongko people in Lembanato for their cooperation and valuable information. This chapter is dedicated to them. Thanks also to Daru from CI Indonesia for reviewing this article and to Herda Hutabarat for English editing.

Information in this chapter is mainly based on my field experience while working on conservation efforts with local communities in the Togean Islands. Some data were collected in personal interviews with the Bobongko people in Lembanato. Other data were collected from internal field reports of the Joint Secretary of the Togean Consortium, who worked for ecotourism development in the Togean Islands during 1998–2000.

Notes

1. Nasikun (2000) mentions that, when communities encounter global business and try to promote sustainable tourism development, it is important for local people to have broader authority in decision-making and to be involved at all levels of the development process.
2. Doubleday also states that traditional ecological knowledge encompasses spiritual, cultural and social aspects, as well as substantive and procedural ecological knowledge. Traditional ecological knowledge also includes customary rules and laws, rooted in the values and norms of its community.
3. Johannes (1993) mentions that there are four essential perspectives or frames of reference pertaining to traditional ecological knowledge in a community: taxonomic, spatial, temporal and social. We can use these perspectives for monitoring and assessing the environmental impact on a community.
4. Conservation International is a non-governmental organization (NGO) headquartered in Washington DC that has an Indonesian Program office in Jakarta. Pijak Foundation is a local NGO based in Palu, Central Sulawesi.
5. The Indonesian Foundation for the Advancement of Biological Sciences (IFABS), whose Indonesian name is Yayasan Bina Sains Hayati Indonesi, is an Indonesian NGO based in Jakarta that works on the promotion of research in the biological sciences. To implement the Togean Consortium's programmes, the CI and IFABS hired nine field officers and established a joint secretariat in Palu. The Togean Consortium's officers acted as the field facilitators who worked closely and stayed with the community in the Togean Islands.
6. Personal interviews and observation.
7. This achievement was published by some national daily newspapers, for example: "Tourism award from British Airways", *Kompas*, 23 July 1998, p. 10; "Environment award", *Media Indonesia*, 27 July 1998, p. 10; and "British Airways sponsored Indonesian tourism promotion", *Bisnis Indonesia*, 28 July 1998, p. 5.
8. Personal interview, 2002.
9. "Salt making attraction in Togean Islands", *Mercusuar*, 3 August 1998, p. 1.
10. Personal interview with Labatjo and Wakatan's members, 2002, unpublished.
11. "Governor proclaimed let's go Sulawesi in Togean Islands", *Mercusuar*, 22 October 1998, p. 1.
12. Stroma Cole (1998) discovered that the recognition of local culture and knowledge by tourists has been one of the positive impacts for local communities, as shown by people in Ngada. Cole noted that villagers believed that tourism is strengthening cultural values (*adat*) and that the children in the village will have the importance of village custom reconfirmed by seeing tourists come from afar to view it.
13. The study showed that, among five locations surveyed, the mangrove habitat in Luok Tingki was the only location with good conditions and without any indication of destructive activities, even though the quality of the trees in Luok Tingki was reasonably good and would be perfect as material to make households' furniture or piers.
14. The Wakai Cottage reported that during 2000–2001 the number of tourists declined by 80 per cent from the previous period (personal interview).

15. Personal interviews with accommodation providers in the Togean Islands. Unfortunately, the Poso District Office of Tourism has no official statistical data on tourist visits.

REFERENCES

Allen, G. and S. McKenna (2001) "A marine rapid assessment of the Togean and Banggai Islands, Sulawesi, Indonesia", *RAP Bulletin of Biological Assessment* (Washington DC: Conservation International) 20.

Cole, S. (1998) "Tradition and tourism: Dilemmas in sustainable tourism development: A case study from the Ngada region of Flores, Indonesia", *Antropologi Indonesia Journal* (Jakarta: Department of Anthropology, University of Indonesia) 56: 37–46.

Conservation International Indonesia and Pijak Foundation (2001) "Participatory study on mangrove ecosystem in Togean Islands", unpublished report, Palu.

Doubleday, N. (1993) "Finding common ground: Natural law and collective wisdom", in Julian T. Inglis (ed.), *Traditional ecological knowledge: Concept and cases*, pp. 69–79. Canada: International Program on Traditional Knowledge and International Development Research Center.

Johannes, R. E. (1993) "Integrating traditional ecological knowledge and management with environmental impact assessment", in J. Inglis (ed.), *Traditional ecological knowledge: Concept and cases*, pp. 33–39. Canada: International Program on Traditional Knowledge and International Development Research Center.

Languha, R. (1998) "Togean Ecotourism Network (TEN), success and obstacles in developing Togean Islands ecotourism", in *Proceedings of a seminar on ecotourism development Togean Islands*, pp. 38–44. Palu: Togean Consortium.

Lindberg, K. and D. Hawkins (1995) *Ecotourism: Guideline for planner and manager*, Indonesian edn translated by PACT and ALAMI Foundation. Jakarta: PACT and ALAMI Foundation.

Ministry of Culture and Tourism (2002) "Ecotourism in Indonesia", Jakarta.

Ministry of National Development Planning (1993) *Biodiversity action plan for Indonesia*.

Nasikun (2000) "Globalization and new paradigm on community-based tourism development", in Chafid Fandeli and Muchlison Yogyakarta (eds), *Ecotourism development*, Indonesian edn, pp. 13–29. Faculty of Forestry, Gajah Mada University.

National Statistical Bureau (1998) *Una una and Walea Kepulauan in Statistic*. BPS.

Suhandi, A. (1998) "Ecotourism development in Togean Islands", *Proceedings of a seminar on ecotourism development Togean Islands*, pp. 27–37. Palu: Togean Consortium.

Supriyadi, D., et al. (1996) "Identification of potency and problems on forest resources in Togean Islands", *Proceedings of workshop on integrated development of Togean Islands, Central Sulawesi, 6–7 May 1996*, pp. 59–63. Palu: Consortium of Integrated Development of Togean.

9

Innovative community-led sustainable forest resource conservation and management in Baybay, Leyte, the Philippines

Victor B. Asio and Marlito Jose M. Bande

Introduction

Forest destruction is the most serious environmental problem in the Philippines today. Of the 160,000 km^2 of forest (covering 54 per cent of the country) in 1970, only about 55,000 km^2 (19 per cent) are left (Center for Environmental Concerns, Philippines 1996). On the island of Leyte it is estimated that less than 5 per cent of the forest remains and this is mostly found on rugged mountain peaks.[1] Leyte's Central Highlands (or Mt. Pangasugan) have recently been identified as one of the Philippines' biodiversity hotspots (Ong and Ibuna 2000). They are a refuge for many endangered flora and fauna (Goeltenboth 1997), and the western region is also home to the community forest management initiative described in this chapter.

The destruction of forests on Leyte island, coupled with heavy rainfall, rugged topography and weak geological material, has resulted in widespread soil erosion, landslides and flooding during the rainy seasons (Asio 1997). The most severe example of this was the great flash flood of Ormoc City on 5 November 1991, which killed about 8,000 people in less than one hour (Eller and Asio 1991). There is also clear evidence to suggest that severe erosion of upland areas has led to siltation, causing marine resource degradation around the island.

Over the past few decades, preservation and reforestation efforts by government agencies and non-governmental organizations (NGOs) have largely failed. One of the major reasons for this is that most of these efforts were driven only by the financial assistance provided by external organizations and they were not sustained when these funds dried up. Another contributing factor has been the lack of substantive community participation. The capacity of government agencies and private organizations to protect and manage natural resources is limited, especially in remote areas (Drijver and Sajise 1992). Natural resource management initiatives that are community based have a far wider potential for success. This is because natural resources are more closely connected to the everyday livelihoods of people at the community level. In addition, it is the residents of communities who possess a profound knowledge of their local environment and are in an ideal position to make effective decisions about local resource management.

Starting around 1998, the two communities of Cienda and San Vicente, in the municipality of Baybay on Leyte island, have succeeded in protecting and managing their forest areas. These successful initiatives were undertaken by the Cienda-San Vicente Farmers Association (CSVFA), an association of farmer-residents in the two communities. Our objective in this chapter is to present an analysis of the innovative initiatives carried out by the CSVFA to solve the environmental problems it faced. Within this analysis we will attempt to draw out the factors that enhanced innovativeness, the specific barriers faced and the role played by external support. We also address the implications and lessons learned.

Environmental problems faced by the communities

The Community-Based Forest Management (CBFM) Program (see the boxed text) area in the Cienda and San Vicente communities includes two small rivers (Gabas and Tubod), which serve as the source of irrigation water for the rice fields, food (fresh water fish, eel, etc.) and drinking water.[2] The protected portion of the watershed is still largely primary forest. It is rich in flora and fauna, much of which has not yet been identified (see the boxed text).

The most serious problem for the watershed, as with most parts of the Philippines, is forest destruction. Until recently, illegal logging[3] was a major source of livelihood for many farmers from the Cienda and San Vicente communities. This practice began as far back as the mid-1970s and, according to some of the old residents, worsened sometime in the early 1980s with the introduction of the chainsaw. After the CSVFA initiated its activities in the mid-1990s, this illegal activity declined dramatically. Some attempts at encroachment by people from other communities do still occur, however, and there is a common perception within the two communities that DENR (Department of Environment and Natural

---

Community-Based Forest Management (CBFM) Program

The CBFM Program was launched by then President F. V. Ramos through Executive Order No. 263 in 1995 declaring community-based forest management as the national strategy to "ensure the sustainable development of the country's forest lands and its resources and achieve social justice". Social justice may be interpreted to mean that the disadvantaged poor farmers who are landless are given the right to protect and utilize the forest. The Program also asserts "that the State acknowledges and supports the capacities and efforts of local communities and indigenous people to protect, rehabilitate, develop and manage forest lands and coastal resources. The State shall provide legal and technical support to ensure equitable access to and sustainable use of natural resources."

(For more details of the Program, see Legal Rights and Natural Resources Center/Kasama Sa Kalikasan 1997)

Resources – the government agency mandated to protect the forest) does not effectively control illegal activities. In some instances, the unfavourable view of this government agency is compounded by the belief that DENR field personnel are actually working with the perpetrators (Alvarez 1992).

Another major cause of forest destruction in the CBFM area during the time that the CSVFA was being organized was slash-and-burn agriculture, or *kaingin*. This was also widely practised by the residents of the two communities as a source of livelihood because many of them do not own land. The effects of this practice varied greatly in relation to the watershed. In some cases it was highly destructive, causing tremendous soil erosion and landslides, particularly on steep slopes. In other instances it proved less destructive, especially when perennial crops such as abaca and fruit trees were grown in the cleared areas.

Another threat to the forest was biodiversity loss brought about by the rampant hunting of wildlife and river-poisoning practices carried out by people both within and outside the two villages. Hunting of wild animals used to be a common activity of community residents in the past and, although this has greatly declined owing to the intensive campaign by the CSVFA, there are still occurrences from time to time. Wild pigs and birds, such as the parrot, are the most commonly hunted because they command a high price, particularly when sold in urban areas. The other destructive community practice was to put poison (usually pesticide) into

---

Geographical background of the Cienda and San Vicente communities

The Cienda and San Vicente communities are villages located on the western side of the Central Highlands of Leyte. The forest there is designated by the Department of Environment and Natural Resources as a Community-Based Forest Management (CBFM) area. The CBFM area covers 22.36 km^2 and is divided into a 12.30 km^2 protected area, a 5.59 km^2 buffer zone and a 4.47 km^2 multiple-use area. Elevation in the area ranges from lowlands, which are only a few metres above sea level, to volcanic mountain peaks of up to 1,263 metres. Only about 30 per cent of the land area is flat (CSVFA 2000). Most of it is sloping, with an inclination ranging from 30 to 80 per cent. The entire area is underlain by generally loose volcanic deposits (pyroclastics). The lowlands are covered by relatively fertile young alluvial soils, whereas the soils on the stable hillsides are old and infertile. The rugged forest areas are covered with mostly fertile young volcanic soils, which are prone to erosion and landslides. Average annual rainfall is more than 2,800 mm, with June to January being generally wetter than February to May, and temperatures range from 25°C to 31°C. As in the other parts of Leyte, two monsoon winds (south-west and north-east monsoon) generally occur, which have tremendous impact on the overall climate of Baybay because they bring plenty of rain to the western and eastern sides of the island, respectively.

(Jahn and Asio 2001)

---

the river to catch freshwater fish, eel and other edible river organisms. This is viewed as the major cause of the great reduction in the fish population in the two river systems flowing through the watershed.

Frequent flooding in the lowland portion of the watershed, where the two communities are located, has been a particularly serious problem in recent years. The cause of this flooding is believed to be the degradation of some portions of the watershed owing to illegal logging and slash-and-burn practices. People became more acutely aware of the connection between flooding and forest destruction after the Ormoc City flood in 1991. Community residents are also aware that forest destruction is the reason for the declining water yield in watershed rivers. Farmers of the Cienda and San Vicente communities first experienced irrigation water shortages in the mid-1980s, and it was this that led them to form the CSVFA in order to protect the watershed from further forest destruction.

Organizational background of the CSVFA

By 2001, the CSVFA boasted a membership of 160 households drawn from the two towns of Cienda and San Vicente, which have a combined population of 1,453. The average family size is six, with an average household annual income of 24,000 Philippine pesos, equivalent to less than US$40 per month. In terms of educational attainment, about 90 per cent of the members attended elementary school, 7 per cent high school, and 2 per cent reached college. The primary means of livelihood is farming, especially rice and vegetable production.

The association's origins can be traced to an informal group that some farmers organized sometime between 1985 and 1987, primarily to protect the forest above the community from uncontrolled illegal logging and slash-and-burn agriculture. During that time, the farmers were alarmed by a considerable reduction in the level of water flowing in the two rivers. This was a particularly immediate concern because the rivers are the source of irrigation water for their 400 hectare rice fields. Farmers were convinced that the rampant cutting of trees, which they had regularly observed in the watershed, was the cause of this alarming reduction in water yield. In 1988, this informal group became formally known as the Kilim Upland Farmers Association (KUFA) under the leadership of active members who became KUFA officers. KUFA's activities were later chosen as a pilot project for the Integrated Social Forestry Program (ISFP) of the DENR.

In the end, KUFA was not able to sustain its activities. This was mainly because of the lack of technical assistance and follow-up from the local government unit, in addition to internal organizational problems. Between 1993 and 1995, after KUFA's collapse, illegal logging activities in the watershed again surged. They were joined by an increase in sand and gravel extraction in the nearby river systems, perpetrated by members of a religious group that had recently migrated to Baybay from the southern Philippine island of Mindanao. In order to tackle the issues collectively, the farmers, under the leadership of a few older and respected members of the communities, revived their farmer organization and established the CSVFA.

Overall leadership within the association is provided by a board of directors composed of eight members (including the chair), who are elected for a term of two years by a secret ballot during a general assembly of all members. The board meets on the last Friday of each month. Its main function is to formulate policies and plan activities that are then presented to the general assembly for approval when it meets on the last Sunday of each month. The board appoints a manager to directly oversee each of the different projects (Bande et al. 1998; CSVFA 2000). As of 2001, the association had nine projects.

Before the CSVFA could begin activities it needed to obtain external support. As the CSVFA had no legal authority to protect, rehabilitate and conserve the government-owned forest (technically called "timber land"), the first step was to gain designation as a CBFM. This designation was awarded to the association by the DENR on 18 January 2000 for a duration of 25 years and renewable for another 25 years.

Technical assistance was also necessary. This was acquired from external organizations, in particular the Visayas State College of Agriculture (ViSCA), which is now Leyte State University (LSU). When the CSVFA was first becoming established it was also approached by ViSCA's ongoing German-funded Applied Tropical Ecology Project, which was looking for citizens' organizations to apply its novel reforestation technology called *rainforestation*.[4]

Activities of the CSVFA

Forest protection

The primary concern of the CSVFA is to protect the forest from further destruction caused by illegal logging and slash-and-burn practices. In this regard, its first challenge was to work out how to do this in such a large area with rugged terrain. Based on their discussions, members decided to form teams of forest wardens who would take turns to patrol and monitor the forest on a voluntary basis. The teams patrolled the forest, giving special attention to areas that, based on their local knowledge, were ideal for timber harvesting. They would usually stay overnight in the forest in order to catch the illegal loggers, who normally transport timber in the night to avoid detection. The foot patrol schedule is irregular and depends upon information passed on to the association by members or other residents of the communities (e.g. the presence of unidentified persons in the watershed).

This strategy has proven very effective, as is evidenced by the 17 apprehensions made by the foot patrols between 1995 and 2001. It is also thought that, in many instances, illegal activity was aborted owing to the presence of the patrol in the forest. With the help of the Environmental Legal Assistance Center (ELAC), an NGO actively involved in environmental advocacy, two illegal loggers have been convicted and imprisoned.[5] In addition, 125 *kaingineros* (slash-and-burn farmers) have been recorded as having encroached into the CBFM area. Many of these *kaingineros*, particularly new ones coming in from other villages, were apprehended and warned to stop their activity in the watershed. Many of the others who succeeded in evading apprehension have either stopped, or at least minimized, their illegal activities.

To make full use of their presence in the forest, the foot patrol teams engage in other activities during their duty to contribute to the protection of the forest. They collect wildlings and seeds of native tree species, particularly Dipterocarp, for seedling production. They also tag the precious mother trees that have been identified throughout the watershed in an effort to at least inform the illegal loggers of their great ecological value, and also to warn them that they are closely watched by the association. The teams also monitor the presence of wildlife fauna, particularly of unidentified species, and report this to the association upon their return to the village.

Forest rehabilitation

The CSVFA has successfully employed a variety of approaches to rehabilitate degraded areas in the watershed. All approaches are based on a common principle, which is the planting of seedlings of native tree species and other plants, such as rattan. This strategy is sustainable not only because of the cost-free availability of planting materials, but also because it results in the very high survival rate of the planted seedlings. As of 2002, the organization had planted 6,817 trees of 33 different species with a survival rate of 99 per cent in highly degraded portions of the watershed.

The association has mostly employed the rainforestation approach developed by the Applied Tropical Ecology Project (Margraf and Milan 1996a, 1996b). In bare areas inside the forest, the association has also employed an assisted natural regeneration (ANR)[6] approach as a means of rehabilitation. For example, it established a 70,000 m^2 ANR site and enriched it by planting 15,000 rattan seedlings with a survival rate of 99 per cent. In a particular effort to stabilize the riverbanks and minimize the danger of flooding during typhoons, CSVFA members also planted 10,253 trees of about 20 species along the riverbanks.[7]

The CSVFA also established a 15,000 m^2 arboretum, where 2,500 trees of 50 different species were planted with the aim of educating local residents, particularly youth, and as an attraction for eco-tourists. A 50,000 m^2 orchard plantation within the protected zone of the CBFM was also established (CSVFA 2001).

Wildlife preservation

As mentioned above, hunting for wild animals was a common practice among the residents of both villages before the CSVFA came into existence. To reduce hunting levels, the CSVFA decided to conduct a strong campaign among both members and non-members of the community on

Table 9.1 List of endemic mammal species of conservation concern found in the CBFM area of the Cienda and San Vicente communities in Baybay, Leyte, the Philippines

Common name	Scientific name	IUCN/CITES status
Philippine tarsier	*Tarsius syrichta*	Endangered (IUCN)
Philippine flying lemur	*Cynocephalus volans*	Vulnerable (IUCN)
		Trade strictly prohibited (CITES)
Philippine deer	*Cervus mariannus*	Endangered (IUCN)
Squirrel	*Sundascirus samarensis*	Vulnerable (IUCN)
Philippine monkey	*Macaca fascicularis*	Trade strictly prohibited (CITES)
Little leopard cat	*Felis bengalensis*	Trade strictly prohibited (CITES)
Philippine warty pig	*Sus philippensis*	Vulnerable (IUCN)

Source: Field observation and monitoring of CBFM area conducted by members of the CSVFA (CSVFA 2000, 2001).

the importance of preserving the wildlife species found in the CBFM area (see Tables 9.1 and 9.2). They used farmer-to-farmer discussions, house-to-house campaigns and meetings as the foundations of their communication strategy.

The main aims of the campaign were to increase people's awareness of the ecological importance of wildlife species in the forest and to inform them of their value for the eco-tourism business. As a part of the campaign, any wildlife species (including orchids and other plants) that were brought down from the forest by any person were confiscated. The association has the authority under its contract with DENR to confiscate plants and animals obtained without permission. Its efforts have paid off, as residents of the two communities no longer engage in wildlife hunting.

The association, which has the mandate to protect the CBFM area against all illegal activities, also banned the use of poison for catching fish in the rivers in the watershed. It also continues to monitor, normally by visual observation during seed and wildling collections and foot patrolling, the movement and presence of any wildlife species in the forest and relays this information to other CSVFA members. Perhaps the most interesting accomplishment by the farmers in the past few years has been the re-discovery of the Philippine tarsier (*Tarsius syrichta*), Philippine flying lemur (*Cynocephalus volans*) and Philippine deer (*Cervus mariannus*) in the protected watershed (CSVFA 2001). The farmers have also reported sightings of animals that they could not identify even with local names.

Table 9.2 List of endemic bird species recorded in 1996–2000 within the CBFM area of the Cienda and San Vicente communities in Baybay, Leyte, the Philippines

Common name	Scientific name	IUCN/CITES status
Rufous hornbill	*Buceros hydrocorax*	Endangered (IUCN)
Philippine eagle owl	*Bubo philippensis*	Endangered (IUCN) Trade strictly prohibited (CITES)
Philippine falconet	*Microhierax erythrogonys*	Endangered (IUCN) Trade strictly prohibited (CITES)
Green-headed racket-tailed parrot	*Prioniturus luconensis*	Insufficiently known (IUCN) Trade strictly prohibited (CITES)
Philippine hawk eagle	*Spizeatus philippensis*	Vulnerable (IUCN) Trade strictly prohibited (CITES)
Taritic hornbill	*Penelopides panini*	Vulnerable (IUCN) Trade strictly prohibited (CITES)
Scops owl	*Otus scops*	Trade strictly prohibited (CITES)
Serpent eagle	*Spilornis holospilus*	Trade strictly prohibited (CITES)
Philippine hanging parakeet	*Loriculus philippensis*	Trade strictly prohibited (CITES)
Philippine grass owl	*Tyto capensis amauronata*	Trade strictly prohibited (CITES)

Source: Field observation and monitoring of CBFM area conducted by members of the CSVFA (CSVFA 2000, 2001).

Livelihood opportunities

To make its activities sustainable, the CSVFA has engaged in livelihood projects that represent a source of cash income for its projects and its members. Members who used to make their living by conducting slash-and-burn agriculture are not financially affluent and they needed to find an alternative source of income to support their families.

Seedling production

The key source of income for the association is the production of seedlings of native tree species. The CSVFA established a nursery on 1,250 m^2 of land (see Table 9.3), using wildlings and seeds obtained from the mother trees tagged during the forest patrols. Some wildlings of impor-

Table 9.3 Total number of seedlings of indigenous tree species and fruit trees produced by the CSVFA, October 1996 to December 2001

Local name	Scientific name	Total number of seedlings
Dipterocarp		
Bagtikan	*Parashorea malaanonan*	82,096
Tanguile	*Shorea polysperma*	24,467
Yakal-saplungan	*Hopea plagata*	24,102
Red Lauan	*Shorea negrosensis*	21,382
White Lauan	*Shorea contorta*	8,561
Yakal-kaliot	*Hopea malibato*	19,433
Mayapis	*Shorea squamata*	19,650
Guijo	*Shorea guiso*	18,781
Mangachappui	*Hopea acuminata*	5,962
Narig	*Vatica mangachapoi*	5,272
Yakal-yamban	*Shorea falciferoides*	13,400
Palosapis	*Anisoptera thurifera*	8,231
Apitong	*Dipterocarpus validus*	1,541
Almon	*Shorea almon*	540
Mangasinoro	*Shorea philippinensis*	3,492
High premium		
Balobo	*Diplodiscus paniculatus*	12,675
Dungon	*Heritiera sylvatica*	10,542
Dao	*Dracontomelon dao*	2,778
Batete	*Kingiodendron alternifolium*	4,418
Tindalo	*Afzelia rhomboidea*	770
Malugai	*Pometia pinnata*	996
Narra	*Pterocarpus indicus*	4,229
Molave	*Vitex parviflora*	5,524
Kamagong	*Diospyros philippensis*	924
Bolong-eta	*Diospyros pilosanthera*	1,134
Amugis	*Koordersiodendron pinnatum*	680
Bunud	*Knema mindanensis*	4,991
Commercial		
Bitanghol	*Calophyllum blancoi*	5,701
Toog	*Combretodendron quadrialatum*	1,048
Mala-cogon		594
Putian	*Alngium meyen*	40
Real Hindang	*Myrica javanica*	948
Antipolo	*Artocarpus blancoi*	5,141
Hingdang Laparan		218
Bagalunga	*Melia dubia*	1,715
Kalumpit	*Terminalia microcarpa*	16,146
Anislag	*Securinega flexuosa*	1,001
Lamio	*Drancontomelon edule*	2,170
Nato	*Palaquium luzoniense*	1,803
Tiga	*Tristania micrantha*	365
Kalutingan	*Pterospermum obliquum*	312
Malakauayan	*Podocarpus philippinensis*	3,960

Table 9.3 (cont.)

Local name	Scientific name	Total number of seedlings
Fruit trees		
Nangka	*Artocarpus heterophylla*	312
Macopa	*Syzygium samarangense*	116
Durian	*Durio zebithenus*	429
Lanzones	*Lansium domesticum*	577
Rambutan	*Nephelium lappaceum*	648
Mango	*Mangifera sp.*	165
Rattan (Palasan)	*Calamus maximus*	9,064

Source: CSVFA (2001).

tant native tree species are delicate and easily damaged and they have a poor survival rate in the nursery. The association's farmers have now perfected a technique based on local knowledge that uses indigenous materials, such as banana or abaca bracts, to wrap and protect them.

Between 1997 and 2001, the CSVFA sold tree seedlings worth 721,514 pesos (approximately US$13,600) to private individuals, government agencies, multinational private companies and NGOs all over the country. In many instances, clients also requested the association to provide the labour for tree planting and also to train local people on seedling production and rainforestation. On some occasions, farmer organizations in other places sent members to Baybay to receive training on seedling production from the CSVFA. Not only has this served as a source of income for the association, it has also enhanced the morale and self-confidence of members and increased their feeling of responsibility for forest protection and management.

Eco-tourism

In order to promote eco-tourism, the CSVFA established an excursion area where it constructed concrete and wooden kiosks along the bank of the river. For tourists interested in experiencing the forest and watching wildlife, the association also established a bunkhouse inside the protected area. This doubles as a watch-tower and a base for patrol teams monitoring the activities of illegal loggers and *kaingineros*. The CBFM area, which the association has promoted as "Jungle Valley", is now a popular destination for local tourists, students and ecologists. In addition, several tourists and students from Europe and Japan have visited the CSVFA and many have received training in seedling production and rainforestation from the farmers. To ensure the safety of visitors, the association always assigns a group of farmers and youth members to guide and assist the visitors during their climb into the forest. When necessary, families of farmer members also assist in the preparation of food for the visitors for a minimum fee.

Organic farming

Members of the CSVFA are actively involved in rice and vegetable production in their respective small parcels of land. The Cienda and San Vicente villages are major suppliers of vegetables to the town of Baybay, which has a total population of 95,630 (NSO 2000). To promote sustainable agriculture, the association also initiated organic vegetable production, with several members volunteering to produce vegetables on their farms without the use of inorganic fertilizers and pesticides. This has caught the interest of many consumers who are concerned about the increasing levels of pesticide residue in agricultural products.

Others

The CSVFA has set up a small convenience store (*sari-sari store*) which sells basic commodities within the village. The store is operated by female members on a rotation basis, with an income-sharing arrangement. The association also operates a small *sinamay* production project. *Sinamay* is a home-made cloth made from abaca (Manila hemp) fibre and is a popular export commodity. The association gets its raw material from the abaca plantations inside the CBFM area.

Factors that enhanced innovativeness

Several crucial factors have enhanced the innovativeness of the communities and contributed to the success of their initiatives, including environmental awareness, volunteerism, empowerment of the people, leadership, use of local knowledge and external support.

Environmental awareness

The level of innovation within the community was enhanced by the high level of people's awareness of the danger of unabated forest destruction. One of the factors that raised people's awareness was the water scarcity they faced in the mid-1980s. It was this scarcity that resulted in the formation of KUFA, which aimed to prevent further forest destruction.

Another factor was the effective environmental awareness campaign conducted by the Regional Applied Communication Project, a foreign-funded initiative of the US Agency for International Development (USAID) through the Philippine Council for Agriculture Resources Research and Development and based at the ViSCA in the late 1980s. The initiative utilized multimedia approaches such as radio plays, songs and paintings to raise people's awareness about the negative environmental effects of deforestation, mining and destructive fishing activities. This was followed by an intensive environmental awareness campaign through seminars and training conducted by the Joint Project on Applied Tropical Ecology between ViSCA and GTZ (German Technical Development Cooperation Agency) and held not just in Baybay but in the whole of Leyte.

Last, but not least, the greatest contributor to people's environmental awareness was the tragic flood of Ormoc City, only 40 km away, which convinced people of the immediate dangers of forest destruction.

The high level of community awareness was evident in people's participation in environmental protests against mining exploration and power transmission projects that would have damaged the last remaining forest of Baybay. In 1997, the Philippine National Oil Company in Tongonan, Leyte, made known its plan to conduct mining exploration in its forest reservation covering a great part of the Central Highlands. Local communities, church organizations, NGOs and ViSCA strongly opposed the plan because many areas in western Leyte, including Baybay, would have been seriously affected. The CSVFA was among the citizen organizations that actively participated in the strong public protest, which resulted in the project being cancelled in 1998.

Between 1999 and 2002 there were also widespread protests by local communities, including the CSVFA, NGOs, church organizations and Leyte State University, against the National Power Corporation's proposal to construct power transmission lines from the geothermal plant in Tongonan, Leyte, to Mindanao and Bohol islands in the south. Protests centred on the fact that the power lines could result in the destruction of a great portion of the last remaining forest in Baybay.[8]

Volunteerism and commitment

Another key factor enabling the CSVFA to implement its highly innovative initiatives was the strong volunteer spirit and commitment of its members. Despite the fact that no clear benefit except the protection of the watershed was recognized, members still proved dedicated to the association right from its initiation. For instance, members volunteered their physical labour to carry materials (bags of cement, steel and other materials) about 10 km into the forest to construct the bunkhouse.

All of the association's projects are run by volunteer labour, including the patrolling of the forest reserve and seedling production. The high level of environmental awareness among members and the existence of a common threat to their livelihood are the main factors shaping their commitment to the project. Members are well aware that if the watershed is not protected the communities will be in grave danger from flooding and from the loss of their source of livelihood. As CSVFA member Leopoldo Alao (or Nong Polding) aptly put it during an interview in March 2003, "the survival of our children and the children of our children is at risk if we will not protect the watershed".

Another factor leading to the strong level of volunteer spirit and commitment is the relatively close personal relationship among most members of the association. They relate to each other like family, with a strong emphasis on the importance of mutual support.

Active involvement of people

Another element that has undoubtedly contributed to the innovativeness and the success of the activities of the CSVFA is the active involvement of members in the planning and decision-making processes. All activities and projects are planned and discussed through focus group discussions and meetings and then subjected to approval by the general assembly. This system gives all members the opportunity to voice opinions about the activities and plans of the association. If a majority of the members think that a particular activity or issue is disadvantageous to them, then it will not be approved during the general assembly.

The CBFM designation awarded by the government through the DENR also had a significant impact on people's attitudes. The right given to the communities to protect and utilize the forest, through its CBFM status, greatly encouraged the members of the CSVFA to participate actively and to work harder to protect and manage the forest.

Leadership

The success or failure of any initiative greatly hinges on the ability of its leaders and their style of leadership. The CSVFA is led by a board of directors whose members are experienced and respected. The board members are very concerned with the welfare of the members of the organization, and their strong leadership has contributed to the success of initiatives conducted by the CSVFA. The style of leadership shown by the board is democratic and transparent, in the sense that all important decisions are presented to the general assembly for final approval. Furthermore, reports on every issue addressed at board meetings are disseminated and explained to all members of the CSVFA.

The election of board members by secret ballot ensures that those elected are the genuine choice of the majority. A two-year term, which is relatively short, also ensures that inactive board members can be replaced at the next election.

Use of local knowledge

Utilization of local knowledge, particularly from older and more experienced members of the organization, contributed to the sustainability of CSVFA initiatives. Local knowledge was invaluable for several of the livelihood projects including, *inter alia*, wildling and seed collection, the raising and planting of seedlings of native species, and the monitoring of wildlife (Bande et al. 1997). Knowledge of the flowering behaviour of some valuable species of trees, some of which flower only very rarely for example, enabled members to collect seeds at the right time. Another example was knowledge about the use of local materials to protect easily damaged wildlings after collection. With regard to wildlife monitoring, it was their experience of the forest that helped farmers to identify wild animals. Local knowledge also played a key role in ensuring the safety of visitors to the forest because it allowed farmers to predict floods based on signals that only they could understand. The farmers were also able to warn visitors of poisonous and dangerous plants in the forest.

Much of this local knowledge was passed down from the parents and grandparents of members, who were also farmers who worked in the forest throughout their lives. The transfer of local knowledge generally occurred in the family by informal means such as daily farm work. It also occurred through informal discussions during public events, such as parties and celebrations that were attended by many association members. The transfer of local knowledge from older members to young people was ensured by the involvement of youth members in many activities.

External support

The availability of external support also greatly enhanced the success of the organization. One key supporter was the Institute of Tropical Ecology of ViSCA (now LSU), which provided voluntary technical support, particularly on the characterization of the bio-physical environment of the CBFM area, and in conducting environmental awareness seminars for CSVFA members. LSU also facilitated financial and technical support provided through the German-funded ViSCA/GTZ Applied Tropical Ecology Program. This project, which ended in 1999, helped the communities to acquire important basic knowledge on rainforestation and provided for the seedling nursery. The provincial government of Leyte provided 100,000 pesos for the water systems in the Cienda and San

Vicente villages in 1999, and another 90,000 pesos in 2001 for the *sinamay* project and abaca production.

An NGO called Voluntary Service Philippines gave 40,000 pesos for the construction of a multipurpose training hall, which now also serves as the association's office. The Haribon Foundation[9] provided technical support for wildlife identification and protection activities. ELAC provided legal advice and lawyers to file court cases against illegal loggers and conducted training for members in order to equip them with basic knowledge on the apprehension of violators of forestry laws. More recently, the European Nature Heritage Fund (Euronatur)[10] provided technical support for the monitoring of the rainforestation site in Cienda. As discussed above, the role of the DENR in designating the area a CBFM site also represented a highly significant external contribution.

Barriers to innovativeness

There were several factors that hindered the capacity of the communities, and the CSVFA in particular, to conduct successful innovative initiatives. Many of these were overcome by the efforts of the association.

The most predominant barrier to the CSVFA's activities was poverty. The average monthly household income, equal to approximately US$40, is below the poverty line in the Philippines. Poverty affected the association in that some of its members could not participate in activities, despite their willingness to volunteer, because it would take them away from their paid employment. In order to address this problem, the association devised an arrangement whereby members acting as tour or hiking guides received a minimum of 150 pesos per day to be paid by the visitors. Members were also assisted financially by the various livelihood projects outlined above.

Another barrier that needed to be overcome was the lack of cooperation by some people in the communities who were not members of the association. The spreading of false and damaging rumours about some members, and about the association itself, occurred on various occasions and resulted in minor misunderstandings among some members. Other conflicts have occurred between members and non-members regarding the interpretation of restrictive policies within CBFM areas. This problem was addressed by inviting non-members to a dialogue and explaining the policies in question to them.

Another barrier to the association's projects was the low demand for the seedlings of native tree species in the Philippines. This resulted in a slowing of seedling production by the association. This low demand was attributed to lack of support by the government for the use of native species in its reforestation projects. Although an increasing number of government officials are becoming aware of the great potential for the use of native species in reforestation, most seedling purchases have been made by private organizations and NGOs. In a few cases, some private companies ordered seedlings but were never able to make payments. This also slowed down seedling production. To avoid such a situation arising again, the association now requires assurance (and some advance payment if possible) from organizations that order seedlings.

The departure of active members has also affected the success of activities. The most recent case was the departure of one very active member who served as the link between the association and the LSU. This member left in 2002 to take up graduate studies abroad. The board has now appointed another active member, who recently graduated from LSU, as the new project manager.

On some occasions, political pressure has taken its toll of the activities of the association. In 2001, for example, when two illegal loggers were caught by the forest wardens and convicted in court, the association was placed under intense pressure from an influential politician to withdraw the case. The officers and members of the association strongly believed that, if they succumbed to pressure and allowed the violators to go unpunished, this would not only greatly discourage members but also encourage potential violators. They resisted political pressure and the illegal loggers were imprisoned.

Finally, the lack of financial resources needed to support projects has also functioned as a barrier to innovation. For instance, one major initiative still awaiting capital is a small-scale mineral water bottling project. The watershed offers high-quality mineral water, but the association is constrained by the lack of capital necessary to purchase the required bottling machine. Such a project would further reinforce the need to protect the watershed to maintain the quantity and quality of its water, while at the same time improving the financial status of the association and its members.

Other areas where financial resources are needed include the securing of communication facilities (two-way radios) to improve the capability of the forest patrol teams and to enhance the safety of members and visitors who enter the forest. Another badly needed project involves conducting an inventory of natural resources (trees, water, soil and wildlife) in the watershed. To address the lack of financial resources, the community, with the help of volunteers from LSU, has sent applications for research and development grants to funding institutions. In September 2003, a modest grant was awarded in collaboration with a university in North America to finance a participatory natural resource inventory in the Cienda watershed.

The implications of lessons learned

Several lessons can be learned from the experiences of this farmer association in the communities of Cienda and San Vicente in the Philippines. This case shows that local communities can be innovative by using their skills to implement new and creative ways of protecting and managing forest resources that are vital to their existence. A strong sense of commitment and volunteerism by community members is a critical factor for success. No amount of funding from external sources can result in such success without this type of community involvement. At the same time, it must be noted that viable livelihood projects to augment the income of the poor farmers were inseparably tied to the successful forest protection achieved by the CSVFA.

It is also clear that, as with any organization, good leadership is essential. The democratic leadership demonstrated by the CSVFA board was a key factor in opening the project up to new ideas from within the organization and outside.

From this case it can also be determined that the sustainability of forest protection and management efforts is highly dependent on the use of local knowledge and locally available materials in reforestation activities. In particular, the use of native tree species adds value to the forest and increases the importance of protecting it.

According to Charles Landry (Chapter 3 in this volume), innovation implies some process of creative or imaginative thinking, for example the capacity to see a problem in a new way. He also argues that communities that are poor and not well educated can still achieve great innovation. What is imperative, rather, is the presence of several other crucial factors, such as environmental awareness, volunteerism and commitment, people empowerment, the use of local knowledge and external support. The imaginative ways in which the CSVFA members have effectively solved their environmental problems clearly support Landry's argument.

Finally, the experience of the CSVFA shows that community-based management of forest resources can be effective, provided there is active support from external agencies and organizations such as local government, government agencies, universities and NGOs. In particular, technical support is necessary to enhance environmental awareness among members and to teach them new methods related to environmental management. Financial support is also key because it provides the community with seed money for livelihood projects. As has been commonly observed in many foreign-funded initiatives throughout the Philippines, however, excessive financial assistance has been counterproductive and has commonly led to failure. Thus, modest financial assistance, particularly for the purpose of obtaining much-needed facilities or as seed money for the livelihood projects of the community, appears ideal.

Conclusion

The chapter has presented an analysis of the innovative strategies developed by the CSVFA to solve the environmental problems faced by two communities. The communities faced a series of barriers such as poverty, lack of government policy to support rainforestation projects and lack of financial resources. This case clearly shows, however, that other salient elements such as environmental awareness, volunteerism, commitment, people empowerment, leadership, the use of local knowledge and external support can enhance the innovative ability of communities and can contribute significantly to the success of initiatives.

The continued technical or material support of external organizations such as LSU, DENR, local government, NGOs and other institutions in the Philippines or abroad will no doubt have a tremendous impact on the future development of the CSVFA and its forest preservation activities. Making the organization a long-term partner in forest resource protection and management, rather than merely the recipient of financial support, would no doubt greatly enhance the further development of the organization. This is particularly the case since the community is dynamic and will continue to evolve as new projects and activities are realized.

Acknowledgements

The writing of this article would not have been possible without the wholehearted support, cooperation and kindness extended to us by the leaders and members of the CSVFA. In particular, we are greatly indebted to the board of directors (Agustino Valenzona, Dominador Polea, Leopoldo Alao, Absalon Betonio, Florencio Tabaranza, Babyluz Napoles and Renato Poliquit) and to Jimmy Pogosa, Mating Bande and Joseph Maceda. We wish also to thank the Innovative Communities project team at UNU for their kind support for the preparation of this article and, most of all, for the encouragement and happiness their visit to the Cienda and San Vicente communities brought to the farmer members.

Notes

1. Leyte has a total land area of 8,000 km^2 and is located between 124°17′ and 125°18′ east longitude and between 9°55′ and 10°48′ north latitude.

2. Some small tributaries upstream are the source of drinking water not only for the community but for more than 4,000 households in the municipality of Baybay.
3. Presidential Decree No. 705, otherwise known as the Forestry Reform Code of the Philippines issued by then President F. E. Marcos on 19 May 1975, prohibits the cutting, gathering and/or collecting of timber or other forest products without a licence.
4. *Rainforestation* is a concept of rehabilitating degraded lands or restoring forests using native tree species. In the first few years, shade-loving agricultural crops are planted in between the trees to provide a source of food and cash to the farmer. It is based on the hypothesis that a farming system is more sustainable when its physical structure and species composition are closer to the local rainforest. For more details, see Margraf and Milan (1996a, 1996b).
5. For more details of the case, see ⟨http//www.elac.org.ph/cienda3-1.html⟩.
6. ANR is a recent reforestation strategy adopted by the DENR involving adding species to the existing ones in a particular site. The naturally regenerated seedlings in the site are allowed to grow, instead of being eliminated during site preparation as occurs in the conventional reforestation strategy.
7. For additional information on rainforestation, see the Earth Report by the Television Trust for the Environment (TVE): ⟨http://www.tve.org/earthreport/archive/doc.cfm?aid=820⟩.
8. The protest actions have slowed down the project and successfully brought NPC to the negotiating table. As of November 2003, negotiations are still continuing between NPC and the other stakeholders. Because of pressure from the national government, LSU agreed in principle to allow the construction of the transmission lines in the university forest reservation provided that no trees were cut and that the university chose the tower sites. But the church and many church organizations in Baybay are still steadfast in their opposition to the project.
9. For the details of the organization, see ⟨http://www.haribon.org.ph/⟩.
10. For the details of the organization, see ⟨http://www.euronatur.org/⟩.

REFERENCES

Alvarez, H. (1992) "Even on the eve of the end of the world, plant a tree", in *Forestry for the people. Field research and theory on environment and development in the Cagayan Valley*, pp. 16–24. Cabagan, Isabela, Philippines: Cagayan Valley Program on Environment and Development of Isabela State University.
Asio, V. B. (1997) "A review of upland agriculture, population pressure and environmental degradation in the Philippines", *Annals of Tropical Research* 19(1): 1–18.
Bande, M. J. M. et al. (1997) "Farmer's knowledge as vital input to the rainforestation farming scheme", paper presented at the International Conference on Reforestation with Philippine Species, MacArthur Beach Resort, Tacloban, Leyte, Philippines, 3–6 March.
——— (1998) "Patag-Gabas-Kilim watershed: A community-based watershed management (the case of Cienda-San Vicente Farmers Association)", paper presented at the International Conference on Applied Tropical Ecology Aspect on Ecosystems Management in Tropical Asia, ViSCA, Baybay, Leyte, Philippines, 8–10 September.

Center for Environmental Concerns, Philippines (1996) "A primer on Philippine environmental data", Quezon City.

CSVFA [Cienda-San Vicente Farmers Association] (2000) "Community resource management framework: 2000–2025", unpublished CSVFA report.

────── (2001) "Summary of accomplishments", unpublished CSVFA report.

Drijver, C. A. and P. E. Sajise (1992) "Local resource management and environmental action research", in *Forestry for the people. Field research and theory on environment and development in the Cagayan Valley, Philippines*, pp. 213–224. Cabagan, Isabela, Philippines: Cagayan Valley Program on Environment and Development of Isabela State University.

Eller, E. and V. B. Asio (1991) "The flash-flood tragedy of Ormoc: A short analysis from a physio-geographical view", *Giessener Beitraege zur Entwicklungsforschung* (University of Giessen, Germany), Series 1, 19: 115–125.

Goeltenboth, F., ed. (1997) "Ecology of Mt. Pangasugan", unpublished material for distribution to government officials and visitors to the ViSCA-GTZ Applied Tropical Ecology Project in Baybay, Leyte.

Jahn, R. and V. B. Asio (2001) "Climate, geology, geomorphology and soils of the tropics with special reference to Leyte island", in F. Goeltenboth and V. B. Asio (eds), *Lecture Notes, 8th International Seminar-Workshop on Tropical Ecology*, pp. 25–43. Baybay, Leyte: Institute of Tropical Ecology, LSU.

Legal Rights and Natural Resources Center/Kasama Sa Kalikasan (1997) *A compilation of laws on natural resources and indigenous peoples' rights: A field handbook (vol. 2)*. Quezon City, Philippines.

Margraf, J. and P. P. Milan (1996a) "Ecology of Dipterocarp forests and its relevance for island rehabilitation in Leyte, Philippines", in A. Schulte and D. Schoene (eds), *Dipterocarp forest ecosystems*, pp. 124–154. Singapore: World Scientific Publishing.

────── (1996b) "Rainforestation farming: A farmer's guide for biodiversity utilization in the Philippines", ViSCA-GTZ Applied Tropical Ecology Program.

NSO (2000) *Census of population, Eastern Visayas*. Manila: National Statistics Office.

Ong, P. S. and N. P. Ibuna (2000) "Highlights of the National Biodiversity Conservation Priority-Setting Workshop", Subic, Zambales, 4–8 December 2000. DENR, USAID, University of the Philippines and Conservation International.

10

Waste management activities in Nagoya City, Japan: Local government and community partnerships

Teruhiko Yoshimura and Rika Kato

Introduction

The past decade has witnessed an important and innovative paradigm shift in the field of urban environmental planning and management in Japan that has resulted in the crucial move toward a resource-recycling society. Key to this paradigm shift has been the now familiar reversal of the top–down approach to planning in favour of a bottom–up approach and the rejection of centralized standardization in favour of local diversity and uniqueness. In particular, the concepts and practices of participation and partnership have been widely advocated.

This chapter examines Nagoya City's waste management system within the context of this paradigm shift. We will show how the leadership exercised by the local government was crucial to the city's dramatic reduction in solid waste. What was also important was that the government recognized very early that widespread community support was going to be a critical factor in ensuring that any innovations in waste management were successful. This is what makes the city of Nagoya an interesting case study. It shows how a combination of a top–down and bottom–up approach can be the most effective with regard to the implementation of innovations in waste management.

The Nagoya case shows how the local government worked in close partnership with an active network of community-based organizations to ensure the widespread implementation of a new waste management system. It was through working closely with these community networks that local government was able to incorporate community feedback into its waste management efforts. This not only ensured greater effectiveness but also facilitated much of the innovation that helped make the new waste management system a success. This chapter will explore these innovations in detail, paying particular attention to the methods applied by local government and the role played by different neighbourhood associations and other citizen-led bodies in Nagoya.

Background

The city of Nagoya is located in central Japan on the Ise Bay. It is a major industrial city and also a centre for international trade via Nagoya Port. As of March 2003, the population of Nagoya was just over 2 million.[1] Like many major cities in Japan, which is a mountainous country with scarce workable land, Nagoya is faced with an excess of solid waste and a lack of space for new landfills. Owing to the large size of the city, it has been more difficult for Nagoya than for other smaller cities to implement a sorting and recycling programme. It is this problem, coupled with the city government's attempt to build new waste dumps in an area called the Fujimae Tidelands, that led to the start of the city's waste reduction programme.

An examination of Nagoya's efforts in waste reduction would be incomplete without first discussing some of the issues relating to the plans for land reclamation of the Fujimae Tidelands. These tidelands are located in a part of Ise Bay and Nagoya Port that has now been designated as a protected site through the Ramsar Convention on Wetlands.[2] The Fujimae Tidelands were the symbol that inspired the citizens of Nagoya to take action and around which they rallied in favour of waste reduction. Although a detailed analysis of both sides of the tidelands dispute is not within the scope of this chapter, which focuses on the waste reduction initiative that followed its resolution, it is nonetheless important to understand some of the key arguments involved.

The city government of Nagoya had planned to reclaim the Fujimae Tidelands area and convert it into a landfill. The government stressed that the current city solid waste disposal site was nearly full and claimed that the tideland area was the only possible site for a new landfill. This move was opposed by local, national and global citizens and environmental protection groups that highlighted the significance of the tidelands for migratory birds and for the ecosystem of Ise Bay. The groups fought hard to prevent construction from starting. In January 1999, Nagoya City caved in to pressure from the groups, and also to criticism from the Environment Agency of Japan, and abandoned its plans to reclaim the tidelands.

The cancellation of the landfill project was a turning point for the city government. The plan for the Fujimae Tidelands project had been in the making for 17 years (Matsubara 2001: 16, 29). During those years, societal concern for the environment and the growing priority of environmental conservation over government development plans became a common theme in the media and in the consciousness of the people. Furthermore, in 1997 a government reclamation project went ahead in Isehaya Bay in southern Japan despite widely publicized citizen protests. This only served to increase community doubt about the prioritization of development over the environment. In the end, the plan to reclaim the Fujimae Tidelands was not able to withstand the pressure of changing public views even though it was slightly adjusted over the years to cover a smaller area (Matsubara 2001: 16, 29).

Prior to the cancellation of the Fujimae reclamation plan, attempts to reduce waste in Nagoya had been based primarily on technological fixes. After 1975, efforts were made to increase waste-processing capacity by improving incineration facilities. In addition, a new system that involved the separate sorting and collection of combustible and non-combustible refuse was initiated. The incineration of combustible waste and the crushing and sorting of non-combustible waste both contributed to a reduction in the volume of waste dumped in landfills. Despite these efforts, however, by the mid-1990s existing city landfills were quickly approaching their maximum capacity.

In the early 1990s, the city had been largely unsuccessful in setting up the infrastructure required for waste recycling. As of 1997, only 7 of the 16 wards of Nagoya were recycling metal cans and glass bottles. The remaining 9 wards separated waste into only three types: burnable, non-burnable and oversized (Matsubara 2001: 56). Through most of the 1990s, recycling activities in Nagoya were largely conducted by a non-governmental organization (NGO) called Chubu Recycle Shimin no Kai (hereafter Chubu Recycle).[3] Beginning in 1991, this NGO set up recycling stations in the parking lots of shopping centres and in local neighbourhoods. Although early efforts to cooperate with city hall were unsuccessful, Chubu Recycle's impressive figures resulted in it being allocated funds from the city in an effort to support its recycling activities. It was in this manner that the infrastructure for recycling in Nagoya was created.

Faced with a dire situation after the cancellation of the Fujimae Tidelands reclamation project, the city of Nagoya issued a "Waste Emergency Declaration" in February 1999. This declaration indicated that the reduction of solid waste had become the city's most important issue. From August 2000, Nagoya City pioneered a new sorting and collection system of recyclable solid waste based on the Containers and Packaging Recycling Law. The main purpose of the new system was to promote the recycling of plastic and paper containers and packaging, which made up approximately 60 per cent of the total of solid waste volume.[4] This law, which had taken effect nationally in April of the same year, was new and untested.

Of the major cities in Japan, only Sapporo and Nagoya enacted the law. In total, only 15 per cent of local authorities enacted the law nationwide and, even then, the city of Sapporo enacted the new law only with regard to plastic and not paper. Nagoya was the only major city that chose to enact the law fully with regard to both paper and plastic packaging and containers (Matsubara 2001: 176). The new law, in all its complexity, required a radical change in waste disposal behaviour by citizens. In response, the city of Nagoya launched an enormous public education and change campaign. The main component of this campaign was conducted through neighbourhood organizations called *chonaikai*.

Local government initiatives

It was the local government that took the lead in initiating the city's new waste reduction programme. Faced with the cancellation of the plan to construct a landfill in the Ise Bay, the city government developed an alternative plan that instead aimed to reduce the amount of waste being produced. City officials realized very early that the programme would have to be implemented city-wide and achieve strong participation from citizens in order to be successful. As a consequence, the plans that were developed and the programmes that were implemented focused explicitly on harnessing the cooperation of citizens.

Introduction of sorting and collection systems

Nagoya's goals for the reduction of solid waste were outlined in the Waste Emergency Declaration in February 1999. This declaration set the city's two-year goal for waste reduction at 200,000 tons, or a 20 per cent reduction. The declaration also called directly on citizens to cooperate in the ongoing "Waste Reduction Effort 100" programme, which was yet to enjoy much success. This programme called upon each citizen to reduce his or her waste output by 100 grams per day. The declaration further called on private enterprises not only to reduce waste but also to engage in better production and sales practices aimed at less waste production (Nagoya City 2002b: 69).

In order to achieve the goals outlined in the declaration, the enactment of the Containers and Packaging Recycling Law was the main policy to be implemented. This epoch-making law recognized that the responsibility for recycling was to be borne by the business entities that produce and use packages and containers. Because the new system required under the law was so complex, the city government began preparing for its implementation about one year before it was to be initiated. The Environmental Affairs Bureau of Nagoya City led this effort, which included various logistical arrangements such as negotiations with concerned authorities, the preparation of educational materials and manuals, and the training of collection staff. At the same time, city officials planned explanatory meetings for each *chonaikai* to ensure that the local people understood the new system. Prior to these explanatory meetings, the city coordinated with municipal health commissioners in the spring of 2000, because they were to act as the go-betweens for city hall and the *chonaikai*.

In the two months leading up to the introduction of the new system, more than 2,300 meetings targeting the *chonaikai* were held. The city government prepared and distributed four kinds of illustrated brochure in five languages to every household. Other methods of campaigning included announcements in newspapers, on billboards and on television and radio, as well as in other media. As a result of the campaign, the city office was swamped with requests for more explanatory meetings and telephone enquiries.

Despite these extensive efforts, the start of the new sorting and collection system caused serious confusion. The implementation of the system also generated much resistance from citizens, who resented its top–down nature. For over a month, the telephones of environmental works offices and other related divisions were constantly engaged. Approximately 20,000 enquiries were made to special hotlines over the first three months after implementation began. If faxes, letters and Internet-based enquiries are also included in this figure, the number of enquiries and opinions doubles. In response to requests, a number of follow-up explanatory meetings were held for *chonaikai*.

Challenges faced

Although Nagoya's new policies have proven to be successful in reducing waste, they have not escaped criticism. The city government made efforts to respond to complaints from citizens to the greatest extent possible. Many of the complaints related to the ways and means of collection, such as location and frequency, and had easy solutions. Based on citizens' requests, for example, the government decided to increase the collection frequency of plastic/paper recyclables from once every two weeks to weekly from April 2001.

Not all complaints were so easy to address, particularly when they related specifically to the details of the Containers and Packaging Recycling Law. From the people's point of view, this new system based on a national law was unreasonable. For example, containers made of exactly the same material had to be separated into different categories of waste, based on criteria such as where the item was purchased or who used it. Further, it was unclear how to handle items containing more than one type of material (for example, paper with plastic coating).

Another major criticism of the Containers and Packaging Recycling Law in general was that it did not reflect the ideals of the Polluter Pays Principle. The cost of the collection, transportation and storage of plastic containers and packaging fell on the local authorities and, as a result, Nagoya City's budget for waste management began to increase. The more the city recycled, the more the budget required for collection vehicles and staff increased. Some people believe that these costs should be paid by the producer of the container or wrapper and then passed on to the consumer through an increase in the cost of the product (*Asahi Shimbun*, 14 April 2003, p. 14).

Although it was difficult for the local government to address these issues in the short term, it made an effort to address the inherent faults of the law in the long term. Both the city government and the city assembly made proposals to the national government regarding improvements in the law. These proposals, which were the result of the shared implementation struggles of both citizens and government officials, were made through the Japan Waste Management Association in 2000.

Community initiatives

Communities and community-based groups in Nagoya played a key role in working in partnership with the city government, and also on their own voluntarily, to implement the waste reduction programme. The central role was played by the neighbourhood organizations, or *chonaikai*, and the municipal health commissioners.

The neighbourhood associations

The neighbourhood association, called *chonaikai* or *jichikai*, was established by the government in 1940. It was established as the smallest governing body to control people's lives under a wartime regime. In addition to being a functional messenger of local government and the smallest unit of public administration, *chonaikai* also dealt with local affairs as a neighbourhood self-governing body. Even though the dissolution of the *chonaikai* was forced during Japan's post-war occupation, social needs such as peacekeeping, public health and the distribution of life's daily necessities led to their re-establishment. They were weakened significantly in the 1960s when high economic growth brought about rapid urbanization and the *chonaikai* had difficulty adapting to the associated changes in life-style. This trend was accelerated by the strengthened social guarantees provided by government and a move away from mutual help activities that related to the reduction of farm work.

In the 1970s, citizens' groups such as NGOs and volunteer groups started to receive greater attention as a new type of community-based organization. This increase in attention was at the direct expense of the traditional *chonaikai*. These new types of organization were composed of individual members who joined on a voluntary basis. They had a clear vision and objectives that were focused on specific activities such as environmental conservation or townscape preservation. Such citizens' groups were playing an increasingly active role in addressing the social needs generated by, among other things, rapid urbanization, environmental deterioration, an ageing society and the lack of governmental support. Although these groups are often praised for achieving good results in specific fields, they are also criticized for not functioning as community-based organizations that satisfy the actual social needs of a community. There is a recent movement to reassess the value of the traditional *chonaikai* and we compare the types of citizens' groups in Table 10.1.

In Nagoya, 10–20 households form a *kumi*, or "group", and approximately 10–20 *kumi* make up each *chonaikai*. Nagoya is divided into 260 elementary school districts, with each district covering approximately 10–30 *chonaikai* (see Figure 10.1). Within the school district, the School District Association acts as the liaison between the different *chonaikai* within the district. Heads of the *chonaikai* are members of the School District Associations, which also include representatives from other groups such as local welfare commissioners, municipal health commissioners, local volunteer fire corps, women's associations, children's associations, crime/fire prevention associations, senior citizens' groups and parent–teacher

Table 10.1 Intermediate organizations between government and citizens

Type of organization	Salient features
Traditional neighbourhood-based association (*chonaikai*)	Household membership – every household within a district is a member (in principle) Deals with a wide range of local affairs
Citizen group, non-governmental organization, non-profit organization, volunteer group	Individual membership – only interested persons become members voluntarily Takes action for specific objectives

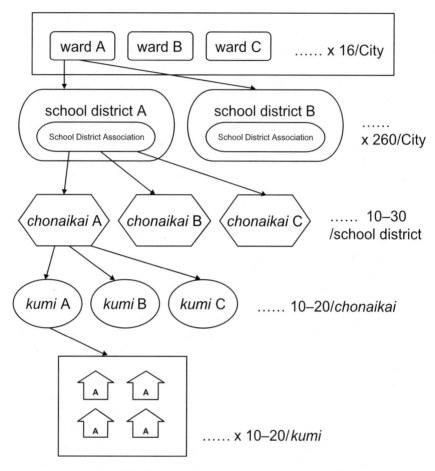

Figure 10.1 Organizational structure of Nagoya City.

associations. People usually join the *chonaikai* in an effort to get along well with their neighbours. Approximately 80–90 per cent of households become paying members of their *chonaikai*, although this percentage varies depending on the district. The situation also differs between urban downtown areas, longstanding residential areas and newly developed residential areas.

Each of the 16 ward offices of the city government have community relations divisions that are in charge of maintaining relationships between various citizens' groups, particularly the School District Associations. Heads of the School District Associations meet with government officials monthly at the ward offices. Any information to be passed down to citizens is transmitted to the leaders of each *chonaikai* in their jurisdiction. Information is then transmitted down to each *kumi* and circulated to every household. This is the system through which each household receives information from the city government.

Urbanization has, in many cases, relegated the traditional community-based organizations of *chonaikai* to a mere formality that functions only at the receiving end of governmental work. Yet, there are still some areas where *chonaikai* are active in conducting self-help activities for community members, even in urban areas such as Nagoya. In 1998, the Nagoya city government conducted a survey regarding the concept of self-governance. In response to this survey, 68.4 per cent of school districts said that they consider these neighbourhood-based organizations to be self-governing bodies and not just the receiving-end of governmental services. In reality, in some areas the *chonaikai* and School District Associations organize many community-based activities, such as athletic meets, festivals and fire drills, in an effort to maintain social harmony. The base of these activities is the community centres that have, since 1981, been constructed in school districts by the city government as a community development project.

In Nagoya, the *chonaikai* functioned as the organization through which the new system of waste sorting and collection was introduced. The community network, which began at the household level and expanded into school districts, functioned well. It was partly because of the extensive and well-functioning nature of this network that waste reduction initiatives were so successful. It should be noted, however, that a considerable gap existed between active and inactive *chonaikai* and the challenge of tackling this disparity is still an issue of concern. For example, the *chonaikai* in the Hibitsu school district of Nakamura ward were so active and innovative that they made an original solid waste collection map and consulted with individual residents for an entire year before the government's new sorting system took effect. Some *chonaikai* considered that every household should attend meetings, and thus organized meetings on several occasions. In other areas, meetings were held merely out of duty; individual citizens were not invited and only *chonaikai* leaders attended. In areas where there was active *chonaikai* participation and commitment, the new waste management system started smoothly.

Municipal health commissioners and ward administration commissioners

Since 1947, municipal health commissioners have been appointed by Nagoya's mayor, based on the recommendations made by the directors of health centres. The role of the municipal health commissioners is to promote citizen awareness and participation in local public health activities. Their duties are to cooperate with regard to: (a) health centre works; (b) environmental works; and (c) other public health works. The commissioners serve for a period of two years and, at present, there are approximately 7,400 in Nagoya.

The municipal health commissioners played a very important role in the *chonaikai* during the implementation of the new sorting and collection system. During the preparations for the introduction of the new system, municipal health commissioners liaised with the environmental works office, obtaining information on the explanatory meetings and then consulting with *chonaikai* heads to set up meeting schedules. Often the municipal health commissioners reserved rooms in community centres, informed community members and kept in contact with officials. The municipal health commissioners played a major role as an interface between local people and the local government. Public awareness regarding the new waste management initiatives depended heavily on the leadership of these commissioners.

Since 1968, the mayor has also appointed ward administration commissioners, based on recommendations from the directors of ward offices. This post was established in an attempt to raise citizen consciousness with regard to self-governance. It was also aimed at increasing citizen cooperation in the administrative work that was becoming more complicated each year. The duties of ward administration commissioners are: (a) publicity for municipal/ward information and the collection of citizens' opinions and their communication to the city; (b) cooperation with disaster prevention activities; (c) local social education activities; (d) promotion of citizens' activities; and (e) cooperation with other municipal/ward works. Approximately 5,200 citizens are commissioned at present, each serving a two-year term. In many cases, ward administration commissioners also serve as head of a *chonaikai*. With regard to the introduction of the new waste management system in Nagoya, the administration commissioners supported the municipal health commissioners by inviting community people to meetings.

The role of NGOs

In addition to the collaborative effort that took place within the governmental framework, the successful reduction of solid waste in Nagoya was due largely to the efforts of community-initiated groups and movements. Chubu Recycle was one of the leading NGOs promoting solid waste reduction and it played a significant role in various city-wide initiatives. Chubu Recycle, along with a number of other NGOs, launched a public campaign through the media and also facilitated and supported local activities utilizing the expertise and experience of local people. As the frontrunners in recycling in Nagoya, Chubu Recycle served as an example of what could be done in the city to work towards a sustainable recycling society. As of July 2002, the organization had 33 recycling stations, and each station collected up to 10 different types of material. The recycling stations were located in supermarket parking lots or other areas, and were maintained by the citizens themselves. Funding and other assistance in the form of publicity were obtained from the business sector and also the city government. The stations not only helped to reduce waste but also served as a catalyst to get the city's initiatives up and going. Chubu Recycle shared its expertise and experience with the city government as it endeavoured to create its own recycling infrastructure. The NGO not only provided advice on technical matters, but also shared its experience in citizen-led recycling. This proved to be a valuable resource for the city government, because citizen participation was crucial for the success of the new waste management system.

Striking results

Waste reduction

The city's efforts, in cooperation with its citizens, were highly effective in reducing the amount of solid waste generated in Nagoya, and the goals set out in the Waste Emergency Declaration were achieved. By July 2001, there was a 23 per cent reduction in the amount of non-recyclable solid waste being generated. The amount buried in landfills was halved (see Figure 10.2). As of August 2000, the per capita volume of waste had dropped to 902 g/person/day, compared with 1,251 g/person/day in 1998. This was significantly lower than the national average and is comparable to the 900 g/person/day of the average person in Germany (Nagoya City 2001: 4). Through its innovative, community-based waste management strategy, Nagoya achieved waste levels that were thought impossible for large cities in Japan. After only two years, the city's new system was being hailed nationwide as a frontrunner in waste management.

The introduction of the new collection system resulted in a steady increase in the amount of plastic and paper recyclables and also led to a reduction in non-recyclable solid waste levels (see Figure 10.3). This reduction in the production of non-recyclables was the result of a change in citizen consciousness with regard to the whole solid waste issue. The introduction of the new waste management system helped the citizens of

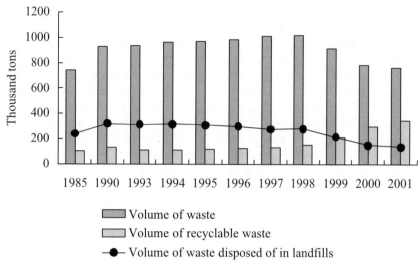

Figure 10.2 Trends in the volume of waste in Nagoya.
Sources: Nagoya City (2000a, 2002a).

Nagoya realize the significance of recycling. The introduction of the new system also stimulated local people to engage in other activities, such as the voluntary group collection of recyclables. Nagoya city government estimates that, as of late 2000, the voluntary collection of recyclable materials by citizens was responsible for approximately half of the reduction of total solid waste (Nagoya City 2000b: 3).

Awareness and community activity

The sorting and collection system that was introduced with the new Containers and Packaging Recycling Law had the effect of expanding the local human network in Nagoya. In order to address the difficulties that arose with residents who did not follow the new system, for example, the local people initiated a number of voluntary activities. These included such activities as putting up signs at collection stations and setting up rotations of guards among residents. The collection stations also turned out to be good places for people to engage in communication with their neighbours, as they discussed with each other the complicated ways and means of sorting. Even the complaints that people had turned out to be beneficial, because deeper communication between citizens and their government officials was also activated. As a result, this communication soon turned into constructive dialogue. Municipal health commissioners

Volume of recyclable waste collected by the city government

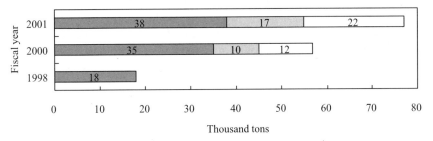

Thousand tons

■ Bottles, cans, PET bottles, and paper cartons ▨ Plastic containers and packaging
□ Paper containers and packaging

Volume of recyclable waste collected by citizens

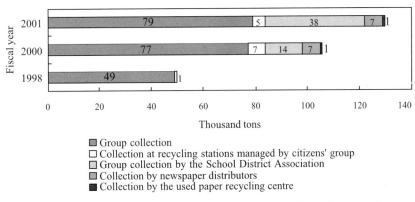

Thousand tons

▨ Group collection
□ Collection at recycling stations managed by citizens' group
▨ Group collection by the School District Association
▨ Collection by newspaper distributors
■ Collection by the used paper recycling centre

Figure 10.3 Trends in the volume of recyclable waste collected by the city government and by citizens.
Source: Nagoya City (2002a).

and heads of the *chonaikai* shared and exchanged opinions and experiences with leaders of other communities at meetings. They used their monthly meetings with government officials as an opportunity to express their opinions and to make proposals and suggestions for an improved collection system.

In these and many other ways, local people in the community initiated activities and began to work together on their own, and also with local government, to achieve the sustainable environmental management of their communities. For example, an elderly group established a non-profit organization (NPO) to look after regional recycling and provide advice to local people. Residents also created an environment-friendly shopping mall in a commercial district and made original eco-coins to circulate within the district. They also cooperated to install a compostor for the recycling of raw food waste in an apartment complex. This shows that local people have both the ability and the capacity to tackle community problems and manage their own environments when internal impetus or external pressure exists. In Nagoya's case, a government-initiated project stimulated residents' voluntary activities to improve their living environment and fostered their sense of ownership of the local environment.

As a result of the introduction of the new waste management system, the consumer behaviour of citizens also changed. According to a survey conducted by Nagoya University and a local NPO, the number of citizens who select their purchases on the basis of simple packaging, labels signifying environmental friendliness and refillable containers is increasing.[5]

Concrete results in waste reduction and raised citizen awareness have both been achieved in Nagoya and any future programmes are also expected to include citizen participation. In May 2002, Nagoya City revised its 3rd Waste Management Basic Plan with the following targeted objectives: (a) maintaining or reducing the total volume of waste (waste and recyclables) to 1,080,000 tons in FY 2010); (b) a 20 per cent reduction in the total volume of waste from 790,000 tons in FY 2000 to 620,000 tons in FY 2010; and (c) further efforts to achieve zero landfill (decreasing to a historically low level from 150,000 tons in FY 2000 to 20,000 tons in FY 2010). As part of the revision process, the city government publicized the new draft plan in December 2001 for public comment. In response, citizens sent in more than 1,000 opinions and proposals, 10 times as many as had been expected. The city government conflated these opinions into 238 issues by grouping similar ones together. These opinions were then reflected in the final plan.

Analysis

The trend toward Machi-zukuri

Recently in Japan, there has been a trend to implement local development efforts called *Machi-zukuri* ("community building/development"). The concept of *Machi-zukuri* is used mainly in the fields of architecture and urban planning. It is quite different from traditional urban planning, which is basically undertaken through a governmental top–down approach. *Machi-zukuri* is defined here as "the overall activities mainly initiated by residents and/or communities/community-based organizations in partnership with local governments, experts, various kinds of intermediary sectors, and the private sectors to enhance and improve the living environment and community environment in terms of its well-being and social development (software approach) as well as physical development (hardware approach)". Although *Machi-zukuri*, along with ideas such as "participation" and "partnerships", has become increasingly fashionable in Japan, there is still a wide gap between the rhetoric and actual practice. Government officials or planners, for example, sometimes believe that it is sufficient merely to go through the motions, to undertake some kind of workshop or establish a policy or institution to promote *Machi-zukuri* activities. In addition, some may be tempted to label their government work as being participatory in approach or as *Machi-zukuri*, merely in an effort to convey a softer image, while in reality their actual planning and management process remains quite conventional. The unfortunate reality is that, in many cases, behaviour and attitudes still reflect an unchanged government-dominated top–down approach.

Machi-zukuri activities are conducted through participation and partnerships. To improve a living environment, active participation and commitment by residents and community-based organizations is seen as indispensable. In *Machi-zukuri*, discussion, reflection and the sharing of common visions among many actors during the formulation, implementation, management, monitoring and evaluation of plans lead to a more favourable and comfortable living and urban environment. The process also leads to better governance and the building of better governance institutions. Through the *Machi-zukuri* process, people's awareness and confidence can be enhanced and their capacities improved. As a result, people will become empowered and social capital can be enhanced.

Machi-zukuri *in Nagoya*

The waste reduction programmes in Nagoya exhibit the characteristics of a *Machi-zukuri* approach in many ways. Both government and citizen groups realized that citizen participation in initiatives was indispensable to success, and thus both groups strove to achieve widespread participation. Although many programmes and policies were initially started by the city government, citizens voluntarily came together to work toward the management of their own environment. As the above discussion demonstrated, in some cases people began their own activities voluntarily, such as voluntary collections or the creation of "eco-coins". There was active two-way communication between citizens and local government, which led to the adaptation of policies and input into future policy-making. Through citizens' involvement and participation in the system, their awareness increased. Although Nagoya may not have achieved ideal *Machi-zukuri*, particularly in the sense that the city government functions as a leader in many ways, the city seems to be heading in this direction. From a national perspective, Nagoya's initiatives serve as a good example of a deviation from conventional urban planning methods.

Innovative aspects of Nagoya's initiatives

Leadership of local government

The success of Nagoya's waste reduction initiatives can be attributed to an effective partnership between local government and citizens. However, it should be noted that, without the local government's leadership and the resources at its disposal, this success could not have been achieved. An examination of the approaches taken by the Nagoya city government, in particular the Waste Emergency Declaration and the adoption of the Containers and Packaging Recycling Law, reveals the innovative nature of the leadership shown by the city government.[6]

Innovation often arises out of crisis[7] and the city government's Waste Emergency Declaration was the first step in spurring the radical changes that were to occur over the next few months and years. The mayor and city officials of Nagoya, having abandoned plans to reclaim the Fujimae Tidelands, and not being able to locate any alternative sites for dumps, were faced with a crisis. It was this reality that led to their innovative next move, which was to declare a "waste emergency". The city of Nagoya had no choice but to completely rethink its waste problem. It was that or face a city full of garbage with nowhere to go. The city was no longer able to calculate the estimated amount of waste that was expected to be produced, factoring in the likelihood of an increase, and plan accordingly for its disposal. With nowhere to dump waste, the city was forced to rethink the problem (i.e. how much waste was being produced) and come up with new solutions (separation, recycling, voluntary emission reduction). To this end, the goals outlined in the Waste Emergency Declaration were set at a high level.

The declaration of a waste management emergency signified a dramatic shift in policy. For years the city had maintained the same view on the city government's responsibilities toward waste management. This view was underpinned by the assumption that waste was a burden for the city and waste management was a service that should be provided by the city without imposing too much of a burden on the people. Past policies also relied almost entirely on technology, such as incineration. With the Waste Emergency Declaration, however, the city made a transition from hard to soft policy. Waste management staff were able to change gear to focus on awareness-raising programmes targeted at citizens and businesses about the need to reduce waste and increase recycling (Matsubara 2001: 134–135). Each additional success in waste reduction was accompanied by a slow change in the mindset of the city government. This resulted in a new appreciation of the role of citizen participation and a whole new way of thinking about who is responsible for waste.

In the summer of 2000, the city of Nagoya enacted the Containers and Packaging Recycling Law. The people of Nagoya now call this summer the "hot summer in Nagoya", referring not just to high temperatures but to the intensity of the "revolution" in waste reduction that ensued. As discussed above, the law was new and untested. Its enactment involved considerable risk and required an innovative approach. Also required was an extensive education campaign in order to address the complexities of the law and the system of separation it required.

Creating a vision for the future was another important step in facilitating innovation. In its ideal form, the people themselves might generate this vision. Yet, in practice, local governments, taking into consideration citizens' wants, often take the lead in creating and enacting plans toward a vision for the future of a city or community. This is what happened in Nagoya's case. As noted above, Nagoya's reputation with regard to waste management changed from "backward" to "frontrunner" in just two years. This was partly owing to the early successes of the waste reduction programme, including the achievement of a high level of citizen cooperation. This image change campaign was also an intentional and innovative approach by the city government. Beginning with the Waste Emergency Declaration, the city made a concerted and intentional effort to remake the image of Nagoya. This was exhibited in the declaration itself, which invites citizens to join in the challenge and to "welcome in the new century as the 'Waste Reducing Forerunning City'" (Nagoya City 2002b: 69). The personality and leadership shown by the mayor himself (often referred to as the "Garbage Mayor") were also significant and contributed to the creation of a new image for the future of Nagoya. Many have credited the leadership demonstrated by Mayor Matsubara as being a key factor in the city's successes in waste reduction.

Citizen-led innovations

Efforts by citizens and citizen groups were innovative in the way that they harnessed the talents and power of the people. As discussed above, voluntary citizen activities played a significant role in the successes of Nagoya's waste reduction programmes. Communities proved that they had sufficient knowledge and information about their local environment, social capital and available resources. Further, communities had the appropriate capacities to understand real situations, to respond to actual needs and to take concrete and collective action. Finally, communities proved to have the ability to forge effective partnerships with all related actors such as local government and NGOs.

The *chonaikai* heads and the municipal health commissioners, and the activism of the *chonaikai* in general, contributed to the transition toward a recycling society. They also contributed greatly to improved human relations within communities, and between communities and local government. In particular, the transformation of the *chonaikai* itself in Nagoya, from the receiving end of governmental services to a voluntary active organization, was one of the main innovations to arise from the city-wide waste reduction efforts.

The efforts of NGOs can be credited with supporting activities and also the participation of local people. Many small and innovative projects emerged around the city as citizens attempted to take local government programmes one step further. For example, an NGO called Namagomi Recycle no Kai (Food Waste Recycle Group) set up compost collectors around the city in neighbourhoods and at schools and developed a system for collection and composting using citizen volunteers. The city, impressed with the group's activities, later contracted the group to conduct the collection of food waste in certain areas of the city on a trial basis. Future implementation of city food waste collection is to be based on the results of these trials.

Synthesis and conclusion

Waste reduction initiatives in Nagoya were successful owing to the effective combination of top–down management by the city (providing a system for recycling) and the bottom–up activities of citizens and citizen groups (voluntary activities of *chonaikai*, NGOs and other citizen groups). First, the leadership of the local government in the midst of a crisis resulted in drastic policy change and attitude shifts in the city's approach to waste management and citizen participation. Further, citizens proved to be cooperative and resourceful, not only in developing partnerships with local government but also in initiating activities of their own. Apart from commendable results in waste reduction, communication among citizens, communities, NGOs and the local government was revitalized. The *chonaikai* were transformed from being only the receiver of public services into groups for collaborative and voluntary activities of citizens.

To create a recycling society in the future, partnerships between community-based organizations (*chonaikai*, NGOs and others) and the local government are a prerequisite. Furthermore, both groups must be independent for the partnership to work properly. The local government cannot make use of organizations such as the *chonaikai* as just an end-administrator. Likewise, residents and communities cannot rely on the central and local government to provide all services. Communities and the local government should have a shared vision and commitment. This begins when residents understand the significance of local environmental protection and wish for a life that values local resources and to be responsible for their own actions. The role of the local government is to provide residents with opportunities to think about the environment and to create better collection systems for recyclables.

The process of creating and implementing a recycling system itself can be a good framework for initiating community-based development of the *Machi-zukuri* approach. Solid waste is an issue in which participation by citizens is key because solid waste is related directly to daily activities and lifestyle. As a problem shared by all, solid waste is a good place to start community-based environmental management programmes. In Nagoya's case, the flexible and frank attitude of the city government contributed to citizens' understanding and awareness and thus led to better cooperation. Further, through action, citizens gained a better understanding of the management of their own environment.

Notes

1. Nagoya City homepage: ⟨http://www.city.nagoya.jp/⟩.
2. The Fujimae Tidelands were designated as Wetlands of International Importance on 18 November 2002. The list of designated sites can be found at ⟨http://ramsar.org/sitelist.pdf⟩.
3. The Chubu Recycle Shimin No Kai was established in 1980. The association has been active in such wide fields as waste reduction and recycling, green purchasing, development and dissemination of environment-related goods, publications and environmental education. In 2000, the association acquired official Specified Non-Profit Organization status.
4. Please refer to ⟨http://www.city.nagoya.jp/06kankyozi/gomipanf/youkirycycle.htm⟩ (in Japanese).
5. Interviews with Nagoya City officials conducted in February 2003 by the Innovative Communities Project team.
6. Although many definitions of "innovative" exist, for the purpose of this chapter the following definition is appropriate: "The qualities of an innovative environment ultimately come down to a few features: taking measured risks, widespread leadership, a sense of going somewhere, being determined but not deterministic, having the strength to go beyond the political cycle, and, crucially, being strategically principled and tactically flexible, as well as recognizing the resources that come from a community's history, talents and products and services. To make the most of this environment, changes in mindset, perception, ambition and will are required" (Charles Landry, Chapter 3 in this volume).
7. In Chapter 3 in this volume, Landry states, "the need for an urgent response to structural crisis or instability may help overcome obstacles to innovation. Crisis situations need

immediate solutions, and it is impossible to insist on old approaches if they are not immediately effective."

REFERENCES

Matsubara, Takehisa (2001) *The one lap behind top runner: The garbage revolution of Nagoya citizens*. Nagoya: KTC Chuo Publishing (in Japanese).

Nagoya City (2000a) "Interim summer report on the recycling of containers and packaging – hot summer of 2000 in Nagoya", October (in Japanese); available at: ⟨http://www.city.nagoya.jp/shisei/jigyoukeikaku/gomi/report/youki/⟩.

Nagoya City (2000b) "Why waste has been reduced in Nagoya? The pain and power of execution of the citizens", December (in Japanese); available at: ⟨http://www.city.nagoya.jp/shisei/jigyoukeikaku/gomi/report/itami/⟩.

Nagoya City (2001) "Nagoya waste report: Nagoya citizens who have turned the adverse wind to the fair wind", July.

Nagoya City (2002a) "Nagoya report on waste management II – Challenge for a resource-recycling society", December (in Japanese).

Nagoya City (2002b) "The 3rd Waste Management Basic Plan", May (in Japanese); available at: ⟨http://www.city.nagoya.jp/shisei/jigyoukeikaku/gomi/jyourei/ippanhaikibutsu/dai3/nagoya00008731.html⟩.

Nagoya City (2002c) "The 3rd Waste Management Basic Plan" (brochure), May (in Japanese); available at: ⟨http://www.city.nagoya.jp/_res/usr/8954/re-style.pdf⟩.

11

People, partnership and profits in managing solid waste in Guimaras, the Philippines

Andrew C. Farncombe, Francis E. Gentoral and Evan Anthony Arias

Introduction

There's an adage popular among elders in the Philippine province of Guimaras that says, "If we all agree, we all stick together." Despite its antiquity, it is a saying that continues to symbolize the spirit of togetherness that has been the island province's most powerful asset in its pursuit of a better quality of life. In the face of the poverty that reigns on the island, the people of Guimaras have forged strong partnerships to move forward an ambitious agenda for development. In the early 1990s, the national government classified Guimaras as one of the 20 poorest provinces in the country. In 2003, after a decade of steady improvement in its socio-economic indicators, the province was commemorating its move out of the ranks of the country's poorest subnational jurisdictions.

The motto "clean and green" has been one of the rallying points for the people of Guimaras. Proud of the civic culture of cleanliness and with a determination to keep it that way, provincial, municipal and community leaders have joined together to make solid waste management a top priority in Guimaras' development agenda. And it shows. Upon arrival on the island from other points in the Philippines, visitors invariably comment on the relative absence of litter in the streets of its towns and villages, along footpaths in the countryside, in its watercourses and at the beaches. With a strong understanding of sustainable development and an acute awareness of the interconnectedness of environmental, economic and social imperatives, these same leaders are counting on Guimaras'

245

clean and green image to make a significant contribution to the growth of the island's fledgling but promising eco-tourism industry. A great deal of hope is also being pinned on this emerging tourism industry to improve the prevailing conditions of poverty.

This chapter tells the story of how one of the poorest provinces of the Philippines – with few resources but with determined leadership and a spirit of partnership – planned for and implemented an innovative solid waste management (SWM) programme. It is also a story of how the province's local government units (LGUs) seized the opportunities presented to them to make a difference for people in the island, first by taking ownership of the powers devolved to them under the country's new decentralization law, and second by joining with the international donor community to provide an infusion of know-how from other places on good local governance and environmental management. What makes this programme, known as the Guimaras Integrated Solid Waste Management (GISWM) project, innovative is the unprecedented and successful partnerships between local governments and community groups that proactively addressed solid waste concerns before they became unmanageable.

The Guimaras development context

The small, pristine island of Guimaras is nestled between the larger islands of Panay and Negros in the Western Visayas region, about 500 km south of Manila in the central part of the archipelago. The pre-Spanish name of "Guimaras" means "to struggle". It was so named because the island, with a geological composition of mainly limestone, posed formidable agricultural challenges to the original settlers who had to struggle to survive. Yet this same reddish and acidic soil that once challenged the original settlers is what today gives Guimaras the perfect conditions for growing what some call the world's sweetest mangos. With export certification under the stringent standards of the United States Department of Agriculture (thanks to the province's well-regulated pest quarantine procedures), the mango-growing industry is flourishing. The island also produces other raw and processed agricultural products, including cashews, coconuts, corn, rice and citrus fruits. Secondary economic activities include industrial lime mining, soap manufacturing, small-scale handicraft making, fishing and aquaculture.

The tourism industry – with an orientation toward both the domestic excursion market and "independent" international tourists interested in Guimaras' ecological and heritage assets – is growing in size and facilities. The industry's increasing sophistication is demonstrated in the provincial government's improved tourism marketing infrastructure. This includes a newly inaugurated tour guide programme, the municipality of Nueva Valencia's unique new heritage tourism initiative, and the island's annual *fiesta* schedule. Guimaras now draws big crowds to its International Mountain Bike Festival (February), the Ang Pagtaltal Sa Guimaras (a re-enactment of the crucifixion of Jesus Christ held every Good Friday), and the Mango Festival (May). For the past eight years, tourist visits have increased at a staggering rate of 92 per cent (Province of Guimaras 2001).

The island is about the same geographical size as Singapore, with a population of about 141,450 spread over 604.57 km^2. There are 96 villages, the two main port towns of Jordan and Buenavista and the inland capital of San Miguel. Located just 3 km across the straight from Iloilo, an urban region with a population of over 500,000, Guimaras can be considered to be a peri-urban region that is increasingly coming under the urban growth shadow. Urbanization pressures are beginning to be felt in settlements along the north-west coast of the island (see Figure 11.1).

About 57,000 of the total population of Guimaras are economically

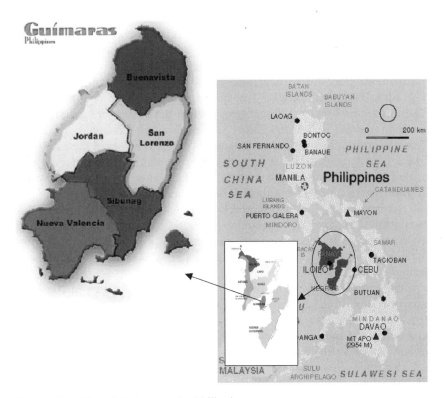

Figure 11.1 Map of Guimaras, the Philippines.
Source: Canadian Urban Institute (1997).

productive (around 69 per cent labour participation rate), of whom just over 28 per cent are employed in the agriculture sector (specifically rice, corn, vegetables and fruit production). Others in the workforce commute daily to nearby Iloilo City for their livelihood opportunities. The incidence of poverty is high in Guimaras, sitting at 69.6 per cent in 2002.[1]

Guimaras is a newly created province in the Philippines. Once a sub-province of neighbouring Iloilo, the national government granted Guimaras full provincial status on 22 May 1992. When it was created it was composed of just three municipalities: Jordan, Buenavista and Nueva Valencia; the two additional municipalities of San Lorenzo and Sibunag were added shortly thereafter. Following its creation as a full-fledged provincial unit, the Philippine government gave Guimaras priority status for development and classified it among the 20 poorest provinces in the Philippines. As a result it has received special financial and technical assistance from national government agencies and priority development assistance from numerous international donors, including the Canadian International Development Agency (CIDA), the European Union's Small Islands Agricultural Support Services Programme (SMISLES), the German Technical Development Cooperation Agency (GTZ), the Australian Agency for International Development (AUSAID) and other international development organizations.

The major infrastructure facilities in the province comprise 14 seaports, 111 educational institutions, 2 hospitals and 67 village health stations. The Guimaras Electric Cooperative (which gets its power supply from the Palimpinon Geothermal Plant, Negros Oriental, through the National Power Corporation) supplies the electricity requirements of the province. The Local Water Utilities Administration provides a stable water supply, aside from other sources such as artesian wells, natural springs, rainwater and the four major river systems. The National Telecommunication Corporation operates a limited landline-based telephone system in the municipality of Jordan, and extensive mobile phone coverage is provided by the three big telecommunications companies of the country. The province has around 366 registered business establishments (Provincial Government of Guimaras 2002).

Guimaras' first governor, Emily Lopez (1992–1997), turned the poverty prevalent in the island into a rallying point to get all people to work together toward social and economic progress. Being a new province, Guimaras had limited human and technical capabilities to meet the demands of rapid growth, to begin reducing widespread poverty and to manage the newly devolved responsibilities under the Republic Act No. 7160 of 1991 (also known as the Local Government Code or LGC). Shortly after taking office, Governor Lopez made a concerted effort to get the local government house in order. She launched an ambitious development agenda and immediately set about seeking international assistance to implement it.

This development agenda had two main components. The first was to initiate, in the spirit of the new LGC, a strategic, grassroots-oriented, participatory planning approach to development planning for the island. After extensive consultations at all levels, this resulted in an umbrella development plan for the island that nested *barangay* (village),[2] municipal and provincial plans under one rubric and tied together economic, environmental, social and cultural issues in the spirit of sustainable development. The second component involved launching a comprehensive capacity development programme, for provincial and municipal civil servants and elected officials, which has resulted in the province moving squarely toward international standards of good local governance. Both components paid significant attention to issues of environmental management and sustainability, including solid waste management. Under her leadership, Mrs Lopez laid the foundation for the holistic, integrated and participatory approach to planning and development that continues to be practised on the island today.

In the spirit of the original island-wide strategic planning exercise, Guimaras' second governor, Dr Rahman Nava (1998–) continued to tackle with fortitude and leadership the wishes of the people to improve their quality of life and to alleviate the conditions of poverty. Under his leadership, the province shifted gear from planning to implementation, with an emphasis on attainable actions that would make a difference for the average resident. With a continued programme of cooperation with international donors and with a multi-stakeholder approach that is seeing new and innovative partnerships for development between local government and civil society and the private sector, the current provincial development agenda is an ambitious but realistic one. It focuses on improving local governance (with a continued emphasis on the use of participatory and strategic planning techniques and a focused capacity development programme), efficient and effective delivery of basic services (in particular primary health care and education), stimulating livelihood opportunities through an economic development agenda focused on agriculture, fishery and tourism sectors, infrastructure development, and improved environmental management (including the solid waste management initiative that is the subject of this chapter).

Decentralization in the Philippines

After 10 years of hard work and determination to improve local governance in the island, Guimaras is now beginning to see the fruits of its efforts. Key to its success has been the process of decentralization, which is the term used to describe a shift in the alignment of democratic powers and service delivery responsibilities between central and local governments.

Decentralization began to occur in many South-East Asian countries during the latter part of the twentieth century, with the Philippines being one of the first nations in the region to embrace the policy (Brillantes et al. 2003). It is occurring for several reasons. These include the trend towards greater democracy, the failure of highly centralized and/or authoritarian government systems, fiscal constraints at the national level, and the growing importance of cities and towns within regional and global economies. Implicit in the concept of decentralization is the principle of subsidiarity, which acknowledges that, where there is a need for the delivery agent to be close to recipients, the delivery of certain services by local authorities can be more efficient and responsive than delivery by more senior levels of government.

Decentralization has brought both benefits and problems. In some parts of the world, new responsibilities and autonomy for local governments have led to innovative solutions to local issues. Decentralization has not only turned local communities into engines of growth and development, but also promoted government–community partnership arrangements that have transformed community groups into crucial partners of local governments in various development initiatives (Gonzales et al. 2000).

In other parts of the world, local governments have demonstrated that they do not have the institutional, human or technical capacities needed to take on an expanded role. And in most countries, decentralization of new responsibilities has not been accompanied by the fiscal resources or revenue-raising powers necessary to deliver the required services. As a result, local governments are having rapidly to build their capacities, reinvent the ways in which their institutions operate, find ways to involve citizens in planning and decision-making to ensure that services are responsive to constituent needs, and lobby senior levels of government for dedicated revenue sources.

The Philippines has a tradition of strong central government power and control that dates back 400 years to the beginning of the Spanish occupation. In 1986 this tendency was reversed by the People's Power Revolution and with the adoption of a new Constitution in 1987. This so-called "bloodless revolution" brought the country into its current era of democratic development.

The Republic Act No. 7160 of 1991 initiated a new trend toward government decentralization, devolution and empowerment of local communities, thereby deepening the roots of democracy. According to the

LGC it is the policy of the national Philippine government that local government units "shall enjoy genuine and meaningful local autonomy to enable them to attain their fullest development of self-reliant communities and make them more effective partners in the attainment of national goals".

Overall, the LGC describes a system of sound local governance based on the principles of openness, accountability, efficiency, equity, respect for the rule of law and subsidiarity. The Code gave LGUs the power and responsibility to deliver basic services that were previously performed by the central government and in doing so altered the hierarchical relationship between the two levels of government. The LGUs were given much greater autonomy, power and responsibilities, and also the sources of revenue needed to enable them to support their devolved functions (Brillantes 1999). Before the LGC was passed, national–local relations had been characterized by strong centralism.

The LGC transferred the responsibilities for the delivery of basic services (including the management of related personnel, assets, equipment, programmes and projects) in the areas of: public health, social welfare, waste management, peace and order, community-based forestry, agricultural extension, some public works (such as the maintenance of roads and bridges, water supply system, school buildings, drainage and sewerage systems), school education, local tourism development, telecommunication and housing programmes for provinces and cities (Brillantes 1999; Tabunda and Galang 1991).

The LGC also mandates that local governments enlist the support of non-governmental organizations (NGOs) and civil society groups (including the private sector) in the formulation and implementation of development policies and programmes. The guidelines of participation that were provided to promote these partnerships include:
- representation of NGOs in local special bodies,
- sectoral representation in local legislative councils,
- mandatory consultations with NGOs for national projects, and
- joint ventures and privatization of local enterprises.

A decade later, the LGC is still considered to be one of the most revolutionary local government reform laws in South-East Asia, although the process of refinement and improvement continues (Brillantes 1999). It has helped to set a policy framework for improved local governance in the country by making certain decentralized provisions to stimulate cooperation among local governments and between local governments and groups within civil society. For Guimaras, the LGC created a policy environment and political landscape that was supportive of the development of successful local partnerships that aimed to improve solid waste management.

Solid waste management issues for local governments

Problems associated with solid waste management have become a major environmental concern throughout the Philippines in recent years. A fast-growing population, rapid urbanization, intensifying economic activities and burgeoning consumerism within the society have all contributed to increased generation of waste, especially in urban centres and within their growth shadows on the urban periphery.

With the introduction of the LGC, the national government devolved responsibility for the enforcement of environmental laws on cleanliness, sanitation, solid waste management and other environmental matters to LGUs. According to the Republic Act No. 7160, 1991:

- *municipalities* are responsible for developing solid waste disposal systems and related environmental management procedures, and for providing services and facilities related to general hygiene and sanitation;
- *Sanggunian Bayan (SB) or municipal legislative councils* are responsible for regulating the disposal of clinic and hospital wastes and for declaring, preventing or abating nuisance; and
- *Sanggunian Panlalawigan (SP) or provincial legislative councils* are responsible for adopting measures to safeguard against pollution, and for the preservation of ecosystems in consonance with approved national standards on human settlements and environmental sanitation.

In 2000, the Philippine government enacted Republic Act No. 9003, the Ecological Waste Management Act, which mandated that ecological waste management should now be the responsibility of local governments throughout the country. The Act provides a further downward shift of responsibility for solid waste management to local government units. Ecological waste management, as prescribed by Republic Act No. 9003, involves the efficient reduction, recycling and composting of waste with the aim of diverting a significant portion of waste away from disposal facilities such as landfills. Under this law, a materials recovery facility must be established in each *barangay* to serve as a primary facility in waste management.

One of the benefits that have flowed from the recent law is that several LGUs have been leading the way in developing innovative new approaches to the management of solid waste. One of the most successful solid waste management systems can be found in Olongapo City, where the municipality charges garbage fees by requiring households and establishments to buy colour-coded bags, each designated for a different type of waste. The initiative in Bustos, Bulacan, Luzon Province, is another success story. Motivated by rising health concerns, the municipality embarked on a solid waste disposal programme before its garbage problem had reached crisis proportions. It did so by addressing each of the different stages of the solid waste stream, from waste generation to storage, collection, recycling, diversion and disposal (Galing Pook Foundation 2001).[3]

The remainder of this chapter will describe some of the innovative approaches to solid waste management that have been implemented by local governments in Guimaras with technical assistance from the Canadian Urban Institute (CUI) and in collaboration with stakeholders from the various sectors and communities on the island.[4]

Toward a clean and green island: Guimaras Integrated Solid Waste Management

During the late 1990s, as the province of Guimaras grew in economic and demographic terms, the need to approach solid waste management activities in a strategic and integrated manner in coordination with its various communities became more and more apparent. This was a contributing factor leading up to the decision to require local governments to develop and manage their own ecological waste management programmes under the Ecological Waste Management Act 2000. Yet, even before this Act was enacted, the 96 villages and the five municipalities of the province of Guimaras decided to take upon themselves the important task of managing their own wastes.

In 1994, a partnership was initiated between the CUI and Guimaras with financial support provided by the Government of Canada through the Canadian International Development Agency. One of the first initiatives of the cooperation programme was to launch an island-wide, community-based strategic planning process. Through a participatory process, the plan defined the vision, mission, goals, strategies and programmes for the province. Approved by all LGUs, one of that plan's priorities was to improve environmental quality and management on the island.

In early 1996, a core group of representatives from the provincial government of Guimaras – drawn from the Provincial Planning and Development Office, the Provincial Engineering Office (PEO) and the Provincial Health Office (PHO), with the facilitation of the CUI – met to formally examine the issues, challenges and prospects for solid waste management on the island. Based on extensive consultation with and dialogue among these institutions, the provincial government officially launched the Guimaras Integrated Solid Waste Management programme in the mid-1990s. The aim of GISWM was to reduce the island's solid waste by 50 per cent and to provide the people with a cost-effective solid waste management system in an environmentally sound manner.

One of the most innovative aspects of the GISWM programme is the fact that the activities were conducted through a strong partnership between the government and the community. In Guimaras, it was the first time that government and community groups had formed multi-stakeholder partnership mechanisms at the municipal and provincial levels. The establishment of multi-stakeholder task forces promoted the coordination not just of planning for solid waste management but also of the implementation process. Although an integrated approach to planning already existed, integrated implementation was a whole new approach.

The project proved to be viable because it gained support from both the past and current provincial administrations. The project was conceptualized, planned and initiated during the Lopez administration, yet implemented and improved upon under the Nava administration. This continuity and sustainability of development programming from one political administration to the next is testament to the commitment by the province's LGUs to good governance and to the strength of community participation as a mechanism to keep local authorities accountable to the public's agreed-upon priorities.

Components and activities

The GISWM programme consisted of the following activities:
• organizing multi-stakeholder task forces as decision-making and coordinating bodies;
• conducting participatory solid waste stream assessment;
• organizing solid waste management planning workshops;
• reviewing and formulating solid waste policies and ordinances; and
• implementing solid waste management demonstration projects.
(Canadian Urban Institute 1997)

Organization of multi-stakeholder task forces

Planning and implementation of the GISWM programme were conducted through the Provincial Implementation Task Force (PITF) and five Municipal Implementation Task Forces (MITFs), composed of representatives of national government agencies, the provincial government, municipalities, barangays, cooperatives, business associations, schools and NGOs.[5] The establishment of the task forces has enabled local governments in Guimaras to enjoy strong political and organizational commitments from various government agencies, at both the national and local levels, and also the voluntary participation of representatives of civil society. Because the PITF and MITFs allowed the government to share

Table 11.1 GISWM task force membership

Sector	Organization
National government	Department of Environment and Natural Resources and Environment and Natural Resources Office
	Department of Education, Culture and Sports
Provincial and municipal governments	Offices of the governor and mayors
	Philippine National Police
	Provincial and Municipal Environment and Natural Resources Offices
	Provincial and Municipal Engineering Offices
	Provincial and Municipal Health Offices
	Provincial and Municipal Planning and Development Offices
	Provincial and Municipal Federation of Barangay Captains
	Provincial and Municipal Social Welfare and Development Offices
	Provincial and Municipal Agriculture Offices
	Provincial and Municipal Councillors for Environment
Civil society and private sector	Good Shepherd Academy
	Guimaras Chamber of Commerce and Industry
	Guimaras Federation of Cooperatives
	Guimaras Cut Flowers Association
	Lopez Foundation
	Organic Vegetable Farmers Association
	People's Economic Council Foundation
	Tricycle Drivers Association
	Vendors Association
	Zambarrano Foundation

Source: Canadian Urban Institute (1997).

power with community groups, governments learned to appreciate that they could yield ownership of the process and that this could produce more meaningful and significant results than when they worked independently or in parallel (see Table 11.1).

Membership in the PITF and MITFs was anchored on institutions rather than on individuals. Thus, if a person representing a government agency or community organization changed, was replaced or became unavailable, the partnership was not affected unduly because continuity could be ensured by simply designating a replacement. Representatives on the task forces usually had a permanent alternate whose role proved to be critical when the main designates were not available. Second-liners also provided back-up support in implementing what has sometimes been

Table 11.2 Roles and responsibilities of the Provincial and Municipal Implementation Task Forces

Roles and responsibilities
Organize provincial and municipal solid waste assessment and action planning activities
Compile, review and recommend solid waste-related legislation and policies
Facilitate the implementation of solid waste projects such as the establishment of effective collection and disposal, reuse–reduce–recycle projects, public involvement activities
Prepare project policies, guidelines and procedures
Prepare plans and regular progress reports to funding agencies and local government units
Prepare plans for sustaining initial activities related to solid waste

Source: Canadian Urban Institute (1997).

a complex and time-consuming endeavour. This arrangement provided expediency in decision-making in the various project activities. The focus on institutional representation proved to be particularly effective, especially after the May 1998 local elections when the provincial government changed and civil servants were shuffled around (see Table 11.2).

Various activities have been conducted through the task forces, ranging from implementing the waste stream assessment, to studying site options for a solid waste landfill, conducting community awareness and education campaigns, designing and launching solid waste demonstration projects, and installing project monitoring systems.

The task forces worked on the premise that each represented organization would share its time, resources and expertise. National government agency task force representatives brought with them the necessary mandate, funds, human resources and knowledge on policy-making and technical expertise in waste management. For example, representatives of the Department of Environment and Natural Resources (DENR) and the Environment and Natural Resources Office (ENRO) provided technical advice when necessary. Local government executives (i.e. mayors) issued orders mandating various government agencies to take part in the project through the task forces, making them much more ready to commit their resources. Different agencies allocated funds in support of project activities, such as public education campaigns, training workshops and the implementation of small-scale demonstration projects. The Provincial Engineering Office made its personnel available to monitor garbage segregation and disposal practices in the province, and municipal governments allocated funds for the establishment of a solid waste landfill.

Participatory solid waste stream assessment

Waste stream assessment is a process designed to identify some basic parameters of the local waste stream, such as the quantity, composition and sources of waste. The results of the assessment provide baseline data for informed programme planning, facility design, regulatory development and financial decision-making.

The waste stream assessment conducted through the GISWM identified the volume, composition and type of waste produced by sample households, commercial entities, schools and farms. Personnel from the PEO, PHO and ENRO acted as the field researchers, teaching households how to segregate collected waste. Provincial and municipal governments selected personnel based on their roles and responsibilities in the solid waste management system as provided for under the LGC.

In order to conduct the assessment, the PITF selected 60 sample households and establishments to participate in the assessment, each of which was required to record the parameters of the waste they produced and to segregate non-biodegradable from biodegradable waste. Participants received a small cash incentive of 100 pesos per respondent for collecting and recording the information.

The assessment involved:

• conducting orientation meetings with the selected households and establishments to inform them of the need, goals and procedures of waste stream assessment and the data-gathering procedures;
• distributing trash receptacles to participating households and establishments;
• distributing instructional forms on how to conduct waste stream assessment;
• weighing and recording wastes per household and establishment using the Solid Waste Record Form;
• collecting waste by garbage truck (non-biodegradable waste was separated from biodegradable waste) – collected wastes were properly covered by a tarpaulin to protect them from rainwater and to avoid spreading of wastes;
• conducting waste characterization and determining waste composition – weighing was done according to prescribed categories;
• preparing terminal reports to be used during the planning workshops.

The results of the waste stream assessment provided the basis for ascertaining the strategies that could be adopted to deal effectively with each type of waste produced. For example, the assessment revealed that 65 per cent of waste is biodegradable, pointing to the potential for composting. The assessment contributed invaluable data for calculating the

size of the proposed sanitary landfill for Guimaras, resulting in the conclusion that the total area requirement for the landfill was 35,000 m^2 for
a 20-year facility lifespan (Link 1997). The results of the assessment also
provided a major source of information for the action planning workshops in a whole range of other areas related to SWM.

Solid waste management planning

Following the waste stream assessment, the project conducted a series
of municipal and provincial solid waste management action planning
workshops drawing in 217 participants representing the *barangays*, municipalities, national government agencies, cooperatives, business entities, schools and non-government organizations (see Figure 11.2). The
goal of the workshops was to formulate concrete and coordinated action
plans concerning waste management. Municipalities prepared draft action plans on waste minimization, collection and transfer, disposal, landfill establishment, information, education and communication, and law
enforcement, which were later consolidated at the provincial level. Technical experts and specialists were drawn from the Department of Environment and Natural Resources and from local NGOs, lending their
expertise in the workshops on waste management, composting, communication and planning. Workshop participants then prepared final action

Figure 11.2 Municipal solid waste action planning workshop.
Source: Canadian Urban Institute (1997).

plans that were linked together in a complementary fashion by way of shared purpose, information, strategy, form and function. The plans were collated and presented to provincial and municipal governments for approval. These authorities then summarily adopted a final integrated plan by allocating budgets for implementation.

Review and formulation of solid waste policies and ordinances

Based on the solid waste management plans drafted in the action planning workshops, the PITF and MITFs provided input into the drafting of comprehensive solid waste management policies and ordinances for each of the five municipalities and for the province as a whole. The aspects covered in the review were the collection, disposal and recycling of wastes, as well as public involvement. The review process included collection of documents on ordinances and orders, codification of the ordinances, and review and formulation of comprehensive new or revised ordinances on solid waste management. The process provided opportunities for the municipal legislative councils to have a consistent scope and coverage as relates to definition of terms, provisions, penalties and procedures for solid waste management. The overarching goal was to ensure consistency in the interpretation and implementation of the ordinances across all municipalities and *barangays* province wide.

The review process included input from 30 participants drawn from the chairs of the Committee on Environment of the municipal and provincial councils, *barangay* captains, NGO representatives, the Guimaras Resort Association, the Guimaras Chamber of Commerce and Industry, DENR, ENRO, the Department of Interior and Local Government and the Guimaras Provincial Planning and Development Office. The PITF and the MITFs selected participants based on knowledge and experience in the various components of the solid waste management system.

Solid waste management demonstration projects

Another innovative project within the broader GISWM initiative was a competition in the field of solid waste management. Using a set of rigorous criteria, the PITF and MITFs issued a call for proposals for small-scale SWM demonstration projects. The provincial government, with funds provided by CIDA, awarded monies totalling 1.4 million pesos (approximately US$25,000) to implement the winning proposals. Among the criteria considered in the competition were the financial and technical feasibility of the project, the ability of the project to promote public–private cooperation, consistency with the integrated solid waste plan and strategies, cost effectiveness and the level of commitment of organizers.

The competition targeted community organizations, government agencies, cooperatives and business organizations, which were all briefed on the results of the solid waste stream assessment and attended strategic action planning workshops to gain background information. All 239 organizations that provided an expression of interest in entering the competition were sent application guidelines.

The next step was to hold a series of two-day municipal workshops with the aim of providing the prospective proponents with a common framework for developing solid waste project proposals. The solid waste strategic plans that had been prepared earlier in the municipal strategic planning workshops became the basis for the projects and activities being proposed. The PITF in consultation with the MITFs approved the design of the workshops and the resource persons assigned. During the workshops, the organizers presented case studies on successful solid waste management projects in the Philippines. These were followed by discussions on project development and management techniques and tips on the preparation of proposals. Following the workshops, proposals flowed in for a range of projects such as solid waste reduction, composting, education campaigns and feasibility studies on landfill locations.

A public review session was then held so that key stakeholders and PITF and MITF members could take a closer look at the 30 shortlisted proposals and rate them using the criteria set forth in the competition guidelines. Of the 17 "winners" of the competition, 14 received project funds of 50,000 pesos (approximately US$900) each to be used for project implementation. Three specific and significant projects received larger amounts of funding. The allocation and management of funds followed existing local government rules and regulations and the competition winners reported to the LGUs on the status of their demonstration projects on a semi-annual basis through the PITF and MITFs. In total, 17 projects received approval and proceeded to implementation (see Table 11.3).

Among the most successful projects was the initiative implemented by the flower growers in Jordan municipality, headed by Josefa Madrones. It has earned a modest 22,000 pesos (approximately US$400) to date through the selling of compost. Through the project, Mrs Garganera, who represents the flower growers, has become a popular lecturer in the province and across the Western Visayas where she promotes the value of composting (see Figure 11.3).

Another winning proposal was submitted by the school children of San Miguel Central School, who spearheaded a waste separation and composting project in their school grounds. The project involved students picking up garbage and drawing posters to highlight the importance of greening Guimaras (see Figure 11.4).

An evaluation of the demonstration projects by the CUI revealed that

Table 11.3 Results of solid waste demonstration projects

Name of project	Proponent/location	Amount granted (pesos)	Results
Sibunag Municipal Collection and Disposal System Project	Municipality of Sibunag (Sibunag, Guimaras)	50,000.00	New knowledge in recycling, composting, and paper crafts making Ongoing composting, recycling and paper crafts projects Established community partnerships
San Lorenzo Solid Waste Integrated Management Project	Municipality of San Lorenzo (San Lorenzo, Guimaras)	219,570.00	Information and education campaigns for community partners Completion of 15 school nurseries
Buenavista Solid Waste Management Information Center	Municipality of Buenavista Buenavista National High School (New Poblacion, Buenavista, Guimaras)	50,000.00	New knowledge in composting and waste segregation Operational school garbage collection system
New Poblacion Composting and Bottle Redemption Center	Brgy. New Poblacion (Buenavista, Guimaras)	50,000.00	Operational bottle-buying centre Institutionalized waste collection by households and tricycle operators Sustained garbage collection and waste segregation project through formulation of new policy and installation of required systems and facilities
Buenavista Cutflower Composting Project	Brgy. Cansilayan (Buenavista, Guimaras)	50,000.00	Operational compost-buying centre Established speakers' bureau for environmental education on composting and ecological waste management

Table 11.3 (cont.)

Name of project	Proponent/location	Amount granted (pesos)	Results
San Roque Composting Project	Brgy. San Roque (Buenavista, Guimaras)	50,000.00	Established and functional community composting sites and facilities
Pre-feasibility study on the establishment of a Guimaras sanitary landfill	Municipality of Jordan (Jordan, Guimaras)	50,000.00	Analysis and LGU approval of sanitary landfill site New knowledge on sanitary landfill operation
Operation "Kontra Basura" (against waste)	Municipality of Jordan (Jordan, Guimaras)	50,000.00	Community-based task forces organized and operating in four municipal areas New knowledge on law enforcement Established institutional structures and facilities to collect waste
Hoskyn Elementary School Solid Waste Management Project	Hoskyn Elementary School (Hoskyn, Jordan, Guimaras)	50,000.00	New knowledge on recycling among school children Ongoing income-generating projects on plastic recycling operated by the school
Establishment of the Bugnay Composting Center	Bugnay Composting Centre (Bugnay, Jordan, Guimaras)	50,000.00	Regular production and sales of composts from agricultural wastes Ongoing community awareness-raising campaign on zero waste management and composting
Farmers Composting Center	Brgy. Poblacion, (Bucao, Jordan, Guimaras)	50,000.00	Regular production and sales of composts from agricultural wastes Ongoing community awareness-raising campaign on zero waste management and composting

262

Guimaras Cutflower and Ornamental Producers Compost Buying and Selling Center	Guimaras CutFlowers Association (San Miguel, Jordan, Guimaras)	50,000.00	Ongoing information and education programme on composting for farmers, schools, school officials, household members and prospective cooperators; Established linkages with cooperators, business establishments and households for the purchase and sale of compost materials; Established of compost buying and selling centre
San Miguel Central School Composting Project	Brgy. San Miguel (Jordan, Guimaras)	50,000.00	Institutionalized school waste collection, segregation and composting system
Poblacion Bottle and Scrap Iron Redemption Center	Brgy. Poblacion (Jordan, Guimaras)	50,000.00	Established *barangay* composting, redemption and education centre
San Miguel Demonstration Center on Composting	Brgy. San Miguel (Jordan, Guimaras)	50,000.00	Established *barangay* composting and education centre
Nueva Valencia Solid Waste Management Project	Municipality of Nueva Valencia (Nueva Valencia, Guimaras)	100,000.00	Established municipal garbage collection and disposal system
Nueva Valencia Improvement of Garbage Collection and Transfer Efficiency	Municipality of Nueva Valencia (Nueva Valencia, Guimaras)	86,418.25	

Source: Canadian Urban Institute (1997).

Figure 11.3 Compost Buying-Selling Center of the Guimaras Cut Flowers
Association.
Source: Canadian Urban Institute (1997).

Figure 11.4 San Miguel Central School pupils using compost in gardening
projects.
Source: Canadian Urban Institute (1997).

7 out of the 17 groups felt that they had increased composting awareness throughout the community; 6 out of the 17 groups also established some type of composting facility based on lessons learned from other communities. One group claimed to have helped formulate ordinance and plans for their solid waste programme. Three groups felt that they had promoted new environmental behaviour and helped to reduce the levels of solid waste generated. Two groups helped to generate income for their local citizens and businesses that almost equalled the initial capitalization of around 50,000 pesos (Canadian Urban Institute 2003).

Community innovation

Government–community partnership

The government–community partnership enabled through the PITF and MITF mechanisms has proven to be an innovative way to employ a participatory, proactive and strategic approach to improved solid waste management in the province of Guimaras. The formation of the PITF and five MITFs defies the traditional notion that managing solid waste is mainly a government responsibility. The task forces provided a platform from which government and citizens in the community shared responsibility. Until then, although government agencies and civil society groups had been engaged in waste management activities, these were not sufficiently coordinated nor did they produce substantial or even sustainable results. In addition, although local governments and civil society have a history of working together on environmental issues in Guimaras, this is the first time that the business sector has also been actively involved.

Embracing good local governance

Another innovative feature of the project has been its sustained participatory approach. Project activities always involved a wide range of stakeholders, and decisions were reached only after thorough deliberation. Solid waste management plans emerged out of a series of community-level workshops, and policies were drafted only after a long process of public consultation and information-sharing. It was participants' full involvement in this extensive process that allowed them to develop a sense of ownership over the project.

A broader output of the project has been to increase community levels of awareness and participation in local governance processes. Nilda Silaya, Buenavista's Municipal Engineer, notes, for example, that village people now come to her office, or to the Office of the Mayor, when garbage is not collected on time. This has prodded the municipal government to make its garbage collection more efficient (Silaya, personal interview, 2001). Improved information-sharing with the national government and the private sector has also fostered greater transparency and accountability in local government priority-setting, budgeting and service delivery.

Partnerships for planning and implementation

The creation of task forces had the result of formalizing good relationships between the government and community groups. Mutually beneficial partnerships were formed by various members, each bringing their own unique contribution to the process, whether this was the necessary mandate, funds, human resources, knowledge of policy-making or technical expertise in waste management. Through the PITF and MITFs, local government agencies had easy access to the local communities by way of the information shared during meetings, workshops and action research activities. The citizens themselves benefited from having ample opportunity, by way of the task forces, to participate in planning and implementing projects in their own communities.

The PITF and MITF members have now been absorbed as members of municipal and provincial solid waste management boards that were created under Republic Act No. 9003, the national law on ecological waste management. Regular meetings of the boards are venues where stakeholders participate in the process of assessing solid waste management performance against the stated objectives of the plan. These regular meetings also give them the opportunity to deliberate on emerging issues and address any problems. Also incorporated into the agenda of these meetings are any issues and concerns that might require the attention of other sectors and agencies. Any differences of opinion are resolved through majority vote among members and, as much as possible, the meetings aim at reaching a consensus in an effort to ensure that the available options are discussed extensively.

In many cases, the issues raised relate to bureaucratic backlogs within government that have resulted in implementation delays. Through regular feedback, however, the government has tried to rectify its inadequacies and has slowly improved its operational performance. In fact, representatives from the government have said that they value this feedback because it helps them improve services and keep up with the expectations of the group in general. Open communications have also made the relationships between board members more comfortable and various professional and personal ties have developed over the years.

Commitment of leaders

The PITF and MITF members became leaders or "champions" of the project in their sector or area. They inspired and influenced others to take part in its various activities. The PITF and MITFs consisted of competent and dedicated members. Participants at the grassroots level have expressed a high regard for the capability of the task forces in managing the project. Since the beginning, task force members have demonstrated a strong commitment to ensure the project's success. Angeles Gabinete, a former project manager, described it succinctly when she said, "Working for genuine development means giving up some of your personal happiness for the welfare of the greater majority" (Gabinete, personal interview, 2001). People's commitment and motivation have been maintained through constant formal and informal communication and through celebration of project successes as often as the available opportunities would provide.

Infusion of knowledge from other places

The formation of the multi-stakeholder community partnership through task forces was inspired by successful experiences from across the Philippines and internationally. The provincial government sent 22 members of the PITF to various areas in the Philippines to observe how LGUs and communities in other places were tackling similar solid waste management challenges. For example, the community-based projects in Olongapo City, Zambales Province, and Puerto Princesa City, Palawan Province, where NGOs and government agencies have tremendous experience in working together to solve waste management issues, were of particular help.

Several task force members also participated in various professional study tours to Canada, organized by the CUI under its CIDA-funded programme. These study tours took them to the Province of British Columbia, Canada's western-most province. In Canada's coastal, marine environment, they were able to meet their peers and be exposed to leading-edge solid waste management initiatives. They were able to view, first-hand, the techniques used in the province's largest city (Vancouver), in towns on Vancouver Island (Victoria and Nanaimo) and in the small-island environment of the Gulf Islands. This provided them with additional knowledge and new insights and inspiration in the spheres of governance and waste management (Gabinete 1998).

With this infusion of know-how, Guimaras communities were able to adopt the lessons learned from other places with regard to composting, recycling and education campaigns and to implement them successfully. As a result, Guimaras has itself become a model for neighbouring municipalities and communities in the planning, implementation, monitoring and evaluation of solid waste management programmes. The provincial government has prepared an SWM manual as a means to share experiences and knowledge with other communities.

Lessons and implications

Numerous lessons can be drawn from the Guimaras case that could be of value to other communities around the world – in particular, the insight gained in building good working partnerships between government and community groups, a feat achieved with impressive results on the island. There are also a number of important lessons that were learned through the GISWM programme and these are worthy of more detailed consideration (Lighid and Gentoral 1999).

A mode for acquiring greater power, capability and results

The experience in Guimaras demonstrates clearly that stakeholders are able to undertake projects beyond the capability of a single organization through the multi-stakeholder task force mechanisms. For example, Edilberto Gange, former president of the Guimaras Chamber of Commerce and Industry, is grateful for his organization's linkage with the PITF. He notes: "Through the PITF, we can work on bigger projects, which our organization simply cannot manage alone. Besides, as a group we have a stronger voice in influencing policy decisions" (Gange, personal interview, 1999). Gil Japitana, the municipality of Buenavista's planning officer, agrees, commenting that, by interfacing various government and community group functions, they are able to be more effective in producing substantial results that meet broad community needs (Japitana, personal interview, 1998).

An arena for resolving conflicts and harmonizing views

The partnership approach pursued through the PITF/MITF mechanism has become a useful venue for sharing information and views, and thereby for resolving conflicts arising from project implementation. This has served, for instance, to mitigate acrimonious protest in the decision-making process over the establishment of a shared landfill in one municipality over another.

An avenue for influencing the reform of local government

As a way of meeting the institutional reform requirements of Republic Act No. 9003, the PITF and MITFs were absorbed and institutionalized into provincial and municipal solid waste management boards. Similarly, the solid waste management action plans prepared at the municipal and provincial levels became the policy documents for charting the ongoing solid waste programming of the respective local governments. By ensuring that both the operational and the planning elements of the project are integrated into the local government machinery in the province, the prospects for sustainability of results have been improved.

A means of tackling issues before they become problems

At the time of project launch, solid waste management had not yet become a visible problem on the island. As a result, during the earlier stages of the project the public did not fully appreciate the importance of addressing the solid waste issue. People did not see it as a serious problem that could have an impact on their daily lives, nor did they see it as an issue deserving top priority. It took them some time to see the link between the province's overall vision for environmental protection and how a proactive solid waste management programme could contribute to that vision. As a result of these dynamics, involving the public in the initial stages of the project proved to be a great challenge. An information, education and communication programme was initiated in an effort to sustain the gains of the participatory approach and to keep public opinion in support of the project. This included the establishment of community billboards, school information campaigns, poster-making contests and other communication initiatives aimed at sharing knowledge gathered during study tours and other key activities.

Setbacks due to resource constraints and bureaucratic delays

Lack of necessary resources and personnel resulted in some setbacks in the partnership process. For government representatives, working on solid waste project activities added additional tasks to their already full workload. Community groups felt hindered by the lack of necessary funds to sustain their participation in project activities and were sometimes stunted in their enthusiasm by delays in approvals and funding allocations. The project surmounted these barriers by creating activities in which community groups could participate and by providing some seed money to support small-scale demonstration projects. To address this matter into the future, municipal and provincial development offices have allocated funds and human resources, although limited, to support solid waste projects and to leverage community participation.

Learning, motivation and relationship-building through study tours

Study tours are an important mechanism for capacity-building, exposing participants to leading-edge innovations and allowing them to see first-hand what might be the end result of their efforts. Study tours have also acted as a major energizer of project participants and a forum for important relationship-building among colleagues (e.g. between a mayor and a director of planning) away from the stresses of political and professional life.

Conclusion

The Guimaras Integrated Solid Waste Management project is about more than just garbage. It is about garbage becoming a rallying point for building government–community partnerships, for harnessing community energies and resources in the face of limited fiscal resources, for joining forces to tackle seemingly insurmountable development challenges, for mitigating threats to environmental health, for taking steps toward reducing poverty, for pursuing good local governance and for improving the quality of life for all residents of the island.

The GISWM project experience has provided a face to the successful implementation of decentralization in the Philippines. The multi-stakeholder, government–community partnership mechanism used in the GISWM project has been shared with other communities across the Philippines and South-East Asia. It has so far benefited local authorities in Thailand, Malaysia and Indonesia. The process of engaging a wide range of stakeholders in solid waste management is already being employed in nearby Iloilo City, where solid waste is a major concern. The process is also being adopted in Boracay Island, the premier tourist destination of the Philippines.

As the country's more than 1,689 LGUs take steps to implement the requirements of Republic Act No. 9003, they can now look to the province of Guimaras as a progressive, home-grown model in integrated solid waste management. The island can serve as an inspiration and as a valuable learning opportunity for local authorities pursuing their own visions for making their communities clean and green.

Notes

1. The formula for arriving at estimates was computed using a new provincial poverty methodology approved by the National Statistical Coordination Board (NSCB) executive board in its meeting on 15 January 2003. The definition of poverty stipulated under Republic Act 8425, the Social Reform and Poverty Alleviation Act, refers to the poor as those families and individuals whose income falls below the poverty threshold and who cannot afford to provide for their minimum basic needs in a sustained manner.

2. With the exception of urban regions, where cities have special provisions and powers under the country's decentralization framework, there are three levels of local government units: the province, the municipality and the *barangay*. A *barangay* is an elected, village-based or neighbourhood-based local government unit, recognized under the Local Government Code.

3. Despite these successes, many local governments in Guimaras are still struggling to deal with increasingly large volumes of solid waste. These challenges include inadequate capacity of existing waste management facilities, financial constraints in the adoption of advanced foreign technological options, and technical, administrative, policy and market constraints that hinder the implementation of locally appropriate composting, recycling and sanitary landfill practices.

4. The Canadian Urban Institute (CUI) is a Toronto-based, non-profit organization dedicated to enhancing the quality of life in urban areas and urban hinterlands across Canada and internationally. With funding from the Canadian International Development Agency, the CUI works with several local government units in the Western Visayas region, as well as with national-level agencies with a local development mandate. The CUI's Philippines project is strengthening the capacity of local authorities to promote sustainable development, pursue good governance and improve community involvement in decision-making. For more information, see ⟨http://www.canurb.com⟩.

5. It is important to note that, although the task forces implemented the activities of the GISWM, support from many other organizations was also instrumental in their success. A group led by the provincial government supervised the task forces, composed of 22 Filipino members. The CUI, for example, provided hands-on support related to management and technical know-how transfer. The project also received financial, technical and research support from the GTZ, the CIDA-funded Canada–ASEAN Governance Innovations Network Program (CIDA–CAGIN) and the Local Government Support Program (LGSP). The LGPS is a Canada–Philippines bilateral cooperation initiative designed to strengthen the capacity of the Philippines to develop and implement policies and programmes in support of decentralization. It is promoting efficient, responsible, transparent and accountable governance in targeted regions of Western Visayas and Mindanao in the Philippines. The programme agenda supports equitable growth and poverty reduction through effective local governance. Notably, the LGSP provided financial support during the participatory waste stream assessment and participatory action planning stages of the project that amounted to approximately one-third of the total budget of 5 million Philippine pesos.

REFERENCES

Babaran, R. P. and J. A. Ingles (1996) "Coastal marine habitats of Guimaras", Philippines.

Brillantes Jr, Alex B. (1999) "Decentralization, devolution and development in the Philippines", UMP-Asia Occasional Paper No. 44. Bangkok, Thailand: Urban Management Programme Asia-Pacific.

Brillantes Jr, A., S. Ilago, E. Santiago and B. Esden (2003) "Decentralization and power shift: An imperative for good governance", University of the Philippines Diliman, Quezon City, Philippines.

Canadian Urban Institute (1997) *Project completion report of the Guimaras Integrated Solid Waste Management Project*. Guimaras, Philippines.

—— (1998) *Integrated solid waste management manual*. Guimaras, Philippines.

—— (2003) *Project evaluation report on Guimaras Integrated Solid Waste Management Program*. Guimaras, Philippines.

Gabinete, Angeles (1998) *Canada study tour report on local governance, environmental management and economic development*. October.

Galing Pook Foundation (2001) *Kaban Galing: Managing the environment*. Manila, Philippines.

Gonzales, J., K. Lauder and B. Melles (2000) *Opting for partnership: Governance innovations in Southeast Asia*. Ottawa, Canada: Institute on Governance.

Lighid, E. and F. Gentoral (1999) *Engaging communities in waste management*. Hull, Canada: Canada–ASEAN Governance Innovations Network Program, CIDA.

Link, P. (1997) *Guimaras Waste Stream Assessment Report*. Guimaras, Philippines.

Province of Guimaras (2001) *Provincial Tourism Office Statistics*. San Miguel, Guimaras, Philippines.

Provincial Government of Guimaras (2002) *Guimaras socio-economic profile*. San Miguel, Guimaras, Philippines.

Republic Act No. 7160 (1991) *The Local Government Code of the Philippines*. Manila, Philippines.

Republic Act No. 9003 (2000) *An Act Providing for an Ecological Waste Management Program*. Manila, Philippines.

Tabunda, M. S. and M. M. Galang (1991) *Primer Q&A: Local Government Code of 1991*. Manila, Philippines: Mary Jo Educational Supply Publisher.

12

Integrated catchment management in the Hawkesbury-Nepean basin, Australia

Amit Chanan

Introduction

Although sustainable natural resource management is viewed largely as a government responsibility, a great deal of community innovation and on-going commitment is required actually to make it happen. In this chapter I explore this reality by providing an overview of the development of an integrated catchment management system in the Hawkesbury-Nepean basin near Sydney, Australia. This river catchment was the focus of strong lobbying from community groups in the early 1990s, which led to the establishment of the Hawkesbury-Nepean Catchment Management Trust (HNCMT). Despite its many successes, this Trust was abolished in 2001. I shall elaborate on the successes enjoyed by the Trust and also explore the challenges it faced. Also of interest are the trials that now face the catchment community as it struggles to build on the good work that was achieved by the Trust prior to its abolition.

Background

The Hawkesbury-Nepean is one of the world's great river systems. Its catchment cradles Sydney and supplies it with fresh food, water and other resources. The catchment drains 22,000 km^2, from Goulburn, south of Sydney, to Palm Beach in the north. The catchment is also home to the world-famous Blue Mountains World Heritage area.

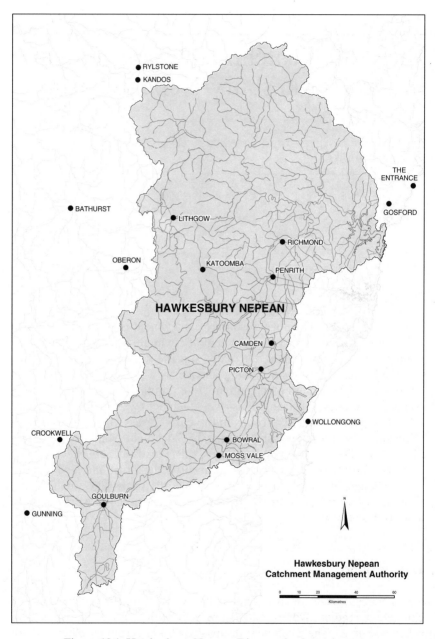

Figure 12.1 Hawkesbury-Nepean River and sub-catchments.

For the past 200 years, Sydney has relied heavily on the Hawkesbury-Nepean River and its catchment for its prosperity. Originally, the river and its catchment provided a life-sustaining food source to the infant colony; today the region contributes some 34 per cent of the nation's gross domestic product (Simmons and Scott 2003).

The Hawkesbury-Nepean River supplies 97 per cent of the water used in the homes and businesses of Sydney, the Illawarra, the Blue Mountains and the Central Coast. Its catchment supplies 80 per cent of Sydney's sand and gravel needs and it also provides the city with much of its fresh fruit and vegetables. The Hawkesbury-Nepean Catchment supports an agricultural industry with a farm-gate value in excess of AUS$1 billion (HNCMT 1999). The catchment is home to almost 1 million people and continues to absorb most of Sydney's urban expansion, as well as much of its waste.

Indigenous communities of the Hawkesbury-Nepean

Some of the earliest evidence of human occupation in the Hawkesbury-Nepean region dates back over 15,000 years (Kohen 1998). Two main indigenous tribes populated the area, the Kuringgai and the Darug. The Kuringgai occupied the land around the mouth of the Hawkesbury along the coast, and the Darug occupied a territory in the upper reaches of the river in the vicinity of the Blue Mountains (Kohen 1998). Both tribes had subsistence lifestyles. Whereas the coastal tribe lived mainly on fish and shellfish, the inland people had a more varied diet based on both the resources of the river and the terrestrial flora and fauna. The indigenous population lived in harmony with the river and its catchment for more than 15,000 years.

European arrival in the catchment

The relationship between humans and the river fundamentally changed some 200 years ago, with the arrival of European settlers in the region (Simmons and Scott 2003). The first European expedition to the area was led by Captain Arthur Phillip in 1789. Within only a few years of Captain Phillip's expedition, the first settlers had cleared the riverbanks of vegetation. In doing so, they were putting in motion a long cycle of erosion in the catchment and of sedimentation of the river channel. By April 1794, 22 settlers had established farms on the Hawkesbury and between them they had cleared about 0.283 km² of land (Simmons and Scott 2003).

European farming methods and equipment proved to be very poorly suited to the intermittent rainfall, extreme heat and meagre soils of the region. Yet this did little to stop the settlers from continuing to clear bush and plant crops along the river flats. By 1830, some 158 households were located along the river (Simmons and Scott 2003). Within half a century of European settlement in the catchment, land clearance for logging and agriculture had resulted in excessive loads of sediments washing into the river. By the 1860s, the river had silted up to such an extent that it could be navigated only by small boats. In 1864, railway arrived in the region and it was now possible to move produce to the markets in Sydney more quickly and reliably by steam engine. As a result of this improved market access, agricultural practices in the region diversified into fruit and vegetable production as well as dairy. This only added to the nutrient loads that were being deposited in the river system.

Mossfield (2000) has highlighted well the forcible imposition of British society on the indigenous population of the catchment. British settlers expressed little concern over their destruction of Aboriginal people and society. The renaming of places, flora and fauna by the new settlers has itself been a process of imposition. "Wianamatta, the Mother Creek, source of life for the indigenous communities for thousands of years, became South Creek, no more than a point on the compass" (Mossfield 2000: 4). Deerubbin became the Hawkesbury, Gedumba became Katoomba, Mooroo Murak became Penrith, and the list goes on. Lost names meant lost meaning, which in turn led to lost ownership of the land (Mossfield 2000). While the indigenous inhabitants, who had been stewards of the catchment for thousands of years, had their land forcibly taken from them under European imposition, the catchment's new inhabitants were struggling to feel at "home". "The heat, drought, flies, dust, smoke, and upside down weather, must have caused a resentment amongst settlers against the very land itself" (Richmond 1976; cited in Chanan 1997: 9). It is likely that these sorts of attitudes contributed to the slow development of the types of understanding necessary for the management of an arid environment. New European settlers lacked the same sense of intimacy with the land that motivated the indigenous inhabitants of the catchment (Chanan 1997). The nineteenth century for the Hawkesbury-Nepean catchment can best be described as the time when the catchment was in effect orphaned while the community profile within the catchment area underwent significant changes.

Catchment and community: The twentieth century

The picture of the river's health was to become even more clouded with the start of the dam-building era in 1907. By the turn of the nineteenth century, Sydney's growing population had outgrown all its local water supplies. In an effort to create new supplies, a state government authority,

Table 12.1 Water supply storages on the Hawkesbury-Nepean

Dam	Year completed	Catchment area (km^2)	Capacity (million litres)
Cataract	1907	125	94
Cordeaux	1926	87	94
Avon	1927	137	214
Nepean	1935	307	81
Warragamba	1960	8,445	2,092
Total			2,757

Source: Warner (1983).

the Municipal Water Supply, Sewerage and Drainage Board, was established to build a number of dams on the upper tributaries of the Hawkesbury River. By 1960, five major water storages had been completed (see Table 12.1). These dams now annually divert more than 600 million litres of water to supply the Sydney region. In dry times these five dams shut off water from 41 per cent of the catchment and, as a consequence, have modified both water and sediment discharges in the river (Warner 1981).

Community awakening

The implementation of the 1968 Regional Plan for Sydney was the starting point of a new era in the development of the Hawkesbury-Nepean catchment. This plan was essentially a project for rapid urban growth in fringe zones (primarily the Hawkesbury-Nepean catchment), which were assessed by state planners as being free of environmental constraints (Searle 1998). The plan in effect gave the green light to indiscriminate development. In the mid-1980s, this unharnessed exploitation of the catchment began to generate alarm among community groups, who were concerned about the environmental costs involved. Given the increased rate of erosion and sedimentation commonly associated with new developments, the community believed that an increase in stress on the river from pollutants and nutrients would occur as housing developments expanded. Not surprisingly, in 1990, not long after the new housing development started, a toxic blue-green algae growth caused a massive fish-kill in a Hawkesbury River tributary (*Sydney Morning Herald*, 21 November 1990; cited in Searle 1998).

Issues and problems in environmental management arise through the interactions between social and biophysical systems. When the net effect of these social–biophysical interactions creates "threats" for an individual or a group, an environmental problem is perceived to exist. This problem can relate to physical well-being, such as changes in culture and social activities, or it can result in changes to aesthetic well-being (Conacher 1980). In case of the Hawkesbury-Nepean, it was the question of aesthetic well-being that finally caused "the penny to drop" for the community, which then recognized that there was a problem and decided to stand up against it.

Community concern regarding the impact that rapid urban development was having on the Hawkesbury River environment led to the local residents setting up the Hawkesbury River Environment Protection Society in 1987. The society started as a group of like-minded people sharing a common concern for the river. The group met regularly to discuss issues relating to river health and to figure out ways to lobby the political leadership to take action. To cover the costs involved in generating a newsletter (*River Watch*), which provided information on proposed and current activities within the Hawkesbury-Nepean catchment, the society charged a membership fee. Within a year it had 109 financial members (Hawkesbury River Environment Protection Society 1988; cited in Searle 1998).

In 1989, concerns over water quality and recurring algal blooms, coupled with the government's lack of response, led to a heightened awareness of the need for some form of action from local communities. As a result, various local community groups joined forces to form the Coalition of Hawkesbury and Nepean Groups for the Environment (CHANGE). This organization comprised 44 environmental groups, including the Hawkesbury River Environment Protection Society and many similar green groups from elsewhere in the catchment. The aim of CHANGE was "to obtain the highest possible water quality for the Hawkesbury-Nepean Catchment System, and protection of all aspects of the Catchment environment" (Hawkesbury River Environment Protection Society 1990: 1). CHANGE took up the concerns of the community and called for an end to unchecked urban sprawl in the west region of Sydney (*Sydney Morning Herald*, 27 October 1992; *Sydney Morning Herald*, 8 February 1993; cited in Searle 1998).

Residents of the Hawkesbury-Nepean catchment, led by CHANGE, reacted against development proposals that would destroy valued local environments. Protests by residents of the catchment, who were acting out of genuine concern about river health, involved a multi-pronged approach that covered both local and state government. Catchment residents, working alongside members of environmental groups, attended local council meetings to protest against development applications. Representations were also made to members of the state parliament, highlighting citizens' concerns.

Organization for total catchment management

The Hawkesbury-Nepean Catchment Management Trust

While CHANGE was actively campaigning against any development proposals that had the potential to destroy the local environment, the state government's response to its demands was less than impressive. Continuous pressure from CHANGE and other community groups did, however, result in a number of significant achievements. Included among these was the announcement by Sydney Water Corporation (then Water Board) in the early 1990s that it would spend AUS$600 million over 10 years to upgrade and expand sewage treatment plants in the Hawkesbury-Nepean catchment (Burgess, c. 1991–1992; cited in Searle 1998). Unfortunately, the upgrading of sewage treatment plants alone was not going to be enough to prevent the river's looming environmental disaster.

It is the leadership of a key individual or group of individuals that often provides the driving force for innovation. In this instance, it was local leaders who recognized that, although community movements such as CHANGE were essential to keeping the issue in the forefront of public policy debate, this did not represent a long-term solution. What was really needed was the establishment of an authority whose sole purpose and function would be to manage the river and its catchment. In an effort to bring such an organization into life, Kevin Rozzoli, a member of the New South Wales parliament and a long-time river advocate, prepared a draft bill calling for a river management authority for the Hawkesbury-Nepean.

CHANGE supported the draft bill and rallied community support to lobby for its approval by the government. In response to increasing community support for the draft bill, the New South Wales government established a Taskforce to consider the available options for better managing the Hawkesbury-Nepean River. The Taskforce was composed of officers from state government agencies such as the Department of Land and Water Conservation, the Department of Planning, the Environment Protection Authority and the Sydney Water Corporation, as well as elected representatives from local and state government. Kevin Rozzoli was elected to the Taskforce as a representative of the state government. The Taskforce recognized that the existing management framework had failed owing to a plethora of agencies involved and, in its report to the Minister for Conservation and Land Management, it recommended the establishment of the Hawkesbury-Nepean Catchment Management Trust (HNCMT). The purpose of the HNCMT was to achieve a healthy and productive river system and catchment (Hawkesbury-Nepean Taskforce 1991).

The Taskforce also recognized that community involvement in, and acceptance of, the solutions developed to help solve the river's problems were essential. The Taskforce recommended, therefore, that the proposed HNCMT must develop effective linkages with communities and interest groups throughout the catchment area and ensure ongoing accountability to the public (Hawkesbury-Nepean Taskforce 1991). These linkages were to be achieved by direct community representation on the HNCMT and by significant community membership on any sub-catchment-based Catchment Management Committees.

The HNCMT was established in 1993 to implement total catchment management in the region. Since its inception, the HNCMT has been advocating the cause of sustainable use, development and management of the catchment. Following the recommendations of the Hawkesbury-Nepean Taskforce, its members were selected on the basis of merit according to their scientific, planning, technical and/or managerial knowledge and ability. Part-time positions on the Trust were publicly advertised, and individuals were selected from a panel of nominees living within the Hawkesbury-Nepean catchment in categories of: landholders/land users, people with environmental interests, people with business and/or commercial interests, local government representatives, and academics. State government agencies such as the Environment Protection Authority, the Sydney Water Corporation and the Department of Land and Water Conservation were also represented on the Trust.

The HNCMT was established by its inclusion in Schedule 1 to the Catchment Management Act 1989, legislation of the New South Wales government, and by the Hawkesbury-Nepean Catchment Management Trust Regulation 1993 made under this Act. This Regulation provided that the purpose of the Trust was to encourage the protection of the Hawkesbury and Nepean River system through facilitating ecologically sustainable development and resource use and fostering orderly and proper physical, environmental and socio-economic planning as the basis of the well-being of the people and all life within the Trust area. The Regulation came into operation on 1 July 1993.

In addition to providing the HNCMT with general powers, the Act provided the Trust with functions relating to:
• preparing advice on environmental planning instruments in the Trust area;
• preparing advice on environmental planning studies;
• advising the Director of Planning on matters that should be addressed in an environmental impact study;
• exercising functions relating to the granting of concurrence to a development if empowered to do so by a planning instrument made under the Environment Planning and Assessment Act 1979;

- formulating guidelines for developers and consent authorities;
- undertaking educational activities;
- maintaining data on the Hawkesbury-Nepean catchment (Trust area);
- facilitating research.

Factors supporting innovation

The HNCMT was able to achieve a certain amount of success in the management of the catchment. These successes were not limited to environmental improvements. Creating and implementing the Trust represented a significant innovation in terms of river catchment management. It was a new and unique approach to river management in which participation by various stakeholders was a core guiding principle.

A key success achieved by the HNCMT was the high level of participation in the organization by community members. This was achieved primarily through the establishment of seven Catchment Management Committees (CMCs) beginning in August 1994. The CMCs were based on the seven sub-catchment regions within the larger Hawkesbury-Nepean catchment. These CMCs were established under the Catchment Management Act of 1989 and, in keeping with the Act, they consisted of a majority of landholders and land users within their respective sub-catchments. The most prominent community activists from the pre-HNCMT era were also given an opportunity to get involved in the management of their beloved catchment by their inclusion on the CMCs. The seven CMCs within the Hawkesbury-Nepean catchment were: Upper Nepean, Middle Nepean-Hawkesbury, Blue Mountains, South Creek, Cattai Creek, Berowra and Cowan Creek.

One of the most humbling experiences for the technical experts involved in the HNCMT and the CMCs was the vast extent of detailed knowledge about the Hawkesbury-Nepean River and its processes that was held by several community members. Some long-term residents of the area had been witness to the steady degradation of the river. They remembered the days when they swam in the river and they had seen the installation of the sewage treatment plants in the region. They had experienced the deterioration of the riverine corridors and the degradation of water quality. Without these walking and talking encyclopaedias of the Hawkesbury-Nepean, and without the opportunity provided by the CMCs for their participation, this information might never have entered the strategy development process and it could have been lost forever. This capacity to capture local knowledge and understanding and combine it with external technical expertise was one of the key factors in making the Trust so effective in catchment management.

In addition to providing useful information on the catchment and the river itself, knowledgeable local residents also performed a vital role as monitors and watchdogs of the river and its surrounds. The sense of ownership fostered by their participation on the CMC in fact resulted in a net increase in enthusiasm for the care and protection of the Hawkesbury-Nepean.

The structure of the HNCMT was another key factor in its success. The establishment of the Trust represented an innovative experiment in catchment management in the State of New South Wales. In spite of being a government body, the HNCMT was anything but a traditional government department. As highlighted in Figure 12.2, the HNCMT involved members from local communities, businesses, other institutional managers as well as government (both state and local) on its board and on the CMCs. It was the board that was responsible for making decisions for the HNCMT. This allowed the Trust to function in a transparent fashion and build up a strong relationship with local communities.

The 16-strong HNCMT board included a chairperson and the HNCMT's chief executive officer. The chief executive officer also acted as a conduit between the board and the other staff of the HNCMT. The technical staff of the Trust included approximately 30 full-time staff, who were divided into four major programme areas, based on the nature of their roles. These programme areas broadly covered: catchment management (including stormwater and wastewater management); catchment planning; catchment education; and catchment science and research.

HNCMT's unique structure was necessary not only to ensure an effective advocacy role, but also to ensure that decisions, resources, policies and programmes were geared towards the long-term and sustainable needs of the river and its catchment (Hawkesbury-Nepean Taskforce 1991). To ensure a degree of accountability, the HNCMT reported directly to the Minister for Land and Water Conservation, who had ultimate responsibility for its direction and control. It was not the minister's role to exercise day-to-day control over the HNCMT.

The seven sub-catchment-based CMCs were responsible for coordinating and advising on natural resource management activities within their respective spheres of operation. Each CMC had a full-time coordinator and limited administrative and project staff. The CMCs were responsible to the HNCMT chairperson. In simplified terms, the CMCs could be said to have acted like a mini-HNCMT within their respective sub-catchments, and they received their funding and strategic direction from the HNCMT. In 1999, after a state-wide review of total catchment management, the state government directed the HNCMT to disband its seven CMCs. Because the Trust was reluctant to lose the strong community linkage provided by these CMCs, it resolved to replace them with Catch-

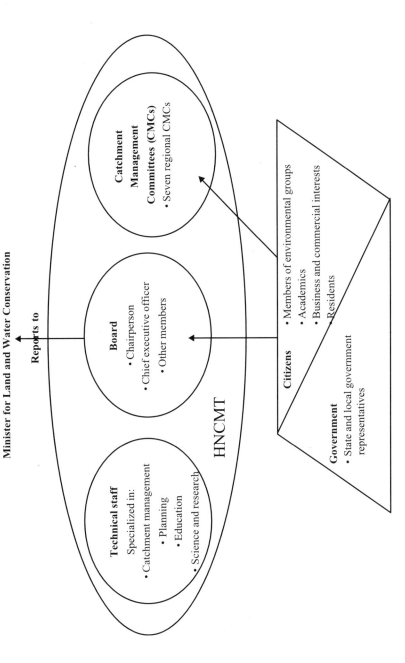

Figure 12.2 The multi-stakeholder structure of the HNCMT.

283

ment Advisory Committees (CACs) and to continue their important function.

Successes of the HNCMT

Within half a decade of its establishment, the HNCMT managed to make significant contributions to community awareness and improvements in river health. The HNCMT placed a particular emphasis on educating the younger generation about catchment management issues, with a view to enhancing children's understanding of their local catchment. Activities jointly organized by the HNCMT and local schools were aimed at developing relationships between the children and their local waterways, a relationship that was all but lost in the rapidly urbanizing environment. Through excursions, by developing a range of education kits and by providing research information, the HNCMT worked with local secondary and tertiary education institutions to educate students about a range of local catchment issues.

In its endeavours to empower local communities and enable them to manage their catchments better, the HNCMT provided support to Regional Habitat Committees within the catchment, including Bushcare and Landcare groups (General Purpose Standing Committee No. 5, 2002). Bushcare and Landcare groups are community-based voluntary groups that undertake reforestation and catchment/stream rehabilitation works. During 1999/2000, some 2,500 volunteers were working on local habitat rehabilitation projects. These groups enjoyed a great deal of support from the HNCMT, both in terms of resources (wherever possible) and in kind. In addition to working closely with the Bushcare and Landcare groups, the HNCMT also worked to strengthen Streamwatch volunteer groups within the Hawkesbury-Nepean catchment. Similar to Bushcare groups, Streamwatch groups operate on a volunteer basis to monitor water quality in the streams. The effectiveness of the HNCMT in encouraging these groups is evident from the fact that by 1999/2000 there were an estimated 5,000 members of 168 Streamwatch groups in the catchment (General Purpose Standing Committee No. 5, 2002).

In addition to algal blooms, severe alligator weed infestation in some parts of the catchment ranked amongst the top environmental concerns about the river health. The HNCMT developed and managed programmes and projects in partnership with the local government to address weed infestation issues. The HNCMT established the Hawkesbury Nepean Aquatic Weeds Taskforce and provided it with start-up funding. The Taskforce has been responsible for initiating a number of local weed control strategies and has been particularly successful in managing the alligator weed (General Purpose Standing Committee No. 5, 2002).

The involvement of local business in catchment management activities is another area where the HNCMT enjoyed a great deal of success. The HNCMT ran an innovative project called the Roofs for Revegetation project, which relied on partnerships with local businesses. The project involved engaging local businesses such as hotels, industries and clubs in growing native saplings on their roof tops prior to their use in riverbank revegetation elsewhere in the catchment (General Purpose Standing Committee No. 5, 2002).

An independent review by the NSW government's Healthy Rivers Commission of the Hawkesbury-Nepean catchment in 1998 publicly acknowledged the excellent work of the HNCMT (Healthy Rivers Commission 1997). This review also specifically recognized the HNCMT's contribution in negotiating excellent working relationships with stakeholders and other agencies. This effective relationship with local communities culminated in a massive volunteer workforce, whose members gave of their time and resources to catchment remediation and revegetation works. According to some estimates, the economic value of this volunteer work far outweighed the actual money given to the HNCMT by the state government.

The Trust received an annual allocation of approximately AUS$3.6 million from the state treasury from 1993 until its abolition. It also succeeded in gaining additional project funding from a variety of other sources, including the Commonwealth government and local government (HNCMT 1999–2000: 15–16). The Trust also received significant in-kind contributions from businesses and volunteers, the value of which was estimated to be about AUS$9.5 million in 2000/2001 (HNCMT 2000–2001: 11).

Barriers to innovation

In spite of all its great work in the catchment, the HNCMT was always treading a fine line between environmental values and economic gains. It was increasingly being squeezed between bureaucratic decisions emanating from the top and community needs being expressed from the bottom. Because of its very strong relationship with the communities involved, the Trust was largely perceived in bureaucratic circles as itself being a community organization. The sub-catchment-based CMCs (later replaced by the Catchment Committees Committees) acted as HNCMT's eyes and ears in the communities, which were often strongly opposed to the state government's development proposals in the catchment. In line with its mandate to improve catchment health and to work with local communities, the HNCMT voiced community concerns in the public arena and empowered community groups. Some critics now believe that it was this function of the Trust that eventually became unpalatable for the state government.

One of the ways in which the HNCMT was particularly effective in empowering the community to work for environmental improvements was by providing people with planning advice and other useful technical information (Powell 2002; cited in General Purpose Standing Committee No. 5, 2002). For instance, a proposal to build a large development close to the water near Brooklyn at Kangaroo Point (estuarine reaches of the Hawkesbury-Nepean) was knocked back owing to strong community opposition to the associated environmental impacts. These environmental impacts were so significant that the HNCMT was opposed to the development and was able to increase the community's awareness of them. In a similar demonstration of its commitment to community empowerment, the Trust was the first public organization to support the Castlereagh community's position that a local toxic tip was unacceptable and it helped to lobby for its closure (General Purpose Standing Committee No. 5, 2002).

In April 2001, without any warning, the NSW state government decided to abolish the HNCMT. A NSW Parliamentary Senate Inquiry set up to investigate this sudden abolition of the Trust has concluded that the "decision was both uncalled for and unjustifiable" (General Purpose Standing Committee No. 5, 2002: xi). The Inquiry found very little evidence in favour of the closure of the Trust, which had become a widely commended organization. If anything, the report suggests that losing the HNCMT was to the detriment of the catchment area and the surrounding communities. Jenny Smith, a former trustee on the HNCMT board, believes that the reason behind the HNCMT's abolition was the threat it posed to the government (Lee 2002). Smith suggests that "the HNCMT was empowering the community, so was allowing the community voice to come forward" (cited in Lee 2002).

The abolition of the HNCMT represented a significant loss for the surrounding communities. In her submission to the Senate Inquiry, Elspeth Murphy of the Movement Opposed to Senseless Environmental Sacrilege (MOSES) describes the situation experienced by the community since the HNCMT was abolished:

We believe the abolition of the Trust has implications for the natural ecology, public health, and social wellbeing within the catchment. Its coordinating, advocacy, and advisory roles have gone.... We do not have the broad range of expertise the Trust encompassed. The two-way education and information exchange has gone – the newsletters and forums have stopped and the Catchment Committees were abandoned. Environment groups no longer have the "one stop shop" advice resource. We are back to the fragmentation of the past! (Cited in General Purpose Standing Committee No. 5, 2002)

In his submission to the Senate Inquiry, John Powell, convenor of The Hawkesbury River Environment Protection Society (THREPS), echoed the views expressed by Murphy when he stated:

There is now simply a vacuum where the HNCMT stood. Its expertise has been dispersed and lost, its voice as an advocate for the catchment is silent, its role as a watchdog is vacant, its monitoring tasks are no longer being carried out, its productive relationship with local government is no longer in place, and its important function as a creator and store of information has ceased. These are all highly significant losses to the catchment. As far as our Society is concerned the clock has been turned back a decade. In common with other community groups we are now obliged to rely solely upon our own very limited resources. It is undeniable that the creation of the HNCMT relieved community groups of a great deal of responsibility, as they were able to rely upon the integrity and independence of the Trust as an advocate for the health of the catchment and, in addition, they were able to seek advice from the HNCMT and draw upon its expertise. (Cited in General Purpose Standing Committee No. 5, 2002)

When asked about the effectiveness of the Trust, Mr Peter Davey, the former chief executive officer, stated in his evidence to the Senate Inquiry into the abolition of the HNCMT:

I think what needs to be borne in mind is that the Trust itself was a unique organisation. It was not a river manager, and that point needs to be made clear. It was not a management organisation. The reason why it was able to perform the role it did was because it was not burdened with or assigned the traditional management responsibilities that normally rest with local government or with State agencies. That is why it was able to maintain that independent role. So to that extent it did not have a traditional management function. It had a coordination, an advocacy function and so forth, but it delivered a whole range of programs to those organisations that did have that management role. (Cited in General Purpose Standing Committee No. 5, 2002)

Future challenges

Hawkesbury-Nepean Catchment Foundation

The disbanding of the HNCMT put catchment management back by a decade to the pre-CHANGE era where no mechanism existed for making community concerns heard. Some former trustees and CMC members recognized the crucial need to fill the vacuum left behind by the abolition of the HNCMT. These key players in the Hawkesbury-Nepean catchment – including Peter Davey (former chief executive of the HNCMT), Jenny Smith (formerly on the HNCMT), Tony Ross (formerly on the Upper Nepean CMC), Sandy Booth (from the University of Western Sydney) and Max Hatherly (formerly on the HNCMT), to name a few – resolved to form a foundation to rebuild community voice in the catchment. Community involvement and activism are the basis of the Hawkesbury-Nepean Catchment Foundation, which was established in 2001, the same year that the HNCMT was abolished. Its members are committed to building an effective organization that promotes catchment management and acts as a watchdog for the river and its catchment.

Of the key challenges that lie ahead for the Foundation, perhaps the most significant one is financial survival. The current source of income for the Foundation is membership fees. This will not be enough for the Foundation to carry out community involvement and education work to the same extent as the former HNMCT and some efforts are under way to try to secure funds from the state government. It is important that, in its attempts to secure finances, the Foundation not forget its underlying principles and objectives. As pointed out by Martin (1991: 781), "if the underlying philosophies are not addressed, the group can end up being too dependent on the Government and the community power may be lost".

Conclusion and discussion

"Problems are not floating around waiting to be recognised. A problem is a problem if there is agreement between people that it is" (Martin 1991: 781). This statement sounds rather simplistic, yet it holds the key to any community movement for natural resource management. In the case of the Hawkesbury-Nepean for instance, uncontrolled land clearance and degradation of river health continued for well over a century before the local communities actually reached an agreement that river degradation was a problem that needed to be addressed.

This lesson will become increasingly important for countries in the developing world that have large river systems, such as India (the Ganges), Pakistan (the Indus) and Indo-China (the Mekong). These countries are all heading down a path of degradation similar to that in the Hawkesbury-Nepean. The communities in these catchments will be able to do something to prevent this only if they understand and acknowledge that degradation is both a genuine and an urgent "problem". Not only does this first step provide the glue that helps community groups work together and cooperate, it also gives them a common goal for which to aim. A shared vision is key to promoting community-led innovation, whereas a lack of such vision can make the achievement of any type of community-led initiative much less likely.

An important observation emphasized by Martin (1991: 781) suggests that "successful community groups, once established, develop into stronger more permanent organisations that become involved in a much wider range of local development". The Hawkesbury-Nepean case study supports this observation. The community movement that started in response to algal blooms in the river resulted in the government setting up the HNCMT, which was responsible for total catchment management in the entire 22,000 km^2 of the catchment. The movement has now transformed into a Foundation, which is carrying forward the work done by the HNCMT.

Ridge (2003) suggests that a healthy river means different things to different people. Although perhaps a little irrelevant to developing countries, the following remarks accurately describe the relationship between an individual and a river in the developed world: "As a child, one's relationship with rivers tends to be centered on the river as a playground, a clean cool place to relax and enjoy. As we get older and busier, we may find that central relationship dwindles to a place we cross over by bridge on our way to work. A place we look down upon, burying thoughts of a vibrant past with a query 'why don't someone look after it better?' " (Ridge 2003: 19). This anthropocentric view of a healthy river is actually crucial for community awakening and action towards improving river health. In the developing world, the relationship between an individual and the river in most cases is much more direct. A river's role in water supply for drinking and irrigation and in removing waste is much more apparent. It should therefore be relatively easier to elaborate on these anthropocentric uses and foster community support.

A significant characteristic of any democratic government is the basic rule behind its policy decisions "to please the masses". Therein lies the strength of community movements. It is important to realize, however, that not all government decisions are made with the environment as the centre of attention. The environment, although vital, is only one of the many portfolios that the government is responsible for. What the Hawkesbury-Nepean experience has proved is that, if the goal of a community movement is to be an independent advocate for the environment, it needs to keep the government at arm's length. It certainly needs to maintain some form of financial independence. As highlighted by the HNCMT experiment, an independent watchdog that focuses explicitly on the environment is bound to have disagreements with the government of the day, which will always have one eye on another agenda.

REFERENCES

Chanan, A. (1997) "Role of GIS and GPS in bushfire management, Cattai National Park case study", MEM thesis, University of Western Sydney, Australia.

Conacher, A. (1980) "Environmental problem-solving and land-use management: A proposed structure for Australia", *Environmental Management* 4: 391–405.

General Purpose Standing Committee No. 5 (2002) *Abolition of the Hawkesbury-Nepean Catchment Management Trust*, Report 14, March. New South Wales Parliament, Legislative Council, Parliamentary Paper No. 8. Sydney, NSW: the Committee.

Hawkesbury-Nepean Taskforce (1991) *Directions towards a sustainable future for the Hawkesbury-Nepean*, Report of the Hawkesbury-Nepean Taskforce, Sydney, NSW, November.

Hawkesbury River Environment Protection Society (1990) *River Watch*, No. 13, Spencer, NSW.

Healthy Rivers Commission (1997) *Independent Inquiry into the Hawkesbury-Nepean River System*, Sydney, NSW: the Commission.

HNCMT [Hawkesbury-Nepean Catchment Management Trust] (1999) "Hawkesbury-Nepean Catchment Management Trust's submission to the House of Representatives Standing Committee on Environment and Heritage Inquiry into Catchment Management", September; available at ⟨http://www.aph.gov.au⟩.

—— (1999–2000) *Hawkesbury-Nepean Catchment Management Trust annual report 1999–2000*. Windsor, NSW: the Trust.

—— (2000–2001) *Hawkesbury Nepean Catchment Management Trust business plan 2000/2001*. Windsor, NSW: the Trust.

Kohen, J. L. (1998) "Aboriginal environmental impacts in the Hawkesbury River area", in Jocelyn Powell (ed.), *The improvers' legacy: Environmental studies of the Hawkesbury*. Marrickville, NSW: Southwood Press.

Lee, K. (2002) "Losing the trust", Australian Centre for Independent Journalism, ⟨http://www.reportage.uts.edu.au/stories/2002/political/trust.html⟩.

Martin, P. (1991) "Environmental care in agricultural catchments: Toward the communicative catchment", *Environmental Management* 15(6): 773–783.

Mossfield, T. (2000) "Saving eco urbia: A Wianamatta perspective", *South Creek Back From the Brink Conference Proceedings*, 22–23 June 2000, University of Western Sydney, Kingswood, NSW.

Ridge, K. (2003) "The community as an active, concerned partner in catchment and river management", in Max Hatherly and Sandy Booth (eds), *Healthy partnerships healthy rivers – Community forum*. Berowra Heights, NSW: Deerubin Press.

Searle, G. (1998) "Contradictions in consumption of the urban environment: Community, state and Sydney's development", *Proceedings of the Environmental Justice: Global Ethics for the 21st Century Conference*, University of Melbourne, Melbourne, VIC, 1–3 October.

Simmons, B., Scott, J. (2005) "The river has recorded the story: Living with the Hawkesbury River, NSW, Australia", in History of water, Volume 1., *Water control and river biographies*. I. B. Tauris Publications.

Warner, R. (1981) "The impacts of dams and weirs on the Hawkesbury-Nepean River system, New South Wales, Australia", *Proceedings of the Second International Conference on Fluvial Sedimentology*, Keele University, UK.

———— (1983) "Channel changes in sandstone and shale reaches of the Nepean River, New South Wales", in R. W. Young and G. C. Nanson (eds), *Aspects of Australian and New Zealand geomorphology*, Group Special Publication No. 1.

13

Water management in Rajasthan, India: Making a difference

Darryl Romesh D'Monte

Introduction

Traditionally, village societies in India enjoyed a harmonious relationship with the natural environment on which people depended. "Common property resources" included village grazing lands, community forests, wastelands, common grounds for threshing grain, drainage, tanks, and rivulets and river beds. These comprised most of the resources available to the community and considerable folklore, as well as religious and cultural associations, was built around them. For centuries, these rural communities also enjoyed a high degree of self-rule. This independence ended with the introduction of British colonial rule, when India's colonial rulers took control of the resources owned by the village communities and deprived them of their traditional administrative and legal powers. After the country regained independence in 1947 this system was largely emulated by the Indian government and, as a consequence, the people living in rural communities lost their capacity to cooperate in the management of their common property resources for mutual benefit.

The lack of capacity to cooperate in the collective management of shared resources is of particular concern in the north-west Indian state of Rajasthan. Common lands play a particularly important role in this arid to semi-arid state because they are a source of livelihood for the agro-pastoral communities, providing for food, fodder and fuel needs. Owing to the excessive control and mismanagement of natural environmental resources by the national and local governments, the rural people of Rajasthan have become impoverished and have been forced to migrate to towns in search of work. One of the most damaging consequences has been a further reduction in the people's belief in their own ability to change their situation.

This chapter describes some of the innovative initiatives that have been implemented in the Alwar district of Rajasthan, which have been aimed at alleviating poverty, addressing the loss of common property, and confronting serious environmental problems such as deforestation and drought. My specific focus of discussion is the community-led water management initiatives that have been implemented through village-level self-governing bodies under the facilitation of a non-governmental organization (NGO) called the Tarun Bharat Sangh. I shall use this discussion to show that the key factors leading to the success of the initiatives were: the utilization of traditional local knowledge, labour and customs; the visionary leadership of the Tarun Bharat Sangh; and the coordination of self-governing bodies at the village level.

Problems faced in Rajasthan

Rajasthan is one of India's "BIMARU" states. BIMARU is an acronym that refers to the Hindi-speaking heartland, comprising Bihar, Madhya Pradesh, Rajasthan and Uttar Pradesh, which is often viewed as lagging behind the rest of the country in terms of its development. The state of Rajasthan is partly covered by desert and is largely poverty-stricken. Although some of its afflictions can be attributed to the vagaries of nature, human intervention has also played a major role in impoverishing the region. Excessive grazing by animals and deforestation are the root causes of the loss of vegetative cover in the state. As early as the 1980s, satellite data showed that only 1.7 per cent of Rajasthan's area was forested. Nearly 40 per cent of the forest cover of the 700 km Aravalli hill range, which runs diagonally across the state, had been lost over the previous decade. The Centre for Science and Environment, an NGO in New Delhi, attributes this high level of deforestation to the "illegal and systematic felling of trees, backed by corrupt government officials" (Mahapatra 2001: 89).

The state's northernmost district of Alwar, just above the state capital of Jaipur, suffers from a similar level of deforestation and degradation. This has occurred despite the fact that the Sariska National Park, which has been designated for special protection as a tiger sanctuary, falls partly within the district. As of 1998, Alwar consisted of 1,991 villages and had a population of 2.3 million (Khalakdina 1998: 6). With average rainfall of barely 62 cm a year, Alwar is described by geographers as "semi-arid". Its meagre green cover consists of deciduous trees and shrublands, and the district has been subjected to almost perennial drought, with rainfall often failing for three or more years in a row. Alwar is home to two tribal groups, the Gujjars and the Meenas. The low-caste Gujjars occupy the hilly ranges, where they raise animals including goats and sheep. The Meenas engage not only in herding but also in subsistence farming on the plains. Each family owns just 1.5 hectares of land on average, which is barely enough to sustain a living given the harsh and inhospitable terrain.

Prior to the implementation of the initiatives described in this chapter, villages in the Alwar district were poorly organized and both poverty and severe environmental degradation were widespread. In part, this was owing to the appropriation by the state of much of the area's natural resources. The Gujjars and Meenas had traditionally been linked closely to their natural environment because their well-being depended on it. This link was completely lost, however, when British colonial rule usurped the local people's rights to natural resources such as timber and fodder. After independence, instead of restoring this link, the Rajasthan government began permitting private contractors to fell trees, which only contributed to the further degradation of the land.

Poverty and the lack of agricultural productivity formed a vicious circle in Alwar, and in the end forced the young men to migrate to the nearest towns in search of work. The harshness of the landscape also took a heavy toll on people's self-confidence and robbed them of the will to launch new initiatives.

New initiatives and challenges

In more recent years, a number of new initiatives have been undertaken in an effort to relieve some of the problems of Alwar and it is these that I shall discuss in detail in this case study.

The first major initiatives undertaken in Alwar took place in the village of Gopalpura, although they were followed by numerous initiatives elsewhere throughout the district. As this case study will demonstrate, the villagers of Gopalpura faced many challenges during the implementation of the initiatives, most of which were owing to conflicts with the authorities. Through their efforts to overcome these barriers, and in rediscovering a local system of water management, the villagers were able successfully to bring about a range of innovations in their communities.

Harvesting the rain in Gopalpura

When the initiatives began, the village of Gopalpura was made up of just 52 families, all belonging to the Meena tribal community. This community was known once to have been rich, with large herds of cattle that provided milk and other products. As the forests surrounding the village were gradually degraded owing to mismanagement and excessive tree felling, the community lost its support system and villagers were forced to migrate with their herds to surrounding areas in search of fodder. In the mid-1980s, the Tarun Bharat Sangh NGO began working with the villagers of Gopalpura to reverse this trend by replenishing groundwater reserves and keeping drought at bay. This effort initially involved three key initiatives: restoring the local mechanisms for water-harvesting (*johads*), repairing a dam and reforesting the catchment areas.

The first step taken by the villagers was to repair the *johad*, the semicircular earthen check-dam, which is a traditional water-harvesting structure. These structures are designed to block the flow of streams during the monsoons and to create a small reservoir behind them. This helps the water to percolate into the ground, instead of running off, and recharges the groundwater. The *johads* ensure that there is sufficient water supply to sustain agriculture even in the dry season (see Figure 13.1).

Figure 13.1 The *johad* in Raika village in Alwar district.
Source: Centre for Science and Environment, New Delhi.

These rudimentary water-retaining structures require regular upkeep in order to function. Many old *johads*, which had been built some 500–600 years ago, lay disused as a result of years of neglect by the Rajasthan Irrigation Department, which operated on very limited funds. Before the monsoons of 1986, the community de-silted and deepened the first *johad* in Gopalpura, which had been constructed at least 300 years ago. Shortly afterwards, the bountiful rains arrived after years of drought and the *johad* was able to retain water for much longer than it had in previous years.

This initial success with the *johad* emboldened the villagers and they embarked upon the more ambitious task of repairing the bigger dam. This new structure was 274 metres long and 6 metres tall. It required 10,000 days of work, and the actual cost of repairing the sluices and over-flow systems was divided equally between the village and the Tarun Bharat Sangh. When all of Gopalpura's nine check-dams were completed, they were able to irrigate 100 hectares of farmland (their earlier capacity irrigated only 33 hectares) and also meet household needs throughout the village.

The restoration of *johads* and the dam did not just result in better financial well-being for families in the village. More importantly, it made the families aware of their own strength and their capacity to overcome difficulties.

The villagers began to realize that the availability of water depended on the overall health of the catchment area surrounding the harvesting structures. After their success in recharging the underground reserves, the villagers realized that they would need to reforest the surrounding areas. This would not only ensure that scant rain did not run off but also yield fodder for their cattle. Gopalpura receives only about 60 cm of rain a year. Since the denuding of the surrounding Aravalli hills, there had been a high level of run-off during the monsoon season. This carried the fertile topsoil down the hill slopes and deposited it in the *johads* located in the foothills. The resulting fall in the water table was reflected not only in poor farm yields but also in empty wells. Land records show that, whereas the village of Gopalpura covers 240 hectares, a little less than one-third of this area was cultivated. Despite only 9 per cent of this culti-vated land being irrigated, groundwater was still rapidly being depleted (Mahapatra 2001: 95–96).

In 1987, the residents of Gopalpura started planting trees in the catch-ment areas of the *johads*. In the vicinity, there was a barren hill that cov-ered 24 hectares. The village assembly collectively decided to afforest the hill and fence it in with a stone wall, both to demarcate the area and to prevent cattle from grazing on the saplings. The villagers also imposed a number of restrictions on themselves. Instead of erecting poles and barbed wire fences to stop animals from destroying saplings, villagers tethered the animals to trees or kept them in barns. They then provided fodder for them instead of permitting them to graze freely. This is known among several greening initiatives throughout India as "social fencing". Within two years of the community beginning these afforestation activities, the desolate landscape had acquired profuse vegetation.

Challenges faced

Although the villagers of Gopalpura achieved early success, they needed to join together to overcome the many challenges they faced along the way. One of their first challenges came in March 1987, when the Rajasthan Irrigation Department served a legal notice on the Tarun Bharat Sangh, declaring that Gopalpura's *johads* were illegal on the grounds that all drains and local monsoon streams were the property of the state. This notice came despite a previous statement from a high-ranking official of the Rajasthan Environment Department that complimented the people on their achievement and noted that he had not witnessed this kind of work anywhere else in the state (Khalakdina 1998: 56).

The reaction to this notice in Gopalpura demonstrated the strength of its people. Having nurtured this resource at considerable cost to the community in terms of labour and money, the villagers were not prepared to relinquish control over it. Instead they stood their ground and refused to let officials destroy the *johads*. In the end, their vigorous protest forced the government to back down. As a result, the state Irrigation Department eventually accepted that the structures did indeed help conserve water and soil and revoked its orders. This incident is proof of the development of self-confidence and self-assertion within the community. Before the initiative to rebuild the *johads* began, the village consisted of individual families, each fending for itself. Once the community banded together in the project, however, it was able to present an effective common front against oppression.

The villagers experienced a number of other problems with the government. After efforts to plant trees in the catchment area began to receive attention, a Rajasthan government land records official inspected the trees that had been fenced in and reported back to the administration and local politicians. The officials levied a fine of Rs 4,950 (US$108) to be paid by June 1989 and issued a notice stating that the protective wall had to be removed.[1] These measures were most likely taken by officials and politicians because they felt threatened by the unprecedented solidarity of the villagers. Previously, villagers had never presented a united front against any official intervention or harassment, and it was relatively easy to intimidate individuals by fining them for minor lapses and on other flimsy excuses. Despite the villagers' protests, government officials felled the trees under the watchful protection of the police. The land was then re-allotted to six families from outside the village.

In spite of these setbacks, the people of Gopalpura continued to stand firm and to assert their rights. With the Tarun Bharat Sangh serving as a catalyst, the villagers demonstrated against the violation of their rights and the transfer of the land they had greened to outsiders. Because the people had invested so much of their own labour and resources in planting the trees, they felt a strong sense of "ownership" over the initiative and this motivated them to protect the area, irrespective of the assistance they received from external organizations (Mahapatra 2001: 96–97). As a direct result of their efforts, the top-ranking official in the Alwar district administration, the Collector, apologised to the people and allotted another 10 hectares and Rs 10,000 (US$219) to the village assembly to continue its greening activities. The people spent the next several months reforesting the catchment and eventually they succeeded in retaining moisture in the soil and averting drought (Sheena and Mishra 1998: 59).

Word of the successes in Gopalpura soon spread to other villages in the Alwar district and kindled people's curiosity. Visitors from surrounding villages came to see what the people of Gopalpura had been able to achieve through their own efforts and expressed an interest in undertaking similar projects to restore their own village *johads*. With the Tarun Bharat Sangh working as a facilitator, similar projects have now been carried out all over the Alwar district.

The roles of different actors

The projects carried out in Gopalpura and throughout the district were a joint effort between the villages and the Tarun Bharat Sangh. In this section I shall outline the different roles played by the various actors involved in the initiatives, as well as the ways in which cooperation between groups was maintained.

Tarun Bharat Sangh

The NGO Tarun Bharat Sangh, based in Alwar town, played a key role as the initiator of the projects in Gopalpura and other villages. The organization was started in 1975 by two teachers in Jaipur, the capital of Rajasthan, who mobilized some like-minded individuals to spread the Gandhian message that people should learn to help themselves. Ten years later, nine members who were frustrated by the belief that their message was not getting across decided to move to a village and actually undertake development work themselves. The activities of Tarun Bharat Sangh have since spread widely, and today there are 7,500 volunteers working for the organization.

When the organization began working with villages in the district, its projects were focused on running schools and health facilities, on the assumption that these were the villagers' priorities. Soon after they started their initiatives, however, the activists of Tarun Bharat Sangh realized that what people needed most desperately was an assured source of water during the long hot summer months. As a result, the members of the NGO decided to assist the villagers in the repair or construction of *johads*. They acted as a catalyst for getting the initiatives up and running in Gopalpura and in other villages around the Alwar district.

Much of the success of the Tarun Bharat Sangh can be attributed to its strong leader, Rajendra Singh. Singh's strength lay in his vision and principles. One of his main principles was that communities should be financially self-sufficient. In 1989, the Tarun Bharat Sangh introduced the policy that a project would be undertaken only if villagers agreed to bear at least a quarter of the cost involved. As a rule, the cost of skilled labour and the necessary materials that were not available in the villages were provided by the Tarun Bharat Sangh. By imposing this condition, the Tarun Bharat Sangh sought to ensure that villagers would not remain dependent on handouts. This arrangement continued until 1997, when the proportion to be provided by villagers was raised to one-third, indicating an increasing degree of self-sufficiency in villages (Mahapatra 2001: 91).

Between 1985 and 2001, the Tarun Bharat Sangh helped in the construction of about 4,500 water-harvesting structures – mostly *johads* and rudimentary small check-dams, in a staggering 850 villages in the Alwar district. This directly resulted in the regeneration of 6,500 km^2 of land.[2] By 1998, these structures had cost a total of Rs 150 million (US$3.3 million), of which as much as Rs 110 million (US$2.4 million) was contributed by the villagers themselves by way of voluntary labour, materials or cash (Mahapatra 2001: 91).

Rajendra Singh has become well known in development circles throughout India and, to a certain extent, abroad. The Tarun Bharat Sangh has also established a solid reputation and has been able to obtain external funding from Panchayati Raj institutions,[3] the state government, individuals and groups in India. Some of the organizations that have funded projects in the past include: various federal government organizations, such as the Council for Advancement of People's Action and Rural Technology; the Central Social Welfare Board; the Department of Science and Technology; and also the Watershed Department of the Rajasthan government. Many international agencies have also contributed funds, including the Swiss Organisation for Development; Oxfam (India) Trust; Swedish Agency for International Development Cooperation (SIDA); and the German Technical Development Cooperation Agency (GTZ) (Khalakdina 1998: 49).

Although many external organizations have provided financial assistance to the initiatives, there is no question that the Tarun Bharat Sangh has been able to mobilize the long-dormant internal strengths of the communities to make them more reliant on raising their own resources than on grants and foreign aid. This approach is in significant contrast to that adopted by many other NGOs in India. Between 1985 and 1999, reliance on internal resources increased fivefold from Rs 40 million (US$880,000) to Rs 200 million (US$4.39 million). Indeed, the entire rationale of Tarun Bharat Sangh is to sensitize the poorest of the poor to realizing their own capacity to change their material situation.

In addition to Tarun Bharat Sangh's strong focus on promoting self-help attitudes among villagers, another feature is its close collaboration with the traditional village self-governing bodies, in particular the village assemblies (*gram sabha*), throughout the implementation of the project. I shall now describe the historical background of the self-governing bodies in India, as well as their role in the initiatives in Alwar.

The village assembly and self-governing councils

The Gandhian emphasis on decentralized rural development has meant that rule by self-governing bodies has spread throughout India, with varying results.[4] In 1992, an amendment to the Constitution required the self-governing bodies to work independently to address various issues, including water, public health, fisheries and education. Importantly, the amended Constitution also reaffirmed the role of the village assembly in ensuring that the self-governing councils, which consisted of elected representatives at the village, block and district level, stayed accountable to all the people of their constituency.

Whereas officials on the self-governing council are elected, the village assembly is made up of adults from every family in the village. Once the village assembly is formed, it elects a head and meets every month as a general assembly of the whole village.[5] One of the unique features of the assembly is that, in contrast to the operations of the self-governing council, the villagers can recall any member for non-performance or misconduct (Mahapatra 2001: 90).

This decentralized grassroots style of democracy represents a crucial innovation in bringing about village self-rule and it marks a clear departure from the authoritative party political system at higher levels. Whereas self-governing councils tend to reflect the power structures within Indian rural society, including influential landed interests and caste hierarchies, the village assemblies are regarded as much more democratic. They provide equal opportunities and voice to the villagers without being affected by the existing political system or social hierarchies.

The 1992 changes to the Constitution also created some problems however. One of the main issues is that the degree of power to be transferred to the self-governing bodies was never clearly outlined. This makes the functioning of the self-governing bodies subject to the vagaries of administrative and political systems. The capacity of self-governing bodies to raise revenue is another problem. According to a study conducted by the National Institute of Rural Development in Hyderabad,[6] between 1992 and 1998 the average village assembly earned only Rs 30,000 (US$660) a year. This is nowhere near enough to undertake any major activities (National Institute of Rural Development 2002). In April 2002, a meeting was organized by the Ministry of Rural Development to mark a decade since the constitutional amendment (All-India Panchayat Conference 2002). At this conference, the Panchayati Raj institutions demanded that state governments devolve funds and functionaries to these bodies, along with adequate control over land, water, forest produce and minerals (Mahapatra 2002).

Despite the problems outlined above, the importance of the self-governing bodies, and the village assemblies in particular, has been increasingly highlighted within local environmental management initiatives in India.

Village assemblies and water-harvesting initiatives

The village assemblies were the forum through which decisions were made and activities were initiated and carried out. This meant that it was vital for the Tarun Bharat Sangh to work closely with the village assemblies in implementing projects, sometimes by sending activists to the villages to attend the assemblies as observers. Although the approaches of different villages varied to some extent, the following discussion provides an overall explanation of how projects were carried out through the village assemblies.

Because it was the village assemblies that were carrying out the projects, each project was designed specifically to suit its community. This is in contrast to government schemes, which assume a uniform model for rural development. The decentralized approach carried out by the village assembly is superior in that it examines the specific requirements of each particular community. Villages vary from area to area. Whereas one village may require land for grazing its animals, another may require wood for fuel. Similarly, where the terrain is inhospitable for some forms of agriculture, an area may need leguminous crops planted simultaneously to fertilize the soil.

One of the approaches adopted by the village assembly was to form a number of committees to carry out the project once it had been designed. For example, when villagers in the Thanagazi block decided to build water-harvesting structures, the first step of the village assembly was to form a resource committee. This committee made a clay model of the village to provide an overall view of its natural assets and then went door to door, assessing the village's problems and eliciting the community's views on the site and size of the *johad*. The construction committee then supervised building activities and decided on the mode and magnitude of the community's participation. The forest committee enforced bans on cutting trees and monitored the regeneration of green cover in the catchment of water structures, and the grazing committee prevented cattle from straying into protected areas. Finally, the water committee looked after the water bodies and distributed this resource between different users. All final decisions were still made by the village assembly.

In afforestation drives, the village assemblies successfully worked in cooperation with herders. To ensure that shepherds did not graze their cattle in protected forest areas, the village assemblies entrusted the herders themselves with the responsibility for protecting the area. This contrasts with the situation elsewhere in the country, where people who are trying to regenerate their surroundings often come into conflict with the herders.

As villages have prospered under the new initiatives, village assemblies have set up a village fund (*gram kosh*), which has provided them with some degree of solvency. The fund was designed to take care of the maintenance of the *johads* as well as the welfare of the community. Each family contributes one-fortieth of its annual income to this fund or provides one day of voluntary labour every month for community work. Penalties for infringements of community-imposed restrictions on felling trees, grazing and the like are also paid into this fund, and anyone who fails to report a transgression pays twice as much.

The societal transformation that has occurred as a result of the water initiatives has also raised some obstacles and caused some conflict among villagers. In Gopalpura, for instance, one of the biggest obstacles was the local moneylender, who realized that if the villagers became self-sufficient this would reduce their need for loans. In addition, the villages are obviously not enjoying perfect harmony because caste divisions have continued. It is also the case, however, that the successful functioning of the village assemblies ensures that these divisive tendencies are brought into the open and resolved within the community, rather than allowed to fester.

Results of the initiatives

The initiatives that began in Gopalpura and spread throughout the district of Alwar had many positive impacts on the natural environment as well as on the social and economic situations of the people.

Reviving rivers

One of the remarkable results of the initiatives, particularly the construction of *johads*, has been the improved flow of the 90 km Ruparel River, which crosses the Alwar district from the hills of the Sariska National Park. By the late 1970s, this river was flowing only after the rains but, once villagers in the district began to build the *johads*, the situation immediately began to improve.

An independent assessment of 36 villages found that a *johad*, which can store 1,000–1,500 m³ per hectare, raises the annual average groundwater table by 6 metres (Agarwal 1996).[7] With funding from foreign donors, other communities in Alwar were able to construct as many as 333 *johads* in the river's basin. As a result, in 1996, the Ruparel River again began to flow throughout the entire year. With the rise in the water table, women and children no longer had to spend considerable time and effort in fetching water every day. Furthermore, the small dams and *johads* created sorely needed employment in the villages because part of the foreign grants was used to pay for labour.

In addition, the rejuvenation of the river forged an umbilical link between people in the catchment area and those downstream, who are the main beneficiaries. Since the former have relatives who live in villages further down, they felt it was their religious duty (*dharma*) to keep the river alive and clean so that it would benefit their kith and kin. Another unforeseen benefit is that the wildlife of the Sariska National Park is much more secure. The animals now have a perennial source of water that does not require them to traverse long distances in summer, exposing them to poachers.

Changing people's lives

Improvement of the water storage structures also brought about positive impacts for agriculture. For example, abandoned farmland was gradually brought under the plough, which considerably reduced soil erosion. Farmers were no longer restricted to crops such as course cereals that consumed very little water, and the ownership of cattle increased as the supply of fodder improved. In some villages, farmers have even begun to stall-feed their cattle, which prevents them from grazing and destroying saplings or crops. In fact, villagers now have surplus milk, which has allowed them to produce clarified butter (*ghee*) for their own consumption and also for sale in the market.

According to a UN survey of six villages that have benefited directly from the water projects, crop production has increased substantially (doubling in most places) and, as a consequence, the farmers have earned a solid return on their investment in the village assets.[8] For every Rs 100 (US$2.20) spent on building a *johad*, the farmers have made a profit of Rs 400 (US$8.80).

Through the initiatives, the Tarun Bharat Sangh has also encouraged the formation of women's groups, which have served to empower an otherwise disadvantaged group. Women were first gradually coaxed to attend village assembly meetings and then started participating in the women's groups, where they were free to speak their minds. By 1998, more than 150 such groups were in operation. In the village of Bhaonta-Kolyala, which is located in the middle of the Aravalli hills on the periphery of the Sariska National Park, women have even formed a separate village assembly. This is not, according to the women, a divisive tendency but rather an attempt to articulate the aspirations of women in their efforts to shore up the regular village assembly.

Perhaps the most significant impact of the initiatives is that people have begun to return to their villages, simply because they have an assured source of water, which is the most basic resource for human well-being. According to one commentator, Vir Singh, "Earlier, people were ashamed to leave as migration was driven by unemployment. Now, leaving the village is seen as a sign of prosperity. As a result, people's self-esteem increased and villages have been reborn, just like the river they depend on" (Singh n.d.: 25).

Innovative features

The initiatives undertaken in the Alwar district, beginning at Gopalpura, exhibit several innovative features. Many of these are evident simply in the approach of the Tarun Bharat Sangh, the village assemblies and the villagers in general. In Gopalpura, the most innovative feature of the initiatives was that the villagers, in cooperation with the Tarun Bharat Sangh and through the village assembly, were able to overcome the lack of self-confidence of a community afflicted with drought, poverty and environmental degradation. This small community consisted of only 360 people but, when their dormant energy was awakened, a spark ignited and the flames of their efforts spread throughout the entire district. It was the small band of dedicated activists from the Tarun Bharat Sangh who acted as a catalyst and played the key role in this process. They enabled the villagers to rediscover their zest for cooperating with each other.

A second innovative feature of the initiatives was the reliance on local resources and the voluntary labour of the villagers. The villagers chose to rely on their time-tested local "engineers" (or, more appropriately, "artisans"), such as architects and stone masons. The Tarun Bharat Sangh helped villagers to identify such artisans and instil a sense of self-worth and confidence in their ability to undertake technical tasks. This is a tremendous achievement in that it resulted in genuine community initiatives, which did not rely on a single conventional engineer. The construction work, from planning to site selection, design and execution, was performed entirely by the villagers themselves. Again, this differs greatly from government-run schemes where construction is carried out by outside contractors, with villagers contributing only unskilled labour. Such recourse to local skills is an important feature in any rural regeneration scheme, because it utilizes available capacities instead of looking for external assistance.

A third innovative aspect of the initiatives undertaken by the villagers and the Tarun Bharat Sangh was their method of raising the consciousness of people through their cultural and religious practices. This represents another sharp contrast to the efforts by the state or by political parties, which are secular in nature and often alienated from the people. In Gopalpura, villagers launched a "Save the Trees" march, which ended on the auspicious Rakhi festival day. Traditionally, on this day, girls tie a decorative thread around the wrists of brothers and male cousins to renew their kinship ties. After the Save the Trees march, people were imaginative enough to tie the *rakhi* threads around the trunks of trees. This etched in the public psyche the symbiotic relationship between the villagers and their natural environment.

One more innovative feature of the water harvesting initiative was the effort made to share experiences with others in the hopes of mobilizing other communities to better themselves. Villagers from several different communities in Alwar, in cooperation with the Tarun Bharat Sangh, have been using the Gandhian technique of organizing marches to raise people's consciousness and awareness of water issues.[9] In many cases, a small band of activists from the Tarun Bharat Sangh took the lead in organizing these marches, and they were joined by varying numbers of local villagers, who would drop in and out of the march as it traversed their region. The people's march lasts for six weeks each year. In 1997, the march passed through 450 villages and prompted 100 communities to start building water-harvesting structures, while another 150 indicated interest. Between 1986 and 1998, these tours visited as many as 650 villages (Mahapatra 2001: 95). In the process of conducting the march, the activists of the Tarun Bharat Sangh also highlighted social and economic problems. Village women cited how alcoholism was taking a heavy toll on their menfolk's lives and driving families into debt. The Tarun Bharat Sangh required the villagers to give up producing and consuming alcohol before it would provide assistance for building and repairing village *johads*.

The ripple effect

The remarkable achievements of the water-harvesting initiatives in the Alwar district have attracted attention both domestically and internationally. For example, a parliamentary committee on forests and the environment visited the village of Bhaonta-Kolyala and awarded the first Joseph C. John prize for the most outstanding environmental community.[10] The award was presented in 2000 by the President of India, K. R. Narayanan, very close to the village itself.

At the international level, the United Nations Inter Agency Working Group for Water and Environmental Sanitation recognized the water-harvesting methods promoted by the Tarun Bharat Sangh as being a "best practice" model. Many UN bodies are keen on introducing the Rajasthan model of rainwater-harvesting in other countries. For example, plans mooted by UN Secretary-General Kofi Annan for the reconstruction of war-ravaged Afghanistan include the replication of what the Tarun Bharat Sangh achieved through the construction of *johads* in India (*The Hindu* (Chennai), 16 February 2002, p. 5).[11] The United Nations Development Programme (UNDP) is also likely to showcase the contribution of visionaries such as Rajendra Singh, leader of the Tarun Bharat Sangh, particularly his work in achieving community involvement to meet developmental goals. The UNDP invited Rajendra Singh to drought-hit Afghanistan to help restore the traditional water-harvesting structures there (*United News of India*, 8 March 2002).[12]

The national and international awards won by the Tarun Bharat Sangh have aroused the interest of other states in India. Several groups of villagers have travelled to the area at their own expense to see for themselves how the barren landscape has been transformed and to discuss with villagers how to manage water resources. Other states have also approached Rajendra Singh for assistance in tackling water shortages. The Tarun Bharat Sangh has now formed an organization called the Jal Biradari (Water Brotherhood), which reaches out to the rest of the country. In Karnataka State, for example, it is helping villagers in the Nagarhole wildlife sanctuary (R. Singh 2001).

Conclusion

The most outstanding feature of the initiative implemented by the Tarun Bharat Sangh and the villages in the Alwar district of Rajasthan is the ability of the communities to harness water and other natural resources by utilizing traditional water-harvesting structures, even in the most trying conditions. By any standards, this area is one of the poorest and most environmentally degraded in Rajasthan. Within India, Rajasthan itself is one of the most deprived states. If the face of the countryside in the villages of Rajasthan could be transformed, the model can be replicated anywhere else in the country or, for that matter, the rest of the world.

The message to be taken away from this case study is that, with a bare minimum of rainfall, any rural area has the capacity to sustain itself. It is not so much the availability of resources as the ability of communities themselves to share the resources equitably and efficiently that can change the face of any area. Alwar district receives just 60 cm of rain a year on average. This may be twice as much as the Sahel region in sub-Saharan Africa, but it is still abysmally low, well below what many would consider the bare minimum for agriculture.

The "technology" that was needed to bring about the transformation of the Rajasthan villages is indigenous, not foreign. Indeed, the technology is based on the rediscovery of traditional methods of harnessing resources, which fell into disuse during the colonial and post-colonial eras. Rather than imposing a burden on the national exchequer, or making the country indebted with loans from multilateral institutions, this approach is labour intensive rather than capital intensive with regard to both construction costs and maintenance. What is required, however, is strong will and the active participation of the community through indigenous self-governing entities such as village assemblies. The success of the initiatives in the Alwar district clearly indicates that, with appropriate guidance and the catalytic role played by an external organization such as the Tarun Bharat Sangh, the communities were able to address their environmental issues themselves. They were not dependent on external assistance but achieved their goals by rediscovering the effectiveness of their traditional methods and promoting self-help attitudes through the utilization of indigenous self-governing bodies.

Notes

1. The exchange rate used in this chapter is US$1 = Rs 45.5.
2. See Rajendra Singh's website at: ⟨http://www.tarunbharatsangh.com⟩.

3. Panchayati Raj institutions are decentralized self-governing institutions at the level of a cluster of villages, as well as for an entire district.

4. Gandhi advocated that villages should learn to become economically self-reliant, rather than depend on towns – and industrialization – for employment. By increasing agricultural productivity, development would be bottom–up, rather than top–down.

5. The meeting is held on a "no-moon" day, which is traditionally devoted to community work.

6. The National Institute of Rural Development is an autonomous institution under the federal Ministry of Rural Development.

7. As an example, in 1985 water around Bhaonta-Kolyala could be found 17 metres underground, but by 1996 it was available at 9.6 metres.

8. The survey was conducted by the United Nations Inter Agency Working Group for Water and Environmental Sanitation.

9. Gandhi organized such marches to come into contact with ordinary rural people in order to enlist their support in the struggle against British imperialism.

10. This was coordinated by the Centre for Science and Environment in Delhi.

11. Cited in ⟨http://data.cseindia.org/news/FMPro⟩.

12. Cited in ⟨http://www.dailyexcelsior.com/02mar09/national.htm⟩.

REFERENCES

Agarwal, G. D. (1996) *An engineer's evaluation of water conservation efforts of Tarun Bharat Sangh in 30 villages of Alwar district*. Alwar: Tarun Bharat Sangh.

All-India Panchayat Conference (2002) "From panchayat to parliament", 5–6 April.

Khalakdina, M. (1998) *The promotion of community self-reliance: Tarun Bharat Sangh in action*. Ahmedabad: Oxfam India Trust.

Mahapatra, R. (2001) "Dramatic turnaround", in A. Agarwal, S. Narain and I. Khanna (eds), *Making water everybody's business: Practice and policy of water harvesting*. New Delhi: Centre for Science and Environment.

——— (2002) "Power to the people", *Down To Earth* (New Delhi), 15 May.

National Institute of Rural Development (2002) *India Panchayati Raj report, 2001: Four decades of decentralised governance in India*, vols I and II. Hyderabad.

Sheena and A. Mishra (1998) *Ripples of the society: People's movements for watershed development*. Field Doc. No. 14, Participatory Watershed Management Training in Asia, Kathmandu, FAO. New Delhi: Gandhi Peace Foundation.

Singh, R. (2001) "Water resources belong to people", interview in *The New Indian Express* (Chennai), 16 December.

Singh, V. (n.d.) *Rejuvenating the Ruparel: From death to rebirth*. Alwar: Tarun Bharat Sangh.

14

Conclusion: Critical elements for achieving community innovation

Makiko Yashiro

The intention of this book has not been to suggest a package of best practice approaches that can be replicated under certain conditions. The aim has been to draw out the important lessons from each case study in order to identify the key elements of an enabling environment for community innovation. It is the existence, or deliberate creation, of such an environment that fosters creativity at the community level and enables the adoption of innovative approaches to environmental and sustainable development challenges. In the following discussion, key lessons drawn from each of the case studies will be combined with the insights provided in the earlier conceptual chapters to highlight what appear to be the critical preconditions for community innovation.

To assist in clarifying the discussion, the editors of this volume developed a table to show an overview of the key elements of the case-study chapters (see Table 14.1 at the end of the chapter). This table categorizes the cases under topic, the approaches used in solving the environmental issues identified, the barriers to innovation, the results of the projects and the issues that contributed to the sustainability of the results.

Multi-stakeholder partnership and participation

Although the importance of multi-stakeholder partnerships and participation has been repeatedly highlighted within debates on sustainable development, it is even more important for successful community innovation.

This is because community innovation requires even greater fundamental changes to the way that individuals, organizations and societies operate. The mechanisms for multi-stakeholder partnership and participation help ensure that the diversity of interests, opinions, knowledge and experience of a myriad of community players are reflected and utilized within the creative process of seeking innovative solutions to sustainability problems.

As many of the case-study chapters have illustrated, multi-stakeholder partnership and participation mechanisms are often both a means and an end for community innovation. On the one hand, partnership and participation among stakeholders are critical for communities in adopting and implementing innovative approaches for environmental management. On the other hand, the adoption of multi-stakeholder mechanisms is itself an innovative process. In many instances, it is a process that requires related actors to understand the views of others and to change their way of thinking, and behaving, in order to establish successful partnerships. The establishment and management of multi-stakeholder mechanisms can be viewed as a learning process through which people exchange skills, information and experiences and develop new ways of doing things. At the same time, continued dialogue encourages people to develop new values and, often, to embrace change and respond flexibly to new challenges (Hemmati 2002).

In Chapter 5, Luc Bellon notes that diversified and conflicting interests are, "simultaneously, the trigger of innovation and the biggest threat to innovation mechanisms". On one level, community innovation needs to be driven by the active participation of different actors with diverse opinions and interests. It is the interaction of this diversity that generates creative ideas and leads to the development of innovative solutions utilizing a variety of social networks. As Bellon notes, the process of innovation is a complex social process through which the diversified objectives of different actors are coordinated and mutually adjusted. On another level, however, and as Nathaniel von Einsiedel discusses in some detail in Chapter 4, the interaction of diversity can sometimes generate a completely different reaction. When communities try to carry out and replicate innovative environmental initiatives, which in many cases require drastic changes in their practices or policies, the diversity of people's backgrounds and conflicting interests can lead to tension among stakeholders and resistance to change. Diversified and conflicting interests can help to generate innovation and change, but they can also represent a barrier to the innovative processes.

A crucial enabling factor for community innovation, therefore, is the existence of mechanisms that allow for the productive and creative resolution of diverse opinions and conflicts of interest. These mechanisms

> **Two main barriers to the innovative process faced by communities in Asia**
>
> • the natural human tendency to resist change
> • the social complexity of the issues being addressed
>
> *(Nathaniel von Einsiedel, Chapter 4)*

must allow people from different sectors to express diversified opinions and ideas, and have them reflected in the planning process, and provide forums where negotiation can take place and a consensus be built. This is the most effective way to ease tension among stakeholders and reduce resistance to change.

Many of the case-study chapters highlighted multi-stakeholder partnership and participation as being the most crucial factor for successful community innovation, although the mechanisms used and the degree of partnership and participation varied. The specific design and scale of the mechanisms, as well as the degree to which they are institutionalized and linked with official decision-making processes, also varied from case to case. As Amit Chanan suggests in his discussion of the Hawkesbury-Nepean river basin in Chapter 12, in some instances multi-stakeholder mechanisms developed with strong leadership by local government. In other cases, such as the Guimaras solid waste disposal management case in the Philippines examined by Andrew Farncombe, Francis Gentoral and Anthony Arias in Chapter 11, it is a non-governmental organization (NGO) that plays the lead role in developing and managing multi-stakeholder mechanisms.

What the case studies have shown is that there is no single recommended model of a multi-stakeholder partnership and participation mechanism that can be applied to any community. As Diane Warburton and Susan Yoshimura note in Chapter 2, there is a wide variety of styles and levels of community participation that may be more or less effective in different types of situation. When designing and implementing a participation and partnership mechanism, it is crucial to consider a variety of factors that will impact on its effectiveness, such as the uniqueness of a community's culture, the availability of resources and the peculiarities of its socio-political situation. To be effective, community participation and partnership mechanisms must be suited to the particular needs of each community and will be determined by its unique conditions. To remain effective, the mechanism will also need to be flexible. The needs and conditions of a particular community are not static; they will develop and transform over time in response to internal and external events and

---

Critical elements for community innovation

- scaling up innovation at the individual and organizational level to the community level by making innovative initiatives mainstream
- creating an "innovative milieu" in which both innovative thinking and project implementation can flourish from any source, and help the chains of innovation spread and gain acceptance
- recognizing the cultural diversity of communities as an opportunity, not a threat to achieving community innovation
- building and sustaining momentum for innovation by creating an "embedding strategy" to develop a sense of "ownership" of an innovative process among various stakeholders

(Charles Landry, Chapter 3)

---

stimuli. It is important, then, that multi-stakeholder partnership and participation mechanisms be flexible and have the capacity to evolve over time and in response to changing conditions and needs.

To be effective, multi-stakeholder participation and partnership mechanisms also need to be sustainable over the longer term. Multi-stakeholder mechanisms are often created only from a short-term perspective with the aim of providing an immediate response to a pressing sustainable development issue. As a consequence, communities often face significant challenges when it comes to ensuring the continuity and long-term viability of their multi-stakeholder mechanisms. This is particularly the case when the continuity of the mechanisms depends upon ongoing external support, regardless of whether this is local or international. It is also the case that continuity can be jeopardized by a loss of motivation among internal stakeholders. It is critical, therefore, that multi-stakeholder mechanisms be designed and managed from a long-term perspective.

A key factor affecting the success of an innovative initiative is its ability to be replicated and scaled up at the community level. Both Charles Landry in Chapter 3 and Nathaniel von Einsiedel in Chapter 4 note that, although it is relatively easy to identify numerous examples of innovative initiatives at the individual and project level, few of these have been successfully scaled up so that an entire community can become innovative.

One of the main barriers to scaling up innovation is that it introduces a greater level of complexity. Applying a small-scale innovation to the broader community requires taking on an even greater variety of interests, cultures, insights, perspectives and power configurations. This is where the need for effective mechanisms that allow diverse opinions and conflicts of interests to be coordinated toward common goals becomes even more crucial. To be successful at the community level, these mechanisms must promote open-minded discussion and communication and allow a diverse range of people to be creative and identify innovative solutions together.

Utilization of local culture, knowledge and indigenous systems

Many of the case studies emphasized the importance of involving people from the communities directly in the decision-making and implementation processes in order to ensure local ownership over the innovation process. This point is highlighted particularly well in the Teruhiko Yoshimura and Rika Kato case study on waste management in Nagoya City, Japan, and also the Darryl D'Monte chapter on water management in Rajasthan, India. Both these cases point to the utilization of traditional and indigenous self-governing bodies, such as neighbourhood associations and village assemblies, being a key factor in successful participatory environmental management. Even when external organizations play important roles in the innovation process, their close collaboration with indigenous self-governing bodies, which have long been managed by locals, appears to be a critical precondition for success. The case studies showed that it is, in fact, the important role played by existing knowledge and understanding that distinguishes community innovation from our general understanding of innovation from a technological perspective.

The generally accepted image of innovation tends to centre on the introduction of new and advanced technologies, whereas community innovation is more likely to be successful when existing culture, local knowledge and indigenous practices are respected and utilized. In this respect, Charles Landry argues that community innovation is a "cultural process" that requires a shift in people's mindsets, values and ideas, and also the ways in which they plan and take action. In many cases this process is greatly influenced, if not largely determined, by local culture and consciousness.

For communities to achieve innovation through the adoption of unconventional methods of planning and implementing projects, they first need to assess their cultural circumstances and assets. These factors, which are an amalgamation of a community's history, talents, products and services, must be utilized fully in order to respond imaginatively to the possibilities presented within a given context. This said, it is important to note that what are considered to be assets and potential are both culturally determined. Successful community innovation depends on how communities

---

Key features of community innovation

- community innovation is a cultural process that goes beyond mere technological innovation, and involves change in people's consciousness and in the value systems and ethics of the society and innovation at every level of decision-making
- community innovation is relative, being both time and space dependent, and requires responses that are unique to the community
- innovations do not necessarily come singly, but tend to cluster in certain places at certain times, sometimes almost accidentally, sometimes as a matter of deliberate policy
- creative solutions and innovations come from any source, including public, private or voluntary sectors, or individuals

(Charles Landry, Chapter 3)

---

assess and utilize their own culture, knowledge, assets and opportunities in their response to emerging problems and challenges.

The utilization of local culture, knowledge and indigenous systems can be singled out as a vital element for the success of community innovation. Bellon notes in Chapter 5 that innovation in the Torghar community in Pakistan was achieved through the full utilization of the pre-existing social structure, customs and negotiating practices of local people. Local governing institutions also played a crucial role in the introduction of new approaches to wildlife management. Similarly, in the Togean Islands case study presented by Sundjaya in Chapter 8, the eastern Indonesian community of Lembanato successfully carried out a number of ecotourism initiatives by making full use of traditional knowledge of the local environment and relying on local culture. When they implemented their ecotourism initiative, the community used the knowledge and the systems that had accumulated through their long and intimate relationship with their physical eco-systems as a means to develop tourism activities and also a number of tourism products.

The forest management initiative in Baybay in the Philippines, presented by Victor Asio and Marlito Bande in Chapter 9, provides another example of how local knowledge, especially that of community elders, played a significant role in facilitating successful innovation. D'Monte also attributes the success of the community-based water management initiative implemented in Rajasthan, India, to the application of traditional water-harvesting structures, reliance on local technicians and the utilization of existing cultural and religious practices. The use of local technologies and knowledge, he suggests, helped people to rediscover the effectiveness of the traditional methods that already existed in their community and at the same time promoted a self-help attitude.

The erosion of cultural assets, such as a community's local knowledge, is a continuing challenge for many communities. Sundjaya, and Asio and Bande, point out that the erosion of local cultural assets has two main causes. It is often due to the intrusion of external culture and the lack of an effective system for transferring knowledge and culture from one generation to the next. If communities are to utilize local knowledge and culture within the process of innovation, it is often the case that they must first enhance their understanding of their own cultural assets and assess the impacts of external cultural influence. They need to understand what they have, in order to be better prepared to protect their cultural assets and respond to the intrusion of external culture. It is also important to make sure that communities have appropriate mechanisms in place to transfer local knowledge to the younger generations. Community innovation initiatives can play a productive role in this regard. In rural communities in Baybay, for example, the forest management innovations that were implemented by the community had the added bonus of promoting the generational transfer of indigenous knowledge and the management of native species. This was achieved through the active interaction of farmers from different generations in their daily farm work and also through informal discussions during public events.

As Landry notes in Chapter 3, one of the key preconditions for successful community innovation is that local communities rediscover and strengthen their relationship with their cultural resources. It is also crucial that these assets, which are often intangible, are utilized within the innovation process using the imagination and creativity of local people. Another key lesson from the case studies is that the processes for community innovation can represent an effective means through which communities can nurture and protect their cultural knowledge and assets and encourage their intergenerational transfer.

Four processes of cultural change to achieve community innovation

- describing possibilities better
- generating a local ethos to drive innovation
- developing innovative projects
- enabling communities to become learning organizations to sustain the innovative momentum

(Charles Landry, Chapter 3)

The role of facilitating organizations

Another key element that affects the success of community innovation relates to the role of facilitating organizations. These organizations, which are often external to the communities, play the role of change agents. They assist communities in their efforts to network with external actors and to locate and obtain external assistance such as funding and expertise. In Chapter 4, von Einsiedel emphasizes the importance of institutions that play facilitating roles in the innovative process. They are often research or academic institutions that have expertise and experience in the area of environmental management and community mobilization. They are also usually well experienced in the crucial task of facilitating consensus-building among different, and sometimes conflicting, stakeholder groups. At their most effective, facilitating organizations work closely with the local leaders and community organizations that play a key role in mobilizing communities.

The case-study chapters have revealed a number of different ways in which organizations can facilitate innovative processes. In Chapter 7, Walter Jamieson and Pawinee Sunalai explore how the technical assistance provided by an academic-based Canadian NGO, the Canadian Universities Consortium Urban Environmental Management Project (CUC UEM), played a lead role in ensuring the success of a sustainable tourism initiative in the community of Klong Khwang in Thailand. Being a neutral organization, unconstrained by government structures and policies, but well experienced in sustainable tourism management, CUC UEM successfully established a collaborative relationship with senior village figures. The institution then helped the headman, other members of the community and local tourism officials to become aware of the importance of sustainable tourism practices and assisted them in the planning and implementation of a number of initiatives. Although CUC UEM provided only limited financial assistance, the technical advice and support it pro-

---

Key elements for achieving community innovation in Asia

Address the issues of social complexity and fragmentation of direction, mission, teamwork and understanding of issues, by promoting coherence among the stakeholders on the understanding of problems, concepts and their respective roles and shared commitments in the innovative process.

(Nathaniel von Einsiedel, Chapter 4)

vided through its day-to-day communications with the community were instrumental in facilitating the sustainable tourism process.

Asio and Bande, too, highlight the critical role played by facilitating organizations in Chapter 9. In this instance the Institute of Tropical Ecology of Leyte State University played two key roles. The Institute provided technical support to the communities and also facilitated their networking with external actors, which helped them to acquire additional technical and financial assistance. In Chapter 11, Farncombe, Gentoral and Arias suggest that it was the Canadian Urban Institute that played the key role in establishing the multi-stakeholder partnership mechanisms that enabled the community of Guimaras to take proactive steps toward resolving its solid waste management issues.

Charles Landry suggests that facilitating organizations play a key role in the innovation process because they help communities to develop, or gain access to, the required infrastructure. It is critically important for communities to have the necessary "hard" and "soft" infrastructure in place to assist in the process of generating a flow of ideas, inventions and best-practice knowledge, and also to provide the capacity for reflection. Hard infrastructure includes resources such as research, educational and advocacy institutes that provide expertise and knowledge on sustainable development for the communities. Soft infrastructure includes the system of social networks and human interactions that support the flow of ideas between individuals and institutions.

Facilitating institutions support the community innovation process by assisting communities to secure both hard and soft infrastructure. They provide technical assistance with their expertise and experience, and help communities to network internally and externally. The support provided to the communities in the development of systems of social networks and human interactions is particularly crucial because it enables communities to learn from, and be inspired by, other communities. It also helps them to acquire the necessary assistance from various external institutions. Both these aspects are critical for community innovation.

Strong leadership

Individuals in possession of strong leadership skills and a pioneering spirit are another critical precondition for community innovation. As Landry notes, when leadership skills and tendencies are widespread within a community, this provides for a high-quality innovative environment. A careful analysis of the initiatives explored within each of the case-study chapters indicates that innovation is often initiated and implemented under the strong leadership of certain individuals. In many cases, these individuals are in the most senior positions within a community or organization. These leaders have a clear vision for the future and are keenly motivated to improve their communities. They can play a wide variety of roles within the community innovation process, for example: clarifying long-term community visions and providing overall direction for the innovation process; generating community principles and a local ethos; legitimizing innovative initiatives through their involvement; motivating and inspiring people; and providing essential support for communities in terms of funding, technology and training.

Luc Bellon provides an example of strong leadership playing a key role in the success of a community innovation in Chapter 5. For the Pashtun community in Torghar, Pakistan, hunting played a significant role in shaping societal structures. The community innovation that was introduced required a radical change in local wildlife management practices, including the prohibition of hunting. Such a measure would never have been accepted by the community without the strong leadership of tribal chiefs. The fact that the hunting ban was launched and implemented under the strong leadership of these chiefs gave it legitimacy. Their involvement enabled the ban to be understood and accepted by the local community without disturbing pre-existing power relations.

The important role played by individual leaders is illustrated well by J. Marc Foggin in Chapter 6. In this case, local community leaders took on several essential roles, including clarifying long-term visions; mobilizing local people through the establishment of a new community-based organization, the Upper Yangtze Organization; and enabling the community to network with, and acquire knowledge from, other communities and external organizations. In Chapter 8, Sundjaya also identifies the leadership of key locals with a strong pioneering spirit as being the key factor that sparked off the innovative process. In this instance, the innovation was initiated when local leaders introduced the idea of ecotourism to the community of Lembanato in Indonesia. D'Monte examines a similar case in Chapter 13 when he describes the role that a local leader, who had a strong sense of vision, played in promoting the principles of financial independence in water management in the Indian community of Rajasthan.

Local leadership, at both the individual and the organizational level, also plays a key role in establishing external links for support and collaboration. Local leaders play a crucial role in terms of establishing and promoting strong collaborative relationships between community members and facilitating organizations. In Chapter 7, Jamieson and Sunalai note that the committed leadership of the village headman was vital to the development of a strong working relationship with the CUC UEM. This close link between the headman and the CUC UEM then became a critical factor in ensuring that the organization and the technical assistance it provided were fully accepted by the community and incorporated into the community innovation process. The village headman understood the concept of sustainable tourism and its potential benefits to the community. On this basis, he was willing to work closely with CUC UEM to introduce the innovative concept of sustainable tourism to the community. The headman helped clarify the ecotourism vision for the community and mobilized its members toward a common goal. His efforts to develop strong links between the CUC UEM and the community, and his strong support for the organization's work, allowed it to play a facilitating role in the community innovation process.

The strong leadership of certain individuals with courage and a pioneering spirit can overcome blocked thinking and encourage the adoption of unconventional development approaches. As many of the case-study chapters demonstrate, leaders assist communities to achieve innovation by introducing new ideas and approaches. More importantly, they help create the conditions necessary to upgrade and mainstream innovation by motivating and inspiring people to become involved in the innovative process. They also provide legitimacy for innovative initiatives and assist communities to network with external organizations or communities to acquire the necessary knowledge and expertise.

Income generation and welfare benefits

One of the biggest challenges for communities is to ensure the sustainability of innovation beyond the short term. As discussed above, one way to encourage sustainability is to strengthen local involvement in, and ownership of, the innovative process. Another way to promote the sustainability of community innovation is to ensure a fair balance at the community level between economic well-being and environmental protection. In poorer communities, one of the best ways to promote this balance and encourage the long-term viability of an innovative initiative is to design and manage the initiative in such a way that it helps to generate income and welfare improvements at the local level.

In the Pashtun wildlife conservation initiatives discussed in Chapter 5, for example, it was the income generated from trophy hunting that provided financial independence to the NGO that facilitated the innovation process. In this instance, the income generated from the initiative was used to provide various benefits to the community, such as improved medical support and the construction of necessary infrastructure. The introduction of the game guards system also increased employment opportunities and monetary compensation for local herders. This generated a lot of local support, and the motivation of local herders to continue the initiative became the critical factor in its sustainability. The Philippine case study presented by Asio and Bande in Chapter 9 also points to the link between income and welfare benefits and sustainable local support for community innovation.

The capacity to generate income from community innovation also poses some challenges. Sundjaya discusses some of these challenges when he examines an ecotourism initiative in the Togean Islands of Indonesia in Chapter 8. He shows that when communities initiate income-generating activities they often face some difficulty in ensuring an equal distribution and sharing of benefits because they do not have proper management systems in place. As Jamieson and Sunalai illustrate in Chapter 7, skills development in the design of income-generating activities is a critical factor, and the assistance provided by external facilitating organizations can play a key role in this regard.

Financial independence

Several of the case studies have shown how devastatingly vulnerable a community-based initiative can be when it relies heavily on a single source of funding and support. Another key way to promote the long-term sustainability of an innovative community initiative, therefore, is to ensure that it maintains a high level of financial independence. Even when communities are provided with seed money to initiate the innovative process, the resulting initiative must eventually aim to become financially independent in order to ensure long-term viability. Without this independence, the innovative initiative, and the communities where it develops, will remain vulnerable to the changing policies and priorities of both external and internal funders.

In Chapter 13, D'Monte uses the Rajasthan case study to highlight the particular importance of limiting reliance on external grants and foreign aid. This point was brought out in several of the case studies, which all noted that a high level of dependence on external financial resources can be counterproductive and hamper the sustainability of a community innovation. In Chapter 9, Asio and Bande also caution against a reliance on external technological assistance. Being dependent on this type of external support, particularly once an infrastructure project has been completed, is a short-term approach that places a community innovation in a very precarious position.

Vulnerability to external change

Several of the case studies showed how vulnerable community innovation can be to external influence and change. Political instability and economic turmoil that occur on the other side of the world are totally beyond the control of communities, yet they can still have disastrous impacts on the communities' innovative processes. In this respect, a high level of vulnerability to external influence and change can represent a barrier to the innovative process. Sundjaya explores this barrier in the Togean Islands case study presented in Chapter 8. In this case, local ecotourism was devastated by a reduction in tourist numbers brought about by social unrest, political turmoil and economic crises in Indonesia in 2000. This, in turn, led to a drastic reduction in local motivation levels, further jeopardizing the long-term viability of the initiative. The Togean Islands case study demonstrates the need for communities to be well prepared for such pressures and changes. They need to make a clear assessment of the external factors and threats that could potentially have a negative impact on their activities and, if possible, develop appropriate mitigation strategies.

Another important element that needs to be highlighted here is the vulnerability of community innovation to sudden policy changes by national and local governments. In this respect, the undemocratic nature of internal political decision-making processes and operations can slow down or even halt the innovative process. In the case introduced by Foggin in Chapter 6, for example, a change in national government policies regarding a poverty alleviation programme looks as though it is going to require the relocation of local herders, seriously endangering the sustainability of their conservation efforts. A similar example is illustrated by Chanan in Chapter 12, which explains the sudden abolition of the multistakeholder partnership mechanism underpinning the management of the Hawkesbury-Nepean catchment area near Sydney. Although a substitute organization was established, the sudden abolition of the partnership mechanism by the state government, without any consultation with related stakeholders, severely damaged the momentum and sustainability of the innovative initiative.

These examples clearly reveal the vulnerability of community innovation processes to undemocratic government decision-making systems in which the communities have little or no influence. The case studies show that the successful and sustainable implementation of community innovation requires not only bottom–up support and effort from local communities, but also top–down support from government. What would also have a significant positive impact on local community innovation would be community empowerment – the enhanced involvement of grassroots communities in the broader decision-making processes that affect their everyday lives and their livelihoods. Local involvement in government decision-making processes would have the added benefit of promoting a greater sense of high-level involvement and association with the community innovation process. As Nathaniel von Einsiedel notes in Chapter 4, a high-level sense of involvement in the process can be just as important as a local sense of ownership, because it can act in the same way to reduce political resistance to innovation and change.

As Warburton and Yoshimura note in Chapter 2, innovation is needed to transform the ways in which institutions, organizations and individuals operate if they are to achieve their sustainable development goals. What the innovation should aim for is the opposite of a top–down style of authoritarian system – i.e. a democratic system that allows people to communicate with each other, try new approaches, take part in decision-making and make changes to the existing system. In essence, the successful implementation of a community innovation requires good governance that provides the community with efficient and transparent institutions through which the active involvement of citizens in decision-making is ensured.

One of the possible measures that might help reduce the vulnerability of communities to these various external changes and influences is to strengthen their preparedness by assessing potential threats and preparing possible responses in advance. The most critical step to be taken to eliminate community vulnerabilities, especially regarding the external threats posed by undemocratic actions by governments, is the shift towards more democratic governance structures through which people in communities take part in decision-making and "own" their innovative efforts.

REFERENCE

Hemmati, M. (2002) *Multi-stakeholder process for governance and sustainability.* London and Stering, VA: Earthscan.

Table 14.1 An overview of the key elements presented in the case-study chapters

Project title/ location/project scale	Approaches	Barriers to innovation	Project results	Factors contributing to sustainability	Top–down/ Bottom–up
Wildlife management					
Chapter 5: "From hunting to sustainable use: A Pashtun tribal group's innovations, northern Balochistan, Pakistan"	Introduction of trophy hunting and the prohibition of hunting	Differing perceptions and conflicting interests within the community	Complete cessation of illegal hunting	Clear understanding by community members of the benefits of the project	Idea: came from a local NGO Implementation: by the community
Location: Northern Balochistan, Pakistan	Creation of jobs and new responsibilities for game guards	Traditional territorial division of mountain resources	Development of the concepts of community goods and ownership, and collective responsibility for conserving mountain biodiversity	Appropriate system and continuous efforts to keep conflicting forces on negotiating terms	
Project scale: Pashtun community living in the Torghar region	Continuous process of negotiation, which led to people's understanding of the need for holistic management of mountain resources				
	Direct involvement of residents in decision-making and the implementation of the project				
	Promotion of equity and collective responsibility				
	Utilization of local culture, knowledge and indigenous systems				
	Active role played by an external facilitating organization				
	Active role played by local leaders				
	Financial independence				

Table 14.1 (cont.)

Project title/ location/project scale	Approaches	Barriers to innovation	Project results	Factors contributing to sustainability	Top–down/ Bottom–up approach
Chapter 6: "Highland encounters: Building new partnerships for conservation and sustainable development in the Yangtze River headwaters, the heart of the Tibetan Plateau, China" *Location:* Yangtze River headwaters, Tibetan Plateau, China *Project scale:* Suojia community, comprising Tibetan pastoralists (4,000 residents)	Establishment of the grassroots organization that promoted the community's involvement in local environmental management, as well as networking and collaboration with government decision makers and international partners Active role played by an external facilitating organization Active role played by local leaders	Lack of understanding or legitimacy given to the non-governmental sector Negative impacts of the central and provincial governments' development policies, which are often decided without careful attention to the situation or to the needs of the community Difficulties in building genuine partnership with external organizations, owing to varied interpretation of the concept of "participation"	Enhanced participation of local herders in planning and implementation process of wildlife management Strengthened communication between the community and the government and international partners	Mutual understanding and genuine partnership between the community and other stakeholders in planning and implementing projects Consistency and sufficient consideration of community needs in governmental policy planning and decision-making processes (still remains to be seen)	Bottom–up

				Bottom–up approach
Tourism *Chapter 7*: "Sustainable tourism planning and management in Klong Khwang, Thailand" *Location*: Klong Khwang, Thailand *Project scale*: Klong Khwang village (about 100 households)	Introduction to the concept of sustainable tourism in community tourism planning and management Involvement of community members in tourism planning and management processes through public consultation Development of a tourism plan with careful examination of its economic, environmental and socio-cultural impacts on the community Development of a tourism plan as an appropriate management structure Equitable distribution of income within the community through the community cooperative Utilization of culture, local knowledge and indigenous systems	Limited experience and skills of the community in tourism management (marketing and promotion)	Development and implementation of a sustainable tourism plan by the community Increased number of tourists, with no negative physical or environmental impacts Both increased and cooperative spiritual and cultural awareness	Continuous and long-term development of community skills on sustainable tourism management, through consultative processes and practical experiences Sufficient access to technical support from external organizations Strong sense of project ownership among community members

325

Table 14.1 (cont.)

Project title/ location/project scale	Approaches	Barriers to innovation	Project results	Factors contributing to sustainability	Top–down/ Bottom–up
Chapter 8: "Mangrove conservation through ecotourism development by the Bobongko people in the Togean Islands, Indonesia" *Location:* Lembanato, Togean Islands, Central Sulawesi Province, Indonesia	Active role played by an external facilitating organization, especially the provision of technical assistance Active role played by local leaders, especially a village headman Introduction of the ecotourism concept, which promoted both the conservation of mangrove habitat and income generation through full utilization of traditional knowledge and methodologies to manage natural resources Establishment of a multi-stakeholder network and a group of key community members, which facilitates the involvement of other community members in	Negative impacts on the tourism market induced by political, social and economic instability at the regional, national and international levels Difficulties in ensuring equal benefit-sharing among community members	An increased understanding of how to utilize traditional knowledge of the natural environment, in order to promote tourism and generate income among the community Increased number of tourists (although it	Prepared for future external changes (political, social and economic instability) Sufficient understanding gained by community members of the opportunities and benefits of the ecotourism project (not only economic but also environmental benefits)	Bottom–up approach

Project scale: Lembanato village – Bobongko ethnic group (243 households/ 1,143 people as of 2000)	tourism activities, with technical assistance provided by an external NGO Development of a system to manage tourism activities (product development, marketing and promotion, and benefit-sharing) Active role played by an external facilitating organization Active role played by local leaders	Limited skills in tourism management (marketing and promotion skills, English ability, etc.) among community members	later declined owing to political, social and economic instability) Improved biodiversity conditions within the community	Continuity of technical and financial assistance from external organizations	Bottom–up approach
Forest management Chapter 9: "Innovative community-led sustainable forest resource conservation and management in Baybay, Leyte, the Philippines"	Acquiring the legal authority to protect, rehabilitate and conserve the forest in the community by registering with the Community-Based Forest Management Programme Acquiring technical assistance (legal,	Limited capacity and knowledge to stop illegal logging Limited knowledge about forest resource management (identification of flora and fauna, etc.)	Fewer incidents of illegal and widespread logging in the area Systematic management of indigenous knowledge related to the availability of	Successful management of community businesses that generate financial resources in order to sustain activities Continuous efforts to	

Table 14.1 (cont.)

Project title/ location/project scale	Approaches	Barriers to innovation	Project results	Factors contributing to sustainability	Top–down/ Bottom–up
Location: Cienda and San Vicente, Baybay, Leyte, the Philippines *Project scale*: 2 towns of Cienda and San Vicente (about 400 households)	scientific and financial) from a local university, NGOs and an international donor agency Development of community businesses to generate income in order to support activities, achieve financial independence and ensure equal benefit-sharing Active involvement of community members in forest management activities by participating in the community farmers' association Utilization of local culture, knowledge and indigenous systems Active role played by local leaders		resources in flora and fauna, and the utilization of that knowledge for sustainable use of forest resources Strengthened collaboration and networking opportunities with external organizations, and the sharing of knowledge and experiences with other communities (through the provision of training on forest management, methodologies, etc.)	strengthen the capacity and knowledge of community members Volunteering spirit and strong commitment by community members	

Waste management

Chapter 10: "Waste management activities in Nagoya City, Japan: Local government and community partnerships" *Location*: Nagoya City, Japan *Project scale*: Nagoya City's population is approximately 2 million (as of March 2003)	Strong leadership role played by the local government, resulting in a huge shift in its waste management policies It adopted the Containers and Packaging Recycling Law as well as issuing the Waste Emergency Declaration, which encouraged the reduction of waste in the city through enhanced cooperation among citizens Extensive education campaigning by the local government in order to promote understanding and participation in the new waste collection processes and schemes Active involvement of community-based organizations (*chonaikai* and municipal health commissioners) and NGOs, and their	Difficulties with informing the entire population of Nagoya City about the procedures of the new waste sorting/recycling programme There were a lot of complaints from residents about the complexity of the waste collection methods Increased costs of waste management for the local government	Dramatic reduction of non-recyclable solid waste and the amount buried in landfills	Shared vision of waste management among the local government and citizens, and their overall willingness to participate in this initiative Efforts by citizens and community-based organizations to form partnerships with the local government and to initiate waste management activities of their own Attitude of the local government in informing	Top–down approach

Table 14.1 (cont.)

Project title/location/project scale	Approaches	Barriers to innovation	Project results	Factors contributing to sustainability	Top–down/Bottom–up
	partnership with the local government Strong leadership role played by local leaders			citizens about waste issues and collaborating with various stakeholders	
Chapter 11: "People, partnership and profits in managing solid waste in Guimaras, the Philippines" *Location*: Guimaras, the Philippines *Project scale*: Province of Guimaras (total population 141,450)	Strong partnership between the local government and the community through multi-stakeholder task forces (PITF and MITF), which promote the coordination of planning and implementation of solid waste management activities Using set criteria, through small-scale solid waste management demonstration projects, to promote competition in this field Development of trainers who can give lectures to	Lack of resources and personnel, resulting in setbacks in the partnership process Lack of funds to maintain enthusiasm and participation among community groups involved in project activities Additional workload for government representatives working on solid	Increased awareness and participation in local governance processes within the community Improved information-sharing with the national government and private sector. This fostered transparency and accountability in local	Institutionalization of multi-stakeholder task forces (e.g. PITF and MITF members have been accepted as members of Municipal and Provincial Solid Waste Management Boards, created under the national law on ecological waste management)	Top–down and bottom–up approaches

other communities and share their successful experiences Increased awareness of community members and their participation in local governance processes Active role played by an external facilitating organization	waste project activities	government priority-setting, budgeting and service delivery Formation of good relationships between the government and community groups, through the creation of task forces	Economically viable projects that have created livelihoods and jobs Creation of "champions" or "leaders" who educated other residents	
Water management *Chapter 12:* "Integrated catchment management in the Hawkesbury-Nepean basin, Australia" *Location:* Hawkesbury-Nepean basin near Sydney, Australia *Project scale:* Residents of Promotion of multi-stakeholder partnerships through the Hawkesbury-Nepean Catchment Management Trust (HNCMT) Mobilization of volunteers and the private sector Increased sense of ownership among community members through active participation in initiatives	Difficulties for HNCMT in maintaining the balance between bureaucratic decisions emanating from the top and community needs being expressed from the bottom Owing to its strong relationship with the communities	Increased awareness among community members, particularly the younger generation, with regard to catchment management issues Improved environmental conditions of the river basin	High level of participation in the initiative by community members Detailed knowledge about the river and its processes among several community members Structure of the HNCMT	Bottom–up approach

331

Table 14.1 (cont.)

Project title/ location/project scale	Approaches	Barriers to innovation	Project results	Factors contributing to sustainability	Top–down/ Bottom–up
the Hawkesbury-Nepean catchment		involved, HNCMT was largely perceived in bureaucratic circles as a community organization, eventually leading to its closure Difficulties in securing continuous financial support to sustain activities, particularly after the withdrawal of support by the government	Active involvement of local businesses in catchment management activities Empowerment of local communities, resulting in the participation of 2,500 volunteers in local habitat rehabilitation projects during 1999/2000	enabled effective collaboration between the government and other stakeholders such as NGOs, academics, businesses and local residents (Because it is listed as one of the barriers to innovation, it should be noted that ongoing support from the local government proved to be essential to ensure the sustainability of the initiative)	

| Chapter 13: "Water management in Rajasthan India: Making a difference"
Location: Alwar district, state of Rajasthan, India
Project scale: Alwar district (consisting of 1,991 villages and a population of 2.3 million) | Promotion of village self-rule through active participation of people in village assemblies
Multi-stakeholder partnerships
Utilization of traditional water-harvesting methodology (johads) and the adoption of cultural and religious practices in conducting environmental activities
Active facilitating role played by local leaders
Active role played by an external facilitating organization
Income generation and welfare benefits gained by the community through the initiative | Regulatory challenges (e.g. the government intervened and hampered the smooth implementation of the initiative, by declaring that johads were illegal) | Construction of 333 johads in the river basin significantly improved the water storage capacity of villages
Generation of job opportunities for community members involved in construction work
Substantial increase in crop production
Return of people to their own villages
Increased self-esteem among community members because the success of activities made them aware of their own strengths and capacities to overcome difficulties | Bottom–up approach
The combination of economic benefits, through increased opportunities for employment and income generation, and social benefits, through improved living conditions for villagers by enhancing water storage structures |

333

Index